DESEGREGATING DESIRE

Desegregating Desire

Race and Sexuality in Cold War American Literature

Tyler T. Schmidt

University Press of Mississippi   Jackson

www.upress.state.ms.us

The University Press of Mississippi is a member of the Association of American University Presses.

Copyright © 2013 by University Press of Mississippi
All rights reserved
Manufactured in the United States of America

Earlier sections of Chapter Three appeared as "White Pervert: Tracing Integration's Queer Desires in African American Novels of the 1950s," in Women's Studies Quarterly. 35.1–2 (Spring/Summer 2007): 149-71.

Frontis: *Champions*, charcoal on paper by Wardell Milan. © 2009 by Wardell Milan. Used by permission.

First printing 2013

Library of Congress Cataloging-in-Publication Data

Schmidt, Tyler T.
  Desegregating desire : race and sexuality in Cold War American literature / Tyler T. Schmidt.
    pages cm
  Includes bibliographical references and index.
  ISBN 978-1-61703-783-2 (cloth : alk. paper) — ISBN 978-1-61703-784-9 (ebook) 1. American literature—20th century—History and criticism. 2. Race relations in literature. 3. Sex in literature. I. Title.
  PS228.R32S36 2013
  810.9'355—dc23
                                      2013011471

British Library Cataloging-in-Publication Data available

CONTENTS

vii   Acknowledgments

3   **Introduction**
        The Half-Told Histories of Desegregation

38   **Ambivalent Desires**
        Elizabeth Bishop, Zora Neale Hurston, and Domestic Desegregation

87   **War City**
        Gwendolyn Brooks, Edwin Denby, and the Private Poetics of Public Space

136   **White Pervert**
        William Demby, Ann Petry, and the Queer Desires of Racial Belonging

179   **Damaged Desires**
        Jo Sinclair, Carl Offord, and the Traumas of Integration

221   **Conclusion**
        Intimate Failures

229   Notes

249   Works Cited

271   Index

ACKNOWLEDGMENTS

I have benefited immeasurably from the ruthless encouragement, intellectual talents, and creative nourishment of teachers, colleagues, and friends from the conception of this project to its completion. My teacher, mentor, and friend Robert Reid-Pharr continues to be an indispensable voice of critique and courage. I am most grateful to Wayne Koestenbaum, Steven Kruger, and Marilyn Hacker, treasured interlocutors who have guided me toward greater intellectual, poetic, and political clarity as a writer and a teacher. Thank you to my CUNY colleagues: Salita Bryant, Terrence Cheng, Shelly Eversley, Jessica Yood, and the members of the Faculty Fellowship Publication Program. Karstina Wong, my graduate assistant, was a welcomed companion in the hunt for archival treasures. Thank you, too, to the students in my spring 2011 graduate seminar, The Integrationist Imaginary, for returning me to many of the inspirations and obsessions on which this project is grounded. Support from the Andrew W. Mellon Fellowship at the Center for the Humanities, the Graduate Center, CUNY, PSC-CUNY, and Lehman College was instrumental in bringing this project to completion. I also thank Polly Thistlethwaite of the Mina Rees Library, Dean Rogers in Special Collections at Vassar College, and the staffs at the Gotlieb Archival Research Center, Boston University, the Schomburg Center for Research in Black Culture, and the Bancroft Library, University of California, Berkeley for their truly indispensable research assistance. Thank you, too, to Walter Biggins of the University Press of Mississippi for his steady enthusiasm and essential guidance with this project. I am grateful to Wardell Milan for granting me permission to use one of his wonderously instructive images of desire for the cover of this book.

The mere listing of the friends who endured the grumbling, read the endless drafts, cooked the meals, shared their homes, or tended to my tenderness is an inadequate expression of the relentless gratitude and love I feel for Amanda Semidey, Jane Sprague, Anne Rice, Clare Hagan and Ray Pultinas, Bertrand Nelson, Hakeem Oseni, Carl Strange, Marcie Wolfe, Delia Mellis, Jason Carey, Jen Weiss, and Peter Lemoine. Thank you to Lisa Rowan, Andy Schmidt, and Tricia Schmidt—siblings extraordinaire—for leaving me to do what I wanted to do and loving me anyway. I give daily thanks to my parents, Rebecca and Ken Schmidt, for their unwavering approval of all my elusive adventures. To my cousin-sister Ingrid A. Eberle, for our intellectual exchanges, culinary schemes, and her shamelessly unending love, I am forever indebted.

DESEGREGATING DESIRE

Introduction

The Half-Told Histories of Desegregation

I always wander back to the scene in Ann Petry's *The Narrows* when Camilo Sheffield visits, for the fifth time that week, The Last Chance, an ungenteel working-class bar in a black neighborhood of Monmouth, Connecticut. A figure of whiteness, marked by her blond hair, she sits among the judging eyes of the black men around the bar, quiet in its afternoon. Camilo, hungry for "her" man, is understood by all of us who have ever been left longing. The scotch is no salve. The just-ended record punctuates the silence and its desperation. She is neither welcomed nor made to leave.

My keeping company with Camilo is the sort of identification—across gender, race, and sexuality—repeatedly voiced in the moment in American literature, the ten years following World War II, that this book explores. If integration is a public act, readily available in our imagination through the iconic images of Ruby Bridges braving the steps of her elementary school escorted by federal marshals or young activists shielding themselves from fire hoses brutally directed at them by unruffled firemen, then desperate Camilo Sheffield, intruding into a male-defined, African American cultural space, in search of reconciliation with Link Williams, the black man with whom she has fallen in love, is part of the invisible tableau of desegregation that this project constructs. If integration is, in part, an act of moving in, inhabiting previously prohibited workplaces, educational institutions, and public spaces, then desegregation might be reconceived as an act of moving outward, most obviously away from discriminatory habits and communities of comfort but also a willed trample, motivated often by desires self-serving and often seemly, across color lines and social prohibitions. The eight writers on whom this book focuses take us into domestic spaces and unsettled public places, revealing new forms of interracial intimacy and sexual difference found there. But rarely is desegregation thought of as a private matter, as a history located not solely in contested public institutions but in transformed homes and personal lives. This study of postwar American literary culture, *Desegregating Desire*, in contrast, conceptualizes desegregation as both a racial and sexual phenomenon, one experienced in public interracial encounters and private interiorities.

In her 1946 primer on race relations, *Color Blind*, Margaret Halsey asserts that "the real basis of segregation is not repulsion, but attraction." Her observation that the social and economic barriers of Jim Crow America were put there not because of a "fear that the Negro would gravitate toward us" but out of "a fear that we would gravitate toward the Negro" reminds us that white Americans' confrontations with racial desire are crucial features of cultural, particularly literary, desegregation (103). Ralph Ellison, observing in his 1963 essay "World and the Jug" that "Southern whites cannot walk, talk, sing, conceive of laws or justice, think of sex, love, the family, or freedom without responding to the presence of Negroes," underscores the psychological interdependencies both crucial to and denied within segregation (163). Following Halsey's contention that segregation systematized and sublimated erotic attraction, I trace the ways that literary texts after World War II employed desegregation as an aesthetic and thematic element that acknowledges these cross-race attractions, that mines the complex emotional interdependencies, some contentious, some pleasurable, that Ellison has recognized as foundational to most interracial relationships in the United States. Desegregationist literature offers a compelling record of these "histories of hidden attractions" (Stockton 150).

Departing from the conventional treatment of the 1950s as a discrete unit, *Desegregating Desire* considers how, between 1945 and 1955, largely private changes in families, racial communities, and sexual practices anticipated and in some ways helped compose the integrationist agenda of the burgeoning U.S. civil rights movement. This inquiry begins with writing from the early 1940s and the cultural shifts that accompanied World War II and ends with work published in 1955, just after the *Brown v. Board of Education* decision and on the eve of the Civil Rights Act of 1957, events that ushered in more pronounced institutional changes. The project focuses on the ways eight divergent American writers desegregated desire in their literary work, a process understood in part as a refusal to bifurcate race and sexuality as well as public and private spheres in their respective representations of emergent postwar identities. Writing in the aftermath of World War II—its impact felt in workplaces, city streets, families, and the private intimacies of bedrooms—the poets and novelists explored in this study imagine and document integration, interracial sexuality, and reconfigured families in the United States.

The war and the subsequent social changes that it spurred transformed the lives of authors on whom *Desegregating Desire* centers. Its interrogation into varied forms of desegregation is organized into four pairings: Elizabeth

Bishop and Zora Neale Hurston; Gwendolyn Brooks and Edwin Denby; Ann Petry and William Demby; and Jo Sinclair and Carl Offord. For all of these writers, the war altered their art and redirected their activism. Hurston participated in the Recreation in War program, speaking to soldiers at segregated bases in Florida. Bishop, living in Key West, a major military hub, wrote of residents displaced by the war and witnessed the Cold War's imprint on daily life from her post as poetry consultant for the Library of Congress in 1949. Novelists Offord and Demby enlisted. After serving in Italy and North Africa, Demby returned to Italy, working there for more than thirty years, while Offord's transnational politics were shaped by his work with the army's Negro Port Company. Brooks's brother, Raymond, was also a soldier, and several of her friends from her South Side writing group also served; these men would later resurface in her war poems. A publicist for the Red Cross, Sinclair described civilian contributions to the war in her short fiction. And although the thirty-nine-year-old Denby was too old to enlist, he covered the war's impact on the arts in his *New York Herald Tribune* dance column, a position offered to him while the regular columnist served overseas.

Wartime upheavals and important public activism helped define the early chapters of the modern civil rights movement. Famously, A. Philip Randolph and Bayard Rustin planned a large-scale march on Washington in 1941, prompting President Franklin Roosevelt's desegregation of the defense industry. In June 1945, Paul Robeson performed at a Madison Square Garden rally in support of a permanent Fair Employment Practices Commission, which would help extend African Americans' recent economic gains beyond the war.[1] Alongside the public acts of courage required in the marches and sit-ins that defined the civil rights movement, another form of activism was less dramatic and more politically imprecise. Desegregation was about social and, more important, economic and educational access, but it also constituted a response to the restlessness of individuals who sought a fuller life outside of Jim Crow structures and repressive ideologies. Northern white liberals such as Halsey, a writer who examined military life with a comic edge, were also seeking new solutions to racial divisions. Attempts by whites to tackle the "Negro problem," of course, were nothing new, but part of what made the years immediately after the war distinctive was a more complex and visible examination by white Americans of the everyday racism that girded segregation. Halsey's *Color Blind* drew on her experience as the hostess of the Stage Door Canteen, an interracial club for American soldiers in New York. The book critiques white supremacy and the sexual mythology and social exclusions assumed within it. At times embarrassing in its earnest tone and racial essentialism, this primer on race relations nevertheless acknowledged the libidinal aspects of segregation and the sexual anxieties of desegregation that few race leaders or activists in the immediate postwar years would publicly address.

Wallace Thurman, of Harlem Renaissance fame, asserted in 1929 that integration is as much a private affair as public social policy: "Wholesale social equality may never become *de rigeur*, but there are constant encroachments of white on black and black on white, with the aggressiveness about evenly distributed. And it is these encroachments, minute and undercover, which will eventually solve the color problem in America, despite the race purists" (282). Taking seriously the claim that "minute and undercover" incidents of racial and sexual encroachments are central to social change and influential in shaping postwar identities, *Desegregating Desire* focuses on domestic upheavals, cross-racial identifications, and desegregated places, both public and private, in American literature of the 1940s and 1950s. The project theorizes desegregation as a compositional and implicitly political strategy that brings sexuality, particularly queer and interracial forms, into new public spaces and broader public consciousness. A central claim of *Desegregating Desire*, pursued in its close readings, is that sexuality, whether queer or interracial, had a crucial impact on race relations of the period in both the public and domestic spheres. Desire, whether explicitly sexual or a more nebulous form of erotic identification, was the catalyst for many of the personal and social transformations related to race found in the literature examined throughout this book. I characterize these novels, poems, letters, and essays as "half-told" histories because they capture private stories that are underwritten and sexual histories that remained a kind of secret in mainstream U.S. culture in the 1950s and to a lesser degree in literary studies still today.

Historicizing a Literature of Desegregation

World War II, as historian Joseph Goulden contends, "brought race relations out of the shadows" (353). The U.S. military's ambivalent wartime desegregation of service units, often taken as the beginning of the "official" story of integration, also provides a useful starting point for contextualizing the desegregationist literature that emerged after the war. The U.S. Army's first interracial combat units were instituted reluctantly in 1944, and then mainly because of personnel shortages rather than ideological shifts. In December 1946, taking rare initiative in correcting racial injustice, President Harry S. Truman formed the Committee on Civil Rights, which provided recommendations on a range of civil rights issues from fair employment practices to antilynching legislation. A July 1948 executive order outlawing segregation in the military was hailed as crucial step in making an integrated America a lived reality, but the fact that Congress failed to act on any of the committee's recommendations reveals how entrenched the country's racial divisions were.

Many of the black men and women and gays and lesbians discriminated against within the military felt acutely the irony of a segregated army waging war against fascism. In response to this hypocrisy, the *Pittsburgh Courier* organized its famous "Double V" campaign, rallying against the Nazis abroad and Jim Crow segregation at home. Despite ongoing hostility and near-total segregation, an estimated 909,000 African Americans enlisted, and although many of the 500,000 black soldiers who served overseas were assigned to noncombat positions, twenty-two African American combat units were deployed in Europe, including the much-revered Tuskegee Airmen (Moore 122–23). Many veterans who served honorably and expected to return home to better treatment and greater economic opportunities instead confronted racial violence, including lynchings. At the forefront of negotiating the racial paradoxes of postwar America, African American veterans, as historian Thomas Borstelmann explains, were emboldened by the war: "Those returning in uniform from abroad, having risked their lives for their country and having survived the often unspeakable brutalities of the modern battlefield, were even less inclined to accept the harassments and indignities of traditional segregation" (54). Intent on fashioning new social identities and shaped by political involvement and economic opportunities, they were forced to grapple with oppressive legacies that curtailed their hard-earned freedoms. A potent symbol in the era's films and literature, the reintegrated soldier paralleled the experiences of African Americans, immigrants from throughout Europe, and gays and lesbians who were also making claims for full citizenship in the nation's reimagined public life.[2]

The war and the social changes in its aftermath altered African Americans' self-perceptions, social practices, and economic conditions in significant ways. Two million black Americans worked in the defense industry, more than two hundred thousand were employed in the federal civil service, and the number of African Americans in unions doubled between 1940 and 1944 (Russell 120; Chafe 19). As a consequence of economic growth and labor shortages during the war as well as industrial expansion in the immediate postwar years, the number of African Americans working in professional, white-collar, and skilled or semiskilled jobs between 1940 and 1960 more than doubled. Migrating to urban centers in the North and West to secure job opportunities that were previously unavailable, more than 1.5 million African Americans left behind the oppressive racial conditions of the South and experienced new levels of social freedom—along with continued racial prejudice. And the North's generally better educational institutions helped facilitate additional social mobility for a younger generation of black Americans.[3] By the end of the war, the majority of African Americans for the first time resided in cities, and many American writers, including Gwendolyn Brooks, Carl Offord, and Edwin Denby, explored this altered urban landscape and its influence on private desires.

Demobilization, however, curtailed many of the economic opportunities that had brought black southerners to northern cities and into middle-class status. Shipyards and factories that were central to wartime production were shuttered after the war, making many of these social advancements short-lived.[4] National reconversion (the return of factories to civilian production after the war) signaled an economic crisis for white women and African American men and women, who lost jobs and faced psychological adjustments to a society in which race, gender, and sexuality had been radically transformed by war. Though rarely understood as connected, reconversion and desegregation were, in fact, entwined and at times competing processes that changed workplaces, homes, and intimate behaviors in postwar America.

Also spurred by the wartime economy, the integration of more women of all races into the public workforce and an expanding middle class altered conventional definitions of family and racial identity. Many African American women who migrated to the North shifted from agricultural work to better-paying jobs in manufacturing. Between 1939 and 1960, the percentage of black women employed in skilled, semiskilled, managerial, and professional occupations increased by more than 60 percent (Russell 120), and the percentage of black women employed in domestic labor also declined significantly, from 60 to 45 percent (Giddings 238).[5] Writing in 1950 in *Phylon*, a journal of African American politics and culture started by W. E. B. Du Bois, Charles King noted that 40 percent of women planned to continue working after their husbands returned from service. Many women who wanted to work nevertheless lost their jobs during the nation's postwar reconversion, a process that not only reshaped industries and businesses but ushered in a return to conservative gender roles.

Accounts of the sexism faced by women who were desegregating workplaces circulated in the popular media. Articles such "Manpower: Sex in the Factory," which appeared in a September 1942 issue of *Time* magazine, reported on the cultural adjustments to women in wartime factories but confirmed gender stereotypes in the process. "Some women take privileges," the article notes, and "powder their noses on company time before quitting, or waste time gossiping in gangs of two or more in the rest rooms" (21). These accounts typically focused on white women's experiences with integrating workplaces and failed to address the gender biases African American women had long experienced, particularly in domestic work often performed outside of public scrutiny. Still, women, white and black, claimed their newfound financial and social independence and began to refashion their public *and* private identities, influenced by progressive sexual attitudes, greater social mobility, and increased attention to issues of racial justice.

K. A. Cuordileone describes the postwar climate as marked by a "heightened female self-assertiveness, nourished by World War II and the space for female autonomy it created" ("'Politics'" 527). Perhaps no writer better documented America's postwar paradoxes and possibilities than Gwendolyn Brooks, whose neomodernist collection, *Annie Allen*, won the Pulitzer Prize for poetry in 1950. The award was a potent symbol of African American writers' creative expansiveness and arrival at mainstream recognition, but the literary accolade did little to relieve the poet's temporary housing troubles. Brooks and her husband spent the winter of 1951 shuttling between homes with their young son until their finances stabilized.[6] Brooks's early poetry and fiction testifies to the impact of the war on American women's lives and their social adjustments in its aftermath. Her protagonist in *Maud Martha*, discussed in chapter 2, clearly embodies the era's increasing social freedoms, but Maud's particular brand of polite if pointed assertiveness in the face of racial hostility highlights the inextricability of race and gender within destabilized postwar identities. Her subtle protests against a racist shopkeeper in the public sphere and her "color-struck" husband in the private, as well as her insistence on seeing a movie at a "white" theater, illuminate some of the ways that African American women both located social change in and were themselves changed by redefined public and domestic places.

These wartime changes—the increased industrialization of the South, hostilities directed at returning veterans and working women, and the altered economic status of many Americans across race—were reflected in novels and poetry written in the decade after the war. The discussion of Elizabeth Bishop and Zora Neale Hurston in chapter 1 touches on the ways both writers nostalgically depict fading southern communities in the wake of the region's rapid modernization. Jo Sinclair and Carl Offord, the focus of the final chapter, critique the fascism taking root in American cities, drawing parallels between Nazism and U.S. racial hostilities. And a central character in Ann Petry's *The Narrows*, Link Williams, is a returning veteran who reintegrates easily into a supportive black community but whose decision to pursue a romance with a white woman reveals the grave risks of claiming broader social freedoms.

Americans' attitudes about race, gender, and sexuality were also profoundly influenced by the escalating tensions between the United States and the Soviet Union after the war. Bolstering "containment" efforts by the U.S. military to deter the international spread of communism, an ideology of domestic containment circulated within popular culture, which encouraged Americans to embrace marriage and child rearing and argued that family stability was foundational to broader national security. This cultural reinvestment in conservative gender roles was reflected in the era's climate of suspicion: Those who deviated from gender, sexual, and racial norms were perceived as potential security threats. Scholars K. A. Cuordileone and Roderick A. Ferguson both have stressed the cultural contradictions that defined sexuality in the early years of the Cold War. Cuordileone notes that "social, economic, and market forces were encouraging a new current of sexual modernism" that existed in tension with "an official ideology that insisted on allegiance to the nuclear family and sexual restraint" ("'Politics'" 531). Enumerating the era's cultural paradoxes, Ferguson reminds us that "the constitution of an American gay subculture during World War II" was emerging simultaneously with "the denial/negation of that subculture by the American state immediately after the war" (234).

As the African American soldiers who were segregated while defending their country potently illustrate, the postwar United States, too, was defined by its racial contradictions. Interracial marriages were becoming more frequent and certainly less taboo. California, for example, dismantled its ban on interracial unions in October 1948. Nevertheless, Hollywood did not lift its ban on depictions of interracial marriage in movies for eight more years, and another year would pass before audiences would see an interracial couple embrace on screen. Despite this cultural ambivalence, American GIs and civilians of all races in changing workplaces and neighborhoods experienced increasingly interracial social circles and sex lives. Public, institutional forms of integration—changing military policies, legislative initiatives, and legal decisions—existed alongside other more subtle cultural shifts reported in a flurry of articles in the late 1940s: testimonies of white patients being treated by African American doctors, proclamations on interracial summer camps ("Negro, White Youngsters Lived Together and Liked It"), and profiles about social clubs (with optimistic names such as Club for Tomorrow and Club Miscegenation) that were formed to combat the ostracism that typically accompanied interracial marriage.[7]

Desegregating Desire pursues the overlap between sexual deviance and racial transgression as one of the ways that race and sexuality are mutually constitutive in desegregation, both public and private. Nowhere is this historical overlap between sexual deviants and social liberals more evident than in the zealous use of "blue discharges" for "disruptive" black and gay soldiers as a means of curtailing interracial couplings and homosexual acts. This classification, neither an honorable nor a dishonorable discharge, denied soldiers substantial GI benefits, including education and housing supplements. Following the war, the so-called panic over American disloyalty often conflated communists, homosexuals, and race liberals into a single figure of deviant citizenry. Roderick A. Ferguson notes that a "national anxiety about communist infiltration and the abolition of segregation created an ideological environment in which the stereotype of the Negro was symbolically congruent with the stereotypes of the communist and the homosexual. The Negro, like the homosexual, was the figure of social upheaval and irrationality" (254). Cold War conservatives centered their suspicions on interracial spaces of liberal politics, avant-garde artistry, and homosexual activity, resulting in the imprisonment or public exposure of many gay civil rights activists and liberal artists.[8] In a moment of destabilized gender categories and racial communities, "the seemingly contagious quality of sexual perversion" was an oft-voiced cultural fear (Kunzel 92). As with staunch segregationists who feared the infiltration of interracial sex into stable monoracial communities, homosexuality was viewed as an unmanageable, often undetectable, force that would destabilize workplaces and homes and contaminate unsuspecting youth.

In his study of interracial American culture in the same period, Alex Lubin argues that "interracial intimacy became a civil rights issue because of the ways that interracial romance and sexuality were at the core of race relations in America and because World War II activism and military service made new forms of intimate relations possible" (*Romance*, 152). This increasing discussion of interracial sexuality coincided with another form of intimate relations made more visible by the war—homosexuality. Sex segregation in the military and the development of screening measures to prevent homosexual men from serving created new homosocial spaces and brought homosexuality to the attention of broader society. World War II, however, was not transformative solely for male soldiers. A 1957 article on lesbianism in the *Chicago Defender* reported that Women's Army Auxiliary Corps as well as the army and navy had "problems with homosexuality within [their] ranks" (Duckett 7). Although gay and lesbian enclaves existed within urban centers before World War II, same-sex military environments, rapid urbanization during and after the war, and a robust discussion among psychologists about sexual difference contributed to a "newly manifest presence of gay men and lesbians in American cities" (Kunzel 86). As the popular media began to acknowledge with less disdain that gays and lesbians existed outside of marginalized sex districts, the battles continued over the meaning of sexual identity. Articles such as *Newsweek*'s "A Delicate Problem" and "Let's Be Honest about Homosexuals," which appeared in the black-targeted *Our World*, educated Americans about the causes of and potential "cures" for homosexuality. By the mid-twentieth century, sexual identity was understood as a matter of object choice and organized within a rigid homosexual/heterosexual binary, a viewpoint that replaced earlier models centered on gender inversion.[9]

Alfred Kinsey's groundbreaking *Sexual Behavior in the Human Male* played a crucial role in the increasing visibility of homosexual cultures, and his research dispelled many of the sexual stereotypes about African Americans and myths about women's sexuality more generally. In his initial 1948 study, Kinsey found "there is no evidence showing differences in sex histories of white and colored in [the] same economic-educational level" (Cherokee, "National Grapevine" 6). And the black-owned *Chicago Defender* reported that the sexologist's 1953 study of women's sexual behavior found that "85 percent of the women have violated some of the legally prescribed sex codes" ("Here's Kinsey's Report" 2). Heterosexual women in the decade after World War II were not only claiming more social freedom but, like gay men and lesbian women, could easily be condemned as transgressive lawbreakers and social deviants. This chipping away at myths about race, gender, and homosexuality became an invitation to postwar writers to more candidly explore the "queerer" forms of sexuality, including interracial desire. In chapter 3 I discuss the convergence of racial treason and sexual perversion in two African American novels from the 1950s and consider the ways that queer sexuality as a threatening contaminant to the social order remained a popular narrative.

The urban landscape for gays and lesbians, no less affected by military activity and postwar prosperity, was also becoming more interracial. Historians, including George Chauncey and Alan Bérubé, have examined an assortment of cultural spaces, both coded and overt, where interracial, homosexual desire became more publicly expressed, including costume balls, bathhouses, military bases, and middle-class, urban bars. In his study of gay and lesbian cultures in Washington, D.C., Brett Beemyn offers an important corrective to the predominant narrative of postwar gay bars as crucial cultural spaces in the coming out process. This research documents the experiences of African American gay men and lesbians, some of whom socialized at house parties and other informal gatherings as a solution to the city's segregation and police harassment. Similarly, Allen Drexel notes "the relatively high levels of interracial socializing within gay male social networks in Chicago" in the decade after World War II but also acknowledges that racist attitudes and racial divisions by no means disappeared in postwar gay subcultures (138).

Gay men and lesbians also began to formalize their activism within new political organizations. The Veterans Benevolent Association, formed in 1945, advocated for the rights of gay soldiers, and in 1950, the Mattachine Society began to provide an affirming place for previously isolated homosexuals. Founded in 1955, the Daughters of Bilitis was the first organization to focus on lesbians' civil rights. The assimilationist politics within many of these early organizations mirrored the rhetoric of universalism evoked by many civil rights activists, including some of the writers discussed in *Desegregating Desire*. Postwar statements of homosexual identity and civil rights, such as Robert Duncan's 1944 essay "The Homosexual in America" (discussed in chapter 2 as a surprising rejection of minority politics) and Edward Sagarin's influential manifesto *The Homosexual in America*, published in 1951, were often formulated in conversation with America's emergent civil rights movement.[10]

In cultural histories and literary studies of postwar America, the increasing visibility of the homosexual, African Americans' social transformations and economic ascent, and the growing sexual and gender freedoms of the 1950s are typically told as distinct narratives. *Desegregating Desire*, however, brings together these often half-told histories. It refigures the stories of Cold War American culture by focusing on connections and overlaps among the gay liberation movement, the feminist movement, and battles over segregation. Postwar writers played an important if sometimes maligned role in forwarding a racially imaginative and sexually expansive politics in the early years of the civil rights movement. Chapter 2 argues that the contested public spaces of the postwar city, as seen in the poetry of Gwendolyn Brooks and Edwin Denby, reflect the concomitant impulses toward racial integration and homosexual visibility in American society. Chapter 3 also makes explicit the imprint of queer sexuality on desegregationist writing, exploring the relationship between racial and sexual deviance through the figure of the white pervert. Imagined in these African American novels as a contaminant eroding the racial integrity and the assumed and publicly named heterosexuality of black communities, this racial and sexual outlaw helps articulate the era's anxieties about integration.

Remapping the Dreary Decade

Allen Drexel has argued that "by focusing primarily on the experiences of white, middle-class Americans," historians "have tended to portray the fifties in fairly stark, sweeping terms as a dreary decade dominated by Cold War ideology and domestic revivalism" (134). So if our sense of the 1950s is wrong or at least incomplete, how can an examination of desegregation in literature help us to see the era in more expansive ways? The ten-year period between the end of World War II and the landmark *Brown v. Board of Education* decision is a moment that critics of American literature have struggled to characterize. James Smethurst calls it a "murky period" (15) in which protest art and social realism were not abandoned but were redefined in response to what Alex Lubin has characterized as "a liminal moment in race formation" (*Romance* xvii). Thomas Borstelmann observes that World War II was a transformative event in race relations, with "many white Americans, particularly soldiers, emerg[ing] from the war with a more acute sense of the injustice of racial discrimination," a process that fostered racial consciousness as they learned about the horrific practices at concentration camps and the shameful treatment of African American soldiers on military bases after their return (42). Local and state governments across the country responded to interracial violence after the war by establishing race relations committees, and interracialism was embraced as "the dominant tactic of the civil rights movement" and was employed in the literature and film of the period (Sitkoff 679).

Racial exclusion became an unavoidable issue for Americans, and writers and editors looked for new artistic approaches for responding to the barriers to and paradoxes of American freedom. Bucklin Moon imagined his *Primer for White Folks* (1945), an interracial collection that stretched from W. E. B. Du Bois to Dorothy Parker, as a book for the "average American who is disturbed by the rising racial tensions which he feels around him and by the paradox of white and Negro relationships in a democracy waging a war of liberation and equality" (xi). Edwin Seaver, editor of the *Cross-Section* anthologies, noted that many of the thousands of manuscripts submitted to its 1944 inaugural volume addressed "the Negro problem," evidence that the country might be ready to confront its shameful history and imagine a desegregated future (qtd. in Jackson 178).[11]

Critics both applauded and cautioned against the interracial dimensions of the literature written in the wake of World War II. In 1950, Arthur P. Davis identified a trend (temporary, he thought) toward "good-will books"—that is, positive propaganda about race relations in which integration seems inevitable (145). In her 1950 survey of postwar African American poetry, Margaret Walker noted a maturation in African American literature that she attributed in part to the racially integrated projects of the Works Progress Administration, founded under the New Deal.[12] Unlike black artists of the 1920s, "creative writers, and poets especially, were no longer entirely isolated from other writers" (Walker 346). Walker's essay was part of the now-lauded collection of critical essays in the 1950 issue of *Phylon*, many of which expressed an "integrationist imperative" (Warren, *What Was* 44). Stacy Morgan identifies the early 1950s as a key moment of aesthetic transition in African American visual art and literature, "vastly understudied" but marked by "a heightened engagement with American high modernism and 'universalist' impulses" (303). In his expansive study of writers influenced by antifascist and Popular Front causes, Alan Wald identifies a "shared yet individualized political commitment" among the era's left-leaning writers despite the varied aesthetics and divergent political critiques found in their literature (14). My readings of Petry, Offord, Demby, and Brooks address these reinventions of modernist aesthetics and racial politics, and I also consider how white writers such as Elizabeth Bishop and Jo Sinclair produced literature that reflected these new beliefs about race and a growing public acknowledgment of Americans' racial interdependencies.

The typical sweeping assessment of postwar writing, particularly the work of African Americans, as embracing the universal fails to acknowledge the ways many writers directly addressed race but explored the affective and communal dimensions of racial identity outside of the conventions of social protest. Wald's impressive three-volume study of postwar leftist writing is a crucial exception, exploring the political development of some of the same writers taken up in *Desegregating Desire*, including Petry, Sinclair, and Offord. Readers today often dismiss the social optimism (which was rarely blind to an equally resonant racial discord) exhibited in many of these works and fail to take seriously the fact that many Americans found the era after World War II both frightening and promising.[13] The integrationist themes found in the work of 1950s writers were distinct from the earlier interracialism of the Harlem Renaissance in both their more hopeful stance about race relations and their more nuanced and less sensationalized treatment of interracial sex and intimate relations. In his canonical survey of African American literature from the 1960s, Robert Bone recognizes in the writing of the "war generation of the forties and fifties" "a wave of assimilationist sentiment" that distinguishes it from the "earlier Negro nationalism" found in much of the work of Harlem Renaissance writers (*Negro Novel* 160). Yet he also acknowledges that the era's racial aesthetics were far from uniform. Rather than embracing "color-blind" narratives, some postwar writers engaged in "a more intensive exploitation of race material for aesthetic ends" (171). While these existential meditations on racial belonging were often seen as a hallmark of postwar African American literature, my discussion of Sinclair as well as the racial poetics of Bishop and Denby illuminates some of the ways that white writers also pushed racial discourse into new artistic territories.

Recognizing, as Walker did, the importance of the Popular Front to changing race relations, Bill V. Mullen argues that the "1935 to 1950 period is better understood as the fruit of an extraordinary rapprochement between African-American and white members of the U.S. Left around debate and struggle for a new 'American Negro' culture" (5). While the rhetoric of interracial unity and universal humanity are evident in the texts I define as desegregationist literature, the debate and struggle that Mullen identifies over the definitional boundaries of American blackness also included an interrogation of whiteness as an identity and practice of privilege. These various challenges to individual and communal identity were crucial strands of literary projects intent on challenging and moving away from segregation. According to George Lipsitz, "More than the product of private prejudices, whiteness emerged as a relevant category in American life largely because of realities created by slavery and segregation, by immigration restriction and Indian policy, by conquest and colonialism" ("Possessive Investment" 370). It follows logically, then, that the process of desegregation institutionally as well as aesthetically must involve the scrutinizing of whiteness and its privileges, pathologies, and histories. A kind of ambassador of white self-scrutiny, southern writer Lillian Smith pointedly named the necessary shift in race relations after the war: "We have looked at the 'Negro problem' long enough. Now the time has come for us to right-about-face and study the problem of the white man: the deep-rooted needs that have caused him to seek those strange, regressive satisfactions are derived from worshiping his own skin color. The white man himself is one of the world's most urgent problems today: not the Negro, not other colored races. We whites must learn to confess this" ("Addressed" 331). This pointed interrogation of whiteness within social critiques by both black and white writers is another feature of postwar desegregationist literature that distinguished it from the interracialism of earlier American literature, and I pursue this thread through the writing of all eight writers discussed in *Desegregating Desire*.

Social realism, reconceived rather than wholly abandoned, remained the preferred aesthetic in the immediate postwar years for many left-leaning writers interested in race, but other artists, moving away from sociological portraits of the "race problem" and reductive definitions of racial identity, began to translate psychoanalytic discourse and existential themes into literary meditations on racial belonging and social alienation.[14] The editorial for the special January 1947 issue of *Survey Graphic* on segregation named it as a pressing social issue because it reflected a "national confusion" with regard to racial matters (Sancton 11). Naming loneliness as a central trope in American literature, Toni Morrison argues that the "school of the alienated hero" that emerged out of World War II was a response to a fragile culture in which Americans "hadn't reconstructed that community. Everything was in doubt" ("Conversation"). Although a welcomed challenge to racial divisions, desegregation also contributed to the unraveling of insular, often protective racial communities, and rendering this cultural dislocation and alienation in its varied racial and sexual forms became an alluring challenge for writers. The growing mainstream interest in psychoanalysis and the embrace of existentialism by intellectuals and artists is reflected in many of the texts examined in *Desegregating Desire*. Fittingly, my readings draw on psychoanalytic concepts to better understand Cold War race relations. Denby's exploration of sexual subjugation in some of his sonnets, for example, is clearly indebted to Freudian theories of the death drive. In Demby's *Beetlecreek*, Bill Trapp's childhood identification with African Americans as lost loved objects helps explain his racial melancholia. And trauma's important role in subjectivity formation is a central idea in both Offord's *The Naked Fear* and Sinclair's *The Changelings*. Underscoring the psychological impact of desegregation, this literature scrutinizes the desire and disdain that animate interracial intimacy.

In his examination of the ways modernization and urbanization "reconstituted the meaning and regulation of black/white sexuality in America," Kevin J. Mumford argues that interracial sexuality shifted from being largely a sociological concern in urban vice districts to a provocative theme explored by avant-garde artists of the 1920s and beyond (xv). Much of the interracialist literature of the 1920s focused on sensationalized encounters across the color line and/or framed race relations as largely hostile and within the conventions of the social protest novel. In addition, expressions of cross-race desire or scenes of interracial socializing were largely confined to the public spaces of the nightclub, workplace, or city street. By the early 1950s, as *Desegregating Desire* documents, literary representations of interracial sexuality were common in both neomodernist poetry and pulp paperbacks, but the taboo was hardly passé. In contrast to earlier writing, novels and poems written during the early Cold War represented a greater range of interracial relations, and these depictions, though perhaps sentimental, were often less sensationalized than their predecessors. In a discussion of 1950s literary representations of interracial relationships, historian Judith E. Smith distinguishes between a more restrained "call for a moderate, paternalistic, contained interracialism" and more candid representations of interracial love that perhaps did not shy away from its sexual dimensions (118). In examining desegregation, early histories of the civil rights movement focused on interracial political allegiances rather than on intimate relationships. *Desegregating Desire* avoids this tendency by looking at varied forms of interracial intimacy and authors' reimaginations of racialized desire in private spaces. Texts focused on domestic and psychological interiors examined race relations outside of a wholly sociological framework and often imagined interracial relations as entangled in new social places neither wholly public or private. In his compelling readings of 1950s comics and movies, Alex Lubin argues that these popular genres treat interracial romance as "a matter of private choice rather than public politics" (*Romance* xvii). If we understand literature as both reflecting and circulating within public life, then we must locate and interrogate forms of interracial sexuality that are present and policed in public places. The novels by Petry, Sinclair, Demby, and Offord discussed in this book explore the porous borders between private and public, specifically showing the tensions and challenges that arise when interracial sexuality is publicly articulated. Our excursion into these sexual geographies finds interracial sexuality unsettling a variety of public sites, from the British pub to the local bar in an African American neighborhood to a teenagers' clubhouse.

Redefining and Rereading Desegregation

Desegregation, a word that even sounds less hopeful than *integration*, encompasses confrontations with and reorientations toward the social Other that demand inevitable reorientations of the self. Noting the distinction drawn by the National Association for the Advancement of Colored People (NAACP) between integration and desegregation, Alex Lubin writes that desegregation "entailed the legal fight for access to public institutions such as schools and transportation. Integration, on the other hand, meant creating social friendships and personal relationships with whites. The NAACP suggested that integration would likely be the result of desegregation but that the fight for desegregation was not primarily a fight for integration" (*Romance* 76). This distinction between the institutional and the interpersonal neglects the affective complexity of desegregation, in which ambivalent desires—fear, attraction, revulsion, and identification—are equally pronounced in citizens' public assertions of their rights, a social reality documented in varied forms by the eight writers at the center of *Desegregating Desire*. Desegregation, we will discover in these literary works, is not a linear narrative of progress but a discourse of failings, trespasses, unreciprocated desires, and personal transformations.

Aiming to trouble the optimism associated with the term *integration*, my critical readings also dissect the alienation, silence, exploitation, and trauma that defined desegregation as represented in American literature written before the civil rights, women's, and gay and lesbian movements had reached mainstream definition. Scholars including Mary Dudziak, Nikhil Singh, and Thomas Sugrue have drawn our attention to earlier chapters in the civil rights movement and previously undervalued activism of the 1930s and 1940s. Still, many of these studies gloss over sexuality as a civil rights issue and an influential factor in the movement. Similarly, earlier literary and cultural scholarship on the Cold War provided important analysis of the era's gender reentrenchment and sexual politics but tended to ignore race or treat it superficially.[15] *Desegregating Desire* emphasizes how race and the ways it was being reconstituted outside traditional communities and across social boundaries were always implicated in the containment politics of the Cold War. This inquiry also reveals how American writing committed to an expansive notion of civil rights often insisted on an interrogation of the sexual mythologies that helped secure segregation. Robert Bone has observed that despite legal correctives to segregation, integration was slow "to be validated in the popular consciousness" (*Negro Novel* 161). My project understands literary works such as Petry's *The Narrows* and Sinclair's *The Changelings* as validating sources in that process of social change. These postwar writers recognized that sexual freedoms must be encompassed in civil rights; therefore, I interpret the imagined intimacies in this literature as political gestures intended to critique and circumvent segregation.

In a landmark study of early twentieth-century African American literature, Siobhan Somerville deftly investigates "the ways in which crises of masculinity and sexuality are linked to negotiations of the imaginary color line institutionalized by Jim Crow segregation" (134), but more critical attention needs to be paid to the parallel strategies employed by American writers after World War II to destabilize racial and sexual divisions. What roles do reconfigured and more publicly articulated same-sex and interracial sexualities play in the dissolution of Jim Crow protocols? This book theorizes desegregation as a response to as well as a refusal of a politics of racial containment. The postwar writing on which I focus typically imagines forms of desegregated desire that extend beyond the critically privileged terms applied to the 1950s of crisis, transgression, and policing. While the interracial romance at the heart of *The Narrows* (a novel as much about insurmountable class differences as racial divisions) is doomed in part by social discrimination, and both Bishop's and Hurston's explorations of women's social ambivalence function as an indirect commentary on the nation's reconversion to gender conservatism after the war, many of these texts also present unconventional sexual identities and interracial relations that are unfettered by communal policing and discrimination. While the homophobia of McCarthyism cannot be downplayed, the literature produced in the ten years immediately after World War II reveals a more complex social positioning for gays and lesbians and leftist artists, both black and white.

The interconnectedness between race and sexuality in American desegregation documented in postwar literature was belatedly covered in the mainstream press. A September 1958 article in *U.S. News and World Report*, for example, noted that the "issue of sex relationships is breaking more and more into the open as the underlying cause of Southern hostility to integration"; the magazine polled a variety of academics and race leaders about the sexual anxieties surrounding integration ("What South Really Fears" 76). The interviews explored the threat of racial "intermixing," the likelihood of a surge in intermarriages, and the fear that African Americans' cultural distinctiveness would be "absorbed" into mainstream white culture (79). Distancing himself from the interviewer's sensationalistic approach to interracial relationships, sociologist Preston Valien stressed the larger democratic goals of integration, of which sexual choice was merely one component: He asserted that "the intent of desegregation" was "to widen the participation of the Negro in American culture" (86). He argued that integration sought a "general freedom from restrictions," including sexual prohibitions (84). Edgar T. Thompson, another sociologist, posited that blacks and whites understood integration differently, with African Americans stressing the possibilities of social change and white Americans wondering how new conceptions of racial identity and racial intermixing would change intimate relationships. Thompson believed that "Negroes tend to define desegregation in terms of citizenship and job opportunities, whereas whites tend to define it in terms of racial status and racial purity" (89). However, these different perspectives on integration were not so cleanly divided along racial lines. *The Changelings* is certainly concerned with the ways that postwar changes in race and sexuality altered a younger generation's sense of American citizenship, and Offord's pulp novel *A Naked Fear* critiques the idea of "racial blood" and embraces a politics of racial indeterminacy.

The fear that integration would promote miscegenation (as conservatives termed it and a term Lillian Smith hated) was a cultural anxiety that liberals as well as conservatives repeatedly addressed. Social scientists and race leaders discussed the likelihood that interracial sex and intermarriage would increase with integration, weighing in on whether the "Negro race" would cease to exist because of intermarriage. In 1956, the *Atlantic Monthly* offered opposing commentaries on whether integrated schools would "lead to mixed blood" (Sass 45). Herbert Ravenel Sass, a conservative southern writer and historian, championed America's "magnificent achievement" under segregation and dismissed scientific findings that race has no biological basis before concluding that "defenseless adolescents" would be "exposed to brainwashing" (49) and "mixed matings would become commonplace, and a greatly enlarged mixed-blood population would result" (48). Rejecting Sass's claim that African American leaders desired intermarriage, Oscar Handlin, a professor of history at Harvard, assured readers that the "notion that Negroes are eager to marry whites is a delusion born of the white man's own vanity and of his ignorance of the real sentiments of his fellow Americans of another color" (53). Disagreeing on whether desegregation would further stabilize American society or turn it upside down, the commentators, perhaps not surprisingly, arrived at the same conservative conclusion: People have a social propensity for sameness, a desire to exist in communities with those of "common cultural, social, and religious backgrounds" (53). Whether they embraced desegregation or resisted it, readers were assured that a society of "mixed-bloods" was not the nation's future.

The eight authors on whom this book focuses are a little less confident about such social stability; they turn repeatedly to figures who reject social homogeny and who desire new social spaces that bridge racial and sometimes sexual difference. The characters in their novels, stories, and poems distinguish and defend their personal desires from those of their communities, choices that usually resulted in social marginalization. By exploring the desires that motivated and the consequences of cross-racial relationships in multiple postwar literary works, we can see that desegregation is not always characterized by assimilationist or conformist impulses. Defying social progressives' assurances that desegregation would not spark rampant interracial sex as well as conservative critics' protestations that racial amalgamation was inevitable, these eight authors explored sexuality as a crucial dimension of interracial relationships with candor, psychological complexity, and in a range of ways: in relationships centered on domestic labor, interracial affairs, unhappy marriages, as well as more socially transgressive and politically problematic attractions that crossed religious and age prohibitions.

Focusing on desegregation as not only a literary theme but also, and more important, as an aesthetic practice permits a reevaluation of the 1950s and foregrounds another predicament of the postwar age: the tension between individual desires and communal belonging. The resolution, reconciliation, and cooperation located in the interracial, desegregated, or tentatively integrated places depicted in this literature reveal a more complicated social landscape in the early years of both the Cold War and the civil rights movement. In particular, approaching desegregation as a concept distinct from integration offers a valuable corrective to scholars' harsh critiques of the naive embrace of a color-blind politics by postwar liberals who made the optimistic claim that social integration, assisted by postwar economic gains, was attainable for African Americans.[16] Characterized as a literature of assimilation, wide-eyed universalism, and diluted radicalism, postwar writing that reflects this liberal idealism is often maligned. One of my intentions is to take seriously (which is to say sympathetically) an integrationist politics—an embrace, even celebration, of interracial cooperation—as a distinct moment in America's racial history that offers a rich literary archive for examining the queer sexualities that often animate interracial relations. Moreover, the range of political perspectives held by these authors and contained, however coded, in their work demonstrates that desegregation was not a monolithic social issue but a complex process that influenced communities, families, and private desires in a variety of ways.

Race liberals of the time may have expressed a now-embarrassing optimism and racial essentialism, but they also recognized that sexuality was a crucial topic to address in forwarding a desegregationist politics. In *Killers of the Dream* (1949), a fascinating meditation on the psychological impact of southern segregation, Lillian Smith insists on a relationship between racial and sexual transgression, finding the prohibitions of segregation echoed in sexual taboos such as masturbation and interracial sex. Exposing the "relentless interlocking of these learnings" (91), her work explores the deeply knotted education southern children receive regarding sex and race. If the lessons of segregation are enmeshed with a child's sexual education, then logically desegregation is another social process inextricably intertwined with sexuality. These eight postwar writers contemplate varied forms of racialized sexuality to rework, unsettle, or blur the color line, a border that often merges with what Smith terms the "sex line" (84). Like Ellison's little man at Chehaw Station who "wants the interconnections revealed" ("Little Man" 499), the poets and novelists in *Desegregating Desire* are attuned to the emotional interdependencies of race and sexuality as well as to gender and class shifts in postwar American culture. For Smith, both segregation and sexual prohibitions are social customs that attempt to constrain the physical body, which is seen as in danger of succumbing to racial or sexual temptations. Writing of the prohibitions on where bodies can go and what they can do, Smith observes, "Signs put over doors in the world outside and over our minds seemed natural enough to children like us, for signs had already been put over forbidden areas of our body" (90). In contrast to this cloistering, desegregation can be conceived as an opening up of the body, permitting mobility and exposure to racial and sexual difference and the possibilities of desire. In mapping desegregation, I necessarily pay close attention to bodies that transgress the borders of segregated places, bodies that meet across racial difference and thereby create new social spaces, and the body's integration of new ideas and ways of being into the most intimate of psychological spaces.

The elasticity of the term *desegregation*, once unmoored from the narrow association with the Jim Crow South, could be a liability for this project but it is also its strength, allowing for an examination of greater aesthetic variance than a focus on texts strictly about the civil rights movement or the "race problem" would allow. Bishop and Hurston, both residents of Florida during this period, write about the vexed interracial relationships found in southern homes, defined by the power hierarchies of domestic labor, which I read as a commentary on both the era's reinvestment in domesticated womanhood and a growing interest in the psychologies of interracial dependence. Denby's poetry and Brooks's domestic epic, "The Anniad," include no direct references to desegregation or the "race problem," yet their rethinking of both poetic form and the sexual and gender identities of postwar urban life provide important evidence of the way sexuality was desegregated and brought into public scrutiny. The midcentury anxiety over sexual desires that exceed the confines of heterosexual domesticity, implicitly monoracial, is both represented and critiqued in Demby's and Petry's experimental narratives about interracial relations and the troublesome eroticism that can define them. Sinclair and Offord, trained in the proletarian protest tradition, depict desegregation as both traumatic and transformative, finding it in symbolic locations—a multiethnic neighborhood in middle America and among troops abroad. These authors collectively offer a rich racial geography in which to consider the changing social-sexual dynamics of public places and private homes.

Desegregation as a Critical Practice

Desegregating Desire enacts its own integrationist ethos, which involves exploring the connections between white and black writers to illuminate the interracialism of this period. Part of a larger commitment to desegregationist criticism that documents the interplay between white and African American literary traditions, this book offers a model for reading post–World War II literature and culture interracially that is indebted to the work of Toni Morrison, Michael North, Ann Douglas, Rachel Blau DuPlessis, and Alan Wald, among others. The juxtaposition of white and black authors is neither a gimmick nor, I hope, forced. The joining of writers typically not associated with each other—Elizabeth Bishop and Zora Neale Hurston, for example—is intended to illuminate the inevitable blind spots in critical projects exclusively focused on race, gender, or sexuality rather than their interdependencies. An integrationist criticism seeks to unearth compatibilities, intertextualities, and tensions across race, aesthetic school, and genre. It, too, implicitly challenges a tradition of segregated scholarship that obscures the ongoing interdependencies between and collaborations among black and white American artists. My pairing of Petry and Demby, two African American novelists, in chapter 3 departs from the interracial pairings in other chapters because their collective conversation regarding white perversion presented a more compelling reason for reading them intertextually than a pairing based on racial difference. Each chapter is organized around a shared set of thematic concerns made richer through an integrationist critical practice that unearths previously neglected responses to sexual and racial changes in American society: For example, poetic formalism, white perversion, and racial damage provide frameworks for reading desegregation as a politics and an aesthetic that connects each pair of writers.

Given the varying aesthetics and pronounced differences in the racial politics of the eight authors examined in *Desegregating Desire*, my insistence on artistic commonalities between writers will no doubt rouse skepticism. What could Brooks, the great poet-witness to postwar Chicago, possibly have in common with New York School dance critic Denby? My answer, in part, is that their reworking of the sonnet, with its private and public structures, is a shared artistic endeavor indebted to the desegregationist practices of their historical moment. In arguing that each pair of writers held not dissimilar understandings of an altered American landscape and dreamed of yet unrealized social identities in which sexual freedoms assisted in the unsettling of gender and racial norms, I highlight the artistic challenges—indeed, failings—of representing sexuality within civil rights discourse or a desegregationist project. In asserting progressive (as well as more retrograde, particularly in the case of Bishop) racial ideologies, the novels and poems discussed in *Desegregating Desire* are certainly less explicit and didactic than later literature about race in America. To some readers, certain texts' relationship to desegregation might seem tenuous, but read collectively, these texts demonstrate the divergent strategies, including cross-race writing rich with psychological complexity, used by postwar American writers to address interracial sexuality and integrated cultural spaces.

Explaining the value of reading disjunctively, outside of racial categorization and narrow definitional boundaries of literary traditions, McKay Jenkins notes, "As with black texts, once white texts are relived of the need to fall into line, to be conceived of as monochromatic and uniform, we can more easily understand the contradictions and nuances of color that exist within them" (186). Similarly, the juxtaposition of authors in this book broadens our understanding of racial aesthetics in the United States in the middle of the twentieth century, revealing the complexity and ambiguities in whiteness and blackness as cultural signs. The stark differences, for example, between literary representations of race and the racial politics of Sinclair and Bishop, both self-identifying as advocates of social change, does not permit a simplistic characterization of white American authors' responses to integration. In disciplinary allegiance with Emily Bernard's call for a "radical reading" of "black-authored texts" to consider "the challenges each and every one makes to our beliefs about and expectations of black authorship itself" (110), my attention to both canonical and minor authors and my valuing of failed aesthetic experiments is also a needed challenge to our understanding of Cold War literature, particularly the racial-sexual dynamics often underexplored in the criticism of the era's literature. I argue, for example, that Petry's and Demby's explorations of the overlap between desegregation and sexual deviance function as a critique of African Americans' racial and sexual provincialism as well as an implicit challenge to the artistic prescriptions imposed on the black writer. Not only does this study signal the rich postwar literary landscape available to scholars of African American literature beyond the monumental work of Wright, Ellison, and Baldwin, but my readings also disrupt simplistic characterizations of both postwar African American aesthetics and the interracial strands of Cold War American literature.

This project, however, is not an excavation of an alternative ancestry of postwar black and white writers, although there is merit in such an endeavor. (Sinclair was influenced by Wright, for example; Bishop reviewed Brooks's second book.) Rather, this collection of writers, canonical and forgotten, permits us to look more holistically at postwar literature in the United States and to see the civil rights novel not as an exclusively black-authored text and responses to Cold War domestic/sexual containment not as purely the concern of white American writers. To better illuminate the ways racial, sexual, and social desires are desegregated in these literary texts, *Desegregating Desire* surveys the integrationist politics and interracial cultural contexts of each of these writers. For example, I note the influence of white mentors on the careers of Brooks and Hurston and the importance of artistic exchanges with African American artists for white writers Sinclair and Denby. Offord's and Demby's interracial marriages are other immediate examples of the transforming and increasingly desegregated American society in which this writing was produced. In certain cases—that is, in my reading of Bishop's and Hurston's racial aesthetics—I rely more heavily on biography to elucidate the changes in race and sexuality that are central to this postwar moment. In mixing biographical details, material from the era's popular culture, and close reading, I conceive of desegregation as a multidimensional, often intimate phenomenon that exists outside of but also perhaps alongside the "official" histories of American integration.

The ways these writers of the war generation, both white and black, were shaped by Jim Crow and translated those experiences into their writing is a related framework used to connect the authors within and across chapters as well as to explore their different racial politics and social positions. For these eight writers, segregation—racial, gendered, and sexual—serves as a departure point for literary visions of a more integrated American life. Many of these texts make visible the ways that racism, sexism, and religious conservatism have permeated even the purportedly private domestic sphere; for many of these writers, the desegregation of desire in the private realm is imagined as the starting point for broader, more public social change.

Locating Desegregation

Although spatial metaphors (invocations of borders, barriers, and curtains) dominate Cold War discourse and critiques of containment culture, segregation—another regime centered on the oppressive manipulation of social spaces—is rarely theorized in relation to the Cold War and its parallel practices of surveillance. Elaine Tyler May and more recently K. A. Cuordileone and Deborah Nelson have examined the ways that containment ideology extended beyond foreign policy to the policing of gender and sexual practices and identities deemed threatening to traditional family life. We must also consider how the containment of social difference influenced racial attitudes and practices, especially the ways that adherence to racial segregation was demanded and the ways that those who embraced integrationist politics and interracial sexual practices were policed. The Cold War suppression of gender and sexual nonconformity overlaps with the sexual monitoring and physical constriction that defined segregation in the United States. African Americans experienced containment policies domestically in northern cities and throughout the South for decades before the Cold War.

Characterizing the Cold War as a "topological crisis," Nelson offers a needed analysis of a cultural moment in which "bounded spaces of all kinds seemed to exhibit a frightening permeability" (26). Given that both the Cold War and desegregation are characterized by the policing and reappropriation of social spaces, we might look for the ways the writers studied in *Desegregating Desire* address desegregation through a critique of gendered and racialized places. These eight poets and novelists understand desegregation as not solely about reconfigured public spaces or the literal physical occupation of previously prohibited places; they also understand the coming together of bodies—socially and sexually—across race as well as the emergent public identity of the homosexual as crucial acts of desegregation, as erosions of social segregation and invisibility. Locating some of the boundaries of and spatial freedoms within the term *desegregation*, this project explores interracial encounters in several locations—Floridian cities, small towns in West Virginia and Connecticut, multiethnic Cleveland, and the urban centers of New York and Chicago.

This focus on desegregated places also helps to distinguish the literature written in in the late 1940s and early 1950s from the interracialist texts and cultures of earlier periods in U.S. history. In looking at desegregated spaces, we can locate new articulations, however tentative, of the interdependencies of race and sexuality, including interracial relations not exclusively defined by sexual attraction or racial hostility. These versions of interracialism feel significantly different from those of the Harlem Renaissance and American modernism of the 1920s. Desegregated places—spaces of interracial contact, interracial collaboration, or tentative integration and the particular desires that animate them—are a thematic thread that connects authors within and across chapters. Each chapter includes some evaluation of each writer's spatial-racial representations and considers the ways these texts conflate and/or rework the division between private and public space and compose models of imagined kinship, new racial communities, and political affiliations. Another connective thread between these widely disparate authors and texts is their shared interest in finding and describing alternative forms of sociality. In their examination of contested spaces—in neighborhood bars, city streets, gullies where children play, movie theaters or hotels, among others—these writers explore the charged attractions and revulsions that unsettle what James Baldwin has poetically termed the "bleak boundaries" (*Notes* 64) that race draws, and they sometimes imagine new forms of intimacy within these socially calcified locations.

In conversation with a broader history of integration that centers on reconstituted public space, this study understands the desegregation of desire as a process that reimagines the borders of public and private spheres. The tensions between private and public discourses has been a frequent focus of recent studies of postwar American culture, including Alex Lubin's *Rights and Romance* and Judith E. Smith's *Visions of Belonging*. In mapping the relationship between public and private, Lubin argues that "postwar culture attempted to confine the explosive potential of crossing the color line by discursively containing interracial intimacy to the domestic sphere of the family. In this case, the space of domesticity—although highly politicized—was defined outside the public sphere in which civil rights debates took place" (xviii). Given African Americans' always contingent access to full citizenship and the historical barriers to their private intimacies, Candice M. Jenkins has argued that "the 'public' and 'private' faces of blackness cannot, and perhaps should not, be distinguished with any great ease" (33). Similarly, Ralph Ellison has asserted that given the racial economy that has shaped America, domestic spaces, even those understood as racially monolithic, are already marked as interracial. African American domestic workers, for example, occupied a marginal status in public life yet were positioned most intimately within white Americans' homes. Naming this position "the listening post," Ellison values the agency within this cultural space, "which puts one in the position of making judgments, of seeing, or of exercising sympathy" ("Indivisible Man" 388). In *The Narrows*, Petry explores this idea of psychospatial contradictions within African American experience—of both centrality to and marginalization within structures of power. Elizabeth Bishop does the same in her early Key West poems.[17] Within this moment of tentative desegregation with its contested spaces, postwar writers logically were drawn to this reconsideration of the binary between public and private, a construct always problematic for African American artists that became increasingly questioned by white and queer artists. In focusing on a variety of increasingly desegregated spaces, both public and domestic, as well as places that could not be comfortably categorized, *Desegregating Desire* challenges the sharp divisions and adversarial relationships conceptualized between the public and private spheres. Focusing attention on interracial intimacy and desiring/desired bodies in desegregated places, this project affirms that for gays and lesbians and African Americans, sexuality has never been a private matter and that the boundaries between public life and private behavior are always tenuous. The writers in this study insist on the muddled and politically beneficial interplay between these spheres. They understand that the desegregation of public space and substantive social change require the reimagining of private spheres where change might be more subtle and fleeting.

Desegregated Writing and Cross-Race Identifications

Christina Klein has argued that rereading the 1950s through the lens of integration offers new perspectives and raises new questions about the era, offering a counterdiscourse that stresses cultural interdependence rather than the much-theorized containment culture of the Cold War.[18] Arguing that such a reframing "introduces a new set of questions about postwar culture," Klein states, "Instead of investigating texts for the interplay of subversion, policing, repression, and paranoia—the familiar thematics of containment culture—we can focus instead on how texts expressed the idea of 'interdependence' among nations and how they fostered a sense of identification between Americans and 'Others' in the non-Western world" ("Sentimental" 154). Scholars including Borstelmann, Von Eschen, Singh, and Dudziak have provided valuable investigations into the interdependencies of the domestic civil rights movement and U.S. foreign policy during the Cold War. Other studies on the postwar family, including those by Judith E. Smith and Ruth Feldstein, have examined the ways race and gender were intimately connected in civil rights discourses and Cold War popular culture. While understandings of Americans' encounters with foreign Others during the Cold War are indeed crucial and the racial discourses that defined Cold War families are considered here, I remain focused on how American citizens dealt with otherness within their own country in the wake of World War II and particularly on the ways alienated subjects formed identifications outside of traditional family structures with people and communities across racial, cultural, and sexual difference.

Revisiting literary representations of the era's changing racial and sexual politics that have been historically neglected or racially segregated in criticism, my project joins Klein's in generating new understandings of American literature in the early years of the Cold War. In particular, *Desegregating Desire* stresses the importance of cross-race writing for both white and black writers as a form of desegregation that insists on the interracial (often sexual) nature of both American homes and the nation's public spaces. To document and enact desegregation, these writers often utilized cross-race writing—writing from the perspective of the previously maligned and distanced Other (a term that is dangerously ambiguous yet readily employed)—but they also reworked traditional literary forms, adapted social protest to render aesthetic and social pressures, and turned to the lexicon of psychoanalysis to do their work. Desegregation, then, provides a useful framework for analyzing the queer identifications and interracial intimacies that though underrecognized were influential factors in both the emergent civil rights movement and in

Cold War popular culture. As an alternative to containment practices that encouraged social isolation and communal suspicion, this project focuses on literature that imagines mutuality, collectivity, and what Katherine Bond Stockton calls "social communion" as well as their impediments (23). *Desegregating Desire* tilts its analysis toward literature that imagines and forwards a complex range of interracial intimacies that both unsettle racial categories rooted in biological essentialism and mine the social potentials within fleeting interracial exchanges and more substantive interracial allegiances.

Identification, particularly in the form of cross-race writing, offers a valuable lens for reading postwar interracial culture within the framework of desegregation. Ralph Ellison's wry observation that "everyone wants to tell us what a Negro is, yet few wish, even in a joke, to be one" ("World" 163) masks the complex, ambiguous racial identifications found in postwar America that some of the nation's writers tried to capture in their essays, novels, and poems. Scant critical attention has been paid in particular to the identifications across race that shaped artists' lives and work. In the next chapter, for example, I consider the ways Bishop's life and early poems were informed by a troublesome identification with African American and Cuban American cultures in Key West. I contrast Bishop's racial ventriloquism with Hurston's in *Seraph on the Suwanee*, which centers on a white woman's sexual repression and consequently required the novelist to forge an aesthetic and psychological identification—what Jonathan Ellis terms "imaginative empathy" (137)—with white femininity.

Identifications, Diana Fuss reminds us, "delight, fascinate, puzzle, confuse, unnerve, and sometimes terrify," and they are often messy, unrealized, and flawed (2). In my discussions of cross-race writing, I have tried to remain equally attuned to the "imperializing character of many cross-cultural identifications" (Fuss 8). Without dismissing the stereotypical portraits of "local color" and emotional projections that often characterize white writers' literary representations of African American lives, my textual readings recognize the psychological attachment and artistic importance of African American culture and of particular interracial relationships to the work of many white American writers. These attachments are central to understanding this desegregationist moment and its aesthetics. This investigation of cross-race identification is one response to Toni Morrison's call to "examine the impact of racial hierarchy, racial exclusion, and racial vulnerability and availability on nonblacks who held, resisted, explored, and altered these notions" (*Playing* 11). Sinclair clearly saw her own struggle for visibility as a Jewish lesbian as intimately connected to African Americans' attempts to claim full citizenship. She was changed by and wrote about their history of resistance. In her novel *The Changelings*, a central focus of chapter 4, African Americans' quest for racial equality was seen as part of a Jewish teenager's journey of cultural and sexual liberation; the narrative explores racial vulnerability across cultures but also imagines interracial allegiances as its antidote. Ellison argued that if "white Negroes" were dedicated to "a basic resuscitation of the original ideals of social and political justice," then "they were Negroes too—if they wish to be" ("World" 178). In this regard, a shared sense of justice might locate writers such as Sinclair, within a metaphorical or ideological (I am reluctant to say spiritual but that, too, is there) identification with blackness.

I am not arguing that white writers who chose to depict black subjectivity and explore African Americans' experiences (however limited those explorations) or whose texts contain racial ventriloquism of black speech wanted to be black. Rather, desegregating desire, as a process in which identifications across race become visible, demonstrates white writers' insistence on highlighting racial interdependency, on acknowledging the libidinal undercurrents within many interracial relationships as part of a desegregationist imperative. Cross-race writing requires writers to inhabit artistically, which is to say psychologically, racial differences—nebulous whiteness or blackness—that remain largely inaccessible to the white writers whom I discuss. In defining identification as a "play of difference and similitude in self-other relations," Fuss points out the ways that writing across difference is inextricable from the processes of self-creation (2). In much of the literature explored in *Desegregating Desire*, we discover that American identity—particularly for white characters—is predicated on a negotiation and even internalization of blackness as central to identity formation. In examining how Bishop's whiteness as a subjectivity and an aesthetic are made visible through multiple identifications with blackness, we can better comprehend Fuss's assertion that "every identity is actually an identification come to light" (2). In my readings, I interrogate often-messy racial identifications and desires animated by sexual longing, racial envy, empathy, or revulsion. Focusing on understudied examples of cross-race writing, *Desegregating Desire* emphasizes the envious identifications that also shaped public and private desegregation, but, like Morrison, I am also interested in the ways that cross-race writing can alter calcified notions of race at a time when definitions of race and sexuality were profoundly destabilized.

These acts of cross-racial identification and composition are also acts of bravado for the white writer. They strut an author's self-confidence in his or her ability to convincingly inhabit another's interiority despite racial, economic, or gender differences. In Bishop's Key West poems, which highlight economic and racial inequalities, and in Sinclair's fictions about African

Americans' social exclusion, one finds a desire to mimic, claim, or interpret a symbolic, fragmented, alienated blackness. These works suggest a need to seek comfort in blackness in ways that are both deeply problematic and politically instructive. The integrationist gesture, then, is a political imperative, an artistic challenge, an expression of intimate identification, and an aspiration to inhabit integrated spaces that are as yet unrealized. The identifications that structure desegregation give voice to the alienated, fragmented, suspicious racial and sexual selves existing in postwar America.

In locating a desegregationist imperative in a variety of texts and in a variety of forms, this project also troubles monolithic notions of whiteness. My readings of racialized sexuality in the lives and works of the white writers in this study and my discussion of white identity in works by all eight writers seek to avoid an easy conflation of "racialized sexuality" with "black sexuality." In insisting that white desires also be read as powerfully racialized, I align myself with a substantive critical tradition that challenges the long-held view of whiteness as being outside race.[19] In articulating identifications with blackness, white writers inevitably call attention to their own whiteness. Bishop's poem "Faustina," for example, illuminates under that glaring lightbulb an unflattering, petty white woman at the eroticized mercy of her black nurse. This study emphasizes the ways that identifications by a white or black subject for the racial Other, despite different social positions and historical trajectories, enact a similar set of emotional responses—longing, revulsion, rejection, and mimesis.

In paying attention to the influence of particular African Americans and black American culture more generally on white artists, however, one risks romanticizing—or worse, ignoring—the historic fetishizations and artistic appropriations that have taken place in American art. As contextual frames for the close readings of cross-race writing in each chapter, I have included cultural snapshots that, while not comprehensive, explore the complex histories, power disparities, and ambivalent desires that inform this writing. Without denying the ways many interracial texts, particularly those infused with same-sex desire, reinscribe the definitional boundaries of homosexual/heterosexual, black/white, I am interested in forwarding alternative theories of racial envy and other forms of cross-race identification rather than in repeating the chastisement that frequently accompanies analyses of cross-race writing. Beyond reading blackness as a "generic commodity constructed by the white imagination for white people" (Gubar xv), how might we otherwise interpret articulations of racialized desire in the postwar American literary imagination? In situating race envy outside of the pejorative, I highlight not only the admirable narrative attempts and awkward confessions inherent in cross-race writing but also the importance of cross-race writing for these writers to a desegregationist politics and broader social change. Lawrence Jackson observes that the years surrounding World War II saw an increase in "imaginative depictions of blacks by white Americans," including Bucklin Moon and Carson McCullers (153). These liberal-minded writers publicly admired black culture, saw its profound social and literary importance, in an era when few artists did. Understanding the value of such admiration within this cultural moment of tentative integration is one of the objectives of *Desegregating Desire*.

Many African American writers of the 1940s and 1950s also embraced cross-race writing as a needed expression of progressive racial politics. This work was often characterized by expressions of universalism, a trend that has been noted by a range of critics, including Sigmund Ro, Bernard Bell, and Emily Bernard, but has rarely been connected to the emergence of the New Critics, who also sought to examine literature free from its social and historical contexts. As I discussed earlier, some critics in the 1950s interpreted cross-race writing as an assimilationist gesture, a desire to be recognized as an American writer outside racial categories. Although Zora Neale Hurston's decision to write *Seraph on the Suwanee*, a "white-life novel" focused predominantly on white characters, has been read as a desire to attract a wider readership, the decision to write "nonracial" literature is an act that in reality both courts publishing success and prevents it. Arthur P. Davis's observation that Richard Wright, Ann Petry, Willard Motley, and other writers moved away from precisely the racial themes that earned them critical success as young novelists suggests the way the integrationist impulse for black writers—a decision to the leave the sanctioned and perhaps lucrative protest tradition—can be seen as a "chosen" failure, an act of artistic independence that forfeits financial reward. Writer Julian Mayfield remained suspicious of integrationist trends in the African American novel, surmising in 1959 that if "integration means completely identifying the Negro with the American images—that great-power face that the world knows better—then the writer must not be judged too harshly for balking at the prospect" (30). For such critics, an integrationist aesthetic risked white emulation and political impotency; writers seeking to avoid racial themes were embarking on a doomed project, striving for an impossibly color-blind postwar literature in which race, if noted, was not given major relevance. This debate, of course, was not new; earlier black writers including Jean Toomer and Nella Larsen explored in their work and struggled in their lives with the economic and emotional liabilities of racial belonging.

The "bard of literary desegregation" (Wonham 4), Ralph Ellison serves as an irreplaceable theoretical framework for my entire project. His persistent interest in American cultural pluralism and articulations of an integrationist aesthetics, referenced throughout my literary analyses, offer the clearest sense of the desegregationist imperative I am tracing in postwar American writing. In his famous response to Irving Howe's confining prescriptions for black writers, Ellison observes that as the Negro novelist "strains for self-achievement as artist (and here he can only 'integrate' and free himself), he moves toward fulfilling his dual potentialities as Negro and American" ("World" 158). The writer's arrival into the cultural mainstream is understood by Ellison as a kind of freedom, but he/she does so only through an aesthetic that does not neglect racial particularities of the American experience but instead insists on them being central to it. Integrationist writers sought to reconfigure American racial identity for both white and black citizens but did not neglect a political commitment to racial justice for African Americans. Desegregationist literature, then, embodies the tensions of race and nation. In the following chapters, I consider how the writing of Ann Petry, Zora Neale Hurston, Gwendolyn Brooks, and William Demby attempted to reconcile the racial particularities of black American life with expressions of universal humanism. Through cross-race writing, these African American writers explored the tense interplay between American citizenry and the subjugation of African Americans necessary for its coherence. I argue that their depictions of whiteness as another form of racial Otherness bypass cultural fetishization in favor of an assertion, often ambivalent, of our common humanity.

Many African American writers of the late 1940s and 1950s who explored themes of alienation, personal resilience, and existential homelessness believed that some white readers would connect to and see themselves in these postwar representations of the human predicament. Julian Mayfield suggests that in mining racial truths, the African American writer could succeed at universal appeal: "He is indeed a man without a country. And yet this very detachment may give him a better position to illuminate contemporary American life as few writers of the mainstream can" (33). Marginal existence, social alienation, and internal discontent, well understood by African American artists, now were seen by a growing number of Americans across racial lines as quintessential conditions of postwar life. White writers also came to understand and attempted to convey in their work a sense that African Americans' struggles for full social integration, repeatedly thwarted, were emblematic of a broader postwar disillusionment in a nation where freedoms—artistic, economic, existential—were often tenuous. Jo Sinclair's *The Changelings* finds blackness, particularly the resilience shown by African Americans attempting to integrate neighborhoods, a powerful parallel to Jewish Americans' search for home and an uncompromised American identity. Postwar novels by African American writers often invited readers to consider the interdependence of racial communities and the pluralistic potential of American society. Hurston's *Seraph*, for example, insisted on the centrality of black folk customs to mainstream American music and literary culture. Elizabeth Bishop's poetry, with its folk aesthetic and blues influences, supported Hurston's challenge to the myth of cultural containment even as it indulged in some of the primitivism that other postwar writers hoped to leave behind. Ann Petry's memorable visions of queer kinship in *The Narrows* challenge the patriarchal models of family promulgated in the mainstream media yet acknowledge the interracial nature of postwar American life, even in an insular Connecticut town.

Such impossible visions of queer kinship can be seen in most of the literature examined in *Desegregating Desire*. A motley band of veterans, nurses, recluses, tomboys, and artistic outsiders emerges from this collection. As Christina Klein notes, "The postwar period saw a proliferation of narratives centering on the creation of families that transcended the boundaries of race, nation, religion and culture. The family became an imaginative framework within which these differences and hierarchies could be simultaneously maintained and transcended" ("Sentimental" 163). Sinclair's vision of an integrated future led by "changelings"—enlightened teens who reject their parents' provincial attitudes about race, gender, religion, and sexuality—provides the most succinct and prescient example of this interest in the reconfigured, socially liberated family. Reading Sinclair alongside Carl Offord's critique of segregation and racial essentialism in *The Naked Fear* makes visible new theories of race and sexuality informed by the era's reinventions of family and community. These new articulations of the family exist within a larger aesthetic turn from narratives of public confrontation to intimate incidents of domestic and psychological trauma.

The cross-race writing taken up in *Desegregating Desire* is not saturated solely with alienation and emotional ambiguities; it often conveys optimism about integration's viability, asserting a vision of a shared humanity and collective desires. In calling integration a "spiritual commitment" more than a lived reality, Arthur P. Davis draws attention to the affective and psychological registers of the desegregationist imperative and the interracial cultures analyzed throughout this study (141). In a 1950 survey of postwar poetry, Margaret Walker, too, diagnosed a search in the modern man for "some definite belief around which to integrate his life and give it true wholeness and meaning," anticipating that African American poets would begin to explore the nation's "religious revival" sparked by uncertain times (353). William Demby's *Beetlecreek* indeed contemplates modern if perverse adaptations of religious reverence in response to the uncertainty of Cold War culture; the novel describes a black adolescent's longing to be protected by an older white man who is marginalized in the community but identified by the boy as "like Jesus Christ" in benevolence. In contemplating the interdependence of religious intolerance and racial discrimination, Sinclair takes these religious reinventions further; Judy Vincent, the protagonist in *The Changelings*, fuses Catholic iconography with her Jewish heritage, modifying both traditions to create spiritual protection in her turbulent world. Sinclair extends desegregation beyond a white/black binary as a religious and cultural issue for Jewish Americans navigating assimilation into white institutions and intercultural families. Characterizing integration in American literature as a spiritual undertaking signals the ways that these artists expressed a faith in an integrated America not yet visible—and, from our twenty-first century vantage point, ultimately unrealized. They believed in the efficacy of their literature to guide reader-citizens toward sustaining bonds across racial, gender, and religious difference, toward an as-yet-unrealized desegregated society.

Each of the following chapters of *Desegregating Desire* identifies the shared strategies employed by a pair of authors for desegregating desire, illuminating the importance of sexuality to these contested and transforming spaces. Chapter 1 critiques the ambivalent desires of domestic labor, examining interracial yet inequitable relationships and liminal places between public and private (in a variety of Floridian locales from hotels to ships to a hospital) in the writing of Elizabeth Bishop and Zora Neale Hurston. The second chapter focuses on desegregated urban places in the poetry of Gwendolyn Brooks and Edwin Denby and considers the ways that both writers transpose private desires into a public imaginary. Brooks and Denby embrace emotional indirection and social silences, a poetics that was less about Cold War censorship than an attempt to render the psychological obfuscations of daily urban life.

Chapter 3 analyzes taboo desires in Ann Petry's *The Narrows* and William Demby's *Beetlecreek*, discussing the ways that insular racial communities were altered by nonnormative sexualities emerging in the decade after World War II. In rendering a particularly queer form of white desire, these novels reveal cultural anxieties about racial mixing and the imagined dangers of integrated spaces and interracial sexuality. The final chapter focuses on damaged desire—the traumas of desegregation—and considers the ways that Jo Sinclair and Carl Offord relocate public upheavals within the private spheres of homes and psyches. My reading of a veteran's racial phobia in Offord's little-known pulp novel, *The Naked Fear*, appropriately returns us to World War II–era violence among integrated troops. Sinclair's *The Changelings*, concerned as well with everyday traumas that accompany social change, documents the first black family in a predominantly Jewish neighborhood. Her novel anticipates the more widespread institutional changes demanded by activists in the civil rights movement and the suburban dreams famously depicted in Lorraine Hansberry's *A Raisin in the Sun*. Several thematic touchstones are examined throughout to strengthen the project's coherence within and across chapters: the centrality of sexuality to race relations; queer sex and/or interracial sex as threats to social stability (the ways writers either affirm or challenge this idea); reconfigured domestic spaces and the reconfigured families that occupy them; and finally the creation of new spaces of interracial sociality (however temporary or transient).

Arthur P. Davis argues that the call for integration, the spiritual commitment to it as aesthetic and social necessities, sent African American writers "in search of new themes" outside of traditional racial depictions (143). Existentialism, sexual freedom, interracial desire, and reconfigured families emerged as political and artistic concerns because these ideas resonated with postwar American writers, both white and black. *Desegregating Desire* argues that the era's dynamic social realities and identities offered these writers a compelling challenge to both document and enact social change. We turn now to their altered America, a literary geography populated with "changelings," race traitors, and deviant dreamers.

Ambivalent Desires

Elizabeth Bishop, Zora Neale Hurston, and Domestic Desegregation

Describing the sublimation of racial and sexual shame as the "dark-town of our unconscious," Lillian Smith in *Killers of the Dream* reminds us that desegregation in American literary culture is located in the interplay between physical spaces and psychological upheavals. Arguing that segregation must be read in relation to suppressed desires and taboo practices, Smith writes, "The lesson on segregation was only a logical extension of the lessons on sex and white superiority and God. Not only Negroes but everything dark, dangerous, evil must be pushed to the rim of one's life" (90). Elizabeth Bishop and Zora Neale Hurston visit this "dark-town of our unconscious" in their writings about home, domestic spaces often marked by the strained bonds between black and white women. Scrutinizing Jim Crow society and signs of its erosion, both writers address the psychological ambiguities of interracial intimacies as well as the resistance to gendered constraints that occurred not only in domestic spaces but also in the reconfigured, however tenuously, public spaces of Cold War America. In this chapter I consider these writers' divergent approaches to cross-race writing as a form of racial ventriloquism and analyze cross-race identifications found in their work as central to a broader desegregationist agenda focused on the interdependencies of race and sex in postwar America.

 Bishop's and Hurston's writing from the late 1940s and early 1950s offers a valuable perspective on the complex ways postwar women writers traced desegregation's imprint on the home as another site of contested racial and gender norms. These writers' creation of alternative domestic spaces in their lives and ambivalent politics regarding integration reveal the social complexities of this cultural moment, particularly for women challenging conservative ideas regarding gender and sexuality as well as race. Focusing on Hurston's "white-life" novel, *Seraph on the Suwanee* (1948), and selections from Bishop's *North and South* (1946) and *A Cold Spring* (1955), I analyze their domestic depictions of racial and erotic identifications at sites typically rendered as deracialized in popular culture's conflation of home building and nation building. In particular, my paired reading centers on their shared interest in the murky interracial relationships of domestic servitude and the ways that racial ventriloquism—speaking for/as the racial Other—challenges Cold War narratives of domestic containment. The chapter concludes with a reevaluation of two neglected texts with an ambivalent, even reactionary, relationship to the era's progressive civil rights discourse: Bishop's essay, "Mercedes Hospital" (1941), and Hurston's short story, "The Conscience of the Court" (1955). In all these critical sites—from these writers' alternative conception of home to the domestic as a place of interracial tension to reimagined public spaces—my primary concern is to illuminate the ways that Bishop and Hurston make visible the private histories of segregation but also begin to compose tentatively desegregated places and render women's ambivalent roles within them. With a retrospective gaze cast on America's shameful racial history, their writings also give shape to the cross-race identifications, equally ambivalent, that inform the nation's aspirations for an integrated future. These works remind us that desegregation was not always a progressive endeavor and that explorations of interracial intimacy could also placate readers who feared the social changes promised with integration.

Hotels and Houseboats: Domestic Reinventions

Historians Elaine Tyler May and Judith E. Smith have argued that the 1950s home often functioned as a stand-in for the nation in both the political rhetoric of the Cold War and the literary imagination. Smith, for example, examines Betty Smith's *A Tree Grows in Brooklyn* (1943), in which "national unity reflects itself in family unity," and considers how other postwar literature, including Lorraine Hansberry's *A Raisin in the Sun* (1959), rewrites the normative models of family to insist on an expansive national identity (73). Describing the reach of Cold War containment policy within the borders of the United States, May observes, "Domestic containment was bolstered by a powerful political culture that rewarded its adherents and marginalized its detractors. More than merely a metaphor for the cold war on the homefront, containment aptly describes the way in which public policy, personal behavior, and even political values were focused on the home" (11). By creating in their lives and literature social places and practices that departed from conservative heteronormative models of home and gender, Bishop and Hurston were among the "detractors" who unsettled containment culture, women who both reenvisioned domesticity and claimed new orientations to public space as writers interested in racial and sexual difference.

Dominant narratives about women in the 1950s are often contradictory: It was an era heralded for women's unprecedented economic and social gains in work and education as well as condemned for its retrenchment into conservative models of marriage and family. Historian Stephanie Coontz describes a gender anomaly at the end of the 1940s in which many women, particularly white women, retreated to social conservatism as wives and mothers: "For the first time in more than one hundred years, the age for marriage and motherhood fell, fertility increased, divorce rates declined, and women's degree of educational parity with men dropped sharply" (25). Women who embraced marriage and motherhood were recognized as valued contributors to national security. As Coontz explains, "A 'normal' family and vigilant mother became the 'front line' of defense against treason" (33). Hidden in this domestic ideology was the assumption that women who did not marry or who rejected traditional gender roles and family structures were at a minimum unnatural and psychologically unhealthy and in the extreme deviants who threatened the nation's social stability.

Many psychologists and the popular press judged the single woman—her social mobility, imagined sexual promiscuity, and abrasive self-assertiveness—to constitute "a potential threat to stable family life and to the moral fiber of the nation" (May 68). Imagining the social and psychological damage single women could cause, a sociologist in 1945 bemoaned the shortage of eligible men, called for healthy alternatives to marriage: "We must find other channels of interest or else run the risk of tremendous emotional and moral chaos" (Harris 82). In a 1948 issue of *Life* magazine, Robert Coughlan raised panic over new postwar gender identities: "The emerging American woman tends to be assertive and exploitive. The emerging American man tends to be passive and irresponsible. . . . They are suffering from what the psychiatrists call sexual ambiguity" (Coughlan 109). Women's rejection of marriage and family life not only posed a risk to national security but represented crisis of gender coherence as well. This gender conservatism suggests the immense social pressure on women to marry and to conform to the role of protector and producer of the next generation of loyal citizens.

Unconventional women who at times transgressed the racial boundaries within American society, Hurston and Bishop also created and wrote about equally unconventional spaces that did not adhere neatly into the category "home." Both Hurston and Bishop were unmarried and childless in an era in which women were expected to conform to Cold War domestic ideologies and become the supportive wife within the secure, nuclear home.[1] Hurston in fact married three times prior to 1944, but each of the unions lasted less than a year.[2] These short-lived marriages and multiple divorces only underscored her unconventional gender identity and defiance of social norms. The writer's fierce independence and passion for her work prevented her from embracing the role of the traditional wife. Writing to Langston Hughes about her first husband, Harold Sheen, Hurston complained, "He tries to hold me back" (Boyd 161). Explaining Hurston's insistence on an identity as a woman defined by artistic achievement rather than maternity, biographer Valerie Boyd writes, "Hurston chose to defect from the demands of marriage and motherhood, but she never once considered abstaining from passion and pleasure" (224). She also refused to limit her career opportunities because of southern segregationist practices, as illustrated by her collaborative writing with Paul Green, a Pulitzer Prize–winning white playwright who taught at the University of North Carolina at Chapel Hill. Writer Richard Bruce Nugent's description of Hurston as "an integrated person" implies appropriately a sexual and racial liberalism—what Valerie Boyd calls the ability to "appreciate human diversity in all its forms" (132). Hurston's friendships with homosexual men—confirmed and rumored—such as Nugent, Carl Van Vechten, Countee Cullen, and Harold Jackman as well as her affiliation with the sexually uninhibited Fannie Hurst and Ethel Waters testify to her sexual liberalism. Biographers have only been able to speculate on the complexities of Hurston's sexuality, noting her three marriages, her friendships with lesbian and gay artists, and her identification with progressive sexual cultures, but it is clear that the novelist cultivated an important network of women with whom she worked and socialized. Carla Kaplan addresses the writer's emotional fervor in the early 1940s for Jane Belo, a fellow anthropologist with whom Hurston worked on a study of sanctified churches in South Carolina. According to Kaplan, Hurston's professed love for Belo in letters and in her autobiography was layered with sexual ambiguity (433–34). Like Bishop's induction into jazz life and its associated social freedoms through her lover, Louise Crane, Hurston's integrationist enthusiasm is closely bound to queer sexual longing, a desire to exist in new social spaces as a reimagined woman.

    Lurking within the cultural marginalization of the unmarried "nontraditional" woman was, of course, an anxiety about lesbianism. Historian Lillian Faderman notes how the social shifts of World War II helped to foster lesbian communities: "Few women who loved other women had serious difficulty during the war, since the military needed all the women it could get who would do their jobs and not disrupt the functioning of the service, and the women understood that if they practiced a modicum of discretion they would be quite safe" (125). Though Bishop's direct involvement in World War II was limited to a five-day stint in the navy optical shop in 1943, the wartime transience and upheavals of work and family made it easier for women to build their own communities and for lesbians to live more publicly. During the war, Bishop was involved with Marjorie Stevens, the estranged wife of a serviceman (Millier 171). In contrast to women who entered the military and discovered new social (including sexual) freedoms, Bishop had already experienced living independently of men. Her social circle of upper-class women helped support her artistic production outside of patriarchal structures. While Bishop was largely discreet about her sexuality, class privilege insulated her from scrutiny, and she could be assured that servants "knew their place" and would remain quiet about such matters. When Bishop began her relationship with Lota de Macedo Soares in 1951, living with her in Brazil for the next fifteen years, she was shielded from social discrimination in many ways by her class and expatriate status. Crafting an unconventional lifestyle, Bishop, like Hurston, did not embrace a life as wife and mother; instead, she explored the social freedoms increasingly claimed by women, who were entering the public sphere as workers and artists in record numbers. Despite her private identity as a lesbian, Bishop would have been read publicly as a single woman outside of the mainstream trends that promoted marriage and motherhood. Bishop's relationship with Marjorie Stevens (domestic intimates yet outside of public pronouncement) took place in and was explained through the geography of Key West. The poem "Anaphora"—with its morning song of birds and factory whistles—was written for Stevens. In May 1942, in part to escape the distressing wartime upheavals in Key West, Bishop and Stevens traveled to Mexico City, where they met poet Pablo Neruda, whose communist sympathies Bishop noted in a letter to Marianne Moore.[3] His political commitments, divergent from her own but evidently not a source of division between the two poets, as well as her sexual nonconformity shed light on the cultural complexities of the emergent Cold War. Bishop, Hurston, and other women who pushed against the era's gender and sexual mores were seen to embody, like homosexual men, the moral and cultural chaos proponents of traditional domesticity feared.

If as Paul Gilroy argues, "The family is understood as nothing more than the essential building block in the construction and elevation of the nation" (128), then Hurston's and Bishop's depictions of home as commentaries on the nation provide useful alternatives to traditional domesticity, challenging whitewashed normative family structures and revealing the racial complexities and gendered restraints that shape home. Bishop's and Hurston's rejections of conservative models of domesticity and the restrictive gender identities contained within them are evident in the places they chose as homes and the nonnuclear families they formed. In the decade after the war, both writers occupied and wrote about hotel rooms, houseboats, boardinghouses, brothels—spaces that muddle the division between public and private and challenged the conception of home as patriarchal refuge. Although my subsequent readings focus largely on Florida as a shared site for Bishop's and Hurston's explorations of domesticity and racial geographies, both women's attraction to mobility as a practice of female autonomy is reflected in their extensive travels outside of the United States. For example, Hurston visited the Bahamas in 1949, the same year that Bishop went to Haiti. The "journeys of subjectivity," to use Eve Kosofsky Sedgwick's phrase ("Response" 239), that both women experienced and explored in their literature were often initiated by literal travel, trips that ruptured both routine and calcified thinking. Travel in fact formed a central part of both women's practice as writers, allowing them to reassess the conservative roles and social places available to women in the 1940s.[4]

Through alternative visions of domesticity and intimacy that accommodated transience, both women experienced greater social freedoms that often strained the color lines of southern segregation. The transience inherent in some of their homes—boardinghouses, houseboats, hotels—embraces a "eerie restlessness" that both Bishop and Hurston found socially liberating rather than pathological, which is how the phrase was applied to discontented American women in a 1947 *Life* magazine article (cited in Mintz and Kellogg 195). While such restlessness was often linked to women's domestic confinement as mothers and wives, particularly since many women were forced to give up employment outside the home after the war, Hurston and Bishop recognized the value of restlessness for their work as writers. In their writing, people are transformed and inspired by mobility as an exercise in freedom. Bishop's "Jerónimo's House," for example, was generated from her strolls through the streets bordering her home on Key West's Whitehead Street and imagines Jerónimo's political marches through the streets. In Hurston's *Seraph*, protagonist Arvay Henson has epiphanies about her life's purpose while out at sea on the fishing boats with her husband's crew, an echo of Hurston's own love of boats.

While living in Southern California, where she wrote her autobiography, *Dust Tracks on a Road*, and worked as a consultant for Paramount, Hurston returned to her beloved home state, collecting folklore throughout Florida in the autumn of 1942. She spent considerable time in St. Augustine, which had previously been home to both a slave market and a Freedmen's Bureau school. Between 1943 and 1945, Hurston lived sporadically on her houseboats, *Wanago* and *Sun Tan*, docked in Daytona Beach. She worked productively when she was onboard, where she experienced "that solitude that I love" (Kaplan 495).[5] Hurston's time on these houseboats succinctly illustrates the ways that the home, particularly for an unmarried African American woman, is never solely private but is subject to public enforcement of the color line. Because of race, Hurston was denied official membership in the Halifax River Yacht Club, but she reported to Carl Van Vechten in the summer of 1945 of the casual transgression of Jim Crow customs: "I have lots of friends in there and am invited to the Club House" (Kaplan 526). At the same time that she was publicly rejecting restrictions on intimacy between white men and black women, Hurston was navigating a still-segregated society as a single, racially progressive African American artist. Social institutions such as the Halifax River Yacht Club were slow to embrace policies that reflected the cultural changes—women claiming social independence, interracial relationships—that were already taking place. The contrast between the exclusionary practices of the yacht club and the relative freedom of living aboard the houseboats, and later on a white friend's boat, illuminates the mutuality of belonging and exclusion within desegregation.

Boats, liminal spaces of privacy on public waters that provided Hurston with a more transient domesticity, are represented as desegregated sites in her writing.[6] The fact that Hurston's vision of interracial camaraderie at the end of *Seraph on the Suwanee* takes place on a boat is no coincidence. In February 1946, while researching her novel, Hurston went out on a shrimping boat.[7] Her patriotic description of the experience highlights its interracial nature, an integrated vision she would emphasize in the novel: "The men, white and black who put shrimp on the table of the nation are made of the stuff of pioneers" (539). This nautical vision of interracial collaboration was in a sense reenacted in 1949, when Hurston lived with Fred Irvine, a white sailor and close friend, on his yacht, the *Challenger*, for five months. She described Irvine as a "perfectly balanced and grand person to work with" and "handsome in a dark manly way" (Kaplan 507, 525). That same year the two traveled to the Bahamas, and Irvine offered to sail his schooner to Honduras, an adventure Hurston spent much of the decade trying to realize.

Irvine and Hurston appeared to enjoy an interracial friendship, quite rare in the 1940s, free of both romantic obligation and racial awkwardness, leaving both to pursue their respective affairs but providing each other with needed emotional support during troubled times. Hurston, for example, sought refuge on Irvine's boat after she was falsely accused in September 1948 of sodomizing three boys in Harlem and faced a devastating trial.[8] And she later returned to Miami to help Irvine "settle his nerves" after "hectic love affairs" had "soured on his soul" (Kaplan 621). Hurston's embrace of an unconventional home and family—living on a boat as part of a platonic interracial relationship—illustrates an approach to domesticity that dominant narratives about women's sexual and social containment fail to include.

Hurston's treasured friendship with Carl Van Vechten, started in the 1920s, also broke taboos against intimacy between black women and white men. He continuously championed Hurston's work in fellowship applications and publishing circles; he defended her during the sodomy trial and contributed to her funeral costs. Hurston paid homage to her interracial friendships in "The Inside Light: Being a Salute to Friendship," a section of *Dust Tracks on a Road*. The publisher's decision to excise the essay, which addresses many white friends, including Charlotte Osgood Mason, Van Vechten, and anthropologist and activist Katharine Mershon, obscures the fact that camaraderie across the color line—expressed explicitly by Hurston in those terms—was important to her development as a writer. Mason's crucial yet manipulative patronage is well known, but Hurston's friendships with fellow anthropologist Jane Belo and writers Marjorie Rawlins and Van Vechten reveal interracial intimacies largely freed from eroticism or condescension.

Hurston's acquiescing to and circumventing of the segregated South, including living with a white man in Miami Beach, and her rewarding friendships across gender and racial lines illustrate the complex racial landscape of the 1940s. As a white northerner, Elizabeth Bishop's encounters with Jim Crow America in both public and private places were less visceral, and her relationships across race were far less equitable, but Key West's unfamiliar social customs proved influential. After making Key West her primary home in January 1938, the poet rented a room in a boardinghouse on Whitehead Street. The accommodations were located near a black neighborhood in an area known as Jungle Town, revealing much about the racial attitudes of the region (Fountain and Brazeau 72). It is unclear if the boardinghouse was interracial, but Bishop's poems and letters reveal that her interactions with African American and Cuban residents became more frequent and certainly less guarded than those in the larger northeastern cities where she had previously lived. This multiethnic landscape—the overheard expressions from African American residents, the hangouts, and Cuban influences—soon began to fill Bishop's writing.[9] Months later, Bishop purchased a home, 624 White Street, with Louise Crane, her best friend at Vassar and occasional yet significant lover in the late 1930s and 1940s. Head of the Crane Paper fortune, Louise's father was a Republican governor of Massachusetts and a U.S. senator, and her mother was a cofounder of the Museum of Modern Art. Crane and Bishop shared a love of poetry and travel, adventuring to Europe and North Africa before settling in Key West. Cuban American primitive painter Gregorio Valdes painted a portrait of the exterior of their home. Bishop, who commissioned the painting, christened Valdes "our new Key West Rousseau" and later wrote an essay about his art, published in the *Partisan Review* in 1939 (*OA* 75).

Valdes's documentation of a space we might claim as a site of lesbian domesticity in an era of increasing conservatism is an interesting juxtaposition to Bishop's poetic voyeurism into a Cuban American home in "Jerónimo's House," a poem defined by its primitivism and prompted by her strolls through the streets bordering Whitehead Street. A silver French horn, spotted during Bishop's snooping and noted in a 1938 letter, becomes the center of this domestic portrait steeped in regional quaintness, with its "palm-leaf fans," "left-over Christmas decorations," and "hominy grits." Bishop imagines the fixed-up horn, "repainted with aluminum paint,"[10] testimony to poverty, as a symbol of artistry and activism. The Cuban speaker says, in the shortest sentence of the poem, "I play each year / in the parade / for José Martí" (*CP* 34). In this assertion of ritualized cultural pride, Jerónimo voices an identity that exceeds the domestic. The reader imagines the man apart from his "fairy palace" and in the collective street (34). He is momentarily both a local resident and an agent within a larger transnational history.

"Come closer," commands the poem's speaker (*CP* 34). With this permission, the reader, the imagined visitor, sheds the discomfort of being the intrusive snoop. But from the vantage point of the public street, outside peering in, Bishop maintains a superficial discretion. Her poetic catalog is limited to the resident's material possessions rather than a rendering of Jerónimo's thoughts, feelings, or details of speech, an interiority that would be a far more risky artistic choice. As an expression of a desegregated imaginary, Bishop's ventriloquism crosses not only race and gender but also the border of public and private, taking on the voice of a Cuban American man within the intimacy of home. Bishop seeks to imagine this encounter between viewer/reader and resident/speaker as welcomed, free of hostility, yet she also highlights the transgression in this cross-race encounter. For readers, it is an intrusion into the unfamiliar. Jerónimo's invitation marks us as strangers, located outside of home and intimacy.

Bishop's excursions into unfamiliar, racially stratified places in Key West brought her whiteness and racial beliefs into increasing legibility, but her retreat into improvised domestic spaces preserved her much-treasured privacy. The hotel room, less eccentric than Hurston's houseboats but similarly attractive for its spirit of transience, was Bishop's chosen site of reinvented domesticity. Though a resident of Key West, the poet regularly took rooms at local hotels "to work in the mornings," away from her gregarious roommate. In June 1940, for example, the poet rented a room in her favorite Key West hotel, "almost deserted this time of year." There she watched navy vessels come and go and the building of a "tremendous airplane hangar" (*OA* 91). The rooms paradoxically offered Bishop both creative solitude and material reminders of the transforming political landscape of the nation: World events and private fantasy are muddled.

A place where the drudgery of homemaking is suspended, the hotel permits fantasies to roam. "The hotel," writes Wayne Koestenbaum, "is blank enough that it has the liberty to pose, anew, questions that have gone stale in regular life" (44). Hotels were regenerative for Bishop, allowing her to explore new territory in her poetry, including fantasies partially animated by race. Bishop composed a poem, "In a cheap hotel," in a notebook from the late 1940s.[11] Although unpublished in her lifetime, the poem is alive with racial and sexual desires suited to the in-betweenness of the hotel room. As a space of purchased privacy unburdened from both domestic restrictions and public judgment, the hotel is an apt setting for the taboo scene of sexual humiliation on which the poem centers.[12]

The syntactical ambiguity of the poem's beginning: "In a cheap hotel / in a cheap city / Love held his prisoners or my love / brought the pitcher of ice— / dropped the quarter in the spidery old electric-fan— / Love the Night Clerk, the Negro bell-boy" leaves open the possibility that Love, the Night Clerk, and the Negro bell-boy are one and the same.[13] The poem's "nameless embarrassment" is revealed as a reoccurring sadomasochistic fantasy of a black hotel clerk holding a (presumably white) guest captive; the poem's speaker confesses, "every night he drags me back to that bed. He chains me & berates me—He chains me to that bed & he berates me" (*Edgar* 83). In revealing the sexual attraction and racial fears underpinning this scene of interracial intimacy, Bishop's fantasy emphasizes the violence—psychological and at times physical—alive in a sexual situation always marked by disparities of power. The poem's invocation of a sexual shame at the hands of a black captor (without overlooking the all-too familiar stereotype of the black brute) complicates conventional formulations of race and power and sanitized portraits of desire, highlighting the overlaps and tensions between racial and sexual shame as well as the convergence of desire and fear that animate much of Bishop's poetry. In an era marked by a growing popular interest in Freudian drives, Bishop inverts the iconography of slavery to imagine an enchained and humiliated white woman. Bishop's call for a private abjection rather than a public confrontation of America's silenced racial history reflects a moment, particularly in literature, in which the exploration of private spaces often supplanted public activism. This fantasy of white supremacy becoming white submission is a poetic allegory for the era's ambivalence regarding racial changes, both fearing and welcoming assertions of agency by African Americans.

Bishop's politics, particularly her racial attitudes, however, can hardly be claimed as progressive. Her poetic imagination, including hotel fantasies, was fueled by her excursions into the unfamiliar world of Key West. Known for its bohemian spirit, the sleepy port town could quite openly embrace a range of sexual behaviors and racial customs, permitting the poet to experience new social freedoms that shaped her writing. She frequented spots like Pena's Rose Garden, a "gathering place," according to fellow Key West resident Steve Boyden, "for all the arty types that were moving down here" (Fountain and Brazeau 79).[14] Bishop and Crane also explored a Key West brothel, the Square Roof. James Laughlin, founder of New Directions Press, recounts a "social" rather than "professional" visit to the brothel with Bishop and Tennessee Williams. Over tea and Oreos, the three chatted with women "of dusky complexion" in church dresses and were invited to see the room of one of the prostitutes, "a light-skinned charmer." The curious visitors found her quaint possessions "touching and sweet"—an "embroidered flower-print rug," a vase with jasmine, and "a row of dolls in dresses that surely the owner had stitched" (Fountain and Brazeau 82).

Located on the margins of respectable society, brothels are pseudo-private sites that typically provide a veneer of domesticity to make palatable the economic transactions at their center. In his history of vice districts in the urban North, Kevin J. Mumford reminds us that these "interzones" of race and sexuality, though a "haven for people stigmatized and relegated to the urban periphery," were nonetheless structured by practices that "recapitulated the ideology of sexual racism" (116). Bishop's visit to a place designed to capitalize on white men's fantasies about black sexuality calls into question her racist erotic projections. The discovery of the makings of home—the woman's attention to visual pleasures and the childhood innocence conveyed in her possessions—ruptures the visitors' voyeurism into this sexualized and racialized space. "What we saw," admitted Laughlin, "there in that room touched us all to silence" (Fountain and Brazeau 82–83). The presence of personal objects disrupts the visitors' assessment of the prostitute as solely a sexual and public figure unburdened by mundane domesticity. Furthermore, the brothel anecdote illustrates Bishop's not atypical role as guide for her fellow cultural tourists into sexually and racially transgressive spaces, a perspective she repeatedly adopts in poems such as "Jerónimo's House," "Cootchie," and "Over 2,000 Illustrations and Complete Concordance," with its reference to the "pockmarked prostitutes" of Marrakesh (*CP* 68), a memory from Bishop's

1936 travels to Morocco. It is not surprising, then, that Laughlin anticipated a poem by Bishop about their visit to the Square Roof, though he never got one.

Writing Jim Crow

As with the other authors examined in *Desegregating Desire*, Hurston and Bishop were educated (one might say miseducated) as artists by the lessons of Jim Crow. Understanding segregation as a psychological process of socialized inferiority as much as a legislated system, Hurston, in her essays and private letters, calls for the elimination of Jim Crow legislation but recognizes that shifts in racial consciousness are also required and perhaps pose the greater challenge. Her description of white supremacist practices as the "unnatural exaltation of one ego, and the equal unnatural grinding down of the other" echoes Lillian Smith and stresses the perverse psychological violence of segregation. If Jim Crow practices depend on physical violence and psychological fear, then desegregation as a counterstrategy requires that white supremacy be confronted, more truthfully examined, and hopefully dismantled. Bishop's and Hurston's restructuring of domestic spaces should be read as part of their larger investigations of racialized spaces and the social divisions that often defined them. In both cases, these women were responding to a changing America and to the stagnant racial protocols in which gender was always enmeshed. Writing about their journeys of subjectivity in Jim Crow America, Hurston and Bishop contemplated their very different experiences of the nation's stratified racial geography, contemplations that informed their cross-race fiction and poems.

In "My Most Humiliating Jim Crow Experience," her 1944 contribution to the *Negro Digest* series in which famous African Americans recounted defining moments of racial exclusion, Hurston directly examines the psychological impact of segregation. Disrupting the tendency to designate segregation as a predominantly southern phenomenon, she writes of the racial humiliations experienced during a visit to a white doctor in Brooklyn in 1931. Not expecting a black patient, the doctor leads her into a "private examination room," actually a closet with a chair and a "pile of soiled linens." Hurston quips, "The room was private all right" (935). For contemporary readers, the closet is always a space associated with the sexual shame metaphorically hidden there, and here it encloses a shameful interracial intimacy. The medical examination, a procedure focused on the body and its difference, cannot be performed in the seemingly private but in reality quite public space of the doctor's examination room. Like furtive homosexuality, the presumed eroticism of a white doctor examining a black woman patient must be closeted in Jim Crow America.

Hurston's vignette precisely maps the interplay of physical space and psychological interiors within segregation. Her black body cannot be left visible in the nominally public space of the "swanky" "reception room" (935), a space conducive to both voyeurism and private ruminations. This encounter brings to mind Bishop's canonical "In the Waiting Room," another incident where private revelation and racial difference clash with public scrutiny. In Bishop's poem, however, black womanhood is safely contained within the pages of the *National Geographic*, exoticized in some nameless distant locale. Yet these "black, naked women" with necks "like the necks of light bulbs" and "horrifying" breasts unsettle (*CP* 159). For both Bishop and Hurston, the waiting room is a place of cross-race encounters, often confrontational, where private desires become public hostilities.

Rather than storm out, Hurston, always the anthropologist, stays to watch the racist doctor contort in discomfort. After his diagnosis, she leaves, stiffing him on the bill. The "reckless angle" of her hat on departure is the only defiant public gesture, a safe substitute for a more reckless and warranted verbal confrontation of the doctor's dehumanizing treatment. The experience, in which Hurston converts shame to defiance, leaves her feeling the "pathos of Anglo-Saxon civilization," a phrase that names both the tragedy and growing impermanence of white supremacy in this era of change. A society built on "a false foundation," predicts Hurston, "cannot last" (936). In writing about public and domestic spaces in flux, public places such as waiting rooms and hotels that enact a form of privacy, Hurston and Bishop document Jim Crow's slow erosion.

Pathos, too, often shades encounters with racial difference chronicled in Bishop's writing. Far from lamenting segregation's demise, both writers evoke the pervasive sadness of people who are connected by economic ties or circumstances but remain intractably emotionally disconnected. In November 1940, while traveling to Florida by train, Bishop wrote in her diary about a turpentine camp in Georgia that she viewed outside her window in the early morning hours, a description full of the allure of transience and rendered with a detached engagement with racial difference that ultimately leaves its witness experiencing a very similar pathos: "I came to about 6:30am, just before reaching Savannah; it was lovely beginning to get light. Everything, field, leaves on the trees, logs, the roofs, seemed to be covered with thick shiny frost. At a little station there were many Negroes—I could hear them talking—carrying lanterns—Everything was dark gray, and the black faces looked beautiful against the *fluorescent* setting. Smoke stood over one little cabin like a big floating {person?} peering down the chimney."[15] The entry, filled with an outsider's predictable romanticization of a southern rural landscape, formed the basis of "Something I've Meant to Write about for 30 Years," a poem Bishop drafted in the 1960s and never finished.[16] But from journal entry to first draft, this writing of an early Georgia morning has some instructive transformations. Bishop translates the landscape of turpentine camps into a charged, literally jolting, intrusion into a space of racial difference. The "black faces" of the town's residents, who in an early draft of the poem actively "lift lanterns like diamonds" and are heard talking "because they love to hear themselves talk," are conscripted by and constricted to an imagined racist geography, a marginal, shoddy neighborhood of "unpainted houses" and "muddy yards" where "all its black people were in bed."[17] Although she characterizes African Americans here as loquacious, Bishop demonstrated little self-consciousness in creating several poems in which she spoke for and as a black women.

The poem's speaker recalls:

> We stopped for just a moment, a small town
> in southern Georgia? Probably—
> we jerked, backward and forward there
> and I woke up—
> Looking right into nigger-town
> then back, then again
> as if to make sure I'd really seen it." (*Edgar* 137)

Whereas the diary entry roams from station to cabin to sky, the passenger in the retrospective poem, divided by the pane, becomes the distanced poet at the window surveying an unfamiliar landscape; her dislocation and sense of racial superiority are emphasized in the hostile labeling of "nigger-town." This racialized geography is comfortably void of the people who, in an earlier version, unsettle boundaries and intrusively "lift" their "black faces to the window." This privileging of the aesthetic at the expense of political critique is typical of Bishop's writing about race. Given the centrality of public transportation within the civil rights movement's demands for social equality, Bishop's reinforcement of racial divisions in this journey through the South (and into white racist consciousness) is unfortunate. Her aesthetic epiphany—"why not *decorate* morning?" (*Edgar* 138)—can be read as a poetic mandate to embellish and rearrange, to dress up racial hostility, tucking it safely into a distanced (and disdained) "nigger-town" and enacting the kind of sublimation that Lillian Smith critiques in Southern social practices.

Engaging in a kind of ocular slumming, the ensconced passenger in "Something I've Meant to Write about for 30 Years" is lured by the mirror-tipped fence whose "Irregular jagged" nature leaves one "disconnected mad" (*Edgar* 138). The reflective chaos of the fence's mosaic suggests that encounters with black cultural spaces and artifacts have the potential to entrance and unsettle. And Bishop's persistence in writing about the memory thirty years later suggests that the imprint of some cross-racial encounters could not be easily removed. This encounter with geographic and racial difference evidences a familiar racial essentialism and outright racism found in many of Bishop's poems and letters about African American culture and interracial exchanges. These problematic portraits of local color nonetheless also acutely document ruptures in social hierarchies. Attention to the negotiations of those excluding and those excluded is particularly valuable to my investigation into the multiple sites and varied politics of desegregation. Though no stranger to racial divisions growing up in New England and studying in New York, Bishop encountered both more expansive sites of African American culture and pronounced social segregation in the South. In many ways, Bishop's desegregationist gestures constituted attempts to remove that pane of glass—that racial and aesthetic barrier. Her racial prejudices, of course, did not magically dissipate, and the interracial relationships she formed and wrote about were not equitable; however, the poet's engagement with race in ways that highlight whiteness and its social privileges are instructive of this cultural moment in which rigid racial divides and calcified social protocols were being questioned and rescripted, and racialized spaces, both public and private, were being reimagined.

Bishop's poem about the Georgia turpentine camps and Hurston's closeted medical examination remind us that a racialized geography is deeply intertwined with a psychological terrain. Segregation, as described by Hurston in her 1945 essay "Crazy for This Democracy," was "the bumps and blisters on the skin, and not the disease, but evidence and symptoms of the sickness" (47). She goes on to conclude that an ideology of white superiority is the actual social illness. For Hurston and with more ambivalence for Bishop, the illness of segregation and the racially "diseased" Americans who supported it were important social realities to address. As witnesses to Jim Crow America, Bishop and Hurston assessed the nation's postwar racial changes. Hurston experienced segregationist practices firsthand as she navigated her ever-racialized body within stratified places of private and public life. Bishop, conversely, could remain the distant witness, observing the changes in racial feeling in aesthetic terms: sailors and soldiers asleep on the train with the all-black Georgia turpentine camp outside but also looming in the imagination.

Keeping House: The Racial Politics of Domestic Labor

In confronting the social complexities of cultural spaces, whether waiting rooms or train stations, imprinted by America's shameful racial history, desegregationist writing has to contend with the subconscious desires, the affective ghosts of exploitation and dependency, that also structured those places, particularly when they are white Americans' homes in which African Americans labor. Both Bishop and Hurston turned in the 1940s to the subject of domestic labor—the vexed relationship between African American domestic workers and white women who employed them—as an important site for commenting on America's history of racial segregation as well as the possibilities of racial change. Heeding Evelyn Hammonds's call for contemporary black feminist projects that include "an analysis of power relations between white and black women and among different groups of black women" (131), my reading links Hurston and Bishop through their shared interest in the affective bonds, identifications, and disavowals between white and black women, particularly in the privacy of the home. As single women living outside of heteronormative domestic arrangements, both Hurston and Bishop formulate home as a site of gender and racial consternation, offering contemporary readers understudied responses to restrictive Cold War gender ideologies. Deborah Nelson argues that containment rhetoric of the 1950s' exaltation of the home as "the symbol and locus of the liberty" and a treasured space of privacy problematically banished it from "public discourse as anything but an ideal" (77). This refusal to acknowledge the ways social tensions, including racial subjugation, extended to the home—indeed, the very public nature of domestic space—came under increasing scrutiny, particularly from marginalized citizens, including African Americans, white women, and gays and lesbians attempting to claim their full civil rights.

The nature of domestic work and its racial dynamics were changed by World War II and the social transformations that occurred in its aftermath. Eileen Boris contends that physical proximity between blacks and whites was accepted in the private realm of domestic work, but in the changing work environments after the war, such interracial intimacy caused alarm (94). As more women, white and black, found jobs in factories and offices and African Americans increasingly moved out of positions as domestic laborers and into the public sector, the social divisions within domestic labor also became an object of public scrutiny in literature. For Hurston and Bishop, a desegregated American literature had to begin in the interracial dynamics of the home. In highlighting the ambivalent relationships between black women and white women confined to the domestic—a private sphere often conceived as removed from the racial politics and hostilities of public life—works such as Hurston's *Seraph* and Bishop's "Faustina" challenge the conception of home as a locus of liberty. rather, it is a space where racial tensions and erotic uncertainties are central.

Lawrence Jackson has argued that the American home, often shaped by African American women and their domestic labor, was one of the "few ritual places of interaction" between whites and blacks in mid-twentieth-century America (197). In Hurston's novel and Bishop's poems, domestic intimacy is structured within the familial and the economic. The affective layers in the relationships between a domestic worker and the lady of the house are revealed to be no less complicated than familial bonds. Alluding to parallels between the turn-of-the-century setting of *Seraph* and the sexual politics of the 1950s, Hurston on one level offers a political critique of southern paternalism and its legacy of objectification and dehumanization of African Americans. On another level, both authors expose the troublesome bonds that exist across race in intimate places, suggesting overlooked sites of desegregationist art. Far from a place of refuge, the home becomes a space of emotional ambivalence and psychological discomfort when seen through the lens of domestic labor, and it is a fitting analogy for a postwar nation grappling with familial changes sparked by reimagined gender identities and racial communities. Affirming Paul Gilroy's contention that the family functions as an "essential building block" (128) for the nation, Bishop's and Hurston's attention to the racial paternalism and the complicated intimacies between white and black Americans in the home reveals familial dysfunction as a symptom of larger national dysfunction, epitomized in democracy's accommodation of legal segregation.

Historically, substantial African American labor took place within or in close relation to the domestic sphere, often in white Americans' homes. For maids, housekeepers, and cooks, work identity, which is typically formed in the public sphere, is obscured within private protocols. Such is the strange intimacy of domestic labor: The economic inequities and exploitation solidify social distance, but the work exists within spaces where intimate knowledge and interactions could be less conscripted by racial boundaries. As a result, many black Americans gained intimate knowledge of white people's practices and beliefs and a privileged insight into domestic negotiations. bell hooks characterizes African American domestic workers as "informants" who "brought knowledge back to segregated communities—details, facts, observations, and psychoanalytic readings of the white Other" (165). This unsettling of racial hierarchies in which white people become the racial Other from the domestic worker's perspective is evident in the inverted perspectives offered by Bishop and Hurston: White femininity becomes the alienated object of scrutiny. In revisiting literary representations of domestic labor produced in the early Cold War, this chapter (and later discussions of writing by Gwendolyn Brooks and Ann Petry) pursues Toni Morrison's invitation to reorient our critical attention from "the described and the imagined to the describers and the imaginers; from the serving to the served" (*Playing* 90). As documentarians of domestic labor who occupy significantly different racial positions in 1940s America, Bishop and Hurston offer a compelling site of cross-race writing to consider how white womanhood and interracial intimacies are scrutinized as part of a desegregationist reevaluation of domestic/familial spaces.

As witnesses to white people's racial psychologies, black domestic workers were also intimate observers of their sexuality. "Housekeepers, bellhops, domestics," notes Ralph Ellison, had a unique perspective on the sexual matters of a home: "outside but right in the *bedroom*" and as such "wise in the ways of human folly and aspiration" ("Indivisible Man" 388). Although it is unclear in Hurston's *Seraph on the Suwanee* how much Dessie and Joe Kelsey as laborers in the Meserve house observed of Arvay and Jim's sexual dynamic, Hurston as a novelist functions as a kind of informant on white people's attitudes about race, marital roles, and sexual submission and aggression. Similarly, Bishop confronts the sexual resonances often layered within the power struggles of domestic workers and their employers. "Faustina" makes explicit the sexual intimacies that sit on the periphery of domestic care.

In "Cootchie" and "Faustina," Bishop zeroes in on the racial and emotional interdependencies, with their often attendant erotic layers, that marked the domestic relationships in which she participated and that she witnessed. The paradox of dependence and exclusion structures "Cootchie," a poem based on the maid of Bishop's landlady, Miss Lula, at the Whitehead Street boardinghouse. Bishop had intended to write a short story about Miss Lula and Mr. Gay, another boarder, and Mrs. Pindar, also a landlady at the Whitehouse boardinghouse (Millier 138). The poet wrote to Frani Blough, a Vassar classmate, about a cook she and Crane had hired, an African American woman who sang in the Island Singers Choir and delighted Bishop by calling her "chile" (*OA* 72). Bishop formed an even more intimate bond with her housekeeper, Hannah Almyda, who worked at her home on White Street and became her "nurse, adviser, and even mother figure" and the focus on many sketches in her writing notebook (Millier 144). The carpenters, cooks, and housekeepers at the service of Bishop and her girlfriend must have been critical, one imagines, of the brassy assertion and needy privilege of these northern-born white women, now living cheaply down South. Indeed, the silence of these workers in Bishop's work is unnerving; the Other remains persistently and silently peripheral.

The racial tableau—black body into white sea—that begins "Cootchie" and the contrasting images of the "sable" mourners and the "egg-white" sky at the funeral underscore the color line (*CP* 46). Less a portrait of racial integration, the first image suggests an engulfment by whiteness. And the poem explicitly names the way racial segregation permeates the domestic sphere: Cootchie is left to eat "her dinner of the kitchen sink / while Lula ate hers off the kitchen table" (*CP* 46). Lillian Smith calls these divisions "invisible lines" that are "electrically charged with taboo" (*Killers* 95). The topographical distance Bishop travels in "Cootchie" is notable, from the expansive seascape to the cramped kitchen counter and back to the "desperate" sea (*CP* 46). The dramatic drowning of Cootchie, whose naming as "servant" (46) emphasizes the disparities of power, is understood as an escape from domestic drudgery. This ambiguous death—perhaps suicide, maybe an accident—hovers between heroic and cowardly, but the grand gesture is undercut by the speaker's ironic concern over how Miss Lula will carry on without her domestic support: "Who will shout and make her understand?" (46). The sand-filled cans, evoking Cootchie's grave in the "marl," are a memorial to Miss Lula's "losses" (46)—the literal loss of a black woman's life eclipsed by a white woman's emotional dependency—but it is also a memorial to the end of this exploitive domestic arrangement. Bishop's subtle critique is found in the syntactically twisted phrase that Cootchie's "life was spent in caring for Lula" (*CP* 46). Less a life passed in dedicated care, hers is spent, exhausted and depleted by this labor. The poem examines segregation as a domestic issue, confronting interracial intimacies that are tense, exploitative, and shameful.

More clearly than "Cootchie," Bishop's much-discussed "Faustina, or Rock Roses" also locates racial difference within the home, in the intimate interior of the white woman's bedroom (nearly smothering for the unnamed visitor, likely Bishop). The poem's central figure is based on a Key West fortune-teller and acquaintance of Bishop's; although her name might suggest Cuban ancestry (or Bishop's romanticized version of it), the poet's writing notebook contains comments only on the woman's blackness, not on her ethnicity. Bishop began the poem in 1948 and continued to revise it until 1955, when it was published in *A Cold Spring*, placing its production squarely within the early civil rights movement. As with much of the literature discussed in this project, it contemplates the relationship between a physical space and racial affect. Its gothic atmosphere, characteristic of much of Bishop's poetry, rejects domestic coziness—the "drowned green" "glow-worms" stuck to the window screen, the worn wallpaper, and the neglected bedside table (*CP* 72). The tattered environment reflects but also elicits the anxiousness circulating between Faustina, her employer, and the visitor: the bedridden woman's fear of death, her paranoia over the imagined revenge behind Faustina's unreadable face, the visitor's embarrassment at observing this awkward intimacy. The white woman's persistent whisper of "Faustina" contains desperation and desire, a contradiction like Faustina's "sinister kind face" (*CP* 73). The ambivalent bonds among all three women support Diana Fuss's assertion that "*every* identification involves a degree of symbolic violence, a measure of temporary mastery and possession" (9). In a similar negotiation to one outlined by Eric Lott, Bishop employs a form of poetic blackface in "Faustina" and "Songs for a Colored Singer" to confront "collective fears of a degraded and threatening" racial Other while "maintaining some symbolic control over them" (25).

The poem is named as a puzzle—"a cruel black coincident conundrum" (*CP* 73)—but is distinct from earlier literature with its predictable dyad of maid/mistress and worn-out fears of a servant's revenge because of its explicit engagement with whiteness, its practices, privileges, and fears. Like the white rags strewn about the room in "Faustina," Bishop confronts a whiteness that is "confusing as undazzling" (73). This scrutinizing of the psychological layers of race and racism, particularly white consciousness, in scenes of subtle interracial conflict reflects one of the aims of many desegregationist texts. "Faustina" focuses on the intricacies of power—the demands of an employer, the sick woman's dependency on her caregiver, the observer's authoritative gaze and complacency. All motives—of nurse, mistress, and visitor—are illuminated and questioned; in the poem's terms, "the eighty-watt bulb betrays us all" (72). Susan McCabe argues that the poem "reveals the more sinister underpinnings of 'care,' especially in contexts of racial and social equality" (125), and Margaret Dickie describes it as "a poem of trust and protection spelled out in racial terms, where trust has always been intertwined with exploitation" (119). Unlike "Cootchie," where racial hierarchies remain unquestioned until the maid's death, Bishop distills social changes through another domestic scenario that contemplates inverted power and white submission. The observer's identification with Faustina is triangulated with the bedridden white woman's clear dependence on her nurse.

Bishop drafted a sequel poem to "Faustina," never published, that underscores the racialized desire that animates the original poem. In both poems, erotic desire is articulated as violence. If a homoerotic reading feels forced, despite its images of "disordered sheets," the mistress's exposed neck, and the nakedness beneath the disheveled nightgown, critic Marilyn May Lombardi's compelling discussion of the poem underscores the sexual resonances of this domestic confrontation. In her notes for "Faustina II," Bishop imagines alcohol running down the black woman's "throat and breast" and writes of loving how "you lift up your black body to its future" and "that darkened (blackened) gibberish you speak" (Lombardi 83). It is, however, Bishop's own "blackened" speech, her racial ventriloquism in poems such as "Songs for a Colored Singer," that reveals an identification with and longing for an embodied blackness tentatively evoked in these poems. This image of Faustina raising her body to a future might solely be read as an expected fetishization, but it might also portend a vision in which fuller civil rights are realized, an act of social ascension that begins in the body.

The power negotiations between black employee and white employer and their sublimated eroticism that Bishop explores in "Cootchie" and "Faustina, or Rock Roses" are mirrored in Hurston's least-celebrated novel, *Seraph on the Suwanee*, and her largely forgotten short story, "Conscience of the Court." Interrogating southern paternalism, these works highlight the gendered aspects of the color line, particularly white Americans' complex engagement with black femininity. Disillusioned by the failed integration of the military during World War II, Hurston locates her version of disturbed white femininity in the turn-of-the-century South still deeply marked by slavery and Jim Crow. Despite its temporal distance, *Seraph on the Suwanee* remains Hurston's most perverse novel and an important but underused commentary on postwar segregation and the psychological landscape of whiteness and its desires and its fears. The novel details the neuroses, many of them racial, of its white protagonist, Arvay Henson, as part of an allegorical vision of racial and domestic reconciliation. Hurston exposes the artifice of race and explicitly names and debunks the muted racial attitudes of many white Americans at the middle of the twentieth century.[18] Lombardi's characterization of Bishop's "Faustina" as an "antiromance" set in the floral lushness of Florida (81) could equally be applied to Hurston's rebuttal to the plantation romance, in which a "Southern cracker," despite the economic and emotional rewards of marriage, remains discontent and trapped within a sadomasochistic dynamic.

Hurston's "whiteface novel," as Claudia Tate terms it ("Hitting" 380), begins in Sawley, where twenty-one-year-old Arvay's loveless, religiously devout life is disrupted by the aggressive wooing of Jim Meserve, an ambitious "Black Irish" turpentine worker. During their courtship, Jim exposes Arvay's feigned sexual hysteria, and the couple rushes to marriage after Jim rapes her. This act of brutality is intended to "break" Arvay of any ambivalence and to assert, oddly, both Jim's commitment and his authority. Her repeated withdrawals and Jim's desertion after failing to achieve his wife's loyalty lie at the center of this unconventional family melodrama. Arvay's emotional transformation at the novel's end, prompted by her mother's death and self-reflection amid the squalor of her family home, brings her back to Jim with the realization that he has loved her generously.

Hurston wrote the majority of *Seraph on the Suwanee* while in Puerto Cortés, Honduras, during the summer of 1947, though some elements, particularly the turpentine camps, are derived from her folklore collections of the 1920s and 1930s.[19] In writing a novel in which African American folk culture, central to both Hurston's aesthetic vision and success, was marginal, the writer placed herself firmly in the era's critical debate over the merits of African Americans turning to nonracial subject matter and "white-life" novels. Writing in *Phylon* in 1950, critic and author Nick Aaron Ford cautions against this literary trend, describing *Seraph* as "unbelievably inferior" to Hurston's novels centered on African American life (375). Ford also asserts that Ann Petry's *Country Place* "lost the naturalness of expression necessary to good art" because it was focused on white experiences too distant from the writer's own (375). Prescriptions to "treat universal themes," he concludes, often result in writing that is too removed from the "genuineness and truth" of racial experiences that the black American artist knew intimately (375).[20] Reviewing one of Willard Motley's novels in 1958, James Byrd assessed the trend in more positive terms, arguing that postwar African American writers, including Petry, Frank Yerby, and Motley, "gained maturity and stature" through successful literary expansions into white subjectivity (433).

When she shifted her attention to a domestic novel centered on white southerners in the late 1940s, Hurston's career was certainly well established and her artistic talent recognized, but consistent publication was still a worry. In a brief stint as a writer at Paramount, Hurston witnessed firsthand the economic benefits of "writing white" and hoped for a commercially successful book that might be made into a movie. A story about white "crackers" with echoes of the plantation romance and elements of the southern grotesque, Hurston may have believed, might have more appeal to white readers and moviemakers than her most recent literary projects, all of which had been rejected. But the marital rape, unsympathetic heroine, and awkward progressions in *Seraph on the Suwanee* unsurprisingly translated into a commercial failure. Despite tempered praise in reviews and its richness for critical study, *Seraph* was a largely forgotten novel until the 1990s.

In conversation with Bishop's poems about black domestic labor, *Seraph on the Suwanee* offers an examination of the complex emotional bonds between the Meserve family and the Kelseys, the African American family they employ. The novel arches back to the history of the southern plantation, whose sexual economy haunts the text's unsentimental interracial encounters. With the exception of her beloved Dessie Kelsey, Arvay maintains a largely antagonistic and condescending relationship with the African Americans and Portuguese immigrants who work for Jim and support her household, insecurely viewing them as competition for Jim's affection. Arvay struggles with a profound alienation from domestic spaces and her expected familial responsibilities as wife and mother, and Dessie often offers Arvay gendered wisdom. The novel addresses the muddled ethics of care through the tenuous bonds between Arvay and Dessie, which are compromised by the white woman's prejudice and her sense of superiority over blacks and her emotional distance from the Kelsey family.

The novel possesses an acute understanding of the South's nuanced racial protocols, where white women such as Arvay often depended on and were affectionate toward black women such as Dessie yet, as Bishop's just-discussed representations of domestic labor illustrate, were also uncritically racist in their behavior and complacent about Jim Crow practices. Explaining to her editor the decision to use *nigger* in Arvay's dialogue, Hurston asserted, "The heroine would have certainly used that word" (Kaplan 555). To mend her psyche and marriage, Arvay must resolve her racial neurosis; her transformation toward mental health, a troubling decision to embrace feminine passivity, depends on and is proceeded by a confrontation of her racial anxieties. In Hurston's depiction of white neuroses, it is telling that Arvay's first act, after her decision to return to Jim, is to make amends with Jeff Kelsey and his wife, Janie, the second generation of the Kelsey family on whom Jim and Arvay have relied for years.

Employing a sermonic style to humorously critique the racial paternalism of the South, Hurston's essay, "The 'Pet Negro' System" (1943), about America's changing race relations is a useful lens for reading *Seraph*. Illuminating the personal, shared loyalties between individual white and black Americans which were marked by racism and class divisions, she concludes that this racial legacy makes current social reforms difficult. "I am not defending the system," writes Hurston, "but trying to explain it" (Kaplan 597). Hurston offers the image of the white southern "gentleman" ready to extend the world to his dear black friend, "as white inside as anyone else," even as he vehemently opposes civil rights for the larger black community ("Pet" 595). This antiquated structure of interracial intimacy promoted the mythology of racial exceptionalism that forfeits a commitment to widespread institutional reform. Hurston, with her own "pet" whites, implicates herself in this individualized cross-race loyalty, admitting, "I have white friends with whom I would, and do, stand when they have need of me, race counting for nothing at all" (599). In this essay, she targets the unruly personal dimensions of desegregation that conform neither to Jim Crow traditions nor to well-intentioned liberal social reforms, surmising that "this friendship business makes a sorry mess of all the rules made and provided" (599).

Hurston's turn to these awkward interracial intimacies of the Old South in the middle of World War II was no coincidence. The paternalism of the southern gentleman had parallels to both the U.S. government's ambivalent role in securing African Americans' full civil rights and its assumed leadership in postwar international politics and reluctant role in the decolonization movements of the 1950s.[21] In "Crazy for This Democracy" (1945), Hurston critiques the U.S. government's racism at home and abroad, including its silence on the anticolonial movements in Africa. She satirizes the rhetoric of democracy—for example, translating *arsenal* to *ass-and-all*—as an ideal supposedly fought for and defended around the world even as segregationist practices persisted on every continent. Exposing the racism beneath Western military campaigns and colonialism, she concludes, "The Ass-and-All of Democracy has shouldered the load of subjugating the dark world completely" (46). Calling for an end to hypocritical American policy, Hurston delineates the psychological function of Jim Crow laws in breeding a sense of inferiority in black American citizens. Such a system could only be eradicated by the repeal of segregationist legislation and by a public confrontation of the white supremacist thinking that informs it. This essay affirms several historians' assertion that black Americans after World War II linked their quest for social equality to the decolonization struggles around the world (see Dudziak, *Cold War Civil Rights*; Singh; Von Eschen). Yet the intellectual contributions of literary artists (with the exception of Wright and Ellison), particularly women, are often overlooked in political histories of the civil rights movement.

Hurston's essays on race relations—what might be called her Jim Crow journalism—trace her complex and at times contradictory racial ideology. Many of these wartime essays, Robert Hemenway notes, "sought to alleviate ignorance by interpreting black subjects for a white audience" (293), but "Pet Negro System" equally confronts white readers with their racial paternalism. In many ways, Hurston was using her journalism in white venues to critique white Americans' prejudices, including the one-dimensional representations of African Americans that publishers and readers embraced. In scrutinizing white supremacist practices, Hurston hoped that changes in postwar American culture would make these dynamics fleeting, but she was also reminded readers that historical oppressions often resurface in new forms. The subjugating loyalties—the tensions and distrust—found in interracial southern friendships or in domestic employment provided an allegory for a nation struggling to imagine new communities unfettered by racial histories at home and abroad. And even more directly, the still rare presence of African Americans in intellectual circles and liberal publications often emulated the "Pet Negro" dynamic.[22]

Hurston returns to this disconcerting idea of the "Pet Negro" in *Seraph* in a scene where Arvay says to her husband that his friend and laborer, Joe Kelsey, "is your pet, I'll bound you." Jim's response—"Kee-reck! Different from every other Negro I ever did see. He's remarkable. Honest as the day is long. Just mighty fine, that's all" (60)—has been interpreted somewhat convincingly as sublimating the homoerotic layers of these southern relationships (Knadler, *Fugitive* 171–75). But a queer reading focused on masculinity neglects Arvay's refusal to see her relationship with Dessie Kelsey within this system of southern paternalism or, more accurately, a maternalism that contains erotic sublimation. Describing poetically the void felt after the Kelseys move at Arvay's insistence because she has concluded that Joe is a corrupting influence, Hurston writes, "When the little house in the grove was empty, Arvay found that its silence left a vacancy in her for days. Joe and Dessie and their children were a part of the pattern of her life" (118). Yet Arvay is too proud to admit her longing for Dessie's company.

Perhaps no one in this era more bravely surveyed the psychoanalytic impact of these segregated intimacies than writer Lillian Smith. In *Killers of the Dream*, she interrogates the complex attachments and shame found between black and white southerners, calling these bonds, including white children and "their" black nurses, "ghost relationships" (116). Smith contemplates the challenge these interracial bonds make to "universal" (deracialized) psychoanalytic theories, concluding that the "dual relationship which so many white southerners have had with two mothers, one white and one colored and each of a different culture that centered in different human values, makes the Oedipus complex seem by comparison almost a simple adjustment" (131). Hurston and Bishop recognize that the black domestic in the white home can function as another type of mother for white women. In "Cootchie" and "Faustina," Bishop shows us emotional dependency that often masks a deeper eroticism, and in *Seraph on the Suwanee*, Hurston places Arvay's struggle to become the matriarch within an extended symbolic family of black workers. These domestic arrangements are additional ghosts in America's racial history not often addressed in scholarship on Cold War families.

"The 'Pet Negro' System" and Hurston's depiction of Arvay's recognizably exploitative relationship with Dessie in *Seraph* and the dynamics between white employer and black maid in Bishop's "Cootchie" appear more rooted in a segregated past than an integrated future. A desegregationist project, however, aims to retell this history to bring to critical light the sexual resonances within these racially charged, socially stratified relationships. For the 1950s reader, particularly women, these texts questioned the meanings and sanctity of home, revealing the complex gendered and racial identifications that shape domestic life. Reminding us of the ambivalence that is central to these cross-race identifications, Fuss writes, "Identification travels a double current, allowing for the possibility of multiple and contradictory identifications coexisting at the same time" (34). From markedly different positions of social power, Hurston and Bishop addressed these bonds of affection, deeply troubling in our current cultural moment, and repeatedly turned to the relationships between black servants and white employers to show the complexities of an American society in which interracial relationships were often animated by ambivalent desires—affection and exploitation, belonging and exclusion. In the wake of World War II, white and black writers more candidly explored the psychological interdependence and hierarchies of power within interracial relationships, both public and private. Postwar authors also wrote about egalitarian relationships and progressive social visions, but their reconsideration of the nation's racist history in intimate terms was an equally important objective. Desegregation necessarily grappled with these racial ghosts to move toward a vision of equality.

Racial Ventriloquism

Critics have often interpreted the decision by authors such as Richard Wright, Willard Motley, and Ann Petry to compose "assimilationist" novels focused exclusively on white characters not only as an aesthetic gesture intended to exhibit their agility with a broader range of subject matter but also as a political gesture by black American artists who refuse to be confined exclusively to racial themes.[23] In his 1948 review of recent books of "raceless writing," Philip Butcher characterizes the praise showered on American writers when they wrote successfully outside of the expected ground of racial themes as a "negative virtue" (113). While the trend among postwar African American writers to attempt the "white-life" novel is well noted, less attention has been given to some of the white American writers from this era who centered their writing on the experiences of African Americans, approaching race and writing in ways different from earlier examples of literary interracialism. The pairing of Hurston and Bishop allows an examination of cross-race writing—what I am calling in these women's work a kind of racial ventriloquism—from a desegregated perspective, considering the corollary moves of black and white writers writing across the color line.[24] This writing can be read as a move to desegregate American culture and its histories by exploring the psychological interdependencies between blacks and whites, but it also reflects a set of shared concerns for black and white artists interested in conveying the potency of segregation as evidenced by reductive representations of racial subjectivity found in much of American literature. By looking further at Hurston's *Seraph on the Suwanee* as a critique of racial and gender domestic practices alongside another text of racial ventriloquism, Bishop's "Songs for a Colored Singer," I illuminate both women's engagement with the era's discourse on feminine neurosis; my main interest, however, rests in the ways these two texts defy the segregationist writing practices of American writers.

Hurston's "What White Publishers Won't Publish" (1950), published a couple of years after her "white-life" novel, offers a useful diagnosis of American literary culture in the wake of World War II and a context for my examination of cross-race writing. The essay speaks to the challenges faced by African American writers who venture into new literary territory and argues for the importance of literature for the nation's stability. Imagining the nation's stereotypes in the "American Museum of Unnatural History," Hurston challenges the "American Negro exhibit" (86) in which two flat figures of buffoonery, the "singing and laughing banjo player" and the "amoral" intellectual "mumbling about injustice" (87), stand in for interpersonally and economically diverse African American communities.[25] The essay offers a rarely considered alternative to the universalizing aesthetic often cited as a postwar literary trend. Hurston argues that conveying the "diverse nuances" of multiple racial communities (the stereotyping of Native Americans and Chinese Americans, for example, are included in her critique) to white Americans is a crucial step not only toward social equality but also toward national security (87). Seeing a relationship between racial politics within America and wider international upheavals, Hurston argues that "this gap in the national literature now has tremendous weight in world affairs. National coherence and solidarity is implicit in a thorough understanding of the various groups within a nation" (85). To articulate, for better or worse, a national identity as Americans, writers must investigate and publishers must support literature that explores the cultural complexities of the nation's citizens, including the troubling intricacies of race. Such a literature, in Hurston's view, becomes in the Cold War a crucial education on racial difference and promotes interracial dialogue.

The decade after World War II was marked by critical disagreement over the purposes and future directions of African American literature. Hurston saw writing by or about African Americans that stays solely in the mode of social protest not only as inaccurate regarding the complex realities of black Americans but also as an impediment to the discovery of shared commonalities necessary for cultural unity. She warns, "But for the national welfare, it is urgent to realize that the minorities do think, and think about something other than the race problem" (87). While her own novel about black entrepreneurialism, *The Golden Bench of God*, bypassed social protest conventions and was rejected by publishers, *Seraph on the Suwanee*, with its focus on the domestic trials and economic mobility of a white family, also demonstrates a refusal to be confined as a writer to the "Negro problem." The novel is Hurston's reminder that her literary imagination expanded beyond racial injustices; however, her shift to whiteness did not erase race from its story line or conform to publishers' preferences for racial essentialism. Folded within *Seraph*'s largely unlikable, neurotic protagonist is a critique of both white supremacy and gender oppression in its everyday forms and an expanded historicization of white identity that references Irish and Portuguese immigration. The novel sits uncomfortably outside of the African American social protest tradition but also diverges from the color-blind and purportedly apolitical stories that came to define the publishing world in the decade after World War II.

In my discussion of Bishop's and Hurston's literary explorations of the affective bonds and tensions between black servants and white employers, I argued that this writing illuminates desegregation as a domestic as much as public issue, but Bishop and Hurston also reveal race as a crucial factor in popular discourses on the changing role of women. In the popular 1947 book, *Modern Woman: The Lost Sex*, for example, the selfish single woman was charged with the unraveling of society's moral fabric. According to K. A. Cuordileone, the volume's authors, Marynia Farnham and Ferdinand Lundberg, "blamed all major social ills—alcoholism, juvenile delinquency, male sexual impotence, female frigidity, the epidemic of mental illness, and homosexuality—on neurotic women who rejected their natural role" (*Manhood* 142). Hurston and Bishop both reference and challenge this figure of the neurotic woman in their literature, and they crafted lives as writers that defied the gender and domestic conformities of the era.

In delineating Arvay's psychological troubles as a form of domestic restlessness, Hurston was careful to describe this neurosis in both racial and sexual terms. Although *Seraph* exhibits the modern folk aesthetic for which Hurston is famous, it is also a classic Freudian case study. Reviewing the novel in the *New York Times* when it was published in October 1948, Frank G. Slaughter calls Arvay a "textbook picture of a hysterical neurotic" (BR24). Ann duCille succinctly diagnoses Arvay as "emotionally ensnared in a state of suspended animation, caught between passion and resistance, desire and defiance" (132). Hurston's depictions of domestic life—the inner turmoil of women living under patriarchal structures and the dynamic between black servants and white employers—reference Freudian theories of masochism and sexual repression to unearth the psychologies of white supremacy. Hurston locates blues material—sexual violence, jealousies, and abandonment—in white lives, fusing a blues aesthetic with psychoanalysis.

Hurston's choice of a white protagonist is an act of displacement that frees the novelist to directly address the popular interest in sexual neuroses, including masochism, without aligning it, as is often done in racist discourse, with blackness. duCille argues that a white context allowed Hurston "to deal with misogynistic attitudes and the issue of sexual violence" without associating these polarizing topics with black masculinity (129).[26] In an era of dehumanizing Jim Crow legislation and mob violence, Hurston purposefully locates the inferiority complex and acts of submission in white psyches and within a white couple's marriage. Hurston explained Arvay's desires and her interest in exploring psychological inferiority, what she calls "a raw sore," in a letter to her publisher, Burroughs Mitchell. Though Hurston confessed to childhood insecurities about her own looks, she also talks about men and women she knew who were intimidated by her confidence and success (Kaplan 558); in writing Arvay, she surely contemplated white women's responses to her unconventional femininity and irreverent racial attitudes, free of subservience or pity. Her firsthand knowledge of neurotic white women, gained from her friendships with Fannie Hurst, Marjorie Rawlings, and Charlotte Osgood Mason, provided a wealth of material for constructing Arvay's neurosis. Her decision to focus on white pathology, to render the expressions of low self-esteem that she had witnessed in white women, is a subversive shift that undermines the pervasive rhetoric of black dysfunction.

This voicing of the sexual neuroses of a white woman, inverts the discourse of racial pathology even as it affirms the feminization of hysteria. In ways compatible with Bishop's "cabaret songs," Hurston uses racial ventriloquism to challenge racial binaries and cultural beliefs about racial distinctiveness. Hazel V. Carby notes the political statement being made by Hurston in having white characters speak expressions "lifted from the mouth of a black character in an earlier novel," exposing the myth of cultural containment (ix). Claudia Tate argues that the insertion of black expressions into white dialogue as well as the vision of a racially egalitarian society on the shipping boat—Jim working alongside his black shipmates at the novel's end—"carnivalizes the presumption that discernible racial differences are the natural basis of segregation and discrimination" ("Hitting" 390). By choosing a white protagonist and including moments of interracial contentment in the text, Hurston jostled readers to accept an increasingly integrated world and to acknowledge the absurdity of white supremacist social customs. In Hurston's novel, integration denotes both psychological wholeness and a social community that unsettles racial hierarchies. duCille questions the sincerity of Arvay's desire to reconcile with Jeff and Janie Kelsey, viewing it as a manipulative move to win back Jim. Tate also complicates Arvay's motives, seeing her shift of racial behavior as part of a race fantasy, a masking of the very real racial strictures of the segregated South in an attempt to assert a utopian vision that erases racial difference. Largely an abhorrent protagonist, Arvay attempts to explain her self-discovery, prompted by the trip to her family home: "I done seen and felt things that I don't want to never see and to feel no more. I don't want to find it in me, and I don't want to find it no where around me. If I got any narrow-hearted littleness is me, I hope to God to cut myself and let it run out" (314). Evoking masochistic imagery, Arvay flatly rejects racist pettiness and pledges to eradicate such divisions from her life. This desire to live free of prejudice might strike the contemporary, jaded reader as naive race rhetoric, but her choice echoes Hurston's commitment to a life unhampered by internalized racism. She refused to accept segregated social spheres and the "narrow-hearted littleness" of Jim Crow ideologies.

When she makes peace with Jim after the death of her son, Earl, Arvay feels that a "great, great burden *had* been wrenched off from her shoulders," a sense of having "worn a shield and buckler for eighteen long years" (158). This cast-off psychological armor is located within a blues sentiment, a testified emotional burden that the speaker hopes to shed by naming it. *Seraph* documents the contours of a white woman's emotional insecurities and masochism but, in an ending true to Hollywood *and* Freud, suggests that marital accord and psychological wholeness can be gained only through a confrontation with and exorcism of the past. Arvay embraces a loyal passivity to Jim only after she buries her mother, confronts the carcass of her family home, and burns it down. She comes to identify with the lyrics of "Careless Love" that moved her on her wedding night: "You cause me to weep, you cause me to moan / You cause me to leave my happy home" (59). Only after shedding familial trauma and confronting her psychological homelessness can Arvay willingly submit to her marriage. Hurston's happy ending, her inclusion of interracial resolution and egalitarian spaces, must not be read simply as conformation to Hollywood formula or solely as subversive social critique.

Reading beyond cynicism or subversion, we can locate Arvay's romanticized transformation within a larger social postwar optimism, compromised by the era's gender conservatism, to move beyond social prejudices.

The trouble with Arvay's transformation is the fact that her independence is facilitated by a dependence on black labor, and her act of autonomous resistance—burning down the family home—is followed by an embrace of a new patriarchy, Jim's household, Jim's ship. Although the novel stresses interracial cooperation and begins to imagine desegregated spaces, its gender politics, unless read as a parody, are hardly progressive. Arvay's resolution to submit to her husband's sexual and economic strength, embracing the role of the dutiful wife, makes it difficult to read the novel as a text of feminist defiance. However, feminist critics have attempted to locate radical possibilities in this seemingly retrograde ending. Both Tate's and duCille's compelling readings of the novel's final scene have pointed to the overwrought dialogue and Arvay's implausible acquiescence to suggest that Hurston is not merely giving us a Hollywood ending of marital accord.[27] I see Arvay's submission to her husband as a reflection of Hurston's ambivalent feminist politics and the larger culture's anxiety about the appropriate role of women. Hurston forwards an integrationist vision of working-class camaraderie but situates it within a restored patriarchal family structure. Because so much of the novel focuses on Arvay's ambivalence about homemaking, *Seraph* can be convincingly read, despite being set in an earlier moment of U.S. history, as a commentary on the cult of domesticity resurfacing after World War II. The porch of Arvay's home eventually becomes her space of serenity, but it is also a symbol of gender conformity, and Hurston reminds us that her domestic contentment depends on the disciplining of black labor. If, as Elaine Tyler May notes, "investing in one's home, along with the trappings that would presumably enhance family life, was seen as the best plan for the future" (165), then Hurston expresses doubt about that future. She certainly experienced domestic contentment herself, but not in traditional forms and not in ways dependent on racialized labor systems. May's use of *domestic trappings* is apt because Arvay is trapped, smothered by the home and the material fervor Jim brings to it. Her decision to burn the family home and her pleasure of playing hostess on the shipping boat, a site of interracial and homosocial culture, suggests an alternative domestic politics with nonnormative gender and sexual practices.

As Hurston did with *Seraph*, Bishop approached the "race problem" through a psychological rather than a sociological lens. While her poems are hardly romances in the conventional sense, their focus on interracial encounters in private spaces construct race relations, as "Faustina" so vividly captures, as a form of domestic intimacy defined by attraction and revulsion. And the first two sections of Bishop's "Songs for a Colored Singer" center on the unraveling of an African American couple's relationship. Her decision to narrate this romance in stilted "black" vernacular deserves attention for what it reveals about desegregationist impulses in American literature and in postwar culture more broadly. Lawrence Jackson describes the white writer of the 1940s who explored African American experiences as being located somewhere between "civil rights crusader and local color portrait-maker" (152). This positioning is apt for Bishop, who certainly cannot be claimed as an activist but whose poems contain a social scrutiny that belies their easy dismissal as quaint racial voyeurism. "Faustina" and "Cootchie" explore emotional dependency in domestic spaces where sexual desire is buried within racial confrontation. These poems make whiteness visible for critique and draw attention to the libidinal dimensions of some interracial relationships. They offer an overlooked and perhaps troublesome white perspective on black women's experiences and, in the case of "Songs," on artistry in the 1940s. These poems illuminate the psychological complexities (and invite us to evaluate the political potential) of white submission.

Published in the September 1944 *Partisan Review*, "Songs for a Colored Singer" caught the attention of Jean Pedrick, an editor at Houghton Mifflin. Pedrick encouraged the poet to send her manuscript to the publisher's first poetry contest, which Bishop won, landing a contract for a first book (Millier 174). The fact that a poem of erotic, racial ventriloquism basically launched Bishop's career is rarely acknowledged or interrogated; however, Bishop's inaugural poetics were defined in fundamental ways by a welding of race and sexuality. Her regular inclusion of black women, not unlike the women she employed in her home, in poems of emergent lesbian identity and identification are crucial layers that are rarely pursued in criticism of her Florida poetry. Despite these connections, Bishop never publicly discussed the racial dimensions of her poetry. Nevertheless, critics including Renée Curry, Camille Roman, and Steven Axelrod ("Is Elizabeth Bishop") have assessed the complex racial and racist dimensions of her work. Despite the risk of breaching social taboo, these literary experiments about conflicted interracial intimacies had economic benefits. When Bishop's writing is read in relation to Cold War politics (another rare approach), the era's racial changes are neglected.[28] Bishop's racial poetics, particularly her attempts to render black subjectivity, should be contextualized within a desegregationist viewpoint; more controversially, her interracial representations should be read as desegregationist acts.

In March 1940, Bishop wrote of working on "Songs for a Colored Singer," calling them "cabaret songs" (*OA* 89). The poet's admission that these songs were "very *vaguely*" intended for Billie Holiday suggests the ways Bishop may have imagined herself as a torch singer performing these works (478).[29] Beyond the tragic mythologies that circulate around her celebrity, Holiday is less often positioned as an icon of integration despite her presence in the interracial circles of the Café Society, one of the few clubs of the era with an integrated policy, in this case dating back to the 1930s.[30] What do we make of Bishop's imagined vocalizing, her performance as the jazz singer? For Bishop, Holiday was emblematic of tragic femininity, unchecked desire, murky sexuality, and an object of racial longing—a touchstone of lesbian desire. Bishop's disjointed four-part poem reflects an investment in Holiday's tragic associations even as it melds racial and sexual identification and writes a space for lesbian desire that is potentially liberating.[31] Holiday's appeal, her marked difference and assumed sexual sameness, illuminates a problematic desire to impersonate black womanhood for the freedom it is projected to offer. The poem performs an identification with a black woman, presented as a marginal figure and therefore resonant for a sexual outsider such as Bishop. Her ventriloquism of Holiday in "Songs for a Colored Singer," then, is both erotic tribute and perverse racial crossing. Here Bishop escapes the body and its gendered tangles and becomes a torch singer, evoking a surreal landscape steeped in the southern gothic tradition.

Though the poem's title indicates songs *for* a singer, the songs, with lines that awkwardly juggle poetic formalism and pseudo-dialect (which slips away almost as if emulating the waning confidence of the poet to render a convincing black voice), appear to be blues lyrics sung *by* the "Colored Singer." Its first two sections both celebrate and critique transience—the ready suitcase, the bus ticket "that will take me anywhere" (*CP* 48). In the spirit of the blues, the hard-luck story is tinged with humor; while Bishop may delight in the odd rhyme of *bus* and *monogamous*, the ironic tone precludes intimacy, and the stilted dialect precludes believability. Toni Morrison argues that we have an "obligation" to consider the reasons that a given artwork "fails" (*Playing* 18).[32] At no point is the reader convinced that a black woman—and certainly not Holiday—is testifying in song, yet to dismiss the poem as an aesthetic failure and an embarrassing racial misstep is to ignore its role in challenging segregation in American poetics. Its attempt to render a racial subconscious and confess an emotional, even sexual, identification across race relies on exhausted racial tropes, but it also tests aesthetic and social boundaries.

The second section of the poem narrates the couple's dissolution and the speaker's decision to "ride and ride and not come back"—an evocation of the freedom found in travel that characterizes many blues lyrics (*CP* 48).

Bishop's performance of blackness rejects heterosexual domesticity; there is perverse pleasure in the woman's decision to "call a halt" to the relationship. Her assertion—"Now I'm pursuing my own way"—both confronts patriarchy and whispers a lesbian alternative (48). The couple's dynamic parallels Hurston's portrait of domestic discord in *Seraph*. In both cases, we have women exerting independence; here, the nameless singer rejects companionship for the road, while in Hurston's novel, Arvay leaves her family to return to her abandoned childhood home to reflect on her commitment to marriage and motherhood. This fantasy of escape captures a blues ethos as well as women's desire for autonomy in an era in which gendered restrictions and new social freedoms often existed in tension.

The poem's final two sections, more mysteriously surreal and erotic, shift the reader away from the overperformed cross-race monologue. The third section is a wartime lullaby, both menacing and soothing. The thin lines of these cinquains operate as sound studies and imagistic meditations rather than narrative-driven confessions, a kind of dreamscape ripe for Freudian analysis. Moreover, the lack of overt racial signification in these latter sections, with their rejections and questions, forwards an integrationist vision. Camille Roman directs us toward such a reading with her observation that the "universal adult and child imagery is inclusive across social boundaries," while the figures' implied race as African Americans "reminds one that society is segregated and unequal in its treatment of its citizens" (71). With these racial and gender ambiguities in the lullaby, Bishop highlights social uncertainty and, like the poem's "big ship," unmoors the reader from racial signposts. The image of the vessel sunken by "lead in its breast" (*CP* 49) evokes both the casualties of World War II and a psychological, almost existential, weight—perhaps segregation's damage or a burdensome sexual longing.

The poem's final section centers on an elusive "shining in the leaves," cycling through images: tears, seeds, fruit, and finally faces (50). The dreamlike quality of the poem conjures the morbid image of the lynched body, an echo, as Roman also notes, of "Strange Fruit," a song made famous by Holiday (75). Bishop's "conspiring root" (50) echoes the song's lyric "blood at the root" too closely to be coincidence. These images build on earlier references to the dark wetness of rain-slicked highways and a face spotted through the rain, evoking a liminal world of near-sleep and unrestrained eroticism. In this poem sequence, Bishop confronts her artistry and, like Hurston, her own version of racial neurosis: the imaginative space where blackness looms prominent and potent. Feeling not anxiety but potential in an identity made "darker, darker" (51), from the "dark and dreary place" of the psyche (50), she encounters her internal, racial Other and claims it as Self. Through the black jazz singer whom the poet clumsily performs, we are invited to contemplate our own racial subjectivity, to test its fluidity, and perhaps to confront the libidinal fantasies lurking "too real to be a dream" (51). Eric Lott's insights into the ways white minstrel performers in the antebellum United States "immersed themselves in 'blackness' to indulge their felt sense of difference" and created a troublesome "imaginary space of fun and license" (51) have relevance to this postwar moment and to Bishop's stilted depictions of African Americans' interior lives. Bishop's constructions of blackness as sites of emotional release and subconscious desire are all too common primitivist stereotypes, but the poem's stylistic shifts and surrealist elements approach race, gender, and citizenship from multiple angles and begin to destabilize these concepts. Rather than trying to reconcile the aesthetic shifts between the sections of "Songs," we might embrace these disjunctures and read the racial mysteries at the poem's ending as a return to the romantic disharmony at its beginning.

Clustering "Cootchie," "Faustina," and "Songs for a Colored Singer," it becomes apparent that black womanhood is central to Bishop's poetics. This fact is overlooked by critics or quickly dismissed as conventional racist cultural tourism, yet these reactions fail to take seriously the desegregating gestures within these poems. In tracing the occluded social consciousness in Bishop's poetry, James Longenbach concludes, "For Bishop, the considerations of gender and sexuality grew to be inseparable from the consideration of nationality and race" (469). The power struggles between domestic worker and employer and depictions of black women's material and emotional lives in Bishop's poetry equally invite us to consider the limits and potentials of women's allegiances and contribute a private narrative of racial change outside the public sphere as part of larger movement of social change. In this postwar moment, we find white writers confronting the nation's racial history, including ideologies of racial superiority and the important, often deeply troubling identifications with African Americans. Although the racial subconscious rendered in Bishop's poetry explores a growing sense of an eroding world, the construction of racial difference found in them ultimately is for the most part about "feeling white." Bishop's "new" version of white southern womanhood still depends on conventional racial imagery. The murky desires and fears of the subconscious that Bishop's poetry repeatedly maps make whiteness visible, but this visibility always depends on reductive representations of black corporeality and speech.

Attributing psychoanalytic significance to Bishop's racial poetics, Steven Axelrod argues, "The mixed feelings Bishop evinces toward Black images—fear and comfort, alienation and love—reflect not only the bias of her culture but also, passing through that bias, her mixed feelings toward her parents and toward herself in so far as she has absorbed those ambivalently loved objects into her subject" ("Is Elizabeth Bishop" 351). Adrienne Rich sees the poet's interest in race as an identification with other outsiders and finds poems such as "Songs for a Colored Singer" and "Cootchie" "honest" and "courageous" (135, 125). Bishop's interest in other races and in the lives of the poor has been interpreted as identification with other forms of oppression, but Bishop was not only interested in blackness as a corollary to her own sexual difference; she repeatedly, though mutedly, locates desire—sensuality, erotic tension—in black women, including Cootchie, the "colored singer," and Faustina. Perhaps these women's marginalization, which Bishop emphasizes in these poems, resonated with the poet's status as a sexual Other, but Bishop's poems, indebted to psychoanalytic theories of subconscious desire, also imagine an expressive freedom in blackness, highlight relationships where power struggles are shaped by sexual forces, and name a racialized eroticism, including objects "ambivalently loved" ("Is Elizabeth Bishop" 351) that complicate characterizations of sexuality in the Cold War as being largely conservative and deracialized. In drawing our attention to the "gendered logic of exchange" in blackface minstrelsy, in which white masculinity is substantiated through the "unmanning" of symbolic black manhood, Lott provides a satisfying lens for understanding Bishop's repeated reductive representations of black womanhood (49). Her focus on the intimacies and power struggles between white women and black women offer another form of minstrelsy that reveals cultural anxieties about changes in racial status, particularly black women's increasing claim to the public sphere. As a result, white femininity is often articulated in an antagonistic relationship to black femininity, and blackness is rendered as crucial to Bishop's articulations of sexual (including lesbian) desire.

While the feminist and racial politics of *Seraph on the Suwanee* and "Songs for a Colored Singer" can hardly be characterized as progressive, the texts share a postwar preoccupation with diagnosing women's changing social positions, unsettling segregationist literary prescriptions to reflect societal ambivalence about these changes. The process of an African American writer composing white characters who speak southern expressions traditionally designated as black—a black woman "talking back" with white characters "talking black"—suggests the complexity of an integrationist aesthetic: an intrusion into the literary mainstream's segregationist practices, a disruption of cherished beliefs in the clear divisions between white and black culture, and a dismissal of racial taboos and propriety. It is within these acts of racial ventriloquism—voicing the Other—that both Bishop and Hurston identify with women testing the boundaries of freedom, a parallel to the creative risks they are taking as writers. Speaking of representations of women's sexuality in popular media, Elaine Tyler May observes, "From the late forties to the fifties, subordination made the difference between good or bad female sexuality" (63). In their literary depictions across race, despite pronounced differences in aesthetics and racial perspectives, Hurston and Bishop explored a shared terrain of the racial subconscious, rendering acts of submission and voicing anxiety that ultimately questioned the viability and desirability of being a "good woman" in a postwar American society still rigid in its gender and racial practices.

Writers who venture across the color line to craft characters outside of their own racial community and particularly to voice the subjectivities of those characters are engaging in an act of desegregation that is likely be treated with skepticism by readers and critics alike. Writers, of course, wrote across race at earlier points in America's literary history, but the pronounced attention to the sexual psychology of these interracial encounters distinguishes these literary experiments from earlier texts. The late 1940s and 1950s, notes historian K. A Cuordileone, were marked by a "wave of Freudianism and existentialism that swept the postwar literary milieu" and included a "fascination with the murky underside of the psyche" (*Manhood* 9). The psychological effects of interracial encounters and the sublimated desires that contributed to segregation's resilience as well as its violations became inviting topics for postwar artists. Desegregation, whether symbolic or actual, made visible Americans' troubled psyches, whether plagued by racism, racial guilt, or interracial desire. This mid-twentieth-century interest in the unseemly layers of the subconscious is evident not only in the dying white woman's fear of Faustina and her "sinister kind face" and in the paranoia that circulates in the final section of "Songs for a Colored Singer" with its "army" of "darker, darker" faces but also in the emotional fragility of Hurston's Arvay.

The confessional poetry of Sylvia Plath and Ann Sexton, notes Deborah Nelson, employs "psychological breakdown as a metaphor and instance of social disintegration" (106). This connection between psychological upheavals and social change is evident in the writing of Hurston and Bishop that precedes the Cold War boom in confessional poetry. While "social disintegration" speaks to the erosion of traditional forms of sociality and the panic over the loss of cultural cohesion after World War II, the term also signals the ways desegregation as a specific form of social change, an erosion of racial divides and practices, caused psychological upheavals of the sort captured by Bishop and Hurston. As writers who did not conform to the era's trends regarding marriage and parenting, Bishop and Hurston wrote about women who experienced social anxieties not with emergent public identities but in traditional domestic roles. Arvay sees marriage as enslavement, blurting out, "I can't stand this bondage you got me in. I can't endure no more! I can't never feel satisfied that I got you tied to me, and I can't leave you" (*Seraph* 218). For Bishop, the domestic space was often rendered void of men but was also threatened by the erotic undercurrents and racial tensions between women. The psychological unease explored in *Seraph on the Suwanee*, "Songs for a Colored Singer," and "Faustina" reminds us that these social and psychological upheavals of home are deeply gendered.

Integrationist Ideologies

Although both women's nonfiction writing has received less attention from critics, Bishop's lyrical essays on Key West outsiders and Hurston's journalism on the era's racial politics offer original perspectives on America's racial history and on the desegregationist ideologies emerging in the late 1940s. They contemplate integration, both emergent and stalled. Published in magazines such as the *American Mercury* and *Partisan Review* that highlighted integration and interracial cooperation, Hurston's political essays and short story "Conscience of the Court" and Bishop's prose portraits of multicultural Key West demonstrate the ways liberal readers consumed integration. In her journalism, Hurston discusses integration as an increasingly pressing issue that needed to be critiqued. Her decision to write opinion pieces on American race issues in mainstream publications indicates a desire to address racial interdependency not solely as a literary project; as a struggling writer, she also may have wanted to capitalize financially on the interest in race relations. In contrast, Bishop chose to write imagistic essays on local artists and obscure institutions in which the racial and sexual divides of Key West were legible, publishing them in literary magazines or not at all. Bishop approached cross-racial connections as an aesthetic experiment that might illicit racial sympathy but avoided pointed political commentary.

This study of postwar American literature begins with Bishop and Hurston not only because their writing and life experiences convey the complexity of racial politics and aesthetics that existed within a segregated nation midcentury but also because their writing represents an early stage in a transition toward new models of citizenship and interracial communities. In examining spaces of tentative racial exchange, many of them marked by suspicion and stereotype, desegregation is conveyed as an unstable and far from utopic process. This pairing of Hurston and Bishop unearths thematic connections—most importantly, the racial politics and gendered practices of domestic spaces; it also illuminates the profound differences in their social positions, complicating a generic sense of desegregation as being solely contained within a progressive politics. Bishop's and Hurston's ambivalence about social change and their conservatism regarding race relations relative to other leftist artists (for example, Carl Offord and Jo Sinclair, discussed in chapter 4) is, in fact, one of their commonalities. Despite the interracial worlds within which both women lived to varying degrees, integration remained a liberal ideal more than a lived reality. If anything, the social strictures of southern slavery had left lasting imprints on St. Augustine, Key West, and other Florida communities. Hurston witnessed that legacy in her daily life and interpreted that ambivalent and often tense racial landscape in her art. Bishop's interactions with and writing about the African American and Cuban American women were far more superficial, evidenced at times in her predictable racial imagery. Like Hurston, however, Bishop recognized the complex identifications and disavowals in the domestic relationships between black and white women. Through their literary representations of these often contentious relationships, both women's larger ambivalence about integration, its politics and promises, is better understood.

During the 1940s and early 1950s, Hurston was involved with community activism in Florida and Harlem, witnessing the effects of World War II and writing about changes in the racial landscape in America. As part of her work with Recreation in War, a project to provide entertainment to soldiers, the writer traveled throughout Florida in 1943 to speak to segregated troops (Kaplan 781). In the fall of that year, she was involved in a plan to build a recreational center in her hometown of Eatonville, hoping to make it "a better place for young folks to be—especially for girls" (Kaplan 496). Hurston's youth advocacy also extended to Harlem, where in the fall of 1946 she helped form Block Mothers of Harlem, a collaborative child-care plan that included field trips and a litter reduction initiative (Mackenzie 14). The community program was started while Hurston was working on the campaign of Republican Grant Reynolds, an "adamant integrationist" running for Congress (Kaplan 441). Like many African Americans, Hurston challenged the hypocrisy of the U.S. government and its reluctance to desegregate the military despite African American soldiers' heroic defense of democratic ideals. She complained to Walter White, executive secretary of the National Association for the Advancement of Colored People, about the substandard conditions for black soldiers who were segregated at the Signal Corps school set up in St. Augustine, Florida, writing that black soldiers, many "college men" who "represent the best Negro families," had been "dumped in this little hole" where they were "insulted and mocked" (Kaplan 470). Her exhaustion with this ongoing racial mistreatment is pointedly illustrated in her comment to

White that "the Negroes have been bitched again" (469). Hurston's gendered comment suggests that racism emasculates and that a desegregated military would produce appropriately masculine subjects and productive citizens.

Hurston's philosophy of individualism, in which identity was shaped within a racial community but never conscribed by that community, is reflected in her position on legal desegregation. She was uncomfortable with the "damage thesis" used to win the *Brown v. Board of Education* case—the argument that psychological inferiority results from segregated facilities (a legal strategy discussed more fully in chapter 4). Sparking controversy, Hurston stated that she found the ruling "insulting rather than honoring" to African Americans. Her fierce racial pride found the idea of forcing white Americans to desegregate institutions repugnant. Refusing to be an object of pity, she boasted, "I can see no tragedy in being too dark to be invited to a white school affair" (Kaplan 740). After being misquoted as supporting segregationist practices, Hurston clarified her views to Douglas Gilbert of the *New York World-Telegram*: In the South, she observed that blacks often "were happy in their social gatherings and had no more desire to associate with the whites than the whites had to associate with them" (476). But she also told Claude Barnett of the Associated Negro Press that she was "ready for anything to overthrow Anglo-Saxon supremacy" (475). As M. Genevieve West observes, Hurston's beliefs about school desegregation were nuanced and easily misunderstood: "She was not opposed to desegregation, but opposed to *court-ordered* desegregation" (227). Hurston argued, for example, that the energy expended to integrate schools should have been channeled toward enforcing compulsory education for black students as well as whites (Kaplan 740).[33] Hurston's 1955 letter to the editor of the *Orlando Sentinel* asserts a long-held belief in black self-sufficiency and ends with a slightly cryptic summary: "Thems my sentiments and I am sticking by them. Growth from within. Ethical and cultural desegregation" (Kaplan 740). Less concerned with racial integration as legislative strategy, Hurston invokes desegregation as a process that acknowledged social interdependence and promoted increased interaction across cultural differences. Desegregation enacted an ethics, a viewing of the racial Other as someone whose well-being all citizens must see as a shared responsibility.

Critics have debated Bishop's political allegiances and commitment to racial equality both in Florida and in her later life in Brazil.[34] It is well known that she viewed herself as an apolitical poet and was wary of dogmatic writing. Biographer Brett Millier characterizes Bishop as repeatedly taking the "uncommitted path" in politics, noting her distancing from the left-leaning poets who supported the Popular Front in the Spanish Civil War during the

1930s as well as her later disinterest in the U.S. civil rights and feminist movements (200). The fact that her first book, *North and South*, did not directly address World War II worried Bishop, and to avoid charges of apathy, she asked her publisher to put a note in the introduction explaining that most of the poems were written before the war began. The collection's oft-noted exception is "Roosters," a war poem confined to the local rather than addressing the global. This gendered allegory was Bishop's preferred mode for addressing current events: imagistic poems with occluded social messages. Despite a reticence toward overtly political poetry, Bishop wanted to be understood as socially aware. In later interviews, she discussed how the widespread poverty of the 1930s spurred her social consciousness: "I had lived with poor people and knew something of poverty at firsthand" (Brown 293–94). The Great Depression, for her and most of the writers in this study, engendered social radicalism. Describing the cultural climate, Bishop observed, "A great many people were communist, or would-be communist" (Starbuck 321). She had tried socialism and anarchism but confessed in 1966, "I'm much more interested in social problems and politics now than I was in the '30s" (Brown 294). Given Bishop's reluctance to be affiliated with any political cause, including the feminist and gay liberation movements that emerged in her later years, it is not surprising that her work in the 1940s did not directly confront the social policies and supremacist ideologies behind the era's segregationist practices. In sharp contrast to Hurston's journalism and letters, Bishop's lack of commentary on civil rights court cases and racial tragedies, including the Scottsboro trial and routine lynchings in the South, is lamentable but also consistent with her avowed aversion to politics in general. While some of her essays and poems contain an implied social critique, Bishop's writing fails to directly address segregation or her privileged position within these socially stratified spheres. Still, the poet's ideas about racial identity and class divisions were folded into a complex aesthetic that repeatedly located interracial tensions within an imagistic, often surreal, but always contested domestic space.

For Bishop, Key West offered a unique site for documenting a nation changed by war. Losing much of its fishing industry and cigar factories during the Great Depression, the racially mixed, sleepy port town was transformed into a bustling military home for thousands of soldiers, including poet Frank O'Hara, when the U.S. Navy moved one of its hubs to the region from Charleston, South Carolina. The "old pirates' haven and new artists' colony," reported *Newsweek*, "hoped to be restored to its onetime prosperity by the nation's biggest business—war" ("War Baby" 27). Bishop witnessed the displacement of residents as the government tore down neighborhoods for military construction. She wrote in 1942, "Some people have received only a day's warning to get out, and there are Negroes sleeping in cars and vacant lots all over town. . . . I don't want to be unpatriotic about it either, but it *is* unnecessary, I'm sure" (*OA* 106). Despite genuine concern and her involvement in a campaign to rally Senator Claude Pepper's intervention in the destruction of historic Key West, Bishop's comments seem to arise largely from a sense of inconvenience and aesthetic assault—all those beautiful houses destroyed. Seeing the city of Key West transformed by military expansion, she wrote in 1940, "The war news fills me with such frantic haste and I am so worried about what may become of Key West" (*OA* 93). Even their commentary on the war's impact on the home front shows a marked difference in Hurston's and Bishop's vantage points: While both commented on race, Hurston was attuned to the mistreatment of soldiers as part of a larger legacy of American injustice, whereas Bishop focused on local dislocations and avoided their connections to larger systems of oppression.

When Bishop visited Haiti in February 1949, she met Selden Rodman, a white poet who shared her interest in black music and vernacular painters, including Haitian artists.[35] Rodman had reviewed *North and South* for the *New York Times* three years earlier. Signaling out "Songs for a Colored Singer," he praised Bishop's precise poetics: "In building up her over-all watercolor arrangements she never strays far from the concrete and the particular" (161). When Bishop wrote to him in November 1947, she inquired about Haitian poetry and expressed her eagerness to visit the country, inspired by his book *The Amazing Year: A Diary in Verse* (1947); she found his section on the island "fascinating because of its strangeness" (*OA* 150). Writing to poet Robert Lowell about the country's racial protocols, Bishop concluded that the "racial situation is the most interesting thing about Haiti." She commented on the mostly bored reactions of black audience members at Rodman's lecture on "Primitivism in Modern Poetry" and was amazed at the racially integrated social events she encountered, noting "thorough mixtures everywhere, at everything" despite a rigid caste system (*OA* 183). This opportunity to observe how race and class operated in another country offered a counterpoint to the social stratification Bishop observed and navigated in Key West. Through her travels, Bishop received a social as much as artistic education, witnessing whiteness jarred from an unremarked universalism and racial difference as nuanced and culturally varied. These journeys and cultural exchanges allowed Bishop to cultivate a life as an artist outside of standard Cold War domestic narratives.

Establishing a home in Samambaia, Brazil, with Lota de Macedo Soares in the 1950s, Bishop again commented on the racial dynamics of a society markedly different from the United States. In her 1962 book on the country, commissioned by *Life* magazine, she noted that "Brazilians take great pride in their fine record in race relations" and praised the country's "racial tolerance" (qtd. in Goldensohn 205). Yet the problematic racial politics that marked her relationships with the domestic workers employed in her Key West homes were replicated in her domestic life in South America. Bishop and de Macedo Soares, for example, played symbolic grandmothers to the children of the gardener, Kyslo, whom Lota had adopted when he was a child. And when the cook named her daughter Maria Elizabeth in the poet's honor, Bishop reported with delight that she had a "Negro namesake" (*OA* 326). Bishop and de Macedo Soares, in fact, considered formally adopting the child because of the family's economic struggles. This lesbian couple's investment in an imagined kinship that transcended racial, economic, and linguistic differences did little to confront or alter their investment in a political system that reinforced these economic inequities. Bishop was disturbed by the poverty she witnessed on a daily basis in Brazil, particularly its impact on children; however, the social critique that animates the 1956 poem "Squatter's Children," as with many of her Key West portraits, is diluted by the poet's reliance on sentimental primitivism.

Bishop's opposition to gender discrimination was more audible than her racial politics, best captured in her lifelong refusal to be published in what she viewed as "segregated anthologies": "When I was in college and started publishing . . . there were women's anthologies, and all-woman-issues of magazines, but I always refused to be in them. I didn't think about it very seriously, but I felt it was a lot of nonsense, separating the sexes. I suppose this feeling came from feminist principles, perhaps stronger than I was aware" (Starbuck 322). Although an anthology of women writers might be read on one level as a feminist statement, Bishop tellingly rejected the practice. Operating from a philosophy of individualism much like Hurston's, Bishop insisted on being read alongside both contemporary and earlier poets regardless of gender. From her perspective, this refusal to highlight gender difference *was* feminist and reflected the universalizing sentiments expressed by many American writers in the late 1940s. This debate mirrors the dilemma of certain African American writers, including Jean Toomer and Ralph Ellison, who sought to be read as American writers outside the designation of "Negro artist." Hurston, too, wanted to be considered within a broader American literary tradition without denying the specificity of race and gender in her writing. Both Bishop and Hurston championed artistic autonomy over political, gender, or racial allegiance, even as they ambivalently claimed membership in postwar communities that were undergoing tremendous changes. Embedded in these rejections of artistic compartmentalization based on race or gender was a precarious reformulation of American citizenship that attempted to reconcile, as did so many postwar literary works, universal humanity and cultural particularities.

This precarious new conception of citizenship is evident in Bishop's "Mercedes Hospital" (1941) and Hurston's "Conscience of the Court" (1955). Though written more than a decade apart, these two works explore social interdependence, locating the problematic interracial intimacies discussed throughout this chapter in the public spaces of the hospital and courtroom, respectively. Situated there, Bishop's Miss Mamie and Hurston's Laura Lee Kimble—black women literally caring for the nation's citizens—espouse an ethics of interracial accountability necessary if the nation was truly committed to social integration. In "Mercedes Hospital," which was not published until after Bishop's death, the author refracts her displacement as a northern white woman through the marginalized spaces of Key West's African American and Cuban residents. After stumbling across the obituary for José Chacón, a drunkard who died in a hospital for the poor, Bishop produced an impressionistic portrait of Mercedes Hospital's present occupants. The essay focuses on the quaint details that attempt to transform this institutional place into something like home: the battered hospital's cross-stitched mottoes, a cigar-box decoration, and a picture of a nearly divine José Martí. The vicarious visitor enters a dreamlike underground; Bishop notes, "The whole hospital has the air of having been submerged."[36] In this otherworldly environment, the poet encounters bodily and cultural difference, typically tinged with tragedy.

The fact that Bishop calls the hospital residents *inmates* rather than patients (at times surrounding this term with ironic quotation marks), contributes to the alienated pathos Bishop attempts to evoke in this surreal, sometimes suffocating, prison-like place (*CPR* 65). Miss Mamie, a nurse portrayed with touches of a folk mammy figure, leads Bishop on her tour. Despite her saintly status, Miss Mamie is depicted in a largely unflattering way: dirty uniform, missing teeth, and a scrutinizing gaze like a "doubtful child" (65). Bishop, in discomfort, notes that the nurse "always stands very close" (65). The nurse's "leer" and "pinch" of the narrator's plumpness suggest a menacing, even molesting, personality (65). Yet this disturbing characterization is balanced by Miss Mamie's loyalty; she has worked at the hospital for thirty years and "has the local reputation as a saint" (63). This piece about a neglected hospital, a public space performing the care associated with home, remains largely focused on Miss Mamie's emotional effect on the narrator. We are told that she "is capable of arousing the same feelings that the saints do: profoundest admiration and suspicion" (69). The narrator's curiosity about this nonwhite woman—her "childlike expression" and "long ascetic feet" (69)—recalls the racialized gaze fixed on other women in Bishop's poems, including Cootchie and Faustina. Tellingly, the narrator concludes that the "absence of tenderness" is the "most consoling thing" about Miss Mamie (70). The nurse's suspicious demeanor is inextricable from her saintliness; in her strangeness, the nurse offers an antisentimentality that Bishop finds refreshing.

Bishop's inquiries into the social fabric of Key West often eulogize an eroding, "quaint" past, including its troubling racial protocols, on which impersonal, modern influences are encroaching. Rather than dismiss "Mercedes Hospital" as serving no political function, we might consider how it reflects a desegregationist imperative by presenting cross-cultural experiences that invite readers to reconsider America's racial landscape and their place in it, much in the same way that Hurston's journalism does. The aesthetic experience of this imagistic essay simultaneously occludes and facilitates shifts of consciousness in ways that more straightforward, didactic journalism might not. Responding to the difficulty of reading Bishop within a leftist, progressive tradition, Betsy Erkkila invites us to reexamine the ways her poetry "problematizes the binarisms" between "formalism/social consciousness" and "private/public" in politically productive ways (285). If we read her essays as a similar form of cultural criticism, Bishop's "Mercedes Hospital" forwards both a critique of economic inequities and racial exclusion and a romanticized portrait of poor and ethnic Others for voyeuristic consumption. In classifying the hospital's residents as inmates, Bishop calls attention to the confining nature of poverty as well as to her identification with imprisonment, a condition echoed in her story "In Prison" and the third section of "Songs for a Colored Singer." In writing about the vulnerable patients of Mercedes Hospital, she insists that locations and lives typically overlooked are worthy of a writer's—and a citizen's—attention. Her essays, however, do little to connect these dignified, struggling people to a larger social critique of race and class exclusions. When Bishop encounters Milton, "a tubercular Negro," at the hospital, Miss Mamie says, "We don't exactly take them, they have a place" (*CPR* 67). While Key West conforms to Jim Crow practices in which everyone "has their place," Milton's presence in this "Casa del Pobre" indicates that poverty carries its own social flexibility, a breakdown of racial protocols that would extend increasingly to middle-class institutions in the next decade. Perhaps in highlighting these sequestered places of the poor, Bishop anticipated and perhaps mourned if not their demise, their inevitable change, folding in a subtle social commentary on fleeting cultural spaces, public and private.

Nearly fifteen years later, Hurston also delineates an ethics of care shaped by America's troubled racial history. Set in a courtroom, one of the most symbolic places of democratic citizenship, Hurston's story, like "Mercedes Hospital," renders a public space where private allegiances surface and demand recognition. Less overt than her journalistic critiques, "The Conscience of the Court," like *Seraph on the Suwanee*, exposes the damage of white supremacy to both white and black Americans. In the short story, Hurston references the human rights discourse central to the founding of the United Nations in 1945 in a seemingly minor legal scuffle that is marked by gender tensions and entrenched racial loyalties of the sort documented in "The 'Pet Negro' System." In this ostensibly humorous tale infused with the superficial patriotism that often characterized the *Saturday Evening Post*'s literary selections, an "unlettered woman," Laura Lee Kimble, prompts a judge to reflect on "something that he had not thought about for quite some time"—that is, the civilizing potential of the law (23). But the tale's irony lurks barely below the surface: Laura Lee's defense of the contested property arises not from a sense of universal justice that the judge conjures in his reference to John Marshall, but from old southern racial practices—specifically, her loyalty to her white employer. Hurston crafts a tongue-in-cheek scenario where the unwritten laws of southern racial conduct clash with the emergent legal discourse of universal human rights. The court's "conscience," in fact, needs to be jogged by the conscientious Laura Lee, described by the judge as a "faithful watch-dog" who will defend her employer's right to an unmolested domestic privacy (122). Ironically, the rights of the individual defended in this case are in actuality a domestic worker's right to protect her employer's property, to insist that the court and Clement Beasley, the man who invaded this domestic space to seize property as compensation for a debt, stay out of private matters.

Within this folksy patriotism, Hurston makes a more radical assertion: Laura Lee, an embodied, headscarf-wearing black citizen, must remind a judge, the symbol of patriarchal, legal authority, of America's—indeed, Western's civilization's—obligation to protect the right of privacy, including its interracial intimacies.[37] Hurston's ironic and even retrograde portrait of a black domestic as the defender of human rights complicates our understanding of the much-discussed universalism of the era.[38] While critics have identified Hurston's choice of a white protagonist in *Seraph* as a universalizing gesture, the invocation of a particularly American version of racial paternalism, embodied in Laura Lee's dogged loyalty to her white employer, is another less recognized desegregationist strategy utilized by Hurston and Bishop for exploring both social freedom and the troubling realities of interracial bonds.

Tracing a postwar anxiety about the erosion of privacy, critic Deborah Nelson notes that many Americans felt that "privacy was dying because it was vulnerable to penetration from without and exposure from within" (11). In this description of external forces trespassing on the private sphere, we might imagine systemic violations by the state or corporate institutions, but as Bishop's poetic voyeurism into Mercedes Hospital and Hurston's ironic tale of domestic trespass illustrate, these intrusions were also aesthetic, affective, and individual and perhaps further reinforced existing racial divisions. Bishop's encroachments at the brothel and the Georgia turpentine camp reveal the way that racism often operates as a denial of privacy for the poor and dispossessed, people who are not allowed to exercise their right to privacy. For Americans outside of privileged whiteness, such rights have always been precarious. Bishop's intrusive gaze and Hurston's indignities when living on a yacht in segregated facilities illustrate how segregation equally structured the domestic sphere and unsettled the boundaries of private and public. Changes in the ways white and black Americans moved within these contested places were central to the narratives both Bishop and Hurston were interested in writing; in these poems and stories, they record both the external assaults on and internal unraveling of privacy.

Writing in 1950 of the "deadly trap of cultural segregation" into which critics and publishers force black writers, Hugh Gloster notes the ways that these conservative pressures work to "stabilize cultural separation" (369) rather than erode it. Placing the cross-race writing of Bishop and Hurston in critical conversation reveals the ways that both black and white writers were questioning the borders of a writer's "proper milieu" to destabilize segregation (369). Complicating the domestic ideologies that dominated popular culture in the decade after World War II, Bishop and Hurston highlight the social places where private desires and public identities overlap; they reconsider domesticity to explore new social possibilities for women claiming their autonomy within a culture attempting to shift away from racial rigidities. Reimagining the experiences of women across race—how they labored, how they loved—was an essential but often overlooked cultural intervention within their ambivalent desegregationist projects. Not only is reading Hurston and Bishop in tandem a departure from segregationist tendencies in criticism of postwar American literature and Cold War cultural studies; their shared interest in the affective bonds within interracial domestic relationships and their articulations of and challenges to white supremacist practices offer an understudied history of desegregation in American literature.

Understanding desegregation as a tenuous and private as much as public process, Hurston's *Seraph on the Suwanee* and Bishop's "Cootchie," "Songs for a Colored Singer," and "Faustina, or Rock Roses" reveal the layers of ambivalence within this cultural moment: the ambivalent desire—identification and animosity—between black women and white women in situations of domestic servitude; the ambiguous position of women, black and white, within the reconfigured family and emergent restructured public sphere; and finally the ambivalent politics of both writers, who, in challenging Jim Crow, remain suspicious of more progressive visions of integration. Perhaps the pairing of Hurston and Bishop is most useful in reminding us of these ambivalent politics, the palpable reluctance to these changes. The aesthetic failings and essentialist racial tropes within these literary works remind us that desegregation was a meandering process more than an arrived reality in the late 1940s.

Reading Bishop's cross-race identifications alongside Hurston's literary experiments with white subjectivity punctures the conceptual boundaries between racial identity and sexual identity and between black and white art. In a literary moment in which writers were exploring with greater candor the psychologies of racial and sexual difference, Bishop and Hurston examined the racial dimensions of the domestic sphere, particularly the labor of African American women in white homes, as an overlooked site of changing racial practices. Florida, perhaps unexpectedly, is a site where both women could locate desegregation not in broad public terms but in the intimate spaces of houseboats, hotels, bedrooms, and troubled minds. In his discussion of its many purposes, Ralph Ellison states that folklore "describes those boundaries of feeling, thought and action which that particular group has found to be the limitation of the human condition" ("Art" 213). These writings about cross-race encounters and fractured social identities are tales of cultural instruction, but they are also modern folktales, indebted to psychoanalysis and reflecting society's changing beliefs about race, gender, and sexuality, particularly the limits of cross-race identifications.

Writing in what Shelly Eversley usefully describes as a postwar "transitional moment when deracialized public space and 'universal' literature seems in reach" (446), Zora Neale Hurston and Elizabeth Bishop offer troubling representations of interracial relations and ambivalent racial politics, desegregationist themes that are pursued differently in the poetry of Gwendolyn Brooks and Edwin Denby. The cultural alienation and tentative interracial allegiances of the emergent Cold War are explored further in the following chapter, which shifts geographic focus from the South to the North to consider desegregation's imprint on the urban landscapes of Chicago and

New York. In ways similar to Hurston and Bishop, Brooks and Denby are interested in revising literary forms—in this case, the sonnet and the lyric poem—to reflect the new racial and sexual identities found in postwar cities. Continuing my inquiry into the psychological layers of desegregation and expressions of cross-racial identification, I explore how public urban places—often marked by racial and sexual anxieties—inform private revelations. Brooks's and Denby's poems explore the interplay between the racial and sexual changes of public spaces and a private poetics of "queer feelings."

War City

Gwendolyn Brooks, Edwin Denby, and the Private Poetics
of Public Space

In the American cultural imagination, the northern city often represents the site of progressive social change, the coming together of urban dwellers across races, cultures, and languages in New York, Chicago, or Washington, D.C. The literary projects of Elizabeth Bishop and Zora Neale Hurston, despite textual excursions into New York, locate desegregationist desires within the particulars of southern domestic spaces. The northern urban centers were experiencing their own transformations after the war. African American women, often the last hired and paid the lowest wages, entered new professions in record numbers during the nation's wartime economic growth and postwar expansion.[1] Through these employment and social opportunities, black women fashioned new public identities within an increasingly interracial landscape. World War II also brought homosexual men and women (to use the era's nomenclature without resorting to the pathologized *invert*) into public awareness in unprecedented ways.[2] The military's discriminatory screening of soldiers' sexual practices offered a named identity as well as a pathology to refute and a tentative community to politically organize. The Mattachine Society, for example, was founded in 1950 as a response to the widespread discrimination against gay and lesbians, particularly in the federal government (David K. Johnson 179–207, 211). The urban landscape bore evidence of these cultural shifts: Black women changed the social climate of factories, department stores, and city streets beyond racially insular neighborhoods. Gay men and to a lesser degree lesbian women of various races claimed luncheonettes, bars, and parks as their own. Urban desegregation, however, is rarely thought about in these expansive ways—that is, as a social reconfiguration of both racial and sexual boundaries.

Describing the postwar transformation of urban centers, historian George Lipsitz notes, "In the crucible of war mobilization and postwar reconversion, changing roles and expectations relating to ethnicity, race, age, and gender turned common and ordinary places like city buses, municipal parks, and housing projects into contested spaces where competing individuals and groups hammered out new ways of living" (*Rainbow* 20). The poems of Gwendolyn Brooks and Edwin Denby were themselves public spaces, evoking the experiences of urban dwellers—most pointedly, for these writers, African American women and white gay men, respectively—who were reshaping cities in the late 1940s and reconciling tensions between private feelings and public identities. Through their poetic depictions of contested spaces, Denby and Brooks consider a range of affective responses to and varied motivations for moving within these socially fraught urban places, exhibiting a range of public and private emotions that extend beyond the competition and hostility rightly pointed out by Lipsitz. Reflecting on the imprint of World War II on American cities, Brooks and Denby desegregate public space in their poems by asserting the interior geography of historically maligned citizens, imagining the social encounters of African American women and gay men in the postwar city, some strained and some affirming. In mapping new understandings of public space and private desire, Brooks and Denby also beautifully conveyed the feelings of dislocation, the questions raised by the alienation from home and community that accompanied these social changes. "Can these wide spaces suit a particular man?," wonders Denby in his 1948 poem, "Summer."[3] In the 1945 poem "One Wants a Teller in a Time Like This," Brooks admits, "One wonders if one has a home."[4] Exploring the spatial and spiritual losses in these poems enables us to better understand the affective landscape of the postwar city for African American women and gay men, who were refashioning themselves in response to major social and indiscernible internal changes.

My reading of Brooks's racial-spatial poetics centers mainly on poems from her second book, *Annie Allen* (1949), particularly writings focused on social encounters and domestic discord in an increasingly desegregated urban landscape. Written the previous year, Denby's debut collection, *In Public, in Private*, revels in a New York City alive with desire, but his poetics fluctuate between coy references to and explicit namings of a visible urban homosexual culture. To better situate the racial and sexual concerns informing their poetry, I also consider some of Denby's dance criticism and scenes from Brooks's 1953 novella, *Maud Martha*. Brooks and Denby have pointedly different perspectives, but both authors illustrate that the desegregation of urban places was both racial and sexual, making possible and publicly visible new forms of desire, both individual and communal. Through this pairing, we also discover a postwar poetics that attempts to reconcile the tension, typical of this cultural moment, between expressions of universalism and the personal idiosyncrasies of race and sexuality. Avoiding representations of "the

Negro" or "the homosexual" as coherent or wholly legible identities, both Denby and Brooks devise neomodernist aesthetics that evoke the private desires of city dwellers and transpose them onto public urban spaces. Interested in the way that this revised formalism operates as "identity-fracturing discourses," to use Eve Kosofsky Sedgwick's phrase ("Queer" 8), I also discuss how their respective poetics simultaneously articulate and occlude the ambivalent, at times shameful, but certainly queer feelings of urban American life of the late 1940s. Together, these poets help us rethink "queer identity," shattering a singular definition by locating its multiplicity in desegregated places, transforming urban communities and murky poetic interiors. This composite portrait of urban life in America in the middle of the twentieth century reminds us of the importance of sexualities and racial desires, both private and public, to the historical-artistic narratives of American desegregation.

Throughout my examination of Denby's and Brooks's poetry in a desegregationist context, I consider some of the "specific subcultural contexts" in which their poetry is "produced, received, and defined" (Schweik 24). In sketching out the invigorating, far-reaching, often interracial artistic circles in which Brooks and Denby worked, I place this chapter's analysis of their shared interest in racial-sexual interiorities in a larger arena of interracial art production, homosexual visibility, and integrationist politics. In situating the poetry of Denby alongside Brooks's writing, I want to relocate him, at least temporarily, outside of the New York School and position Brooks momentarily outside of the African American social protest tradition—that is, to understand the two poets as neglected contemporaries through my own desegregationist gesture that takes perverse delight in their illogical juxtaposition. The pairing of Brooks and Denby complicates the standard picture of mid-twentieth-century American poetry, revealing innovative approaches to war poetry as well as to poetic representations of race and sexuality, overlaps that have been obscured by segregationist criticism.

Both Brooks and Denby might be understood as transitional figures, part of an older generation of artists taken with and taken up by the artistic movements of younger poets. Inspired by the candid racial poetics of the Black Arts movement in the 1960s, Brooks began to modify her ornate style and left Harper and Row in the late 1960s for the black-owned Broadside Press. For many years, Brooks was envisioned as a solitary phenomenon, tentatively linked, despite few similarities, to poets Melvin Tolson, Robert Hayden, and Margaret Walker, transitional figures who serve as a bridge between the Harlem Renaissance and the Black Arts movement; alternatively, Brooks was placed within a trajectory of black women writers but envisioned quite alone as a modernist innovator who documented the Cold War sentiments of black women.[5] Denby suffers from the opposite phenomenon, habitually placed within the New York School milieu. Known primarily today as a dance critic, if at all, Denby is a "poet's poet," known and celebrated by New York School writers such as James Schuyler and John Ashbery and influential to a second wave of writers including Ron Padgett, Alice Notley, and Ted Berrigan. In addition, Denby's placement at the intersections of dance, poetry, and visual art offered a model of artistic and urban engagement for these younger New York School writers. Although Denby's *In Public, in Private* has been described as the "first book of poems published by a New York School poet" (Diggory 240), little attention has been paid to his poetic particularity and associations with other New York artistic circles, including the New York City Ballet and Andy Warhol's Factory.[6]

The Queer Spaces of Desegregation

The urban landscapes that Denby and Brooks depict continually depart from conventional iconography of the city in their attempts to evoke the emotional undercurrents—whether erotic longing or racial hostility—as well as the fragmented ways of knowing and transient identities that define queer aesthetics. The homosexual, Harold Beaver has argued, is a "prodigious consumer of signs—of hidden meanings, hidden systems, hidden potentiality. Exclusion from the common code, impels the frenzied quest; in the momentary glimpse, the scrambled figure, the sporadic gesture, the chance encounter, the reverse slippage, the lowered guard. In a flash meaning may be disclosed; mysteries wretched out and betrayed" (105). Denby, too, advocated a different kind of seeing, a sort of queer vision. In his beautiful essay, "Dancers, Buildings, and People in the Street," he writes, "I make a distinction between seeing daily life and seeing art. Not that seeing is different. Seeing is the same. But seeing art is seeing an ordered and imaginary world, subjective and concentrated" (201). Though the idea that everyday life is art has become clichéd, Denby's poems model a queer attentiveness, distilling the emotions and meanders of daily living into poetic artifice. Equally, Brooks's *Annie Allen* reminds us that black women were also adept readers of cultural signs, navigating the racially and sexually problematic moments of postwar urban life. In similar ways to gay men, these women were exploring a different set of peripheral images and tentative psychologies. In fact, many reappropriations of public space by gay men, lesbians, and African Americans, including black gay men and women, have occurred at the level of language, retooling political, artistic, and medical discourses almost always girded by heterosexual and racist assumptions.

As a cultural critic and poet, Denby reinvented social spaces—concert halls, late-night cafeterias, the subway—where an intellect and an aesthetic candidly marked by homosexual sensibilities, distinct from sexual practices, could flourish. In many cultural histories of the American postwar city, queer spaces are defined by such venues, but places of transient interracial contact, both welcomed and hostile, might also be read as queer spaces: restaurants, movie theaters, or the streets. Brooks's depictions of segregated places, fleeting integrated moments, and disclosures of black women's interior struggles are also poetic constructions of defamiliarized and thereby "queer" space. Though focused on a later moment of cultural production, Judith Halberstam's definitions of queer space as the "place-making practices within postmodernism in which queer people engage" and as the "new understandings of space enabled by the production of queer counterpublics" (6) are helpful for examining the desegregated places and the desires that animate them found in Brooks's and Denby's poetry. How might we read Brooks within this queer context, considering the ways her poems document the place-making practices of postwar African Americans claiming urban places as well as literary spaces in unprecedented ways? How might Denby's poems be read as a queer counterpublic, both to the dominant representations of postwar urbanity in which desire, particularly homosexual desire, is invisible and to the aesthetics of the New York School and Beat poets, in which homosexual identity is more explicitly named? Both writers engaged in projects centered on the desegregation of public space, making room for shunted citizens and for an affective realm that included not only pleasure and belonging but also longing and shame.

Though she was born in Topeka, Kansas, in 1917, Gwendolyn Brooks's artistic identity has become inseparable from Chicago. Writing of her love of the city in her autobiography *Report from Part One*, the poet declares, "The city is the place to observe man *en masse* and in his infinite variety" (135). Much of her writing—from her first collection, *A Street in Bronzeville* (1945), to her urban epic, *In the Mecca* (1968)—is set in and was informed by the South Side neighborhoods in which she grew up and lived as a young wife and mother. Her son was born in 1940, before the publication of her first book of poems. After the success of her first collection, Brooks received Guggenheim Fellowships in 1946 and 1947 to support work on *Annie Allen*, her second book of poems, which won the Pulitzer in 1950. The following year, Brooks and her husband, Henry Blakely, welcomed a daughter into the world. This simultaneous burgeoning of career and domestic life became one of the complexities Brooks explored in her writing; her novella, *Maud Martha*, in particular, narrates the pleasures and indignities of marriage and motherhood as well the navigation of a larger racially stratified society that shapes them.

In their respective studies of political activism and artistic production in Chicago, Robert Bone ("Richard Wright"), Bill V. Mullen, and James Smethurst situate Brooks within a socially conscious community of black writers and visual artists working in the city in the late 1930s and 1940s. While left-leaning African American artistic circles were central to her development, Brooks's early career was also shaped by the interracial networks in which she wrote: She was mentored by white socialite Inez Cunningham Stark and published alongside such white liberals as Jack Conroy and Earl Conrad.[7] A regular attendee at parties hosted by Conroy at his home on Green Street, Brooks was part of an interracial guest list that included journalist Studs Terkel, editor Fern Gayden, and African American writers Margaret Burroughs and Willard Motley (Wixson 462). Blakely, also a writer in the workshops at South Side Community Art Center led by Stark, was a "lifelong integrationist" and did not embrace the nationalist stance adopted by his wife in her later career (Melhem 9). In his memoir, *Livin' the Blues*, poet Frank Marshall Davis recalls meeting Brooks and her husband in the summer of 1948: "We met often, usually socially and informally, at their second-floor apartment above a store on 63rd Street" (303). Davis, an important activist-artist in Chicago's leftist circles, was likewise living an integrated life; two years earlier, he had married a white activist involved in the American Youth for Democracy whom he met in his jazz history class at the Abraham Lincoln School, which offered courses for Chicago workers.

A critical influence on Brooks's politics and intercultural aesthetics were the integrated writing workshops led by Inez Cunningham Stark, a reader for *Poetry* magazine. Writers in Stark's 1941 poetry class included Brooks and her husband, Margaret Burroughs, Margaret Danner, William Couch, and Conroy, one of several white writers who also participated in events at the South Side center. Mullen's *Popular Fronts* details the fascinating interracial history of the institution, which was linked to a network of Works Progress Administration art centers. It was founded by Peter Pollack, who exhibited black artists at his North Side gallery, and was dedicated by Eleanor Roosevelt on May 7, 1941. Its board, the South Side Community Art Center Association, was composed of an eclectic, interracial group that included judges, labor leaders, and socialites. For many African American visual artists and writers, the center was a place to assert self-consciously racial rather than universal art. Of the shared communal sense between artists and the larger South Side community, Burroughs wrote, "We believed that purpose of art was to record the times. As young black artists, we looked around and recorded in our various media what we saw. It was not from our imagination that we painted slums and ghettos, or sad, hollow-eyed black men, women and children. They were the people around us" (Mullen 86). In his profile of the center's opening, Alain Locke praised the visual art produced there: "Without being out of step with contemporary modernism, it is both nationally characteristic and racially distinctive, a happy and fortunately compatible combination" ("Chicago's" 372).[8] This aesthetic negotiation of the country's broader social changes and the particularities of racial experience is equally evident in Brooks's poetry.

Brooks's merging of African American imagery and language with modernist compression and syntactical play—an integration of voices and influences—would become a dominant feature of her poetics.[9] Already influenced by the romantic poets and the black vernacular poetry of Langston Hughes and James Weldon Johnson, whom Brooks credits with introducing her to the modernist poetics of Eliot, Pound, and Frost, Brooks followed Stark's encouragement and became a voracious reader of modern poetry (Kent, "Aesthetic Values"; Melhem). In an unpublished essay, "Has It Been Hard Miss Brooks?," the poet answers with an acknowledgment of her white mentors on the page and in the classroom: "From many white writers I have had impartial respect, and sympathy in its highest sense. I treasure the early interest of the late Inez Stark Boulton, for example, who in 1941 started a unique poetry writing class here in Chicago, giving her enthusiastic students a better understanding of modern poetry. I am much indebted to the 1944 criticism and market suggestions of Iowa University's Paul Engle."[10] In her autobiography, *Report from Part Two*, Brooks recalls the "white white white" authors, including Emerson, Locke, and Donne, on her childhood bookcases as well as the role of Paul Laurence Dunbar, *The Crisis*, and Booker T. Washington in shaping her racial and poetic education. In interviews, Brooks identified the time between her "chiefly white" high school years and 1957 as her "integration stage" (Madhubuti 74). In a 1971 interview in *Essence* magazine, Brooks pessimistically assessed those early years, remembering the interracial parties at their apartment: "I believed in integration," Brooks admitted, "I thought it was the way to live. I wrote, these people wrote, we saw each other, we talked about writing. But it was white writing, the different trends among whites" (Lewis 62). The invisibility and silences surrounding her racial aesthetics and experiences as an African American writer reveal the social limitations of the era's integrated social circles and would become a crucial feature of *An-*

nie Allen, a collection in which sublimated desires and gendered silences are central.

Brooks published her early work in this interracial context. Alongside Owen Dodson's integrationist poem "Open Letter," the first two poems in her series "Gay Chaps at the Bar" appeared in the March–April 1945 issue of *Negro Story* (published between 1944 and 1946). These poems, resonant for wartime readers, had already been published the preceding autumn in *Poetry*. Both journals were committed to desegregated literary culture and introduced Brooks to a diverse range of readers through her poems about African Americans' wartime experiences, which fused modernist experimentation with social protest. Fern Gayden and Alice C. Browning, editors of the short-lived *Negro Story*, welcomed Brooks's early merging of aesthetic traditions. Her "Chicago Portraits," an uncollected prose mosaic that complements Brooks's famous Bronzeville poems, was published in the literary magazine's inaugural issue. *Negro Story* accepted submissions from emerging and established writers, both white and black. According to the editorial statement in the July–August 1944 issue, its mission was "to publish creative writing which would reflect the struggle of the Negro for full integration into American life as well as the many aspects and aspirations of his life. This is indeed a challenge to the Negro writer and the interested white writer" (Browning and Gayden 1). The editors recognized that desegregation and the changing face of race relations were compelling subjects for both black and white artists who were diagnosing the social shifts of postwar America.

Much of the fiction by white writers in *Negro Story* addressed integration as an aspiration, but interracial encounters were typically sites of conflict rather than collaboration. Helen Herbert, a white writer praised for her "good insight into Negro life," contributed "Masterpiece: A Story about a Colored Girl and a White Man." Conrad, a white novelist, civil rights activist, and teacher of African American history, included his poetic tribute to Paul Robeson, "I Heard a Black Man Sing." Conrad's assessment of *Negro Story* illuminates the relationships among interracial experiences, desegregationist politics, and increasing candor about sexuality. Linking the magazine to what he calls "blues writing," he praises *Negro Story*'s direct look at "issues of segregation and protest, the complexities of Negro-white labor relationships, intermarriages, and all matters of color, 'race,' caste, class, and sex" (Mullen 124). Conrad's extension of a blues protest aesthetic to include interracial culture, convoluted by its sexual dimensions, not only describes the work of Elizabeth Bishop and Zora Neale Hurston but also instructs us on the social redefinitions and sexual confessions found in the poetry of Brooks and Denby. While these poets redirect language in ways that do not conform to Conrad's idea of "blues writing" (and to the narrow aesthetic spectrum used to define "radical" or "proletarian" literature, which overlooks writers with less overt leftist politics or an aesthetic in which social critique is not central), they do mine the connection between desegregation and sex that he mentions.

For the writers in *Negro Story* who explored interracial sexuality, fulfilling romances were often depicted as impossible situations destined for failure. In Herbert's epistolary tale, the flirtations between a white author and an admiring fan end abruptly when Mr. Britton discovers that Mary Lincoln is a black woman and refuses to meet her—a reaction she anticipates. Frank Harvey's "The Bedroom Door" takes on the controversial topic more directly, imagining a narrowly avoided affair between John, a white economics teacher, and Joan, an African American artist, each of whom has a spouse of the same race. Joan appears to give in to John's persistent advances but then refuses at the last minute. The sensationalistic treatment proved effective with readers; the next issue of *Negro Story* mentions the objections of white readers who expressed concern about the story's impact, particularly the "subconscious anger stirred by the fact that a white man might be insisting and a Negro girl resisting" (Browning and Gayden, "Just" 61). While that particular reader saw an updated version of slavery's sexual oppressions, we might equally argue that Harvey's story of marital infidelity and Joan's independence in navigating her desire typify new postwar American perspectives on race and sex. In these desegregationist texts, interracial sexuality is more candidly explored, and black women's desires are more openly expressed, yet the solidity of racial boundaries is also affirmed. Still, integration was a delicate business for postwar writers; the troubled history of American race relations, including its sexual politics, confronted writers and readers even in stories focused on the contemporary moment.

World War II also looms in the journal's submissions, and many of the readers and contributors were soldiers. For example, the first issue included Lieutenant William Couch's poetry alongside Aldon Bland's "Let's Go Visiting," a story of a black couple's failed, humiliating attempt to socialize with a white couple. Bland was serving in the U.S. Navy at the time, and Brooks's "Memorial to Ed Bland," which opens *Annie Allen*, commemorates his death during a mission in Germany in March 1945. Davis Grubb's "Rest Stop" depicts the war's palpable racial tensions in a confrontation between soldiers at a Mississippi rest stop. Esta Diamond, a student of Conrad, reveals the hypocrisy of America's patriotism in "Something for the War." In the story, Lily, a maid for Mrs. Lloyd, plans to donate blood for the war effort with residents from her building, many of them with family in the service. Mrs. Lloyd, irritated that her plans for a bridge and "bandage rolling" party have been spoiled by Lily's polite refusal to work on her day off, is left with a disturbing question, "They wouldn't give Negro blood to our boys, would they?" This tale not only succinctly reveals the power negotiations between economic classes and their divergent approaches to wartime activism but also depicts whites who see integration as a contaminant that pollutes not only blood but also racial borders and social customs. This metaphor of tainted blood, of course, reverberated with early twentieth-century anxieties about interracial marriage and the children of such unions.

The integrationist enthusiasm of *Negro Story*, however, was short-lived; it ceased publication in April 1946. The magazine's "radical biracial politics," according to Mullen, "began to sound hollow" in light of the racism and continued employment discrimination faced by returning black veterans as well as African Americans who lost their stable industrial jobs to white soldiers returning from the war (123). This hypocrisy was succinctly cataloged in Frank Marshall Davis's biting poem "Peace Quiz for America." Davis later recalled that the Pentagon tried to keep the training-camp tensions between black and white soldiers, which often escalated into major clashes, hidden from the American public (*Livin'* 269). The "wave of intimidation, terror, and death" that white southerners unleashed on returning black veterans raised questions about the U.S. role in defending human rights internationally (Borstelmann 55).[11] Biracial politics, radical or liberal, did not, however, simply fade away; rather, integrationist politics, including a growing skepticism over their viability, and interracial subject matter continued to broaden American literature in the late 1940s and early 1950s. And new representations of urban sexual subcultures were a crucial part of this artistic expansion.

Brooks described *Annie Allen* as "a book of extensive experiment" (Hull 96). Representative of Brooks's integrationist politics, the collection shuttles between a desire to assert a common humanity and the particularities of black women's experiences in postwar urban America. Maria K. Mootry describes Brooks's sonnet sequence "Gay Chaps" as a kind of "vocative and visual architecture" (134). Taking this cue, we might recognize how Brooks creates a kind of poetic public space—artifices of street and mind—shaped by war and changed by desegregation. In her poetry and prose writing of the 1940s and early 1950s, Brooks often examines a privacy created in public space—in restaurant booths, an enclosed car in the white suburbs, the imagined solitude of the movie theater seat. In these locations, she details the psychological impact of desegregation. Her poetic attention often returns to sites of what Brooks calls "solace" (*BL* 276)—the kitchenette, the beauty shop, or the veteran's tavern—black-defined spaces that nurture despite the indignities of segregation.

Mullen finds *Annie Allen* "almost destitute of geography" (184) in comparison to her debut collection, *A Street in Bronzeville*. However, in moving away from the urban folk portraits of her first volume, Brooks does not wholly abandon an attention to urban space by concentrating on the interior world of her protagonist, Annie. Her famous kitchenettes still evoke a cramped domestic reality, but they increasingly become psychological spaces of gendered resistance. In the middle of "The Womanhood," the final sequence of *Annie Allen*, Brooks offers mirrored images of desegregated spaces ("I love those little booths at Benvenuti's" and "Beverly Hills, Chicago," poems set in Chicago's urbanscape). One can assume that these are scenarios witnessed and experienced by Annie Allen as an adult navigating public spaces under transformation, interracial encounters that leave her irked. In these two poems, Brooks locates desegregationist desires—curiosities of both white and black Americans—in public urban spaces, encounters that might extend to the erotic but are more often animated by resentment and hostility. These "ugly feelings" also contribute to the unsettled queerness of these desegregated places.

In "I love those little booths at Benvenuti's," Brooks imagines white Chicagoans journeying to a supper house in the African American neighborhood of Bronzeville in hopes of "observing the tropical truths" of "dusky folk" (*BL* 126). The title itself functions as a bit of overheard conversation, a snippet of racial ventriloquism in which, one imagines, a white diner raves about a delightful Italian place in an African American neighborhood. Safely "boothed-in" (126), the cultural tourists leave the restaurant disappointed, "overwhelmed by subtle treason" at the discovery that "the colored people will not 'clown'" (127). This imagined scenario of stunted interracial contact—more voyeurism than meaningful affiliation—illuminates the persistent stereotypes held by many white Americans about black life as well as the increasing erosion of segregated places necessary to maintain these mythologies. Though motivated in their excursion to the black side of town by a desire to have their notions of blackness affirmed, these white visitors to Bronzeville must now reconcile the banal realities of African American life with their racial fantasy; they are forced to rethink not only their racial assumptions but also their understanding of their white identities.

The rudely curious white patrons of Benvenuti's sit in a queer space of desegregationist tension and a racial hypervisibility previously unknown. The poem comically inverts the racial gaze—whites become the Othered

"They." While much of Brooks's writing remains focused on the particularities of black, working-class women, here she documents the intersections of black and white social practices, highlighting African Americans' intimate perspectives on and privileged knowledge of whiteness. Brooks asserts, "We know the conditions of your gums because we have been so long between your teeth" (*Report from Part Two* 127). "I love those little booths at Benvenuti's" invites the reader to dissect the racial fantasies of these cultural tourists as they attempt to consume a blackness imagined as "clamorous," "colorfully incorrect," and "straining in sexual soprano" (*BL* 126). But these racialized desires are flatly refused, and the white patrons leave disappointed, their racial assumptions unconfirmed: "But how shall they tell people they have been / Out Bronzeville way? For all the nickels in / Have not bought savagery or defined a 'folk'" (127). The poet's clever conclusion to the poem—an image of African American diners marked by normalcy and decorum ("Handling their steel and crockery with no clatter, laugh punily, rise, go firmly out the door" [127])—becomes an ironic act of civil disobedience.

Excursions into insular racial communities, of course, were not a new phenomenon. In the 1920s, white New Yorkers famously went "slumming" at Harlem clubs, bars, and rent parties, but cultural commentary on crossing the color line in postwar America typically avoided this sensationalism. Stripping interracial encounters of their exoticism, columns such as Alfred E. Smith's "Adventures in Race Relations" in the *Chicago Defender* showed the absurdity of white and black Americans' racial myths about each other. In "Slumming," Smith chuckles at the shocked cabdriver who delivers a white man, the chair of the interracial American Veterans Committee, to a black neighborhood in Washington, D.C., warning him to be careful. In on the joke, the reader is assured that the work of racial justice continues and that such backward beliefs about race would soon be history (13).

In "Beverly Hills, Chicago," the follow-up poem to "Benvenuti's," Brooks again assesses this changing urban landscape and the unsettling of traditional understandings of racial identity. The title refers to Beverly, a South Side neighborhood (now racially integrated), whose large homes, tree-lined streets, and "golden gardens" were a potent symbol in the 1950s of middle-class domestic contentment (*BL* 128). Brooks again positions whites as scrutinized cultural objects for an African American family on a scenic drive, noting the privileged environment of white suburbia, where "even the leaves fall down in lovelier patterns" (128). George E. Kent argues that the poem imagines blacks as "self-contained and cultivated observers" of whites, whose "patterns of behavior also become art objects" ("Aesthetic Values" 40). Resentment is repeatedly denied in the poem: "Nobody is furious. Nobody hates these people" (*BL* 129). Despite these assurances, their ambivalent observations and disavowals of course contain a social critique. The narrator does not want to deny these white people their lovely homes but concludes, "It is only natural that we should think we have not enough" (129). In the car, a space of racial security and homogony, Annie and her family subtly seethe with anger, evident in their voices becoming "a little gruff" (129). As mirrored images of tenuous interracial spaces marked by ambivalent desegregation, these poems succinctly render the emotional complexity of the era's cross-race encounters: curiosity, envy, aggressive refusal, polite irritation, rationalized hate, and disappointment. But in their focus on encounters within an elastic color line, they also destabilize the notion of racial containment and the insularity of racial communities, white and black, questioning their viability and perhaps, for an integrationist-minded readership, their desirability.

Brooks's interest in the psychological impact of desegregated space continued in her novella, *Maud Martha*, published in 1953. Originally conceived as a teen novel with a working title, *Daughter of the Dusk*, that emphasizes color prejudice as a central narrative theme. The poetic bildungsroman follows Maud from childhood to adolescent romance to marriage and motherhood. One might conceive of the novel, despite its poetic densities, as a more transparent elaboration of the domestic concerns and psychological tensions raised in *Annie Allen*. Throughout Maud confronts the intimate workings of race, including skin color prejudice within the black community, the racist "slip" of a white saleswoman, and mistreatment by an employer and a sales clerk. In many of these scenarios, Maud is the silent observer whose physical presence as a black woman—as girlfriend, as employee, as customer—upsets long-standing racial protocols. These vignettes, alongside Brooks's articulations of Annie Allen's sexual complexities, contribute to a desegregationist project in which African American women attempted to find an expanded freedom and greater self-fulfillment in previously hostile domestic and commercial spaces.

In one chapter "We're the Only Colored People Here," Maud and her husband attend a movie downtown at the World Playhouse. The scene is framed by the pair's painful self-consciousness, fretting over their presence in this nearly all-white space. Maud worries about her husband's discomfort while the white women in the lobby scrutinize Maud's outfit "with which no special fault could be found" (*BL* 218). After the film, they "hoped they would meet no cruel eyes," and, uplifted by the movie, the couple fantasize about an effortless interracial exchange as they leave the theater: "They wanted to laugh, to say warmly to the other outgoers, 'Good, huh? Wasn't it swell?'" But the fantasy quickly dissolves in the chapter's final line: "This, of course, they could not do. But if only no one would look intruded upon" (220). Knowing that such a natural banter between races is impossible, the couple would be satisfied by a lack of open hostility. Brooks meticulously conveys the awkwardness felt in these interracial spaces, the sense that integration is often perceived by whites and wrangled with by blacks as a kind of cultural trespassing. For Maud and her husband, seeing a movie downtown rather than in a neighborhood theater that caters to African Americans also holds cultural significance, a claiming of desegregated space despite emotional discomfort.[12]

In a tribute to the movies in her second memoir, *Report from Part Two*, Brooks dissects the humiliation of and identification with African American actors performing one-dimensional buffoonery in Hollywood movies: "They came onto Our screen, Our wonderful, clean, elegant white-folks screen, Interrupting personal Escape, Interrupting personal white-oriented Dream (which dream, of course, was unreal 'even' for whites)" (16). Maud's desire to claim the movie theater as a space where her blackness recedes in the dark and whiteness can be vicariously experienced is equally unraveled by racial intrusion. Sensitive to the invisible color lines although she is trying to ignore them, Maud is unable fully to enjoy the cinematic escape she desires. Yet in highlighting the encounter's comic absurdity and the couple's largely effortless resilience, Brooks is careful to avoid positioning Maud and Paul as objects of pity. This scene of tentative integration deftly captures the tensions between public space and private desire, personal indulgence and social insult, and the delicate balance between public pride and personal shame—negotiations that characterize much of the poetry discussed in this chapter.

Maud Martha's hunger for the indulgent pleasures of life, unencumbered by racist strictures, is again humorously explored in the chapter "Maud Martha and New York." As a young woman, Maud imagines herself as New York–bound on every passing train, "lean[ing] back in the plush" (*BL* 189). Vicariously living through magazines and the New York papers, the eighteen-year-old "was on Fifth Avenue whenever she wanted to be," taking in the decadent foods and expensive trinkets that she imagines every New Yorker possesses (191). Maud is fascinated by the commercial presentation of these private indulgences and imagines herself as an equal consumer: helped from taxis, sighted in front of theaters, found "before velvet-lined impossible shops" (191). For Maud, the narrator explains, New York "stood for what she thought life ought to be. Jeweled. Polished. Smiling. Poised. Calmly rushing!" (192). These vignettes celebrate the claiming of public space but remain attuned to the difficulties of and resistance to these appropriations. Though void of explicit racial commentary, Brooks's New York fantasy, like "Beverly

Hills, Chicago," engages in a subtle social protest; Maud's fantastical journey into the freedom of urban consumption defiantly though naively transcends the class barriers indelibly built around race and gender. "Upward mobility, and the accumulation of material good as its measure," notes Paula Giddings, was often interpreted as evidence of African Americans' patriotic embrace of mainstream American culture, including a conservative gender ideology that encouraged women's consumerism as a form of self-fulfillment in the public sphere.[13] While Maud appears motivated by a similar materialistic impulse, her fantasy of conspicuous consumption in New York is a fantasy of escape from domestic obligations as well as a subtle commentary on the economic inequities faced by African American women that leave such luxury goods far from reach.[14] In Maud's imagined urban adventure, wealth erases the era's indignities of racial discrimination as well as its strictures of domestic duty.

Annie Allen and *Maud Martha* address the emotional indignities of Jim Crow in the urban North but do not do so through conventional forms of public protest. Within these public places of integration, Brooks still emphasizes interiorities, creating portraits of convoluted emotions found in insular spaces: booths in which the white voyeurs ensconce themselves or the closed-up car as it meanders in white suburbia. The city's investigative potential, with its opportunities to witness new spaces and reimagine one's place in the urban landscape, anchors these poems. Still, Brooks reminds us that the increased mobility of postwar life—including voyeuristic jaunts to the suburbs or excursions into recently integrated movie theaters—did not erode racial division or produce an easy social harmony. Interracial encounters of the postwar city, in fact, often triggered queer feelings of dislocation, though they were left unvoiced.

Just as Gwendolyn Brooks has become inextricably linked to Chicago, New York was central to Edwin Denby's poetic imagination. Born in 1903 in China, where his father was a diplomat, Denby shuttled between China, the United States, and Europe as a child and young adult. He attended Harvard sporadically but never completed his studies, returning to Europe to explore his interests in dance, gymnastics, and psychoanalysis. In the mid-1930s, he moved to New York City's Chelsea with photographer and filmmaker Rudy Burkhardt, whom he met in Switzerland in 1934. Burkhardt's 1936 film, *145 West 21*, was named for the address of the loft that they shared in the 1930s, which remained Denby's home for most of his life. The cast of *145 West 21* included some of the celebrated artists who would come to define white gay culture in the United States at midcentury: Aaron Copland, Virgil Thomson, and Paul Bowles, who composed the film's music. Burkhardt and Denby became collaborators and intimate friends—a model of artistic and emotional intimacy that circumvents restrictive, conventional definitions of both homosexuality and family. Burkhardt's photographs accompanied Denby's poems in his second book, *Mediterranean Cities* (1956), and the poet appeared in many of Burkhardt's short films, including *The Uncle's Return* (1940) and *Crime Makes a Down Payment* (1952). Though Burkhardt later married, Denby and the filmmaker shared a lifelong, oft-noted closeness; they continued to travel together—Italy, Morocco, Greece—and Denby spent most summers in Maine with Burkhardt's family. To many, their intense closeness was assumed to be that of lovers (and in the early years of their friendship, they likely were), but the two kept an intimate, somewhat mysterious, bond despite Burkhardt's marriage and their geographical distance. After Denby's death, Burkhardt explained their partnership: "What was Edwin to me? Not a father. Not an older brother. Not a teacher, though he opened my eyes to many things over the years. Not much of a lover; neither was I. Rather, a friend I could always rely on" (14). His assessment that Denby was "not much of a lover" appears compatible with Denby's handling of his sexuality, which remained a deemphasized part of his public identity but an explicit and coded part of his poetics.

Historians including Charles Kaiser, Alan Bérubé, George Chauncey, and Nan Boyd have documented the increasingly recognizable gay and lesbian urban cultures emerging throughout the United States during the twentieth century. Discussing the impact of Alfred Kinsey's research on male sexuality and the transient, same-sex socializing during the war on gay visibility, historian K. A. Cuordileone notes that despite Cold War sexual policing, "the rise of gay and lesbian urban enclaves and communities in the postwar years suggests the extent to which the war, and the accelerated social and economic changes it provoked, helped to establish a larger or at least more noticeable gay subculture in America" (*Manhood* 71). Certain hotel bars, luncheonettes, city parks, and avenues served as meeting places for men, particularly those interested in having sex with other men. The importance of the city as a homosocial space is evident in the queer style of Denby's poems. Alice Notley, a fellow poet and longtime admirer of Denby's poetry, observes, "The one thing, as I have said before, that everyone seems to leave out of discussion of the New York poets is the fact of New York. Edwin just loved that city, and the city is what most of his poetry is about" (email). In fact, Denby's most significant erotic relationship may well have been with the city. He wrote, as did Brooks, within a tepidly integrated art scene, but he was also influenced by the city's increasingly visible homosexual subcultures.

Fellow writers including Frank O'Hara and Ron Padgett have commented on the primacy of urban space in Denby's poetic imagination, but they have failed to consider its connection to gay men's shifting relationships to New York City's public space. Bars such as the Oak Room at the Plaza Hotel, the Savoy Plaza, and the Astor were crucial spaces where middle-class men could meet one another, provided they adhered to the demanded discretion of these establishments. Most of these bars, however, did not cater to an exclusively gay clientele; the famous San Remo, in Greenwich Village, for example, attracted a racially and sexually diverse group of artists, including James Baldwin and O'Hara. Brad Gooch notes that many writers—among them Tennessee Williams, Allen Ginsberg, James Agee, and William Burroughs—patronized this "mixed, talky bar" over the years (201). According to Gooch, "Denby and O'Hara spent many hours at Carnegie Tavern, the bar across the street from City Center, discussing the ballets they had just seen" (220). Denby also frequented Martens Bar, a "traditional New York Irish workingman's bar" in Chelsea, according to Rudy Burkhardt's son, Jacob, a filmmaker who used Denby's poetry to begin his film, *Martens Bar*. Leery of the "sweater bars" on the east side of Midtown, which were filled with the zealous fans of Broadway musicals, O'Hara reportedly preferred to visit the gay bars of Eighth Street—particularly Mary's and Old Colony— before cruising the night streets for sexual adventure. "His taste for men whom he thought were straight, especially straight black men," notes Gooch, "often led him outside the perimeters of the established gay bars" (195). Such practices reveal the pervasive gender and racial segregation of 1950s urban nightlife and remind us of the interracial sexual relationships that remain outside of many histories of gay urban culture.

The title of Denby's debut work, *In Public, in Private*, names the poet's central obsession with the social and spatial contradictions of the American city. In his study of pre-Stonewall public sex, Ross Higgins discusses a "growing awareness among gay men in urban North America after 1945 that they belonged to a large social group which shared a common language, symbolic systems, interests, and values distinct from those of the surrounding society" (191). Though it is debatable whether Denby would have agreed with this idea of a distinctive homosexual culture, the substantial contributions of gay writers to the New York School's aesthetic insured that much of the art not only celebrated urban consciousness and speech but was infused with queer language and erotic expression. A 1948 article in the *Pittsburgh Courier*, in fact, speculated that the urban environment itself might foster homosexuality: "It is thought that there is something distinctly neurotic in the lives of city males which turns them to perversion. It is possible that urban civilization always accents the effete and unmasculine attitude" (Gorham 15). For his part, Denby's status as a critic and poet made him a kind of historian of city life in its public forms: He described regular citizens (many of them, though covertly identified as such, homosexual) and their urban rituals in parks, luncheonettes, bars and performance halls and even on jaunts in the city's streets.

Like many of New York residents, Denby frequented and wrote about the city's all-night cafeterias and lunch counters, spaces particularly important for gay life in the mid-twentieth century. Writing of his time living with Denby in the late 1930s, Rudy Burkhardt recalls, "We stayed up most of the night, sat in Stewart's Cafeteria taking with Bill [de Kooning] and his friends, watched the dawn on Madison Square" (12). Elaine de Kooning remembers, "None of us lived a domestic life. We worked in our lofts and went to cafeterias and the Automat to eat. We would meet in the street or at meals and have conversations that would stretch on for hours" (29). According to George Chauncey, in the wake of the police harassment that accompanied the 1939 World's Fair, cafeterias and the counters at drugstores "continued to serve as gay haunts" because they were not subject to liquor regulations. These venues provided gay men with "places where they could gather with gay friends, gossip, ridicule the dominant culture that ridiculed them, and construct an alternative identity" (*Gay* 163). In the poem "Lunchroom," Denby pays tribute to the "strange tables" of these homosocial spaces:

> buoyed upbuoyed with pieces of familiar shoulders
> fragments bear bear up fondly pillows warmly bear
> and smoke and grey soft fleshly and carrying
> and friendly muscles buoy near ignorantly
> like breathing like bleeding feathers
> in pores at strange tables (*DCP* 46)

The light-hearted near pun of "buoyed" exposes a queer sensibility, as do the surprising line turns, repetitive utterances, and sexual innuendos. Barely about a lunchroom, the poem captures the elastic mind of a diner distracted by the "friendly muscles" of the fellows around him.

Such appropriations of urban places by gay men and lesbian women, Chauncey argues, can be understood as "part of a more general challenge to dominant cultural conceptions of those boundaries [between public and private space] and of the social practices appropriate to each sphere" (*Gay* 204). These spatial intrusions, however, are rarely theorized as a form of desegregation despite the fact that in the decade after World War II, many African American and gay and lesbian writers were engaged in compatible projects to broaden the definitional boundaries of domestic and public places as well as the sexual geographies within them. This is pointedly illustrated in "Standing on the Streetcorner," where Denby details the expansive streets and bustling walkers, native and tourist, and the sky itself; the poem ends with a contorted couplet: "Time in every sky I look at next to people / Is more private than thought is, or upstairs sleeping" (*DCP* 6). These inversions of public and private, of body and mind, of linguistic sense, articulate the queer spaces of desegregation.

For Denby, like Brooks, physical and by extension social movement in the city sparks psychological insights, generates intimacy. Padgett writes that Denby "was throughout his life mobile and fascinated by mobility, the mobility of travel, of dancers, of his cats, of strolling through the streets, and of thought" (xv). This love of transience is succinctly captured in such poems as "The Subway," "People on Sunday," and, of course, "Elegy—The Streets." In "The Subway," Denby infuses sexual innuendo into a seemingly conventional portrait of city life. Alive with action—"dive," "roar," "rocked" (*DCP* 5)—the poem re-creates the bustle of the city commute but is equally attuned to the movements of erotic energy between riders. Written in the second person, the poem drops the reader into the "peculiar space" of the subway car: "You dive from the street, holing like a rabbit" (5). Mimicking this penetration into the bowels of the city, the act of "holing" mischievously suggests homoerotic movement into the most tabooed holes of the body. (These orifices are echoed in Brooks's equally erotically suggestive poem, "flags," with its query, "I pull you down my foxhole. Do you mind?" [*BL* 74]) The perverse strands of Denby's poem are confirmed by the passenger's attention to "a square of bare throat" and to "the fold at the crotch of a clothed human being" (*DCP* 5). This corporeal fragment incites animalistic desire; the poem's speaker mischievously predicts, "You'll want to nuzzle it, crop at it like a goat" (5). Despite an increasing anxiety in the late 1940s over sexual perversion as a national security risk, Denby boldly conveys the perverse pleasure of urban travel, including the naughty delight of cruising bodies on public transportation. In this image of transience lies an even more subversive message that sexually desirous bodies, like the queer imagination, cannot be contained.

Kenneth E. Silver's credible argument in "Modes of Disclosure: The Construction of Gay Identity and the Rise of Pop Art," that an abstract expressionist aesthetic evokes rather than explicitly names can be productively extended to Denby's handling of sexuality and his development of a queer language. His poem "Summer," for example, captures an urban landscape of private desires. Its speaker "stroll[s] on Madison in expensive clothes," taking in the sights of New York City—the "ostrich-legg'd" shop clerks, a storm brewing over the skyline, men asleep in the park (*DCP* 9). While such images might suggest a rather conventional ode to the city, this dandy's jaunt is alive with eroticism. The "loping clerks" who cast a "glance nude as oh in a tiled shower" (9) mimic the homoerotic flirtations of a locker room, but these knowing glances have migrated to the city sidewalk. The "bulging pea-soup storm" in midtown foreshadows the bulges of the "grass sleepers" in Central Park, including a "soldier, face handkerchiefed, an erection / In his pants" (9). Denby's flaneur is alert to the libidinal energies of the city, particularly the more public expressions of male sexuality that were also transforming the social practices of the postwar city.

The worlds of ballet, theater, music, and visual art, which Denby knew intimately, also provided opportunities for gay men to share their artistic passions and their now less-than-covert sexual interests. "Opera and dance performances," notes Chauncey "drew large numbers of gay men" and offered spaces beyond bars and cafeterias for same-sex flirtations (*Gay* 351). As a former dancer, respected critic, and lifelong art patron, Denby socialized with "gay" men who were renowned artists in the New York City arts world: Lincoln Kirstein, cofounder of the New York City Ballet; composers Thomson and Copland; choreographer Jerome Robbins; and fellow writers, O'Hara and John Ashbery.[15] Today Denby is probably best known not as a poet of the New York School but as a celebrated dance critic. He established himself at the *New York Herald Tribune* from 1942 to 1945, when he wrote as guest critic for Walter Terry, who was serving in the military. Thomson, who worked as a music critic at the *Tribune*, had recommended Denby for the position. Kirstein praised Denby's rigorous dance criticism as "highly technical reporting which heretofore had only been enjoyed by music, boxing and baseball enthusiasts" ("Comment" 27). Though married to the sister of painter Paul Cadmus, Kirstein was quite candid about the gay relationships he maintained throughout his life and was a prominent fixture in New York gay society. Cadmus, also part of this extensive artistic circle, painted a ballet series—*Arabesque* (1941), *Reflection* (1944), and *Dancer* (1945)—based on his visits to the School of American Ballet. Commissioned by Kirstein, gay photographer George Platt Lynes also produced a series on the dancers of the New York City Ballet. Infused with this queer sensibility, American ballet was a site of creative inspiration, and Denby was there to document it.

This queer sensibility, however, was for the most part a white one. As remains true today, the ballet world of the 1950s was on the whole closed to black dancers. After studying with Lester Horton in Los Angeles, African American choreographer Alvin Ailey came to New York City in 1954 to study with Karel Shook, who had one of the few studios that admitted

African American ballet dancers. Shook, a white dancer formally with the City Ballet, later founded the Dance Theatre of Harlem with Arthur Mitchell, who in 1955 became the first African American male dancer with the New York City Ballet. Denby enthusiastically noted Mitchell's performances in his dance columns.[16] In a classic review of "Three Sides of *Agon*," Denby wrote that Mitchell's pas de deux with Diane Adams "startles by a grandeur of scale and of sensuousness." But he made little fuss about the interracial pairing, admiring that it was "neither stressed nor hidden" but merely "adds to the interest" (123). Such color-blind praise reflects Denby's approach in much of his cultural criticism and more broadly the era's embrace of integrationist art.

Denby's columns concentrated on ballet, but his coverage of modern dance included several reviews of Katherine Dunham and Pearl Primus, prominent African American dancers during the 1940s.[17] His predecessor, Walter Terry, also sent home a dispatch, "Dance Critic at War," for the 19 March 1944 issue of the *Herald Tribune*, in which he describes the excitement over Josephine Baker's "series of sold-out performances for the benefit of the Fighting French" in Cairo the previous fall (Terry and Denby 8). Terry also commented on the performance's interracial dimensions: "Baker's partner Frederick Rey danced exceptionally well in good, slick night-club style, his blondness used as a sort of human spotlight to illuminate the dusky Baker in their duets" (8). Gwendolyn Brooks also uses *dusky* to describe whites' perceptions of the African American diners in "I love those little booths at Benvenuti's" (*BL* 126). Familiar with white people's racial tropes, she transforms racial exoticism, implicit in Terry's review, into a satirical social commentary. As a critic, Denby was much less likely to comment directly on a dancer's race. His approach to racial identity conformed at times to the limited vocabularies of the era, but he also searched for new language to describe the interiors of human experience.

"The question of the interrelation of dance and poetry in Edwin's work (and life)," Padgett notes, "is a huge and interesting one about which an entire book could be written" (Simon Smith and Padgett). Illuminating his poetics, Denby's art criticism also offers insight into racial attitudes that are too subtle to discern in his poetry. For example, he offers high praise for Dunham's choreography and her introduction of Brazilian and Cuban dance vocabularies to American audiences; he describes the "African Negro dancing" at a 1943 festival as a "completely civilized affair" and defines non-Western cultures as "primitive communities" ("Miss Dunham" 362).[18] Primus, one of Denby's favorite performers, was associated, like Billie Holiday, with the interracial milieu of the Café Society. Applauding Primus for her attainment of a "fine

Negro grandeur," Denby calls her "native Negro quality—an unction and a spring" (*Looking* 366, 341, 378). These reviews reflect typical cultural biases of the times, an era where black dancers were more often praised for "verve" and "vitality" than technical skill or choreographic innovation. But Denby's tastes were admirably democratic. He did not treat ballet as an exalted form, and he paid attention to various modern, African, and Asian dance traditions as well as emergent musicians and visual artists and recognized African Americans' important contributions to American dance.

In his 1943 "Miss Dunham in Review," Denby questions the dancer's success in her tropical dance revue at synthesizing African dance elements with the conventions of American choreography—what the critic characterizes as the tension between a Western emphasis on "varied gesture[s]" and an African use of "plain reiteration" (368). Denby admits, "To reconcile two such different expressive methods is a big problem. It is a problem that faces all those racially conscious artists who insist on reconstructing a style whose creative impulse is foreign to their daily life" (368). At a time when artists across multiple racial categories and communities were increasingly merging cultural forms and traditions—artistic experiments that also functioned as a form of desegregation—Denby, whose reviews relied on limited racial vocabularies, did not ignore the potential failings of such work when reconciliation was not achieved.

For artists such as Dunham, artistic desegregation joined seemingly incongruent influences, a fusion of forms necessary for representing new, amalgamated American identities. Through these cross-cultural experiments, New York School poets and visual artists often intersected with African American musicians, dancers, and writers, an interracial history rarely recognized. Revered composer and jazz musician Billy Strayhorn, a longtime collaborator with Duke Ellington and author of the melancholic song "Lush Life," created a musical adaptation of García Lorca's romantic allegory, *The Love of Don Perlimplín for Belisa in Their Garden*, at the Artists' Theatre in 1953. Alfred Leslie, an abstract expressionist, designed the sets for Strayhorn's production, which included an all-black cast.[19] The Artists' Theatre, started by Herbert Machiz, boyfriend of art dealer John Bernard Myers, was a central venue for New York School artists, including Ashbery, James Schuyler, Elaine de Kooning, and Grace Hartigan. O'Hara's play, *Try! Try!*, a spoof on postwar melodramas adapted from a Japanese Noh play, was produced in the same inaugural season as Strayhorn's adaptation of García Lorca, which the composer intended to be a "black-gay statement" (Hajdu 126). Interested in transnational projects, both O'Hara and Strayhorn translated revered literary texts into modern narratives that reflected a post–World War II sensibility about race and sex.

Translation was emblematic of many interracial exchanges of the 1950s. In his early career, Ailey choreographed *Morning Mourning*, based on the writings of Tennessee Williams. Like Strayhorn, the young dancer found emotional and perhaps sexual resonances in the work of García Lorca, and would later create dances based on his tales. Lincoln Kirstein, seemingly interested in establishing a gay literary canon, connects Denby's poetry to García Lorca's, as well as to Hart Crane's. Ailey's New York breakthrough took place in a 1954 musical, *House of Flowers*, based on a story by Truman Capote. The project typified the integrationist projects commonly envisioned in the 1950s and like Strayhorn's musical centered on interracial relationships. The production involved director Peter Brook, Capote, and choreographer Herbert Ross and starred Pearl Bailey and Diahann Carroll; Mitchell was one the dancers.[20] These examples indicate the underrecognized importance of interracial/intercultural collaboration to postwar American art and racial activism.[21]

These intersections between black and white artists were increasingly commonplace in the 1950s, yet their degree of significance in Denby's life and influence on his work remains unclear. The poet certainly was making cross-cultural connections of his own. Painter Alex Katz recalls taking Denby to a Mahalia Jackson concert, after which the poet compared the gospel singer's inflection to Gertrude Stein (23–24). A modernist innovator whose experiment with cross-race writing, *Three Lives*, sparked controversy, Stein was a major influence on both Denby and O'Hara.[22] Denby, in fact, intended to work with Thomson on a German translation of *Four Saints in Three Acts*, the composer's collaboration with Stein. An opera for "Negro voices," *Four Saints* purportedly was inspired by Jimmie Daniels, a café singer and Harlem club owner whom Thomson admired. In the late 1940s, Daniels worked as a host at Bon Soir, a West Village club that attracted a racially and sexually mixed clientele (Kaiser 42). In 1952, the American National Theatre produced the first major revival of *Four Saints*, featuring Dunham's dancers (Watson 302). Though the German production never materialized, Denby's interest in creating a transnational production of *Four Saints* suggests further possibilities for reading his art within a previously unrecognized interracial context that includes figures such as Daniels, Stein, Mitchell, and Thomson as well as Ailey, who contributed minor direction to a 1973 production of Stein's opera at Lincoln Center.

Although a fuller history of African American artistic production in the 1950s is beyond the scope of this chapter, my purpose in turning briefly to

Strayhorn, Leslie, Ailey, and Mitchell is to acknowledge the wider interracial artistic networks that remain largely unexplored and to encourage further investigations into the exchanges between New York School artists and African American artists working in musical theater, modern dance, and jazz as another node of desegregation. These tangled connections—the seemingly incestuous history of the New York School and African American dancers and musicians—risk becoming a history built on gossip, but they are apt for a poetics, like O'Hara's, that embraced rumor, innuendo, and the casual encounter. Indeed, Denby's name-dropping poem "Postcard" revels in a web of interpersonal, interracial connections; its references stretch from Elaine de Kooning to that perpetual icon of an integrationist ethos and postwar alienation, Billie Holiday.[23]

In the decade after World War II, African American artists were beginning to create and perform within mainstream, mostly white-operated, institutions; this art often centered on the experiences of African Americans, but just as frequently, black performers and visual artists were part of integrated performances and exhibits that did not highlight the significance of race. Unlike the white patrons in the jazz bars of 1920s Harlem, audiences in the late 1940s and 1950s were experiencing African American art outside of the context of African American communities, at times struggling to respond to these artists outside of habitual racial perspectives. Not only did many black artists, including Gwendolyn Brooks, stress the universal relevance of their art and downplay the primacy of race in their artistic ventures, but white audiences were learning to see African American dancers, painters, and writers within emergent aesthetics that were not racially defined.

The poetry of Brooks and Denby from the late 1940s often transposes a private, emotional landscape onto public places, thereby changing those spaces. Though stylistically divergent, the two poets explore the tensions and false distinctions between public practices and private desire found in desegregated, urban spaces of the late 1940s. In "I love those little booths at Benvenuti's," Brooks uses the semipublic space of a restaurant to imagine the internal response to an ambivalent integrationist moment—specifically, the emotional upheavals for both white and black Americans of crossing the color line. An inversion of typical narratives of black migration into white spaces, the poem questions white Americans' private desires that fuel and limit public acts. In his study of interracial intimacy during this same period, Alex Lubin identifies this public positioning of interracial desire as a crucial political strategy that "pushed certain civil rights questions into the public realm, where they could be dealt with through public policy" (*Romance* 123). Brooks's poetics and politics, however, are more complicated: She not only expands the idea of intimacy beyond the sexual but also illustrates the fragility of interracial intimacy in the public realm. And in reading Denby, we are reminded that interracial and queer desires and urban sexuality more broadly have often been treated as public matters, scrutinized and policed. In "Summer," the exaggerated public nature of spaces such as the street and the park are compromised by an intimate attention to the seemingly private sexual and social urges that are often felt and evoked within these spaces. Here, the privacy of sexuality is amplified and performed in public space, thereby changing its publicness. Denby's observation that the park contains "only men, the women don't nap there" (9) names not only the homoerotic possibilities of the era but also its gendered restrictions of urban public space. Emphasizing these social contradictions, Brooks and Denby depict sexual and racial desegregation in ways that both highlight and transgress the racial, gendered, and sexual borders of public space.

These artistic connections and integrationist experiments provide a framework for understanding the reconstituted urban places in the poetry of Brooks and Denby. This framework situates Brooks within a layered interracial context that has been neglected by critics who insist on reading her as a proto-black nationalist. In addition, this framework places Denby's work within a network of gay artists, many interested in racial themes, thereby foregrounding the racialized whiteness and sexual resonances contained in his work. As these integrationist contexts for their individual explorations of urban space make clear, Denby's and Brooks's circumstances as artists differed markedly. Denby's poetry debut, for example, went largely unnoticed, while Brooks's second book won the Pulitzer Prize, strengthening her career and making African American poetry more visible in the broader cultural landscape. Racial desegregation for Denby was often something witnessed on stage and in the collaborations of fellow homosexual artists, yet the parallel claiming of public space for diverse forms of sexual expression was a cultural shift noted in his poetry. For Brooks, desegregation was reflected in the social fabric in which she wrote and socialized, but her poetry remained solidly in African American experience, and her politics never embraced the era's color-blind sentiments. Still, both of these writers illuminate a changing postwar society and contribute in meaningful ways to the broader history of American desegregation, which includes black literary magazines fueled by integrationist missions, the interracial art scenes of Chicago, New York's diverse dancers and musicians, and other gay subcultures, often interracial, that existed in increasingly public ways in both of these cities in the decade after the war.

The Universal Particulars of Feeling Queer

In addition to their attention to the racial and sexual resonances of urban space, both Edwin and Gwendolyn (even the pairing of their names offers poetic pleasure) noted the unavoidable imprint of World War II on their respective cities. Locating the war's aftermath in the alienation and longing of urban citizens, Denby's *In Public, in Private* and Brooks's *Annie Allen* rewrite the genre of war poetry in important ways. In both collections, these poets merge the contemporary language of the city with traditional poetic forms, making visible the ways the war altered Americans' experiences of race, gender, and sexual identity. Disclosures of hidden meaning and sublimated emotion—whether spiritual dislocation, racial grief, muted sexual desire, or ambivalence over promised integration—are central ideas in these poems, which memorialize the war, its varied legacies, and its queer affects. In their revisions of war poetry, Denby and Brooks remind us of the urban survivors of the late 1940s—returned death-haunted soldiers, melancholic women, and discontented, sometimes discharged, queer military personnel. Through their attention to the private, traumatic registers of social change, both racial and sexual, we discover neglected strands in the histories of racial and sexual desegregation.

Brooks and Denby are poets of urban history, documenting the changing public and personal practices in postwar Chicago and New York City, as well as artists of social protest, writing postwar poems of formal reinvention and psychological disclosure about segregation, gender oppression, and gay invisibility. These two documentarians explore a similar melancholic register of queer feelings, often evoking the private turmoil and everyday rituals of black women and white gay men as they navigate public spaces transformed by the social changes of World War II. Historian Charles Kaiser notes that the military's screening policy during the war created "a new kind of official stigmatization," but military service also "provided gay men and lesbians with a dramatic vision of their diversity and ubiquity" (27). As writer James Schuyler's discharge from the U.S. Navy because of his homosexuality makes clear, the experience of World War II was paradoxical for many gay men (see Mlinko). Denby attempted to enlist but was refused by the recruiting officer; Rudy Burkhardt surmised that Denby "would have made a terrible soldier" because he was too "extravagant" (14). In his poem "On the Home Front—1942," Denby addresses the domestic impact of World War II, where the "the small survivor has a difficult task" (*DCP* 52). Conveying the psychological ambivalence of the time, the poem recognizes that civilians have their own battles, including the "duty to keep control" (52), a struggle for restraint and public respectability we find echoed in Brooks's "thousands—killed in action" (*BL* 110). The nameless confessor in Denby's poem offers this melancholic reflection:

> Anybody can make it, that's democracy, sure
> The hard part's holding on, keeping fit, world of difference
> You know war, mass hysteria, makes things insecure
> Yep a war of survival, frankly I'm off the fence (*DCP* 52)

For the disillusioned citizen, navigating this "world of difference" is a kind of mental warfare, but this state of psychological turmoil offers a subtle kind of resistance, a confrontation of political, even sexual, ambivalence in the disclosure "I'm off the fence." Denby's suicide in 1983 is both an ironic epilogue to this "war of survival" and the final act of the artist-citizen who has lived fully yet tires of "holding on" (52).

In "On the Home Front—1942," Denby performs his own version of military service, "answering the questions great historians ask" (*DCP* 52). For Denby and Brooks, the poet is the paradoxical civilian-soldier who records history and, as Denby insists, offers answers. Those answers often voice the experiences and the psychological battles of African American veterans, African American women battling discrimination on the home front, and gay and lesbian artists intimately changed by World War II, even as these populations are perceived as tangential to it and often written out of its official histories.

A black soldier, one of the "Gay Chaps at the Bar" in Brooks's melancholic poem "mentors," answers back to those cultural exclusions and speaks of the haunting of war, including its homoerotic registers. Brooks's ventriloquism of black masculinity centers on a man who cannot be mentally or physically present with his date, "fragrant as the flower she wears." Instead he confesses, "For I am rightful fellow of their band. / My best allegiances are to the dead" (*BL* 69). His loyalty to his cohort of soldiers—ghosts and a memory of homosocial protection—expresses a queer longing, a postwar lament, for male companionship that perversely borders on necrophilia. Susan Schweik's observation that the soldier "rejects the imagined seductiveness of a present woman for the company of dead, remembered fellow soldiers" (131) can be taken further to acknowledge the queer desire of its speaker to walk in "the midnight that is mine and theirs" (*BL* 69). In this unregulated night, men, haunted with memories of wartime bonds, seek solace and perhaps find it in sex. O'Hara's "A Modern Soldier," written in 1951, renders this wartime solidarity in even more explicit terms. In the lines "but the landscape with a gun / in your hand becomes friendly, sucking you / down, 'aint that your idea of good fun?'" (70), battle and blow job merge.[24]

In her much-admired study of feminist poetics during World War II, Schweik argues that Brooks's war poems utilizes a gaze developed during the war: "The crisis of war disturbed, redefined, even sometimes drastically altered, women's understanding, and their culture's understanding, of their roles as nourishers of the symbolic order; 'looking' records and responds to that upheaval" (127). In writing *Annie Allen*, Brooks, however, turns away from the public mandates of war poetry, from the "overtly topical, directly political, stubbornly public poems" as Schweik identifies them (24), to gaze on the domestic front, foregrounding private, gendered protests over racially charged scenarios of social change. As with Denby, Brooks's poems advocate on behalf of a new way of seeing. Despite its explicit references to war, including its "loose-leaf war diary" (*BL* 110), *Annie Allen* has not been characterized as a gendered, domestic commentary on the war and the racial changes in its aftermath. Claudia Tate observes that most of the volume, particularly the first two sections, contains "no explicit social statement regarding race, caste, or gender" ("Anger" 141), yet Brooks's references to domestic discontent and racial identity—the "tan man" and his "maple banshee" (*BL* 103, 104), for example—are, in fact, part of the collection's social critique of domestic containment.

Brooks's revision of traditional poetic forms expands the definitional borders of war poetry and its subject matter. For example, the final section of *Annie Allen*, "The Womanhood," with its masterful five-part sonnet sequence "The Children of the Poor," is a regendered version of "Gay Chaps at the Bar." Published in the March 1949 issue of *Poetry*, its first three sections showcased Brooks's negotiation of formal innovation with social consciousness, a modernist sensibility welded to a protest against economic injustice. The expansive fifteen-piece suite "The Womanhood," which includes the desegregation poems discussed earlier, collectively offers a pioneering statement on black female subjectivity in poetic form. Brooks confronts postwar experiences not from the perspective of soldiers but from within the domestic and social spaces of black women navigating tenuous citizenship and persistent poverty. Brooks's resistance to an abundance of racial references in these poems communicates an ambivalence about postwar identities and politics organized around race as much as an embrace of universalizing modernist aesthetic.

Brooks and Denby were, to use George E. Kent's phrase, "cultivated observers" of public spaces in postwar cities ("Aesthetic Values" 40), but their shared interest in formalist poetics, particularly the sonnet, also reveals a relationship between poetic structure—as another form of desegregated space—and the era's politics of containment. In fact, Kent's suggestion that African Americans in Brooks's poems exist in a "self-contained" state (40) reminds us that although seldom seen as such, Brooks and Denby were Cold War writers whose poetry collections circulated within and commented on an expanding ideology of domestic containment. Both Denby and Brooks experimented with a highly stylized, insular form that might be similarly characterized as contained, a poetics suited to both queer feelings and occluded social protest. In his now-canonical study, *Containment Culture*, Alan Nadel argues that containment as a Cold War narrative "describes American life in numerous venues and under sundry rubrics during that period: to the extent that corporate production and biological reproduction, military deployment and industrial technology, televised hearings and filmed teleplays, the cult of domesticity and fetishizing of domestic security, the arms race and atoms for peace all contributed to the containment of communism, the disparate acts performed in the name of these practices joined the legible agenda of American history as aspects of containment culture" (2–3). Considering that desegregation in its legal, informal, and imaginative forms intersected with domestic containment in the late 1940s, the absence of race in Nadel's instructive list is striking. Underscoring the influence of Cold War containment on race relations, writer Margaret Burroughs commented on the erosion of interracial allegiances within the American Left after World War II: "Black and white people were together all the time. We visited each other's homes. . . . The thing that broke that up was the 1950s and the McCarthy scare. The McCarthy period came on and certainly any black person who had a white friend was a Communist" (qtd. in Morgan 22). Reminding us of the overlooked racial dimensions of containment culture, Burroughs's explanation also challenges critics to document the ways interracial allegiances survived (the examples discussed earlier from the New York dance and theater worlds provide some counterevidence) but were reimagined in the literature from the early years of the Cold War. The compressed poetics of Brooks and Denby constitute a reflection of—and, more important, a refutation of—the containment politics and racial suspicions noted by Nadel and Burroughs.

Both poets' interest in social alienation reflects Americans' larger preoccupation with the psychological consequences of World War II and the racial changes that accompanied it. In her survey of mid-twentieth-century African American poetry, writer Margaret Walker notes a departure from racial themes and a growing interest in the "intellectual themes of psychological and philosophical implications which border on obscurantism" (350). Pointing out that the "strong note of anxiety" in the aftermath of World War II "was not felt at first in the literature," Walker cites Brooks as part of an emergent group beginning to explore the conflict's psychological impact (348). The psychological dislocation in Brooks's poetry, however, documents wartime anxiety within domestic crises: marital infidelity and sexual anxieties both personal and cultural. Markedly different than the aesthetic of *A Street in Bronzeville*, her second collection explores the psychological dimensions of desegregation not only in scenes of interracial contact but also in domestic and emotional interiors that transpose public events and private desires. Denby was equally interested in a coded confessionalism within the public sphere, but his poetry generally avoids conventional depictions of the domestic. Reflecting a cultural climate of uncertainty, these poems enter the troubled psychological interiors, the queer emotions, of citizens dislocated by racial or sexual difference in a moment defined by suspicion and cultural upheaval. Both poets embraced a neomodernism alive with the contemporary speech of the city, an effective aesthetic for rendering postwar subjectivities outside of essentialist categories. Indeed what unites *In Public, in Private* and *Annie Allen* is their mutual ambivalence about traditional communities and subcultures organized around race or sexuality, an ambivalence evoked in the transient places they represent and neomodernist forms they reinvent.

Feminist Appendectomy

Annie Allen remains Brooks's most disputed and least admired poetry collection. Early critics failed to consider the radical possibilities in *Annie Allen*'s formalism and often took Brooks to task for its obscurity. Reviewing the book, J. Saunders Redding confessed, "I do not want to see Miss Brooks' fine talents dribble away in the too obscure and the too oblique" (7). Don L. Lee (later Haki Madhubuti), Brooks's "spiritual son," felt that many of the volume's poems lacked "the feel of home" and offered this blunt assessment: "*Annie Allen*, important? Yes. Read by blacks? No" (17). Brooks repeatedly dismissed her second book as too ornamented, too crafted, too oblique, ranking it below *A Street in Bronzeville* and *The Bean Eaters*, both of which she believed had "more humanity" than her epic homage to Annie and postwar America (Terkel 7). These aesthetic assumptions—that black women should write with a transparency, a domestic coziness, unlike poets such as Eliot or Pound whose cryptic verse is praised as modernist achievement—reveal a gendered and racial double standard. "Memorial to Ed Bland," the book's introductory poem, appears to anticipate critics' ambivalence regarding *Annie Allen* with its line, "Calling what they can't clutch insanity / Or saintliness" (*BL* 80). Incomprehension, then—what we cannot "clutch" in Brooks's work—might be read as craziness or prophecy, but her embrace of a formalist aesthetic suits her project: a depiction of the post–World War II city not in public spaces but in feminist interiors alive with emotional ambiguity and psychological dislocation. Occluded by and pushing against the sonnet's rigid cage, the queer feelings of postwar America were becoming increasingly audible in Brooks's poems.

Although Brooks's reorientation of public space was a central approach to desegregation, Tate's observation that Annie refuses to "externalize her internal life" ("Anger" 145) reminds us that black women's relationship to postwar urbanity was not a simple claiming of public space or an increased social visibility. In an era of growing gender conservatism, Brooks's poetics offer a model in which racial and gender issues—for example, a critique of color prejudice and sexual discontent—are voiced through a poetics of indirection. It is a desegregationist strategy—bringing these historically silenced experiences to a postwar readership—that muddles private disclosure and public pronouncement. Brooks's desegregation of the domestic sphere, positioning it within larger public changes, makes visible black women's sexuality in unprecedented ways, but she also risks its exposure to public scrutiny. As a result, Annie's discontent regarding sexuality and domesticity is obscured in the modernist meticulousness that characterizes *Annie Allen*. The crafted obscurities of these poems, described by Kent as a shift from "the simple representation into the symbolic" (*Life* 83), however, are suited to a desegregationist moment in which African American women were reenvisioning their communal and familial structures.

Brooks speaks of being "technically passionate" in her early work, her politics "crowded back into language" (Hull 96; Tate, "Interview" 106), but she does not elaborate on how this technical obscurity, what she calls a "close-textured" poetics (Fuller 68), hides the ambivalent feelings of loss and longing, the racialized textures of feeling of African American soldiers and mournful women found in *Annie Allen*. The desires found within these physical and emotional sites of dislocation reflect a range of queer feelings—self-pity, envy, grief, and anger. The poetry of Brooks, as well as of Denby, highlights the relationship between textual obscurity—what Fred Moten calls the "desire for misrecognition" (Rowell and Moten 959)—and an affective landscape where secrets (in this case, often objectionable, unheroic feelings) are expressed. Brooks, unlike Denby, often bypasses typical images of the urban streetscape, instead delving into spaces of emotional ambivalence—about patriotism, religion, racial integration, and femininity.

"The Anniad," Brooks's intricate epic of forty-three septets, is a stunning commentary on domestic containment, particularly the gendered constraints on women as wives and sexual subjects, but it is rarely read this way. Tate's description of "The Anniad" as a series of "domestic crises" ("Anger" 147) reminds us that the epic and its "Appendix to the Anniad" are war poems focused on the home front as well as a coded resistance to Cold War sexual containment and gender conservatism. When the war is explicitly named in "The Anniad," it is often layered with sexual consequence:

> With his helmet's final doff
> Soldier lifts his power off.
> Soldier bare and chilly then
> Wants his power back again. (*BL* 103)

The implied impotence suggests that the black soldier, out of uniform, is once again vulnerable to the "bare and chilly" racism of the nation, but he is also struggling to regain power in the home and bedroom. Brooks brilliantly reveals the overlap between racial retrenchment, domestic containment, and sexual conservatism.

"The Anniad" is a puzzle whose cryptic compactness mirrors its heroine's sexual repression: "Think of ripe and rompabout / All her harvest buttoned in, / All her ornaments untried" (*BL* 99). The "tan man" returns from war fueled by longings both social and sexual: "Hies him home, the bumps and brindles / Of his rummage of desire / Tosses to her lap entire" (102). The musicality of this fairy tale sings of innuendo, bumping desires land in Annie's lap, shuttling between sexual expansiveness and the gendered containment of those desires. In a passage that succinctly aligns marital discord with the emergent Cold War's climate of suspicion, Brooks writes of "vaunting hands" no longer attentive, "now devoid" (102). The "paradise" of both nation and coupledom is "paralyzed and paranoid" (102). Americans' panic over communist allegiances and sexual deviance has trickled down to (or is just as likely rooted in) intimate, domestic places. Annie's internal negotiations reflect a longing that is both sexual and existential, a cultural space where both "idea and body" "Clamor" with advice for domestic contentment: "Skirmishes can do. / Then he will come back to you" (102). The marriage is altered not only by the ruptures of war but also by suspicions of infidelity and a sexual awkwardness that leave body and mind to question the satisfaction of the veteran's return. Brooks invites the ambiguity of *skirmishes*—alluding to larger international conflicts that claim Annie's husband for military service while also emphasizing the marital discord ("Not that woman!" [104]) explored throughout "The Anniad."

The skirmishes of marriage, in fact, are found throughout Brooks's writing.[25] In *Maud Martha*, Paul neglects Maud for the lighter-skinned women at the Foxy Cats Club. And in a 1951 essay in *Negro Digest*, "Why Negro Women Leave Home," Brooks distills many of the important cultural changes that shaped this desegregationist moment—interracial sex, public discussion of homosexuality, and women's social and economic empowerment. Notable in its particularization of the needs of "Negro Women," the essay also performs its own desegregation, bringing private matters to public scrutiny.[26] Brooks discusses extramarital affairs across the color line, noting that black women, particularly "university or artistic women" (28), were exploring the "white male market" (27). Acknowledging that sexual troubles, including a husband's homosexuality, might dissolve a marriage, Brooks concludes that black women's reasons for marital dissatisfaction are neither financial nor the result of infidelity; rather, they illustrate a psychological desire for validation. She pronounces, "A wife whose husband respects her as a person, instead of 'humoring' her as though she were a chattel or a slightly idiotic child, is not likely to leave him" (28). Defying the reentrenchment into conservative gender roles that defined Cold War domestic containment, Brooks writes that a woman who continues working after the war "was deserving of [her husband's] respect and tact" and a woman who stopped working "still expected her husband to think of her as a cooperating human being and treat her accordingly" (28). This call to respect women's economic and sexual choices—to argue for emotional validation as the center of marital contentment—is mirrored in Brooks's literary projects, where Maud and Annie navigate their desires within a racist public sphere and sexist domestic sphere.

Despite critics' charges that Brooks distanced herself from leftist affiliations during this period, the feminist sentiments in Brooks's writing from the early 1950s can be read collectively as a critique of domestic containment and racial segregation as dependent forms of social control. In later years, Brooks departed significantly from these feminist and integrationist sentiments. In the 1980s, she spoke of the idea of "racial grief," arguing that black women "are not going to be winners on account of leaving their black men and going to white men, to themselves or to nobody" (Tate, "Interview" 110). This insistence on racial loyalty and the privacy of intraracial "family matters" complicates black women's struggles for autonomy, which Brooks so movingly portrays in earlier work.

At a moment when many African American artists explored an aesthetic that balanced universal statements with cultural specificity, black women writers faced the even more complicated task of expressing the particularities of gender and countering their invisibility as artists. James Smethurst's description of Brooks as a "cold-war poet of anger and self-repression par excellence" (164) reminds us of the historical forces constraining African American women after World War II. However, the poetic playfulness in which Brooks addresses sexuality demonstrates that repression was not the singular or even dominant trope in *Annie Allen*. In her discussion of the impact of the Cold War on family life, Elaine Tyler May draws a distinction, noting that "sexual containment—unlike sexual repression—would enhance family togetherness, which would keep both men and women happy at home" (99). Brooks also does not repress her racial critique in "The Anniad"; she addresses it not as a generic, largely public "race problem" but sees its influence within intimate relationships: the way Annie's self confidence is shaped by color prejudice within African American communities or the bruised ego and indiscretions of her "tan man." Here, the black soldier is not only the insulted hero but also the neglectful husband. *Annie Allen*, then, points to the failings of sexual containment and the ways the home can be refuge from and a microcosm of larger social problems.

The overlooked and occasionally dismissed "Appendix to the Anniad" offers another gendered site in which to document the psychological impact of World War II on domestic life, a parallel to the more studied tribute "Gay Chaps at the Bar." A reworking of social protest, the "Appendix" examines a woman's—presumably Annie's—response to World War II. Her queer feelings are as much personal as political. Illuminating the feminist impulse that is central to all her work, Brooks wrote in 1996, "I cite, star, and esteem all that which is of woman—human and hardly human" (*Report from Part Two* 131). The three tiny poems of the "Appendix," an appendage to the epic, might be read not as an epilogue or a transition, as some critics have argued, but as a poetic detour like the corporeal sac the name evokes. An appendix suggests not only a supplementary text but also the too often peripheral social space occupied by the woman writer in the rhetoric of war and its grand narratives. Brooks notes and bemoans women's role in war, aware of her assigned place within sentimental forms outside of the epic; like her troubled women, alive with queer feelings, Brooks's poetics is hidden in the bowels of contemporary culture.

The first of the poems—parenthetically titled "thousands—killed in action"—conveys, in second-person address, the urgent need to mentally process the war's causalities announced in this newspaper headline. "You"—and we are thrust into the subject of this poem as war observers—feel, like Annie, forced to negotiate a "proper" response to this massive death. Denial—"the clever evasions of the vagueness"—personal selfishness and secret horror preclude the "proper" and "sweet" face of public stoicism (*BL* 110). The opening line, "You need the untranslatable ice to watch" (110), suggests both a ruminative walk by a lake in winter and a frozen emotional state that cannot be publicly shown or understood. This icy lake—tellingly bruised "purple and black" (110)—amplifies the slippage between landscape (here one is outside of racial culture) and interior and the need to loiter in a sublimated world below the ice with its "healthy energy of decay" (110). Brooks renders a state of emotional abeyance, imagines the interiority of a woman fumbling toward braveness on the home front stunned by the thought of her soldier in those dying masses. These ruminations, evasions, are necessary before grief can be, in Brooks's terms, "other than discreet" (110). This transformation is speedy: "Quickly you are well" (110). But her handling of wartime loss is new and disorienting: The poem concludes, "How you yawn, have yet to see / Why nothing exhausts you like this sympathy" (110). This sympathy, the expected public performance, Brooks suggests, is tiring because it requires a censoring of one's own psychological musings, a denial of self and one's inappropriate—selfish, horrified, angry—feelings. The reader lurks between those killed in action and the woman at the frozen lake actively suffering in her ice-like stasis.

The contours of sentimentalism and emotional repression are expanded in the second poem of the "Appendix." Its first section, with echoes of Dickinson, imagines war-divided lovers meeting in God's "wide Parlor" (*BL* 111), but the poem ultimately rejects both religious rhetoric and sexual repression, opting for an erotic immediacy suggested in the image of the pleasure-seeking couple. These "worshippers of life" are described in the urban landscape as "masters of the long-legged stride, / Gypsy arm-swing" (111). George E. Kent dismisses this passage as a cliché of "gusto life" popular on television (*Life* 86). Suspicious of Brooks for drawing on this mainstream (white hegemonic) imagery, he fails to consider the appeal of such fantasies—the projection of a free-spirited, self-fashioned identity into public urban space—particularly in wartime and particularly for African Americans, who have been historically precluded from claiming these spatial and emotional freedoms. The poem's *we* is one of coupledom, not racial collectivity. The suggestion that the couple "never did learn how to find white in the Bible" (111), while clearly suggesting racial resistance, speaks ultimately to religion's futility as a wartime salve for frustrated libidos. The poem's social intervention rests in its refusal to privilege the overtly political over the emotional, the collective over the individual. Rejecting wartime restraint, the couple demands, "We want nights / Of vague adventure, lips lax wet and warm, / Bees in the stomach, sweat across the brow. Now" (111). Brooks aligns the anxiety of war, including its racial injustices, with the nervous energy and physical exertion of sex; in so doing, she points to another indignity of war: youthful sexual expression mutilated by deflating death. The overlooked sexuality of "The Anniad" and its appendix are partially a coded subversion of containment ideology, but these poems also provide a countercurrent to the concern over black middle-class respectability that characterized the decade after World War II.

The final poem of the "Appendix," "sonnet-ballad," Brooks's invented form, is a first-person portrait and excessively sentimental. A daughter, mourning with her mother, pines, "They took my lover's tallness off to war. / Left me lamenting" (*BL* 112). Even if he does not die, the woman realizes that her man will return unrecognizably scarred, haunted by the death he witnessed. The soldier's encounters with killing are imagined as unfaithfulness; he would "have to court / Coquettish death, whose impudent and strange possessive arms and beauty (of a sort) / Can make a hard man hesitate—and change" (112). War twists romance into a kind of necrophilia, recalling the "remotest whispers" of the "reproving ghosts" in Brooks's poem, "mentors" (69). The poem's excessive romanticism and melodramatic register ("Oh mother, mother, where is happiness?" [112]) have made it an easy target for critics. Don L. Lee quipped, "This poem is probably earth-shaking to some, but leaves me completely dry" (17). Such a comment not only dismisses Brooks's inventiveness but misguidedly concludes that women's interior musings and romantic sentiments, severed from political outrage, are fundamentally dull. Lee's implied preference for the unornamented racial affirmations of Brooks's later career should prompt us to celebrate these disparaged poems all the more for their romanticism, a strand of urban poetics often maligned in the literary marketplace that still largely applauds African American work of explicit social protest.

The "Appendix" is an essential document of Brooks as an experimental romantic. Moten notes that "courting miscommunication" or keeping a secret often has had political and aesthetic utility for African American writers; misunderstanding, he argues, saves poems from being "bare romanticism" (Rowell and Moten 960). Poets perhaps can write sappy love poetry but need to be technically sophisticated and aesthetically oblique in their execution. Brooks's obfuscations through metrical formalism can be read as a subtle intervention into the ritualized expectations of war poetry, and the aesthetic offers the poet a public place to critique domestic discontent and sexual longing while still averting public scrutiny. Departing from her own portraits of heroic soldiers, bruised by military racism and struggling to reacclimate to American urban life, Brooks turns to the emotional ambivalence of African American women navigating loss and the shifting racial and gendered locales of urban life. Here, sentimentalism, unapproachably packaged, protests both war and its traditional poetics. In subtitling her appendix "leaves from a loose-leaf war diary," Brooks suggests both the intimacy and impermanence of women's writings of war. Like the sheets of a diary ripped out and attached to the "Anniad"—her intricate, more psychologically guarded epic—these poems might be read as a feminist appendectomy, the harvesting of private sentiment, now provisionally displayed as public confession.

Edwin Denby's "Filthy Double"

Although I have focused largely on Brooks's three-sonnet appendix (a war diary that takes confessionalism and queer sentiments of racial belonging in new modernist directions), one of the generative connections to Denby's writing is their shared use of the sonnet sequence. In "Children of the Poor," a sonnet chain, Brooks uses children, favored figures for her political-poetic commentary, to challenge the postwar narratives of economic abundance and domestic refuge. The poem's line "queer / Whimper-whine" (*BL* 115) is a pointed descriptor for the emotional tone of Denby's "A Sonnet Sequence: Dishonor," which performs a similar task of upturning narratives of postwar optimism. Hardly celebratory of the homosexual's arrival into popular culture, Denby explores the underbelly of queer emotion, an embrace of abjection that is surprisingly at home with current queer thinkers. This testimony of shame, on one level, is suited to the embrace of psychoanalysis as a lens to explain humanity's destructive potential, so disturbingly evidenced by concentration camps and atomic bombs. "A Sonnet Sequence: Dishonor" might be a portrait of that hungering id. But what, on a secondary level, does it reveal about a queer poetics and nonnormative sexuality in post–World War II culture? And, in furthering my inquiry into desegregation and the new routes for racial and sexual discourses, how do Denby's sonnets invite today's critics to broaden their investigations into racial aesthetics of the period to acknowledge a racialized whiteness found in his work and in that of his contemporaries, including Allen Ginsberg and Frank O'Hara?

Many of Denby's poems, particularly the later sonnets, capture the intimate, compressed emotions—shame, anger, longing—that define the psychoanalytic session. As a young man, Denby pursued psychoanalysis for several years because of suicidal feelings; in Vienna in the 1920s, he was a patient of Paul Federn, an analyst who studied under Freud. Denby later concluded that analysis was "quite painful" but "very good for many people who are alone and have nobody to talk to intimately" (Gruen 163). Both elegy and autobiographical lament, the lonely "New York dark in August, seaward," one of his later sonnets, perfectly exemplifies the poet's melancholic tendencies. The

"Creeping breeze" like an intrusive ghost of death finds the speaker, clearly Denby, reminiscing: "Old poems by Frank O'Hara / At 3 a.m. I sit reading" (*DCP* 165). Overcome with emotion ("Heart in my mouth"), the poet heads to bed at dawn feeling "Inside out like a room in gritty / Gale" (165). Less laudatory than most of Denby's urban odes, New York is described as the "the lunch hour city / One's own heart eating" (165), recalling the cannibalism of his "Dishonor" sonnets. The final lines—"Complicities of New York speech / Embrace me as I fall asleep" (165)—imagine the poet coddled by language but also, more morbidly, perhaps embraced by the death that circulates breeze-like throughout the poem. This scene of the lonely urban night leaves contemporary readers feeling pulled inside-out by their own insomnia-induced reminiscences. Like the urban solitude of Edward Hopper's paintings, an aesthetic link that Lincoln Kirstein also notes ("Comment" 27), Denby evokes the psychology of emptied places and bare emotions.

The quiet rage and sublimated desires in Brooks's poetry are also steady forces in Denby's work. In "A Sonnet Sequence: Dishonor," with its unsettling spectrum of erotic desires and queer violence, the physical city retreats, and fragmented snapshots of emotional unease become central. Alice Notley writes of the evolving psychological textures of the "Dishonor" poems, "The sonnets of the second sequence are totally self-absorbed because self-absorption, pain and near-constant self-knowledge, which makes the self divided, is their subject matter" ("Edwin Denby" 4). As the sequence's introduction explains, these poems are concerned with the unresolved self, "the filthy double of me who attends / To the secret matters I don't care to treat" (*DCP* 17). The perverse mixing of the erotic and the grotesque that marks the expansive twenty-two-part sequence is gruffly evident in its initial first lines: "I hate you, I feel your flesh suckling flesh / Here between my fingers the flesh I wanted to eat" (18). Readers are uncertain if they are witnessing an act of cannibalistic violence or an utterance of sadomasochistic sexual bravado. The language is fixed on the tactile and the impulsive, but the nature of consumption is ambiguous, both sexual and violent. The poem's "bleating" and "Howling" speaker, the "pumping meat" of the heart, the "boiling dreams," conjure both a lover's passionate release and a psychopath's rage (18). We recoil at the poem's frank physicality; its "pus" (18) reminds us that the secretions of a wound are not unlike those of the ejaculating penis.

Section 16, with its obsessive attention to orifices—"Smelling or feeling of the several holes / Above the jawbone and below the belly" (*DCP* 33)—also asserts the primal body, propelled by unchecked drives. Echoing the sexual consumption of the sequence's first sonnet, No. 16 finds the speaker probing mouth, eyes, and ears, looking for the soul's "sweet jelly" (33). But "when it's lower down the lover comes / He's washed all through by something awfully sweet" (33). Enacting Freud's polymorphous perversity, the poem disorients the reader within this "research," this erotic investigation. Again one is left sullied and sustained by the body's saccharine fluids.

But sexual beings must formulate an ethics, as Denby reminds: "Each lover must deceive himself at will / Must falsify, forget, betray, besmirch" (*DCP* 33). Such a list reminds us of the psychological negotiations, the emotional contortions, that we perform in asserting our sexual selves. As Notley observes, "I think Edwin's homosexuality sharpened his moral sense—he was very much a moralist. He saw humans as somewhat disgusting creatures redeemed by their art. Not so much that sex is disgusting, as that the postures we force each other into to express or repress ourselves sexually are often unbeautiful, degrading, even hurtful to others" (email). These poems invite us to consider the beauty in the abject and the psychological redemption sought not only in art but also in sex itself. And as Notley suggests, Denby may designate our social relations as much as our sexual practices as filthy. These humiliations within intimate relationships recall Annie's painful introspection in Brooks's collection. For both poets, the underbelly of emotions, whether sexual discontent or erotic dislocation, also define this era of reconfigured social and psychological space.

In a 1949 essay, "Against Meaning in Ballet," Denby argues that both dance and poetry deliver "an aspect of the drama of human behavior" that cannot be understood from "a rationalistic point of view"; though dance offers the "finest images of our fate," Denby suggests, its meanings evade us (192). Art and the subjectivities it renders can be understood only through impressionistic, often fragmented, means. The sonnet series "Dishonor" is not unlike a choreographed dance sequence, employing the physicality of language to illuminate human desires that are both admired and maligned. In the same essay, Denby describes watching dance as an "especially attractive form of feeling social consciousness" (34). In exploring ugly feelings and human perversity in his poetry, Denby, like Brooks, nudges readers toward another kind of social consciousness, one that contemplates the interplay between the corporeal and cerebral and stretches the aesthetic boundaries of both modernist and protest art. "A Sonnet Sequence: Dishonor" perversely upsets Denby's reputation as the modest, respectable purveyor of the arts. Adopting the psyche of "Death's own bisexual self-polluting pimp" (*DCP* 17), Denby acquires a social freedom in which to explore the intersections of thanatos and eros, crafted art and lived life, and public persona and secret self. These explicit sonnets, in turn, inform our reading; when we return to Denby's more benign city poems, the sexual innuendos, violent undercurrents, and sublimated longings are brought into clearer relief. In a desegregationist context in which homosexuality, previously shamefully private, finds an unprecedented publicness, these depictions of abject sexuality bypass more respectable models of gay identity, expressing sentiments dangerously close to the rhetoric of the sexual pervert circulating in this same period. Denby's reference to the "filthy double of me," then, indicates a suppressed alter ego that has found voice as well as a duplicity within homosexuality itself, an identity both banal and menacing.

Notley identifies the "sound of personal peculiarities" ("Edwin Denby" 4) in Denby's work, but one of the few critic-poets to register sexual particulars within his writing is contemporary poet Nicole Mauro, whose "Ode (to Edwin Denby)" is a sonnet sequence in the spirit of Denby's aesthetic, including startling images and syntactical twists. The overt sexuality in Mauro's poems repositions Denby as the erotic, sexually embodied poet who has been largely invisible. Mauro's first sonnet begins, "The secret of life is leaking / Into my penis (Homeric and chapped, yes a little)." Alluding to Denby's line "The airless secret I strangle not to share," from No. 17 of the sonnet sequence "Dishonor," Mauro's contemporary homage aims to name sexual secrets as a way of recognizing Denby's contribution to a queer poetics.

Despite the overt exploration of libidinal desires in his writing, Denby's sexuality remains troublingly hidden in the few critical accounts of his work and his influence on the New York School.[27] Private. Discreet. Eclipsed within good manners. In contrast to Joe Brainard's and Frank O'Hara's bold assertions of homosexuality, Denby was part of an older generation with a different relationship to gay identity and public expressions of homosexual desire. Recalling Denby's sixtieth birthday party, Joe LeSueur cattily describes the poet's sexuality as "vicarious and voyeuristic" (92). Much more guarded than O'Hara, a younger, more autobiographical poet, Denby did not write explicitly about cruising for anonymous sex or openly share his homosexual encounters. It is tempting to imagine the older poet living through O'Hara's sexual escapades, including those with anonymous African American men, the stories of the mailman and subway clerk as naughtily dished by LeSueur in his memoir (40, 56–58, 60, 185–87). Denby, in fact, was an important but often overlooked figure in O'Hara's artistic development. His tribute in honor of Denby's sixtieth birthday, the poem "Edwin's Hand," before all else, celebrates a disembodied, fragmented sense of Denby, an artist who is "Easy to love, but / difficult to please" (*Collected Poems* 238). O'Hara's description of his mentor "in the midst of spectacular" (238) aptly locates Denby's centrality to the New York School art scene as it was unfolding, a witness to the memorable sexual, social, and artistic freedom claimed by many of the movement's artists.

The artist as voyeur is celebrated in Denby's prose poem, "Aaron," likely a portrait of composer Aaron Copland, a friend who "had a passion for the lost chord" and "preferred to look when nobody was watching" (*DCP* 39). Denby had collaborated professionally with Copland, writing the libretto for his 1937 opera, *The Second Hurricane*. But this poem remains private, literally set within the intimate world of home and imagination. The poem narrates Aaron's mysterious activities up in his bedroom: "He closed his eyes and shivered, enjoying what he did. And he went on doing it, until it was time for something else, saying 'I like it.' And he did. He liked a good tune, if it lasted" (39). Full of sexual suggestion, "Aaron" is also a tribute to Gertrude Stein's linguistic playfulness. The ambiguous eroticism folded within its straightforward narration recalls the queer innuendos of Stein's "Miss Furr and Miss Skeene," another soundscape of queer desire. Denby's poetic tribute to a friend (recognizing the poem's Aaron as Copland requires a social familiarity) also toys with the boundaries of public and private; here, private queer intimacy becomes public adoration.

Persistently elusive, Denby occupied a loft apartment on West 21st Street for most of his life.[28] Thinking of Denby's "modestly furnished" austere all-white space, John Gruen observed that "the economy of his writing was paralleled by the sparseness of his life style" (161). Mimi Gross recalled, "Walking into his single, extremely spare room, the feeling was white" (89). Taking up this notion of "feeling white" and the minimalism implied by his friends' comments on his white space, I consider the convergence of racial poetics and queer affect in Denby's poetry to place it in a desegregationist context in both racial and sexual terms. Denby's poetry, in addition to its expansion of unconventional sexuality into the public realm, offers another approach to postwar racial aesthetics. Whereas O'Hara's identification with African American culture and his attraction to African American men are quite discernible in "Easter" and other poems, Denby's quirky approach to sexuality and his racial indirections make him a challenging figure for theorizing a poetics of whiteness. My interest is, in part, an extension of the influential work of Rachel Blau DuPlessis on the racial poetics of modernist writers, including Wallace Stevens and Vachel Lindsay, in which the legibility of whiteness is no longer denied. Denby's writing is also a useful counterpoint to the white subjectivities found in Elizabeth Bishop's poems and Zora Neale Hurston's narrative. In illustrating the breadth of approaches to racial poetics, Denby's contrast to Brooks's more overt though equally experimental racial representations is also instructive.

Denby possessed a memorable whiteness. Tributes to the poet, often note his thin physicality, his paleness, his intense pale blue eyes. Gruen mentions his "lean, almost spectral look" (161). Ron Padgett recalls, "His slender build, silver white hair, white skin, and blue eyes, his graceful manner, his attractive modesty, his inwardness, surprising in so public a man—all went toward giving him a kind of radiance, or spirituality" (xxvi). Deborah Jowitt describes him as a "fragile, white-haired heirloom" (30).[29] Whiteness, like the poet's much-noticed paleness, appears central to his memory and his aesthetic. More muted than his dance criticism, Denby's poetry also engages the discourse of race. Imagine a spectral loner, the city's nocturnal wanderer, as the speaker in his sonnet "Meeting in the Postoffice," which begins, "Was it you or myself I saw, white in the postoffice / The white face hung in the air before the government marble—" (*DCP* 53). Departing from the literal realm of the post office, this nebulous whiteness imagined as the "crazy face" of the subconscious holds the grotesque, the surreal, and, of course, the erotic, suggesting a casual hookup between pale, "dazed" strangers who "left that soapy government erection." The poem ends on the street where "Heat and brightness and reflection / Play in the distance and in your look, doing no harm" (53). Heat playing in the eye, the white gaze cruises.

The unease in placing Denby's poetry within a context of racial aesthetics convinced me such a reading was necessary. The queerness of his poetics—both the homoeroticism and textual occlusions—insists on an expansive theory of racialized desire. The desire, images, and sentiments in his work are expressly white, the specter of his pale, physical frailty looming on the edges. His poems and criticism help define a mid-twentieth-century queer aesthetic in which whiteness is predictably assumed and central. However, an interracial cultural history, including the contributions of Billy Strayhorn, Alvin Ailey, and Jimmie Daniels mapped out earlier in this chapter, challenge monochromatic histories of gay artistic expression in the 1950s. Not unlike Elizabeth Bishop's tentative gestures to make whiteness visible in her poems, Denby's evocations of white corporeality contribute to a subtle racial poetics that is often ignored. We can see this in the later sonnet "Writing poems, an employee." In the poem, a "white old man" and "employee" of verse, looks back on his youth, comparing his passport picture with its "soft vague boy's smile" to the "Current boys nineteen, their beauty / Of skin" (*DCP* 135). Skin here is itself a kind of passport, suggesting not only the access afforded white flesh but also its role as the tactile trigger to memories of that "Vague-faced boy." I am thinking here of the heartbreaking image, in Denby's "The grand republic's poet is," of white-bearded Whitman sitting in his underwear in Denby's loft. In these seemingly raceless poems, whiteness is racialized, dislodged from a nebulous universalism.

Noting that only a "refracted" whiteness can be critically viewed, critic Mason Stokes argues that an "unsettled and disturbed whiteness" is "most revealed, most instructive, most worth learning from" (191). This unsettled whiteness often becomes legible in the cross-cultural comparisons found in Denby's dance reviews. In his essay "Dancers, Buildings, and People in the Street," written in this same period, Denby catalogs, in a moment of cultural essentialism, the different ways people around the world inhabit their bodies: the "miraculous" stroll of blacks in the Caribbean, Italians' "extraordinary sense of the space they really occupy," and Americans who "occupy a much larger space than their actual bodies do" (197). This love of the dance in everyday life is found in the "girls' easy-sided gait" and "loping clerks" of Denby's poems (*DCP* 14, 9), but references to racial and cultural difference slip away, recede to assumed whiteness in many of his poems. His "People on Sunday" is a collage of communal city life that uncharacteristically names ethnicity: young men play ball; others in "fresh shirts" wait for their dates; bums "sit quietly soused in house-doors"; and "Greeks laugh in cafes upstairs" (11). Elaine de Kooning notes that "Edwin's consciousness, through his poetry, was always of people, of human relationships, of power, no matter what he saw. Whether it was dancers, buildings, or people in the streets, it was always humanity" (30). Yet the racial boundaries so crucial to understanding these relationships of power are tellingly unacknowledged in his poems. Denby was more willing to specify cultural and racial differences in his criticism. Despite the unspoken ethnic diversity within New York City in the late 1940s, his streetscapes are generically peopled, universally human in an unspecified whiteness. Resisting a realist documentary portrait of urban life and eschewing racial referents, Denby embraces the language experiments that characterize many of the later New York School poets: twisted syntax, coy erotic reference, and touches of surrealist imagery. Elizabeth Lee's proposed mode of "identifying a queer presence in art" by "demand[ing] the detection of certain subtleties, which often only appear in an indirect reference or exaggerated detail," can be usefully applied to the reading of race in white writers (320). The racial discourse in Denby's poetry is sometimes prominently announced through racial references but is equally shaped by the corporeal and cultural signifiers lurking on the edges of his urban landscapes.

The poetry of Brooks and Denby documents as well as remaps public space as part of a response to desegregation that is still undervalued in studies of postwar American poetry. Illustrating George Chauncey's thesis in *Gay New York* that gay men have historically shaped public space for private needs, Denby's poems highlight the intimacy, the private moments, within public space. Brooks, conversely, turns from the concrete urban geography of her first book to record interiorities, prominently feminine, and interracial public spaces of World War II and urban life. I have conceptualized Brooks's poetry as another form of queer place making in part because it constructs a social space for African Americans, particularly women, that similarly blurs heteronormative ideas regarding the division between public and private. In documenting the public sexuality of gay men in Atlanta in the 1950s, John Howard characterizes the city as a competitive space in which "a burgeoning gay male culture, limited in its alternatives, visibly and assertively made its stake along with other often competing interests on the city's publicly contested terrain" (169). Brooks's attention to the urban spaces that African American women inhabited or attempted to access in the spirit of desegregation remind us that as part of this contingent of "competing interests," black women were also occupants of queer spaces, contested and precarious. In both Brooks and Denby, we find the transgressive, ambivalent, and transient spaces that define desegregationist writing. Through poetry, these writers could capture the affective landscape that remains largely invisible in the histories of gay men and lesbians and African American women in postwar America.

In his essay on the ballet photographs of Alexy Brodovitch, Denby writes, "He took neither official portraits of the stars in their emphatic moment nor the designed effects of choreographic climaxes. What he took, what he watched for, it seems, were the unemphatic moments, the ones the audience does not applaud but which establish the spell of the evening" (Brodovitch 11–12). Both Denby and Brooks engaged in art of the "unemphatic," of private, often banal, moments of the everyday—the cat sleeping in the apartment, the glances exchanged in a luncheonette, the Sunday drive in the segregated suburbs, or the date at the racially mixed movie house. Both writers use these moments to conjure the melancholic mood and the hushed-up indignities of urban life. With these interiors—actual and psychological—Brooks and Denby, like Brodovitch, employ a poetics that casts spells. They capture the moods, the emotional geography of postwar American life. Sometimes in this poetics, the city itself slips away, leaving only the queer, ambivalent feelings of its urban wanderers.

Some readers, I anticipate, will object to the possibilities and improbabilities of reading Denby's work within an explicit, though perhaps peripheral, multiracial context or the corollary challenge of "queering" Brooks's writing from the late 1940s and 1950s. Denby's poetry, like Bishop's, was for many years viewed as irrelevant to race studies, and while criticism on Brooks often focuses on gender, issues of sexuality and particularly its queer manifestations have been largely unidentified. While I want to avoid recklessly forcing such interpretations on these writers, both poets, like many of their contemporaries, were interested, at least tangentially, in racial and sexual difference, their parallels and overlaps. Denby's dance reviews of an increasingly vibrant African American modern dance scene that included Josephine Baker, Katherine Dunham, and Pearl Primus certainly confirm the interracial connections that shaped his art.[30] And Brooks's sustained attention to the complexities of black masculinity as well as the social strictures, including color prejudice and gender conservatism within black communities, that influenced black women's sexuality have clear relevance to current theories of racial affect and sexual difference. Clippings and copies found in Brooks's archive, apart from a 1972 *Chicago Today* article about parenting and homosexuality, also reveal an admiration of poetry by several gay American writers, including poems from Tennessee Williams's 1956 collection *In the Winter of Cities* and clippings on Allen Ginsberg. Moreover, the homosocial world of black men depicted in Brooks's war poems shares the urban landscape of queer desire represented in Denby's poetry.

I conclude by returning to a discussion of poetic form to further solidify the connections between Brooks and Denby. These poets were engaged in complementary visibility projects that remapped the public sphere to account for the sexual resonances and racial shifts in urban life after World War II. The courted miscommunication, as Moten describes it (Rowell and Moten 460), found in Brooks's critiques of sexual repression and domestic restraint are also evident in the sexual desires sublimated in Denby's city poems. His treatment of race—at times an explicit naming of whiteness, sometimes a circumvention of it in the rhetoric of human universality—enacts a similar obfuscation. Their reinventions of a modernist aesthetic, then, respond to desegregation that is both racial and sexual; however, the era's conservative cultural politics as well as the emotional complexities of postwar urban life that Brooks and Denby sought to document required a poetics of indirection.

In discerning a "growing perspective beyond the point of view of race" in African American poetry of the late 1940s (349), Margaret Walker noted that this universalism was "coupled with another definite mark of neo-classicism, the return to form" (350). In the anxious, policed cultural moment of the 1950s, both Brooks and Denby embraced neoclassicism, particularly the sonnet, to experiment with a new forms of social critique that reflected their shared interest in postwar negotiations of private emotions within urban public space. Sonnets, as "containers of polite protest," to use George E. Kent's description ("Aesthetic Values" 40), require condensed language and compressed emotions as well as an attention to the rhetoric of the cultural critique being made. Both Brooks and Denby experimented with the relationship between form and voice, often refusing to reconcile the two. The "elliptical or truncated lines" that Walker observes in Brooks's work (351) have much in common with Denby's syntactical experiments, and both were clearly influenced by Gertrude Stein's poetics.[31] Notley speculates that Denby chose the sonnet "because he could adapt it best to suit his speech patterns. He spoke in a highly compressed, precise manner. The Later Sonnets sound just like him" (email). In a review, O'Hara also notes Denby's precision of voice, praising *In Public, in Private* for the "risks it takes in successfully establishing a specifically American spoken diction which has classical firmness and clarity under his hand" ("Poetry" 179). Through a neomodernist style that welded traditional rhyme schemes to modern diction—the voices of contemporary urban culture—Brooks and Denby enacted the era's tension between social restraint and affective release, between occlusion and confession.

Insisting that emotional complexity required technical sophistication, Denby and Brooks grappled with the paradoxes of form and feeling, exploring how modern desires could be contained within but also exceeded the bounded structures of the sonnet. The characterization of Brooks's aesthetic as self-contained makes clear the ways that her exploration of black female subjectivity enacts sexual containment through a rigid formalism, but this approach also unsettles social-aesthetic constraints by approaching black female subjectivity in unprecedented ways. The ambiguous images and twisted phrasings found in her *Annie Allen* and Denby's *In Public, in Private* emulate cluttered emotional interiorities that avoid simplistic representations of identity or flat-footed social commentary. In their adoption of the sonnet sequence, they find a poetic structure, simultaneously contained and sprawling, in which to excavate an emotional landscape of shame, disavowal, and disconnection that defined this desegregationist moment in American culture. Both poets explore the aesthetics of high modernism, with its reinvented poetic forms and textual obscurities; however, in their fragmented portraits of postwar psychological upheaval, their poetry helps define a particular version of late American modernism. The interplay of formalism and rupture in their poems in many ways anticipates the activist and postmodern art of the late 1960s.

Brooks's and Denby's turn to a neomodernist style might be understood solely as response to a conservative cultural moment of political and sexual repression, a way "to express radical politics without drawing the attention of the antisubversive governmental investigators" (Smethurst 51), but I have argued that their indirection and formal complexity has social and political value for the ways it enacts fragmented, at times lyrical, consciousness as more truthful representations of modern subjectivity. The anti-identitarian strands within these projects express sentiments, public as well as private, that are not exclusively the result of sexual and racial silencing and that offer inspiring (a quality literary critics seem to readily dismiss) expressions of being and belonging. Roderick A. Ferguson argues that unlike the Popular Front writers before them, postwar "avant-garde writers insisted on a representational complexity that strained toward the unique and the unpredictable" (237). One of the conclusions that can be drawn from a paired examination of Brooks and Denby is that in reimagining public space to reflect racially and sexually marginalized citizens' emotional responses to such places, both poets' quirky adaptation of high modernist forms challenges the coherence of these minority identities as well as the divisions between public and private that mark those identities. For Brooks, her poetic experiments are a rejection of a reductive definition of "black woman"; for Denby, unbraided formalism is a route away from asserting "homosexual" as the newest cultural minority.

This reevaluation of fixed social identities in many ways mirrored the ideological battles of postwar American artists and political activists. In their political writings in the wake of World War II, homosexual activists Donald Webster Corey and Robert Duncan evaluated parallels between racial and sexual oppression and the shared minority status of "Negroes" and "homosexuals." Corey initially decried homosexuals' "caste-like status," noting that their lack of civil rights had much in common with other oppressed minorities (D'Emilio, *Sexual Politics* 33).[32] In his pioneering 1944 essay, "The Homosexual in America," Duncan, however, rejected an identity politics that centered on difference or defined homosexuals as a social minority. He believed that the homosexual needed to emphasize *his* (the attention to lesbian identities being wholly absent) common human experiences over sexual peculiarities. Duncan asked how gay artists and critics might handle sexuality and concluded that they must convey, like African American or Jewish artists, universal humanity over difference.[33] This negotiation of the universal and the particular has much in common with shifts in African American literature immediately following World War II. Kent ("Aesthetic Values"), Sigmund Ro, and Walker have all observed that postwar writers increasingly asserted the universal significance of black subjectivity as the quintessential perspective for citizens of all races facing profound social and political change and psychological alienation. In taking up the correlation between homophobia and racial prejudice, Duncan's and Corey's work also asserts an integrationist sexual politics: Their (homo)sexual manifestos complement the era's universalizing literary gestures by African American writers that future critics would come to see as naive visions of assimilation.[34]

This political and aesthetic interest in the intersections of race and sexuality and the growing aesthetic emphasis on universal humanity over racial and sexual particularities provide further contexts for reading Denby and Brooks collectively. Denby's refusal to depict an explicitly named homosexual identity or sexual practices affirms Duncan's prescription that the homosexual artist must remain devoted solely to "human freedom, toward the liberation of human love, human conflicts, human aspirations" (322). "To do this," Duncan instructs, "one must disown *all* special groups (nations, religions, sexes, races) that could claim allegiance" (322). Likewise, Brooks's decision to foreground the gendered realities of black women as representative of the wartime experience and disillusionment of many American women, irrespective of racial and economic differences, challenged critics to broaden the definitions postwar feminist poetics and the boundaries of the African American protest tradition. Writing before identity politics had solidified, Brooks and Denby not only documented the racial and sexual particularities of urban places but also attempted to reconcile a broad humanist vision with the specificity of postwar urban existence. Despite their different perspectives, the pair reinvigorated traditional poetic forms and crafted a poetics of disclosure that was both personal and eccentric. In the contested spaces of their poems, we find a range of "inappropriate" emotions—including erotic desire, racial grief, buried rage, and sexual shame—that defined mid-twentieth-century American cities. Desegregation is an act of unsettling, a moving into previously prohibitive places—both physical and psychological—but it is equally a moving from the sharp divisions of public and private and from the traditional confines of community and family and the sense of emotional separateness that they foster. In many of their poems, Brooks and Denby name the dislocation and profound doubts regarding one's place in the expanses of city and in the clutches of home.

The reading of Brooks and Denby collectively as an alternative, poetic form of civil rights discourse as well as Robert Duncan's early attempt to find commonalties between the burgeoning movement for gay and lesbian rights and the civil rights movement offer a broader context for reading the treatment of sexual deviance in the black press and in 1950s literature discussed in the following chapter. In focusing on the figure of the white pervert in two novels by African Americans, I further delineate the overlaps between racial desegregation and sexual integration that my readings of Brooks and Denby explore. Chapter 3 also considers the role sexual deviance, particularly white perversion, played in both impeding and facilitating integration. Located in small towns far removed from the erotic freedom celebrated in Edwin Denby's city poems, the white pervert in novels by Ann Petry and William Demby represents the sexual anxieties of this integrationist moment, embodying the queer feelings lurking in the poetry of Brooks and Denby.

White Pervert

William Demby, Ann Petry, and the Queer Desires
of Racial Belonging

The preceding chapter explored varied articulations of sexuality—queer abjection, the erotics of public space, and the intimate negotiations of marriage—by African American women and white homosexual men in American cities transformed by World War II. In exploring Gwendolyn Brooks's poems and prose in which black women reimagine both domestic duty and their public identities, I considered that African Americans' desegregation also can be a queer intrusion, arousing similar feelings of defiance, doubt, shame, and pleasure to those experienced by gays and lesbians in their own claims to public space. The representations of and resistances to sexual containment in the poetry of Brooks and Edwin Denby provide further evidence for one of the central premises of this book: Sexuality was central to these writers' documentation of social change, particularly desegregation, in the decade after World War II. This entanglement of race and sex within desegregation is most clearly seen in the anxiety over interracial sex, a concern addressed in the many journalistic assurances that "miscegenation" would not be the inevitable outcome of desegregationist laws and practices. In a 1958 *U.S. News and World Report* article, "Leading Sociologists Discuss Sex Fears and Integration," experts assured readers that a groundswell of sexual experimentation across the races was an unlikely outcome of desegregation. Integration was about access and economic equality, the article concluded, not sex.[1] For an October 1957 article in the *New York Times*, reporters interviewed residents of thirteen southern states to better understand the hostilities toward integration, centering much of the coverage on attitudes about interracial sex and marriage. Black schoolteachers, rural white Christians, university faculty, and community leaders discussed reactions to interracial intimacy in their schools, communities, and families. Several African American respondents reminded readers that the idea of racial purity was a national fantasy long since eroded. These anxieties regarding interracial sexuality as well as rejections of the idea that integration would promote it circulated alongside another vexed site of desegregationist panic: the growing presence of the sexual deviant, often imagined as the perverse homosexual, who threatened historical racial boundaries and normative sexual practices. Shuttling back to some of the regional resonances of desegregation discussed in the work of Elizabeth Bishop and Zora Neale Hurston—a necessary reminder that the homosexual is not solely an urban creature—this chapter considers the figure of the white pervert in African American literature from the early 1950s as the embodiment of larger cultural anxieties about sexual and gender differences and racial changes.

In a cultural moment of refigured work, family, and sexual cultures, African American literature and journalism of the immediate postwar era are dotted with discussions of the queer outsider. Taking inspiration from Ellison's critique of archetypes in "Change the Joke and Slip the Yoke"—specifically, the darky entertainer as a figure of white imagination—and Richard Dyer's tribute to the sad young man in the essay "Coming Out as Going In," I situate the white pervert alongside journalistic accounts of postwar sexuality as a way of considering how the queer citizen—often both homosexual and interracialist—in this integrationist moment exists as a convoluted figure of racial trespass, sexual deviance, and familial threat, a potent archetype that complicates our understandings of race, gender, and sexuality. Arguing for the ways that the white pervert both facilitates and impedes integration, I evaluate his presence in two African American novels, Ann Petry's intricate, often experimental, novel of interracial romance, *The Narrows* (1953), and William Demby's existential narrative of stunted lives in rural West Virginia, *Beetlecreek* (1950). In particular, I am interested in the ways that both novelists unravel romanticized portraits of racially hegemonic communities and the traditionally gendered family structures that define them. In an era that increasingly championed family life (always heterosexual, always nuclear) as the locus of both self-fulfillment and national security, Petry and Demby explore other bonds of kinship across race, age, and sexuality, composing family structures that correspond to the alternative models found in the work of Brooks, Demby, Bishop and Hurston.

The Narrows and *Beetlecreek* highlight the perverse resonances within interracial sociality and cross-race encounters, reminding us how deeply threatening these desegregationist acts were to the Cold War ideology of containment. Critiquing the provincialism of segregated racial communities, in which private matters quickly become public scandals, Petry and Demby use a range of queer desires—interracial, same-sex, pedophilic—to expose, critique, and at times defend the cultural anxieties regarding racial and sexual integration. Their attention to both sexual deviance—represented by the white pervert as well as by black characters who depart from heteronormative identities—and racial transgression, including violations of segregated spaces, cross-race allegiances, and interracial sex, foreground the libidinal dimensions of integration. Contemplating the attraction, revulsion, fear, and melancholia that often prompt crossings of racial borders, these novels also acknowledge the subconscious desires that arise and are sublimated within integrated spaces. Continuing this project's focus on topographical symbols of desegregation, this chapter traverses desegregated places, from barbershops to hotel rooms, with particular attention paid to the ways Demby and Petry document the subtle hostilities that accompany the erosion of racial lines, particularly in locales traditionally understood as providing racial solace. Discussing social and domestic places that are marked as queer because of racial transgressions that are often coupled with sexual perversion, my analysis illustrates the crucial role that queer desires played in desegregating the domestic and public places of these small towns. Although departures from normative sexual and racial protocols (at least by the standards of dominant culture) are imagined, particularly in the figure of the white pervert, as threats to an increasingly fragile social order, I also argue that both novelists imagine the possibilities for positive communal change within interactions, intimate or hostile, across the color line.

The Narrows and *Beetlecreek* solidify as much as challenge the prevalent attitude in 1950s America that the homosexual was still fundamentally a pervert, a deviant figure on society's fringes. The idea of the "sexual psychopath," historian Estelle Freedman argues, was constructed in the 1940s and 1950s to delineate a "strict boundary between heterosexual and homosexual males, labeling the latter as violent child molesters" (211).[1] Historian David K. Johnson writes that "'sex deviation' became a staple of public discourse in the decade after World War II with fifteen states establishing commissions to study the problem" (56). An anxious fascination with the "sexual menace," almost always imagined as male and white, circulated in the era's films, popular journalism, and literary works. Journals of psychology and criminal justice outlined symptoms, causes, and treatments. Psychotherapist Benjamin Karpman, for example, argued in 1951 that the "paraphiliac" (a term he preferred to *sexual psychopath*), unlike the "average normal person," possesses a "compulsive, insatiable, unremitting, unbridled" sex drive, a desire so strong that normal life becomes impossible (191). Karpman's analysis of sexual deviance was progressive for its time; he believed that perversions such as homosexuality, exhibitionism, and transvestism should be dealt with through psychological treatment rather than legal means because "the law fails to prevent, correct, or deter sexual criminals from their activity" (194).

Such studies suggested that homosexuality, although framed as pathology, required medical sympathy, not social hysteria, and helped to bring sexual difference to mainstream attention.

While histories of sexuality in postwar America have largely neglected African Americans' responses to shifting social attitudes, news articles in the black press about juvenile sexual delinquents, hermaphrodites, and southern men passing as women suggest African Americans' significant interest in the nation's transforming understandings of interracial sex, gender identities, and family life as well as perversion, homosexuality, and racial deviance. An October 1957 article in the *Amsterdam News* polled Harlem residents about whether they accepted "the new English theory on homosexuality," which contended that "sexual perversion is a homosexual's personal business as long as he does not violate the law or molest non-homosexuals" (De Vore, "Singer" 1). Among those polled, the program secretary of the Harlem YMCA—ironically, a hotbed of hidden homosexual activity and a historically significant site for African American artists—argued that homosexuals should be "forced to take corrective treatment" to "protect the innocent," while a minister believed the community should reach out to those "plagued by perversion" (1). Adrian Jarvis, a "somewhat 'gay'" patron of the Apollo Bar, believed that the number of gay people was increasing and classified the homosexual into types, including the "bum or lazy," the "frivolous teenage type," and the "gentlemanly" version, carefully distinguishing "undesirable 'gays'" from those living respectable lives ("Singer" 23). A follow-up article characterized Harlem homosexuals as "reserved" with "good jobs" and named a "popular nitery" for the "'gay' set" (De Vore, "Article" 28). This piece perhaps inadvertently normalized homosexuality in the African American community, viewing it as not necessarily deviant but already integrated into Harlem's stable social fabric. This article appeared literally alongside a report on FBI intervention in school integration in Little Rock, Arkansas, a juxtaposition that pointedly illustrates the rapidly changing postwar society and the simultaneous emergence of public homosexuality and integrated institutions. Among images of integration in the popular press of the 1950s—wedding photos of interracial couples, integrated summer camps, and black doctors lauded by white patients—we find discussions of homosexual practices, interracial sex scandals, and changing teen behavior in African American communities.

While Freedman's "'Uncontrolled Desires': The Response to the Sexual Psychopath, 1920–1960" and John D'Emilio's "The Homosexual Menace: The Politics of Sexuality in Cold War America" are foundational to my reading of the white pervert, few literary critics have considered the ways that integration and America's increasingly interracial culture have shaped post–World War II cultural depictions of homosexuality. Robert Corber's analysis of James Baldwin in *Homosexuality in the Cold War*, Frederick Whiting's "Stronger, Smarter, and Less Queer: 'The White Negro' and Mailer's Third Man," and Robert Reid-Pharr's *Once You Go Black: Choice, Desire, and the Black American Intellectual* are notable exceptions; their investigations into the often ignored racial dimensions of masculinity in the early Cold War broaden established narratives about postwar sexuality in the United States. But *Beetlecreek* and *The Narrows* remain underrecognized contributions to larger mid-twentieth-century discussions of homosexuality and the meanings of perversion. This discourse was shaped in part by the publication of Havelock Ellis's theories on sexual inversion in 1942, Alfred Kinsey's findings in the next decade, increasingly common interracial marriages and interracial sex, and a growing scientific interest in sexual pathologies and more public homosexual identities. These novels are uncommon in their focus on the regional nuances of sexual identity and attitudes in small segregated towns and rural communities; they locate a now well-documented midcentury anxiety about the homosexual in spaces often overlooked in critical studies focused solely on urban gay culture, such as Chauncey's indispensable *Gay New York*, or histories of postwar homosexuality, including D'Emilio's *Sexual Politics, Sexual Communities*, which focus largely on white cultural sources.

In much of the criticism of African American literature from the early 1950s, literary explorations of homosexuality were seen as frivolous distractions, and race (magically extracted from sex generally and perversion specifically) was understood to be *the* substantive topic and dominant concern for African American writers. As we saw in the discussion of Gwendolyn Brooks, the belief that a turn from social protest or even an embrace of sentimental themes or more lyrical forms of representation indicated a vacating of racial duty or social responsibility was a political and aesthetic conundrum faced by writers (black and white). Postwar African American writers, including Petry and Demby, interested in exploring interracial desire and emergent sexual identities risked condemnation from the many literary critics in the 1950s who treated homosexuality as a trivial subject. Taking issue with novels that joined racial conflict and homosexuality, critic Charles Glicksberg, writing in *Phylon* in 1953, naively urged, "Let us right off divorce the racial problem from that of homosexuality; there is no reason why the two should be conjoined, as if they offer a common basis for fictional treatment" (388–89). Writer and activist Julian Mayfield argued in 1960 that writers were neglecting "the great questions facing the people of the world" and instead writing about such seemingly minor topics as "the foibles of suburban living, the junior executive, dope addiction, homosexuality, incest, and divorce" (32). This odd list is reminiscent of Ellison's classification of homosexuality—along with parricide, fratricide, and incest—as a "problem at the base of personality" ("Twentieth-Century" 94); in "Change the Joke and Slip the Yoke," he also accuses Leslie Fiedler of (mis)using homosexuality symbolically as the "most terrifying name for chaos" (105). Both Ellison and Mayfield link homosexuality to incest and familial violence, indicating the potency of the homosexual as a symbol of social deviance who threatens family, racial community, and eventually nation.

Despite Glicksberg's assertion that homosexuality is a "minor issue" next to race and that joining the two subjects is a "perversion of the art of fiction" (389), Demby and Petry chose to examine the interdependencies of race and sexuality through the figure of the white pervert, a sexual body on which to pin the racial and sexual anxieties of the immediate postwar and with which to explore the limits of freedom and fear. Petry believed that literature inevitably interrogates societal practices and values, arguing in "The Novel as Social Criticism" (1950) that writers must illuminate the ways characters are "formed and shaped by the sprawling inchoate world in which they live" (95). The inventive and often lyrical narratives of *Beetlecreek* and *The Narrows* explore racial perversions and psychologies of whiteness and subvert African American literature—the rigid boundaries of the protest tradition, its racial provincialism, and the historical silences about homosexuality.

In asserting the white pervert as a complex sign within interracial encounters, Petry and Demby acknowledge the erotic dimensions of desegregation, but their representations also argue for a more subversive reading of the integrationist as race traitor, positioning him or her as a more transgressive symbol of social change than the conventional, assumed white, liberal intellectual. In articulating the anxieties of integration through a racialized figure, visibly white, Demby and Petry not only critique the racist discourse of an assumed black sexual pathology but also perversely gesture to their own artistic transgressions as black intellectuals, existing as outsiders within largely white liberal circles yet also maligned within segments of the African American community for their perceived artistic and political perversions. The black American writer interested in troubling African American traditions by candidly addressing the queer facets of black sexuality and incorporating cultural representations and artistic traditions from outside of African American contexts was also understood in 1950s America as a social deviant.

I am particularly interested in the ways that Petry and Demby, as black intellectuals, articulate their own positions as outsiders and craft their individual aesthetic perversions. Demby, for example, cites the influence of a

European intellectual tradition where pedophilic sensibilities were openly acknowledged; furthermore, his conception of African Americans as a fallen aristocracy seeks to illuminate the roles perversion and historical shame play in black cultural production. He readily admits that Bill Trapp, the sensitive reclusive in *Beetlecreek*, is a projection of his "secret self" (interview). For Petry, the postwar black intellectual necessarily views the world askance. In invoking Rose Jackson, a woman from Petry's childhood, as a symbol of the outsider, she, too, privileges the black intellectual's marginal position and the vision it affords. Both novelists' identification with racial and implicitly sexual marginalization aligns the African American writer with the skewed vision of society that the social deviant is assumed to possess.

Perverted Domesticities

Pharmacist, journalist, and fiction writer, Ann Lane Petry, best known for her feminist-tinged novel of social protest, *The Street* (1946), occupies a unique and increasingly recognized position in American literary studies for her documentation of mid-twentieth-century African American life, particularly the racial and sexual politics of small-town New England. Petry began to receive sustained critical interest in the late 1980s and early 1990s, when her novels, *The Street* and *The Narrows*, and short story collection, *Miss Muriel and Other Stories* (1971), were reprinted. Her second novel, *Country Place* (1947), focused mainly on white characters, has been of particular interest to contemporary critics interested in postwar sexual politics and whiteness studies, and its depiction of a veteran's struggle to reassimilate into his New England town makes it a crucial text in Cold War studies.

Born in 1908, the daughter of a pharmacist, Ann Lane grew up in the predominantly white town of Old Saybrook, Connecticut, an insular locale on which she modeled much of her fiction. Following family tradition, Lane became a pharmacist, working during the 1930s at the drugstore started by her father in 1902. After marrying George D. Petry in 1938, Ann Petry moved to Harlem and worked as a journalist for the *Amsterdam News* and the leftist weekly *People's Voice*, where she wrote a weekly column, "The Lighter Side." Her reporting on urban culture, particularly the experiences of New York City's black women, provided the inspiration for her best-selling and most-analyzed work, *The Street*, the story of Lutie Johnson's futile attempt to save her son and herself from urban corruption—the kind of novel of social criticism that Petry defended. Her embrace of a fatalistic social realism, an aesthetic from which she would later depart, is seen in one of her earliest stories, "On Saturday the Siren Sounds at Noon" (1943), in which a man jumps in front of a train after his child dies in an apartment fire because of his neglectful wife. While Petry's work often reflects, like much of American naturalism, pessimism about race relations, her novels strive to convey characters' psychological complexities—their burdened histories, desires, and fears—outside of a solely sociological framework. "I write about the walking wounded," Petry observed.[2] The emotional landscape of her fiction, nuanced and expansive, reveals the imprint of economic, gender, and sexual forces—both internal and external—on postwar identities.

Like most African American writers of her generation, Petry's political consciousness and inevitably her aesthetic were shaped by segregation and activism focused on its dissolution. As part of the *Negro Digest* series "My Most Humiliating Jim Crow Experience"—Zora Neale Hurston was another contributor—Petry wrote in the June 1946 issue about her school picnic at a Connecticut beach, which abruptly ended when local residents, including children spewing racist epithets, protested her presence. As the only African American child in her class, the traumatic incident, despite a protective teacher, was clearly life altering. Of her early education in racial prejudice and social policing, Petry lamented, "Here in America they teach us when we are very young" (64). The racial education and its convergences with sexual education that African American children acquire in the navigation of daily life became a central inquiry of her novels and short stories. Petry acknowledged how small-town New England—an "essentially hostile environment for a black family" ("AP" 257)—shaped her artistic vision. She called her short story about white violence, "Doby's Gone," "another expression of the outrage that has stayed with me all these years" (256). Like the seething anger of Gwendolyn Brooks's *Maud Martha*, the ethical outrage in Petry's writing, with characters often sublimating their fury, is often overlooked in critical studies of the author as well as in scholarship about the Black Arts movement that focuses solely on masculine expressions of anger.

Incidents of racial confrontation are woven throughout an autobiographical essay Petry wrote in 1988: her father's refusal to be intimidated by Old Saybrook residents upset by a black pharmacist, the violent taunts of schoolchildren, and her sister's graduation from Brown University despite the lack of housing for black female students ("AP" 257). In documenting segregation's imprint on her family history, Petry tells the story of Sister Rose Jackson, whose gravestone she discovered in her hometown's cemetery, in the back and facing the wrong direction—"the nineteenth-century equivalent of the back of the bus" (256). Petry seizes Rose Jackson's memory as an emblem of racial indignities—often absurd social practices—and as a symbol of a shared legacy of defiance. Within her Whitmanesque catalog of multiple identities—her grandfather, a runaway slave; her resilient father; her resourceful sister—Petry lyrically asserts, "I am Rose Jackson, 'a colored woman,' buried the wrong way round near the swamp of that ancient burying ground" (268). Jackson's positioning also is a metaphor for another way of looking—a deliberately skewed perspective, often from the borders between conflicting racial, gender, and economic spheres, that Petry as a black artist cultivates. This vantage point of the cultural outsider is found, too, in much of her short fiction and children's literature. Petry uses these experiences of segregation and cross-race conflict to fuel the four books she wrote for children, possessing an activist impulse to provide young people with role models and a too-often neglected history.[3]

Petry's compelling self-presentation as a "survivor and a gamble," "an outsider, a maverick, not a member of the club" ("AP" 256, 254) directs us toward a radicalism not often attributed to her by critics intent on seeing her as a rather restrained middle-class New England novelist. Her claim of not being a "member of the club" is complicated, however, by the reality that she had membership in a variety of Harlem organizations in the late 1940s, including the Harlem Riverside Defense Council, the National Association of Colored Graduate Nurses, the American Negro Theater, and Negro Women Incorporated, where she served as executive secretary (Jackson 143).[4] Indeed, the social renegades of Petry's literary imagination parallel Petry's self-definition as an outsider. The novelist's personal navigation of racial segregation and commitment to racial equality informs her analysis of the shifting social practices that transpired in part because of World War II: interracial dating, African Americans' economic advancements, and women's sexual independence. The novelist cofounded Negro Women Incorporated with Dollie Lowther Robinson. This consumer group sought to "help women get their money's worth" ("AP" 268). The group was affiliated with the People's Committee, an organization founded by Adam Clayton Powell Jr., who went on to represent Harlem in the U.S. Congress.[5] Inspired by her aunt, Anna James, one of the first women pharmacists in Connecticut, her mother's entrepreneurial ways, and her sister's educational achievements, Petry embraced a feminist cultural shift that ushered women into new professional roles. Like Hurston, Petry also briefly applied her writing skills to the film industry: In 1958 she worked on the Columbia Pictures screenplay *That Hill Girl*, a film slated to star Kim Novak that was never produced.[6]

Petry's first critics understandably focused on the gendered social constraints on her women characters, finding feminist parallels to Richard Wright's school of naturalism. But Petry's interest in the complexities of masculinity, shaped by region, class, race, and sexuality, is equally central to her feminist project. Her satirical essay "What's Wrong with Negro Men?" (1947), which should be read as a feminist companion to Brooks's "Why Negro Women Leave Home," written a few years later, illustrates how empowered versions of black womanhood are asserted indirectly through a pointed critique of patriarchal practices. Within Petry's predictable caricature of the male species (the essay adopts a comic anthropological tone) is an astute articulation of women's exploitation: their inequitable share of domestic labor and men's refusal to recognize them as intellectual equals. Referencing readers' preoccupations with the emergent Cold War, Petry critiques the socially progressive man who is retrograde on gender issues at home: "He flatters himself an expert on such diverse subjects as OPA, income tax, world government, military strategy and what's-wrong-with-the-Negro. But he will run like a rabbit if his wife suggests he prepare a simple meal" (5). In a swipe at the domestic retrenchment of women after the war, Petry surmises, "Deep down in his heart he subscribes to the ancient belief that there is a special place in the world for women, and certain kinds of work for which they are eminently suited" (5). Petry's challenge to women's assumed station in life is connected, of course, to broader social segregation in a cultural moment when civil rights activists increasingly were challenging the customs and laws pertaining to African Americans' "proper place" and demanding access to more social, educational, and economic spaces.

These gender critiques, masked in humor, were regular features in the African American press and reflected interest in changes in marriages and family. Roi Ottley's "What's Wrong with Negro Women?" (1950), also published in *Negro Digest*, reveals the sexist assumptions, despite advances in education and employment, faced by African American women. Invoking the era's political rhetoric in his essentialist analysis (women are frivolous and lack self-esteem), Ottley describes women's distrust of each other as a "common kind of cold war between females" (72). His problematic conclusion that African American women are focused on "meaningless teas, fashion shows and bridge playing" rather than the "race fight" (73) is tempered by his acknowledgment of a few activists and artists, among them Mary MacLeod Bethune, Katherine Dunham, and Lena Horne. Petry, in contrast, avoids composing a didactic novel centered on a race woman—although Abbie does irk Link with her relentless concern over properly representing "The Race" (*Narrows* 138). Unlike Ottley's monolithic sense of black womanhood, *The Narrows* depicts women from a range of social positions: some socially repressed, others sexually expressive, but all living outside of traditional patriarchal domestic life. Building on the gender critique offered in "What's Wrong with Negro Men?," Petry not only shows independent business owners such as Frances

Jackson, Abbie's confidant, who rejects traditional domesticity altogether, but narrates the struggles of an interracial couple whose private and public bond challenges the practices of racially exclusive places.

Petry's final novel, *The Narrows*, documents a wide social spectrum. Examining the lives of an eclectic group of white and black residents in Monmouth, Connecticut, the text focuses on Abbie Crunch's adopted son, Link Williams, a Dartmouth graduate returned home, and his socially prohibited affair with the white heiress of Treadway Munitions, Camilo Sheffield. Weaving together stories of Abbie's middle-class propriety, bar owner Bill Hod's role as surrogate father to Link, and the marital negotiations of a working-class couple, the sensual Mamie Powther and her husband, Malcolm, an earnest butler, Petry disrupts monolithic representations of African American life. Her experimental narrative with its nonlinear structure and collage of stream-of-consciousness monologues captures the complexities of class, gender, and race in American life at midcentury.

While I am concerned here largely with Petry's depiction of white perversion, her perceptiveness about divergent gender identities, less-than-ideal familial reconfigurations, and class stratifications within racial communities are equally relevant to the larger integrationist themes explored in this project. In particular, the representations of masculinity throughout Petry's writing, which include the white pervert and nonnormative, sometimes effeminate black men, direct us toward useful expansions of feminist and queer scholarship on African American literature. In what he terms a "masculinist" reading of Petry's short story "Miss Muriel," Keith Clark aptly notes, "Petry broadens the discursive treatment of masculinity by dramatizing the many spaces where black men attempt to re-center themselves as subjects and potential perils they face when embracing deformed and deforming constructions of masculinity" (83).[7] Clark's thoughtful analysis of the effeminate and suggestively queer character Dottle, a figure he reads as "a variation on the patriarchal and heteronormative family structure" (89), does much to illuminate Petry's feminist concerns, recognizing her career-long interest in gender matters. Similarly, the queer masculinities of Howard Thomas and Weak Knees in *The Narrows* complicate notions of race, masculinity, and family. In her reading of the novel, Hilary Holladay calls attention to Petry's gender disruptions: Abbie Crunch and her best friend, Frances Jackson, Link's "surrogate female parents," are replaced by the "father figure" Bill Hod and "motherly" Weak Knees, lifelong friends who live behind The Last Chance bar. But Holladay's reading fails to explore the queer significance of these non-normative familial configurations.[8] Farah Jasmine Griffin's reading of the novel is the only one to align these "alternative family formations" with Petry's depictions of interracial sex and homosexuality, other important aesthetic challenges to 1950s cultural norms ("Hunting" 140). Within these queer family units, Link witnesses unconventional gender behavior: Frances is a no-nonsense successful owner of a funeral business, and Weak Knees is a man of emotional gentleness who embraces domestic life. Forwarding a nonnormative understanding of family, Petry writes about Link's informal adoption by Bill Hod and Weak Knees as well as his legal one by Abbie and Major. Without embracing the rhetoric of broken families, Petry shows that African American families that do not adhere to the nuclear model can be nurturing and flawed but not pathological. These alternative families (a troublesome phrase, but they certainly are not deviant) offer an implicit critique of the era's embrace of restrictive gender identities and traditional heterosexuality.

These visions of nonnormative sociality further complicate the social and aesthetic significance of Petry's depiction of the white pervert, which comes near the end of the novel. Kidnapped by Camilo's mother, Link senses his impending murder for having an interracial affair that violates social protocols, but he flashes back to the summer when he was twelve and did housework for the Valkills, an eccentric white couple on the edge of town. His adoptive mother, Aunt Abbie, found him the job, believing that "every boy should know how to keep a house clean" (*Narrows* 392). More than learning responsibility, as Abbie Crunch had hoped, Link is educated in bohemian excess, homosexuality, and the economies of desire, including the sexual exploitation that many African Americans historically have battled in white employers' homes. The scene reiterates the rifts between Abbie and Link that we see throughout the novel: she sees "fine rich people," while Link sees "fine slave drivers" (391). Abbie is baffled when she hears of Henry Valkill's impropriety, thinking he had "the loveliest manners" (396), but Link slowly comes to understand the intentions behind the tanned man's escalating advances: His teasing and invitation to rest on their private beach, the couple's favorite pastime, fail to mask his predatory desires.

Sauntering into the kitchen, Mr. Valkill, with his "bright blue eyes always filled with laughter" (*Narrows* 392), changes his manner and voice around Link. The "thick blond hair on his tanned chest" fascinates Link but is described as "something not to look at, to be avoided looking at" (393). The adolescent perceives whiteness, like many of the descriptions of racial difference I examine in this project, as something both alluring and grotesque. The twelve-year-old begins to understand an unfamiliar form of male desire, one both racially and sexually prohibitive. For a tea party, Mrs. Valkill asks Link to wear a silk kimono "made of a sleazy thin material" that smells like the musty house. Her husband admires the boy in costume and "how attractive a Japanese kimono can be" (392). Link begins to see his blackness and masculinity through his white employers' sexualized projections. Within their bohemian sensibility, Link is disturbingly eroticized as a submissive geisha. Invoking Shakespeare, Valkill calls Link "Cassius" because he has a "lean and hungry look," a comment that says more about his fetishistic desire than literary wit (392). When the inevitable happens and Mr. Valkill takes advantage of his wife's absence to put his hand on Link's arm, the teenager is initially confused: The hand reminds him of Bill Hod, a man he deeply admires, but he is disturbed by the whiteness of his employer, the hair of his forearm like the "blond fur" of an "ape"—"revulsion made him move" (394). The teenager, schooled by Weak Knees, remembers that there "ain't never no disgrace to turn tail and run" and flees from Valkill, resolving to quit despite Abbie's insistence that he honor his commitment (394).

Experimenting with the temporal layers of consciousness, the novel employs many flashbacks: This memory of sexual trauma and racial affirmation in its aftermath is folded within the novel's dramatic ending.[9] Link, blindfolded in the back of a speeding car, must confront his own violent death, a seemingly inevitable consequence of his racial and sexual transgression, from which he cannot run. The juxtaposition of Mr. Valkill's coded proposition with Link and Camilo's interracial affair suggests that Link's sexuality and much-desired masculinity are always threatening to and threatened by the social order. Both relationships arise from inequitable power dynamics; the differences in age and racial status thwart Link's social autonomy. Both are moments when racial desire is expressed, disavowed, and policed as perverse.

The menacing homosexual, typified in Henry Valkill, was increasingly visible in African American magazines and newspapers of the 1950s. Coverage included a self-professed straightforward article "Let's Be Honest about Homosexuals" in the August 1954 edition of *Our World*, a publication sometimes described as the black *Life* magazine, that warned, "If you are looking for sensationalism and pornography, you will not get it here" (48). The article, surprisingly for the period, attempted to be factual and avoided hysterical homophobia despite its aim of redirecting the "potential homosexual" (49). Readers, assured that homosexuality no more prevalent in black communities than white ones, are told that "between one-third and one-half of today's normal men and women have had homosexual experiences" (48).[10] The article also seeks to educate parents on the differences between normal adolescent same-sex socializing and homosexual impulses but spends most of its time delineating the causes of homosexuality, introducing homosexual vocabulary ("drag," "camp," "crushing," and so forth) and lamenting the lack of cures.

Though "mental unbalance" (48) is offered as the main cause for homosexuality, environmental factors, including poor housing, "broken homes," absent fathers, "seduction by irresponsible adults and 'street corner' sex education" are also acknowledged (49). Informed by such cultural beliefs, perhaps Abbie Crunch, widowed and left to raise her son alone, feared the homosexual's corrupting influence. But Mr. Valkill, whose whiteness was naively equated with respectability, fooled her. Within the popular thinking that homosexuals were made, not born, white perverts like Henry Valkill pose a threat to fatherless black children, tempting adolescent boys into racial and sexual deviance.[11]

As one might expect, the representation of a sexual menace within the African American context of Petry's novel differs from popular psychological portraits. Her depiction is informed by the sexual oppressions of slavery and its legacy, including the exploitative nature of domestic work that many African American women experienced as well as the stereotype of a hypersexualized blackness still dominant in white popular imagination. In Petry's imagination, the pervert is not the perpetrator of a public act of molestation—the strange man in the park—but one's employer gradually testing social limits in the privacy of his home. *The Narrows* offers a reinterpretation of the domestic servant's cautionary tale, referencing a history of sexually exploitative white employers, but it also reflects the increasingly public presence of the homosexual. Instead of an African American maid, here we find a black male adolescent resisting the advances of the white employer, emphasizing the double vulnerability of African American children.[12] Mr. Valkill's sexual advances, Petry reminds us, are part of a legacy of African Americans' exploitation as domestic workers in white homes, but her depiction of sexual deviance is also rooted in a contemporary set of social issues.[13] In an era concerned with wayward youth, Abbie is the dutiful mother who wants her adopted son to learn responsibility. And the Valkills, their bohemian ways distinctive from the moneyed set accustomed to servants, are emblematic of a growing racial liberalism. Their desire to hire Link, as they likely saw it, was well-intentioned, a sign of their social progressivism, rather than a continuation of historical economic exploitation. On one level, the traumatic incident confirms Abbie Crunch's naïveté, her unquestioned belief in the moral superiority of the white middle class; on another level, Mr. Valkill's advances remind us that interracial intimacy, shaped by the nation's troubling history of racial and sexual subjugation, can often be an impediment to rather than a means toward social equality.

Highlighting the potential dangers of integration and the need to protect youth from predatory homosexuality, Petry clearly is not offering Valkill as an admirable figure, celebrating sexual difference; however, this conflation of pedophilia with homosexuality provides an important example of the ways that homophobia and the anxiety about integration were entangled in this era. The home, as in Hurston's and Bishop's writings, is imagined as a contested site for unearthing anxieties about desegregation, including the inappropriate sexual intimacies it might foster. When Bill Hod hears of Link serving tea in a kimono, he reads it as behavior that suggests a larger perversion and demands that the boy quit the next day. In Weak Knees's worldview, "Some things is natural and some things is against nature" (394). As Link's surrogate (and ironically queer) parents, Weak Knees and Hod are disturbed by the idea of the boy's emergent black masculinity being domesticated, feminized by white bohemian ways. The traumatic interracial encounter affirms Weak Knees's and Hod's belief in white people's depravity.

Petry's location of this sexual predation within the home draws attention to this unseemly side of interracial intimacy as well as highlights the troubled relationship between masculinity and domesticity. In his discussion of a "1950s model of masculinity that stressed domestication and cooperation" in child rearing (*Homosexuality* 6), Corber notes that many postwar critics, including Irving Howe and Norman Mailer, viewed "black male rage as a form of oppositional consciousness" to these new cultural norms (173). While many African American men have viewed the home in part as threatening, connecting hegemonic domestication to larger social regulations of their masculinity, critics have only begun to adequately theorize the expression of black rage by queer subjects. As E. Patrick Johnson notes in his study of black gay men's appropriations of the home, "Simultaneously included and excluded from its discursive and material reach, 'home' has always been an ambivalent site for black gay men" (79). Both black masculinity and queer sexuality—with shared histories of relentless social regulation—have been viewed as tangential and, in the extreme, paradoxically threatening to domestic protocols; therefore, even as gender stereotypes often locate gay men, always imagined as effeminate, within the domestic sphere, the black gay man can be understood as the most threatening of domestic presences, a potential renegade who comfortably brings his rage home. Link's flight from the Valkills' home can be read as a racial protest against the hegemonic domestication of men during the 1950s, but his escape also highlights sexual insecurities, a discomfort with the sexual ambiguities and tainted masculinities of home. For Bill Hod, Link's work in Mr. Valkill's home suggests a domestication that threatens both the boy's blackness and his heterosexuality. Simply put, it is the kind of work, the kind of space, that will make him queer.

Although *The Narrows* centers on the prohibitive interracial affair between Link and Camilo, Petry's consideration of sexual deviance expands beyond Mr. Valkill's pedophilic advances. Critics, including Nellie McKay and Hilary Holladay, have explored Mamie's and Abbie's contrasting sexualities, Bill Hod's violent anger about Link's visits to the local brothel, and the dangers of interracial desire that frame the novel, yet the queer dimensions have been largely ignored. Mr. Valkill's sexual deviance—doubly signified in that it is homosexual and pedophilic—needs to be read alongside the novel's interracial romance, another sexual taboo increasingly explored by novelists, playwrights, and filmmakers in the 1950s. In 1949, James Baldwin theorized on the "present untouchability" of the homosexual, concluding that "his present debasement and our obsession with him corresponds to the debasement of the relationship between the sexes" ("Preservation" 595). Baldwin's insistence on the necessity of the homosexual for heterosexuality's rearticulation helps illuminate Petry's project, where conventional heterosexuality and femininity are contested or absent at every turn—most prominently in the furtive affair between Link and Camilo, but also in the unconventional marriage of Mamie and Powther and the ambiguous relationship (familial, sapphic) of Abbie and her best friend, Frances. Thus, in *The Narrows*, the white pervert's "ambiguous and terrible position in our society," to use Baldwin's terms ("Preservation" 595), comes to symbolize postwar America's larger discontent and ruptured definitions of race, gender, and desire.

In locating interracial heterosexual desire within a larger terrain of sexual expression, including transgressive forms, Petry affirms the interdependency and, in Eve Kosofsky Sedgwick's words, the "irresolvable instability" of the hetero/homosexual binary (*Epistemology* 10). *The Narrows*, then, draws attention to the slippage between black sexuality specifically and queer sexuality more generally, including their shared history of perceived deviance as unregulated desire outside of white, disciplined heteronormativity. Dyer has argued that "inter-racial heterosexuality threatens the power of whiteness because it breaks the legitimation of whiteness with reference to the white body. For all the appeal to spirit, still, if white bodies are no longer indubitably white bodies, if they can no longer guarantee their own reproduction as white, then the 'natural' basis of their dominion is no longer credible" ("Matter" 25). Through this process, interracial desire threatens the reproduction of whiteness and its myths of unmolested purity and cultural superiority; homosexuality, in turn, threatens the presumed stability of heterosexuality, also imagined as contained. Moreover, Petry's depiction of white perversity is disturbingly linked to interracial pedophilia; in this case, the anxieties of desegregation are inextricable from cultural concerns about children's exposure to social vices. Interracial and queer desires have the potential to disrupt the era's political preoccupation with stability and containment, wreaking havoc on social orders and vulnerable adolescents.

As a writer experimenting in *The Narrows* with a multivoiced narrative outside a social realist structure, Petry was committed to treating interracial romance—the prohibitions against it, the motivations that define it—with psychological complexity rather than sensationalism, and her writing journals offer a fascinating window into her venture into new artistic territory. Creating *The Street*, a process clearly applicable to *The Narrows*, Petry remembered, "I rewrote these chapters again and again, working on the dialogue, the characters, tightening the plot, trying to strengthen the story line" ("Great Secret" 217). Challenging the conventional wisdom that writers should write what they know, Petry advises, "first find out what you know, find out what it means, and then set your imagination to work on it, transforming it, dramatizing it" (216). Rather than being bound by personal experience or even inherited cultural boundaries, the writer necessarily ventures across race, gender, and geography. Petry's writing notebooks for *The Narrows* illustrate her continual revision and acts of imaginative transgression, refining of dialogue and background details, and striving to understand interracial desire and her characters' social risks. For example, the novelist struggled with her characterization of Link, wanting to make sure that he was sufficiently complex ("a believable male—more action than introspection")[14] and that his motivations for pursuing a white woman were plausible. She modeled him after her husband and Carl Offord, both of whom, as Petry's daughter notes, were "veterans and grew up without their mothers" (84). These details suggest the importance of alienation—national and familial—to Petry's characterization of Link. His restless spirit and pain from Abbie's emotional absence texture his pursuit across the color line.

In her notebooks, Petry also lists famous interracial marriages (Walter White and Poppy Cannon, Paul Robeson Jr. and Marilyn Greenberg, Prince Seretse Khama of Bamangwato and Ruth Williams), muses about liberals' objections to such marriages, and sketches out Camilo's psychology and interest in Link. She also contemplates the public sensationalism regarding interracial sex: "Why the alarm—the hysteria—the interference—the public open interference in the form of photographs, reporters, radio—everybody must know—white men can marry Chinese, Indians, Japanese, etc.—let a Negro marry a white woman and the pack is in full cry." Interrogating the power of the taboo, she writes, "interracial marriages, miscegenation (what a term!)—as man is not free, his personal freedom is neither assured or safe as long as at any moment he may brush against, no matter how lightly this greatest of taboos. The taboo is so powerful it effects Negros as well as whites—and frightens both."¹⁵ In arguing that sexual autonomy is central to the practice of social freedom more broadly, Petry reveals the larger stakes of her project and the necessity of an interracial relationship within a plot centered on a young African American man's attempt to claim his own freedoms outside of family and communal expectation.

Petry's reservations about her ability to represent subjectivities and experiences far from her own—Link's attraction to Camilo as literal and symbolic white femininity, for example—go directly to some of the questions that initially motivated this project: Where are the limits of one's own subjectivity, and to what degree can we move aesthetically and psychologically beyond them? What is the value, compulsion, or necessity for writers and ordinary Americans (whoever they are) in the late 1940s and early 1950s to make these intersubjective leaps as part of a social transformation that includes desegregation? This embodying of personhood outside of one's own culturally named gender, race, sexuality, or so forth is an age-old task of the writer, a kind of desegregation of creative consciousness, pushing its limits, but it is a process and artistic challenge that has further resonance in an era when civil rights advocates were trying to locate, as part of a political strategy, a shared cultural identity across these differences.

To represent these shifts of consciousness within desegregated places, Petry employs two dependent and counterintuitive strategies regarding public and private spheres. First, she locates homosexual perversion within the home at a time when popular culture imagined the sexual deviant in the shadowed public of streets and parks and homosexual activists sought visibility and acceptance in less marginalized public places. Second, she takes interracial sex, a taboo subject left in the hush of private talk, and holds it up for public scrutiny. The inversion of Link's entrance into white domesticity (and queer perversion), Camilo engages in several acts of transgressive desegregation within "black places." First, she visits the lively Moonbeam Café, where Link takes her for a drink after their initial meeting on the fog-filled docks, her whiteness implausibly undetected. Through the black clientele's indifference to the interracial couple, Petry reminds us that African Americans have long been accustomed to whites' intrusions into their communal spaces. Later, in her hungry search for Link after their breakup, Camilo goes ritually to The Last Chance, the bar owned by Bill Hod where Link bartends. Camilo's class as much as her race marks her as an intruder in this multiracial working-class bar, whose customers are described as "dockhands and cooks off the barges, hunkies and Swedes and sometimes a foreign nigger off a river tramp" (*Narrows* 299). Again, oblivious to her intrusion, she is publicly treated with indifference, but through characters' private musings,

Petry reveals varied responses to interracial intimacy and these spatial transgressions. "Somebody ought to tell that little white bitch to stay away from here," grumbles Bill Hod (304). "Tell her to go do her huntin' in her own part of town," suggests a regular, Old Man John the Barber (304). Tellingly, the socially uninhibited Mamie is most sympathetic to Camilo's longing and accepting of interracial sex, thinking, "If there is anything I can't stand it's a whole lot of mess about who is sleeping with who as though it made any difference to anybody" (304). Camilo's intrusions into African American establishments, often sanctuaries from the racist mistreatment of the larger segregated world, are tolerated, but when she is discovered in Link's bed—blunt evidence of the desires that motivate these visits to segregated spaces—Abbie passionately ejects her. Camilo has violated a space too private, too beloved.

When Abbie sees the naked Camilo resting her head on Link's chest, the older woman is shocked by the sexual, racial and spatial violation. Indeed, house and bodies are entangled in her fury: "Yellow hair on his chest, his shoulder. A white girl. How dare he? In her house, her house" (*Narrows* 249). The danger of desegregation, the much-debated interracial sexuality it would or would not promote, is distilled here as a domestic trespass. "Yellow hair on my pillowcases, the bridal ones, the ones that I made with my own hands" (250) is the potent symbol of an intrusive whiteness that Abbie cannot banish. She assumes Camilo is a prostitute, for in Abbie's worldview, only a "hussy" (249) would agree to such a transgressive crossing of racial boundaries.

Historically, the division between public and private has been porous for African Americans. Petry's exploration of a purportedly private affair between a black man and a white woman that was repeatedly thwarted by public scrutiny and policing illustrates within an interracial context the falsity of these separate spheres. It is curious, then, to read Petry's deep convictions about privacy in a 1977 letter to her daughter. She attributes her "strong feelings about privacy" to "having been born a female—for generations and generations women had no right to property or privacy—these days Congress, the President, state legislatures are still determined to violate a woman's right to ownership of her body" (Elisabeth Petry 61). The right to privacy, Petry suggests, should be impervious to state control and cultural condemnation and needs to be defended, but she recognizes that this ideal has historically always been corrupted. Petry's observations on the gendered significance of privacy are reflected in Abbie's rage over Camilo's presence in Abbie's home. In the act of tossing her out the door, Abbie is distracted by snippets of her husband's deathbed worries: "The house, Abbie, the house" (*Narrows* 249). Left to step in as the patriarch, she has struggled to find the economic means to maintain the house, but she must also defend it. Interracial sex is seen as a violation of this treasured right of privacy, a traumatic reminder for Abbie that neither her son's desires nor ubiquitous whiteness can be excluded from black domestic space. At a moment when mainstream discussions of civil rights and the state's infringement on them were becoming more audible, the novel offers a unique perspective on the crossroads of sexual and racial freedoms and the rights of privacy.

Void of explicitly sexual scenes to tantalize a 1950s reader, *The Narrows* defines interracial sexuality in the mid-twentieth century as largely a matter of navigating racialized space, concluding that there are few places, domestic or public, that interracial couples can inhabit. Camilo and Link exist as an interracial couple largely within the pseudo-privacy of a Harlem hotel, with its purchased discretion. The hotel room, as I explored in my discussion of Bishop, is a space neither fully private nor public that is intended to accommodate prohibited social practices. Petry's description of the "fifteenth-rate hotel" (*Narrows* 265) in Harlem makes clear the liminal space between public and private that hotels occupy as well as the range of social transgressions such a purchased privacy permits: "The Hotel knowing that these rooms would be used for assignations, for the consummation of illicit relations between males, between females, between males and females, for rape, for seduction, sexes arranged and rearranged, mixed up, mismatched, and so charged Waldorf-astoria prices for thirdrate fourthrate accommodations" (283–84). A site of same-sex desire, interracial sex, sexual violence, and perversion, the hotel represents both an alternative to domestic containment and an escape from the surveillance of public street. Indulging a fantasy of suspended social restrictions, the hotel room exists perversely as the most genuinely desegregated of places.

But it is no utopia. Petry's rendering of Link's growing resentment of Camilo's white privilege is masterful; her nonchalant interactions with black hotel employees, labor that facilitates their sexual affairs (and the racial desires that animate them), are framed within the sexual politics of slavery. Link's discomfort at being sexually objectified, of course, also recalls the predatory desires of Mr. Valkill. In the Harlem hotel, Camilo is described as "friendly and unselfconscious as though all her life she had been looking for men, black men, big black men—plantation bucks (stud) look at his thighs, look at that back, look at his dingle-dangle—as though all her life she had been looking for colored men to whom she was not married, to whom she would never be married because she was married to a nice young white man" (*Narrows* 288). The correlation between the sexual objectification endured by African Americans under slavery and a white woman's fantasy-filled excursions outside of white domesticity and marriage in the 1950s doubles as commentaries on both the racial politics of white liberals and the racial objectification and economies of desire that inevitably, at least for Petry, define those politics. In refusing to see interracial intimacy as solely progressive and liberating, Petry forces her readers to reflect on the uncomfortable history of racialized sexuality that has too often been avoided.

As early as 1945, Langston Hughes lamented the sensationalist turn to interracial sex in literature and Broadway shows of which Petry's *The Narrows* was a part, arguing that it occluded more pressing concerns for African Americans. "When Broadway mixes up sex with the race problem, it makes for good drama, to be sure, but I wish the problem of jobs could be dramatized as excitingly as sex. Most Negroes prefer a good job to a fine white woman," Hughes writes. He then goes on to conclude that "the real arena of the race problem is NOT a bedroom, but economics" (1). But Petry's psychologically attuned scene in the Harlem hotel shows the intimately intertwining of sex and economics. Link's attempt to be a modern man and the freedoms it offers—to sleep with whomever he wants, to make a family in his own way—is circumscribed by a racial history of economic and sexual exploitation that cannot be easily distanced and rejected.

My discussion of *The Narrows* has concentrated on two areas in which Petry explores broader social changes within desegregated public places and the domestic sphere: the growing public discussion of interracial sexuality, and homosexuality as a form of both racial and sexual deviance. *The Narrows* imagines perversion perpetuated by a bohemian white man as a threat not only to familial integrity but, even worse, to Link's heterosexuality and his attendant racial authenticity. This is evident in the fact that, after the sexual advances, Link runs to the Last Chance and the comfort of Bill Hod, the man who "re-educated him on the subject of race" (144), instilling in him a pride about blackness. It is also the place where he made his home as a child after Abbie's neglect.[16] Interracial romance, the second stigmatized topic that the novel addresses as an inevitable outcome of desegregation, is a doomed rather than liberating social act. Given the novel's tragic conclusion, readers are assured that the pace of racial integration would hardly be hasty. But, as her extensive preparatory writing about interracial sex and its prohibitions illustrates, these sexual taboos were as much writing conundrums for Petry as sensationalistic terrain for enticing readers. Despite contemporary critics' assertions that sexual matters were a trendy distraction from African American writers' more pressing critiques of racial and economic injustice, Petry recognized that to document the changes occurring within African American communities—increasingly nonnuclear, nonpatriarchal family arrangements, women entering new professions and social identities, a younger generation both damaged and emboldened by social encounters across race—was an irresistible artistic challenge in which sexuality in its myriad of forms and prohibitions must be addressed.

The Narrows ultimately offers another model of civil rights literature as well as an alternative approach to a Cold War climate of sexual repression. Petry's commentary on domestic privacy and its limits is also an assertion of women's right to sexual autonomy. While Abbie's expulsion of Camilo from her home might be read as part of the older woman's racial and sexual conservatism, which is expressed throughout the novel, she does recognize love in the language of Link's and Camilo's interlocked bodies: "I saw the immorality, the license, the wantonness, but I saw and remembered, just that quickly their bodies, the perfection" (252). Furthermore, her decision at the novel's end to report to the police that Camilo might be in danger, fearing that Bill Hod will seek retribution for Link's murder, is not solely an act of racial betrayal; it is also an act of gender allegiance, across race, insisting on a woman's right to sexual freedom. In expanding civil rights discourse and the desegregationist imaginary to encompass both destructive and affirming forms of interracial intimacy, Petry questions the provincialism of racially insular communities, both black and white, but ultimately suggests that even the most conservative of citizens, including stodgy Abbie Crunch, are capable of moving beyond the charged yet invisible lines of segregated America.

Race Traitor

A counterpoint to the unsettled racial dynamics of Petry's Monmouth can be found in the segregated West Virginia town in which William Demby's debut novel, *Beetlecreek* (1950), is set. Born in Pittsburgh in 1922, Demby moved with his parents to Clarksburg, West Virginia, after high school, a migration from northern city to southern hamlet that mirrors the life of the novel's central character, Johnny Johnson. After military service during World War II in Italy and North Africa, Demby completed his studies at Fisk University, where he studied with poet Robert Hayden. A proponent of experimental writing freed from worn racial tropes, Hayden was a critical influence on Demby's avant-garde experimentation. Hayden's 1948 chapbook, *The Lion and the Archer*, part of the Counterpoise series, which he founded, was illustrated by Demby, who pursued his interest in visual art and jazz music before committing fully to writing. Returning to Italy in 1947, Demby worked as a screenwriter and translator and served as assistant director on Robert Rossellini's *Europe 1950*. Establishing Italy as his main home for the next thirty years, he married writer and translator Lucia Drudi in 1953, and they had one son. His second novel, *The Catacombs* (1965), is set in Italy, and its postmodern collage of newspaper clippings, interracial romantic escapades, and philosophical detours continues to interest critics and puzzle readers with its blurring of fiction and autobiography: Its main character is the expatriate William Demby. Demby returned to the United States and taught at the College of Staten Island from 1969 to 1989. In 1978, he published *Love Song Black*, an oddly humored romance filled with the masculine postures of the 1970s that has received almost no critical attention. Dividing his time between Sag Harbor, New York, and the Italian countryside, he continues to work on a novel tentatively called *King Comus*.[17]

Because of the disparate styles of his novels, Demby's writing has resisted placement within a single literary tradition. *Beetlecreek* is mentioned in critical surveys of the African American novel, along with other postwar narratives that depart from literary naturalism, but most scholarship has focused on the avant-garde qualities of *The Catacombs*. Distinguishing *Beetlecreek* from "assimilationist novels" that completely avoid African American life, Robert Bone locates Demby among postwar writers who "turned to more intensive exploitation of race material for aesthetic ends" (*Negro Novel* 171). Not only does *Beetlecreek*'s existential focus on racial belonging broaden the aesthetic possibilities for conveying racial psychologies in the postwar era, but the novel's attention to sexual longing and cross-race identifications—their origins and their dangers—offers a social commentary on the anxieties of integration, particularly the queer desires that might facilitate it.

The exploration of interracial desire in *Beetlecreek*, more ephemeral than Petry's in *The Narrows*, is folded within an existentialist inquiry into freedom and its impediments, a philosophy of growing popularity among intellectuals, galvanized by Jean Paul Sartre, after World War II. In an era fixated on national security and risks to it, Demby's tale of tentative integration imagines the white pervert as a race traitor, the social and sexual deviant whose identifications and loyalties lie outside of traditional racial protocols. Like many postwar African American writers, Demby attempts a new racial aesthetic, what Sigmund Ro calls "a sensibility relevant to a new age of moral uncertainty and global racial-ethnic integration" (233). Experimenting with the bounds of racial identity and sexual stability, the novelist resituates black subjectivity, asserting it as emblematic of the wider culture's alienation.

Beetlecreek shuttles among the existential emptiness of three characters: Johnny Johnson, a fourteen-year-old African American boy who is visiting his uncle in the small West Virginia town of Beetlecreek; his uncle, David, a man bitter from unrealized artistic aspirations; and Bill Trapp, a white recluse who has lived invisible and undisturbed for fifteen years on the outskirts of the black community. The novel pursues their individual anguishes and attempts to find social connection; the three develop a sense of a shared misery, a Freudian mourning and longing for psychic contentment. Johnny hopes to find a surrogate family—his own mother sick and miles away in Pittsburgh—in a group of rough, adventurous local boys. Bill Trapp recognizes this longing and breaks out of his seclusion to befriend the boy. A shared identification as social outsiders, including a palpably queer attraction that is both familial and spiritual, exists between the older white man and the black adolescent. This tentative bond—rooted in a mutual cross-racial curiosity—is severed when Bill is accused of molestation by a white girl, Pokey, after his interracial picnic, a momentous attempt to break from isolation and facilitate integration in a racially polarized town. As the black community decries the racism in a suspected pervert being left uninvestigated, the adolescent gang, with Johnny, seeks vigilante justice by burning down Trapp's home. At the same time that David is forming a tentative friendship with Trapp, David's college girlfriend, Edith Johnson, the symbol of all the tangible risks not taken, returns to town for her mother's funeral. Her arrival compounds David's discontent with his wife, Mary, whose sole ambition is to be an envied leader in her church community.

Apart from the interracial picnic that Trapp (his name also a spatial metaphor of emotional imprisonment, but he is also a kind of trap for a lost child such as Johnny who is ensnared by the older man's odd ways) organizes, Beetlecreek's color line remains largely impenetrable. The clubhouse of a teenage gang, the Nightriders, the barbershop, and the church festival that Mary eagerly helps to organize are all places of racial homogeneity. In the popular imaginary, barbershops and churches are viewed as sites of racial solace and intraracial fellowship, but Demby is far less romantic. Like Brooks's depictions of the beauty parlor and the dance hall in *Maud Martha*, these social spaces are defined by their exclusions and intracommunal prejudices as much as racial cohesion. The men in the barbershop clearly enjoy the camaraderie of discussing local events, and despite the petty competitive undercurrents, the women of Mary's church are clearly a community. Fundamentally, however, these racially bound places and their occupants, who are suspicious of any encroaching difference, leave David and Johnny feeling estranged from the community and their racial identity within it. Johnny's revelation that "coming from a barber always made him feel ashamed" (*Beetlecreek* 36) explains not only the nakedness he feels after a fresh cut but also the vulnerability felt from the men's interrogation of his origins and association with Bill Trapp. Not unlike the bars frequented by the black residents in Petry's

Monmouth, the regulars at Telrico's tolerate the occasional white customer, including Bill Trapp when he is brought there by David. The confession that nobody thought about the bar's Italian owner, Telrico, "as a white man, but he never forgot it himself" (154) reflects the puzzling fluidity and rigidity of race and its imprint on the town's geography. The relentless murmur at the barbershop and bars about everyone's affairs and this stratified geography emboldens David to leave town with Edith and propels Johnny to find racial community with the Nightriders.

A tale of reverse integration, albeit one that fails, *Beetlecreek* narrates a white man's attempt to find social acceptance and emotional connection within this insular African American community. Rather than focusing on systemic racial oppression, as do many social protest writers, Demby critiques the provincial attitudes and racial biases within the black community, an orientation with pronounced similarities to Petry's commentary on the failures of racial allegiance. In his reading of the novel, Bone argues that "readers experience racism chiefly on the rebound, through the antiwhite sentiments" of the black community (*Negro Novel* 196). Living alongside blacks, more tolerated than accepted, this white protagonist can be viewed as a race traitor, transgressing the social boundaries and the purportedly rigid categories of race. Critic Edward Margolies argues that Trapp is "as much a Negro as the others—a pariah, an outcast, all his life he has known shame and fear and self-contempt" (179). Secluded by personal choice and social necessity, Trapp is segregated from both the white and black communities, but his proximity to African Americans makes his whiteness visible and maligned in ways unknown to most white Americans.

The novel's tension between a rigid racial geography and a certain fluidity of racial identity is further complicated by the author's observation that Bill Trapp "is probably myself . . . the secret self. The persona that I had created for my own consumption was probably someone like that" (interview). In this integrationist moment, the social pariah is a convoluted figure of both racial indeterminacy and sexual deviance, a potent symbol in which the African American intellectual can explore the psychology of difference, the previously unspoken internal creations of self that transgress restrictive public racial and sexual identities. Through these racial and spatial inversions, Demby offers a unique figure through which to comment on Jim Crow customs as well as speculate on routes to refuse them. *Beetlecreek*, however, like Petry's novel, is ultimately a cautionary tale about integration and interracial allegiance. Bill Trapp's desire to reach out to the black community, particularly to Johnny, and host an interracial picnic for the town's children leads to a sex scandal involving a white girl and ultimately to his rejection, not social acceptance. David, Johnny's uncle, had warned Trapp about the picnic and "the danger of interfering with things as they were" (*Beetlecreek* 181). Jim Anderson, in the barbershop, sums up the suspicions of many of the town's residents: "Somethin mighty funny about a white man livin round darkies when he got good places over there in the white part of town. Don't make no sense, must got something up his sleeve" (32–33). In the end, both the white and black communities read Trapp's racial transgressions as a symptom of an even more disturbing sexual deviance; his integrationist urges, they fear, mask sexual motives. Johnny's willingness to spend time with this marginalized figure makes him deviant, even queer, by association.

The banishment of the race traitor—his ghostly absent presence in the collective imagination—as represented in Trapp's seclusion and in the intellectual's necessarily peripheral stance is echoed in *Invisible Man*'s critique of racial allegiance. Ralph Ellison's queer Emerson Jr. betrays familial and racial loyalties when he tells the nameless narrator about the damaging content of Dr. Bledsoe's letters and the campaign against him, an act he says his father would consider "the most extreme treason" (192). Betrayed by his "own," schooled by his grandfather for a life of "treachery" among whites (17), the Invisible Man is befriended by the clearly deviant young Emerson and invited to join the interracial, queer, cosmopolitan jazz world of Club Calamus. The homosexual's ironic quip that Bledsoe's northern contacts were "all loyal Americans" mocks the McCarthy-fueled Cold War paranoia over "sex perverts" in the government, who, as potential objects of blackmail, were seen as "dangerous security risks" ("Federal Vigilance," 3; William White 8).[18] This pervasive federal witch hunt, however, was far from humorous for the gay and lesbian Americans targeted. "Between 1947 and 1950," historian David K. Johnson notes, "1,700 applicants were rejected because of a 'record of homosexuality or other sexual perversion,' more than four times the number of incumbent employees dismissed on similar charges during that period" (167). In the logic of the Cold War, explains Johnson, homosexuality and communism were "perceived as alien subcultures that recruited the psychologically maladjusted to join in immoral behavior" (38). The era's anxieties that impressionable youth, dislocated from their families, would fall prey to the queer perversities of white America are articulated in Valkill's sexual advances, in Emerson Jr.'s coy invitation, and in Trapp's socially unacceptable affection for Johnny.

Bill Trapp's interest in Johnny and physical discomfort around him are disturbing for their ambiguity—as much sexual as paternal. When Johnny, the embodiment of this longed-for blackness, visits the old man, curious after their initial meeting, Trapp rushes to meet the boy and takes his hand, noticeably "nervous and shaky" (*Beetlecreek* 68) Like awkward lovers, "the old man caught Johnny's eyes and Johnny flushed" (69). Their discomfort might be attributed to race; however, the community's suspicions about Trapp, Johnny's awakening sexual identity, and the oft-remarked emotional charge between the two suggests the social awkwardness of interracial intimacy in mid-twentieth-century America and alludes to the possibility of a shared identification as sexual outsiders. Johnny is worried that the gang has "branded him a sissy" (121) for his sensitive ways and for "hanging around old peckerwood" (127), as the boys refer to Trapp. He knows that an accusation of a more menacing queerness might lie behind the boys' cruelty.

Johnny observes that he "felt comfortable, as if he belonged" sitting next to Bill Trapp (70). When looking at "the old white man," he experiences "the feeling of his father's face," a sense he sometimes felt on the street when exchanging "glances with men" (69). The tension between the homoerotic cruising that the description evokes and the familial identification across race that Johnny feels illustrates the psychological ambiguities of integration's queer desires. The fact that Johnny finds comfort in whiteness and identifies it with (black) paternity offers a disturbing and potentially radical commentary on racial belonging, but their connection is further complicated by the possibility of a shared sexual identification, an unspoken queerness each senses in the other. Demby's narrative, however, seems to retreat from this homoerotic layer, noting that the attraction might be spiritual in nature. Johnny sees Trapp, with his white hair and generosity, "like Jesus Christ" and desires to "put his arms around him and hug him and be protected by him, wanted to be contained in the old man's kindness" (125). Here, Trapp's fatherly appeal is translated into a kind of religious fervor.

Despite critics' reluctance to consider the sexual dimensions of Trapp's oddness, his unconventional racial attitudes and awkward bond with Johnny convey a queerness that potentially extends to the homoerotic. Though Demby leaves Trapp's sexuality largely allusive, the figure, whose interest in children cannot escape pedophilic association, embodies the era's concern with the sexual predator. Furthermore, Trapp's characterization as a race traitor aligns him with popular representations of the homosexual in the 1950s—predatory, socially eccentric, and unconventional with regard to racial protocols. Like Ellison's inclusion of the white pervert, Emerson Jr., in *Invisible Man*, a scene that toys with the pedophilic symbolism of Huckleberry Finn and Jim (and parodies Leslie Fiedler's 1948 queer reading of Twain's novel, "'Come Back to the Raft Ag'in, Huck Honey'"), Demby's novel uses pedophilia—both rumored and symbolic—within a larger exploration of familial reconfigurations and sexual difference, major concerns of writing of the 1950s.

Demby appears to welcome the ambiguity between affection and sexual desire in his description of the exchanges between Johnny and Trapp. During his time in Europe during World War II, he observed that the "idealized pederasty of European intellectuals and priests . . . was very much present, both in the film, articles, and the literary and in the aristocrats that you would meet" (interview). He "was conscious of this idealization of boys. And some of it must have crept into *Beetlecreek*" (interview).[19] In this postwar moment, as Demby suggests, long-held racial and sexual taboos were eroding, and the convoluted psychologies of perversion were being documented. A 1965 study of sex offenders, for example, interprets same-sex desire as a form of familial substitution: "Some homosexually inclined males desire young boys not only as sexual objects but as son-surrogates; they need to find some boy to help and tutor, upon whom to lavish affection" (Gebhard et al. 299). Ruptures in domestic life and familial instability were viewed as potential causes of "individual maladjustment," including homosexuality (D'Emilio, "Homosexual Menace" 233). It is, then, no surprise that we find the white pervert in these "fatherless novels"—and orphans appear repeatedly in 1950s texts—as part of a larger exploration of masculinity and the black family. Trapp recalls his shame at being an adopted child, situating his childhood alienation within an emotional connection to blacks as a young adult. Fatherless, he now recognizes a similar longing in Johnny, yet his emotional connection is muddled by erotic undertones.

In *The Narrows* and *Beetlecreek*, homosexuality is rendered as an alien threat not to national security but to the racial security of the black family, already destabilized by the legacy of slavery and the changes in gender and domestic life initiated by World War II. Men such as young Emerson and Bill Trapp who embraced interracial allegiances and expressed no loyalty to their whiteness (and by extension to their nation) and whose sexuality seemed deviant were often branded communist sympathizers. Indeed, in part to justify their relentless screening, monitoring, and removal from the federal government, homosexuals were conceptualized as a subversive mob undermining social norms and political stability. R. G. Waldeck, for example, imagined a collective of homosexuals he called the International, warning, "Welded together by the identity of their forbidden desire, of their strange, sad needs, habits, dangers, not to mention their outrageously fatuous vocabulary, members of the International constitute a world-wide conspiracy against society" (453).[20] This paranoia over a supposed pan-national homosexual cult parallels the increasing worry about international black liberation and anticolonial movements, also imagined as subversive subcultures building alliances across borders. In being aligned with African Americans—historically America's subcitizens whose patriotism also was repeatedly questioned—figures of white perversion embody the perceived social danger of the race traitor, illustrating the slippage between betrayals of race and of nation vigilantly policed by the government and media.

Though critics, from Bone in the 1960s to Robert Washington more recently, have observed the traces of existential philosophy in *Beetlecreek*, few have looked at the specific connections to sexual alienation. The novel's existential concerns are most directly seen in each character's confrontation of the question "Why go on?" The novel connects each stalled life: David's unrealized dream of becoming an artist; Johnny's need for familial attachment and increasingly sexual expression; and Bill Trapp's social isolation. The uniqueness of Demby's approach to existentialism lies in its expansion of the philosophy's racial implications into the interracial and prohibitive relationship between a white man and black boy. Bill and Johnny's companionship, despite differences in age and race, is marked by a shared sense of melancholic loss. Their existential predicament is a struggle to be both racially and sexually free. Bill Trapp's identification with blacks is inextricable from (and in some ways names) his queer demeanor, understood by his disconcerting appearance and twitchy ways. His early memories are rich in both existential and psychoanalytic implications: He connects black Americans to the longed-for comforts of early life, lost objects of racial memory that partly explain his melancholic state. But this identification is complicated when Trapp explains his existence as connected to blacks through a perception of shared shame.

As a young man working for a circus, Bill Trapp first encountered African Americans: "From the slit in the corner of his tent, he would watch them. Even from that distance, he felt close to them. Watching them secretly as he did he could see that they were always dodging something, were ashamed of something just as he was; they were the same breed as he" (*Beetlecreek* 55). In "Existential Dynamics of Theorizing Black Invisibility," Lewis Gordon argues that when the "morphologically white man" tries to define himself in relation to an "inferior Other," an existential crisis inevitably results from such intimacy: "Such 'knowledge' has an impact on who or what he is perceived to be in his totality. His flesh becomes 'black flesh'; his thoughts, 'black thoughts'; his 'presence' a form of absence—white absence" (71).[21] *Beetlecreek* explores these conundrums of racialized existence, extending the epistemological and social interdependencies of black and white identities into the psychological realm. Bill Trapp's existential alienation is framed by the mourning of his lost blackness; his reaching out to Johnny can be understood as an attempt to fill this affective void.

Demby's narrative is radical for the 1950s in that it dislodges whiteness, not unlike Petry's *The Narrows*, from a nebulous universalism by imbuing Trapp with a conflicted racial identity within a largely black social context. These two novels represent forms of white racial subjectivity that are more complex, compelling, and troubling than those in the poems of Elizabeth Bishop and Edwin Denby. In *The Melancholy of Race*, Anne Anlin Cheng usefully considers how the processes of racialization can be illuminated by psychoanalysis, a framework that understands "private desires to be enmeshed in social relations" (27). Trapp's cross-racial identification similarly flutters among desires for social acceptance, familial belonging, and erotic contentment, between the symbolic and the political. His position within the community, simultaneously privileged and marginalized by his whiteness and social oddness, invites new investigations into the groundbreaking theories of racial melancholia explored by Cheng, David Eng and Shinhee Han, and others. In *Beetlecreek*, like other integrationist novels of the 1950s, conventional explanations of assimilation are unsettled, and the causes of racial melancholia are redefined. Bill Trapp, marked by social transgression, is emblematic of a different sort of melancholia, whose "ambivalent identifications," to use Eng's term (1279), with African Americans resonate with shame and fear as well as familial and more subversively erotic longing. In extending Cheng's compelling analysis of "dreams of impossible perfection" (79), symptomatic of racial melancholia in Asian American culture, to Demby's novel, we find a useful illumination of Trapp's equally perverse dream of an impossible blackness. This desire for a counterassimilation into blackness, however, is hampered by charges of sexual impropriety; through this public scandal, Demby pursues the cultural fear that desegregation will expose the libidinal underbelly of race relations.

The circulation of incest and other Freudian narratives of familial rupture with same-sex deviance (overt and symbolic pedophilia) in both *The Narrows* and *Beetlecreek* is troubling, potentially homophobic, terrain. In two different moments, Bill Trapp is conflated with a parental figure. In addition to the scene where Johnny sees his father in the white man's face, his mourning for his mother later merges with an attachment for Bill, described by critic Stephen Knadler as a moment in which "maternal regression is associated with a homosexual longing" (*Fugitive* 165). In an uncanny connection, Link in *The Narrows* also associates the predatory hand of Mr. Valkill with Bill Hod, his surrogate father figure. Exposing the emotional failings of the nuclear family, both young men express a familial yearning that surfaces in an interaction with a white man who is associated with perversion. Without reinforcing compelling Freudian readings of this longing for and ultimately extinguishing of the father figure, we might consider how black male adolescents in both novels, in discovering intimacies outside of kinship and even race, desegregate familial desire. These narratives offer an important political and aesthetic departure at a cultural moment when both the traditional family and racial unity were being heralded. These interracial episodes, marked by queer desire and in white-defined spaces, enact desegregation, but in Link's and Johnny's literal flight from these perverse identifications with the white father, integration is deemed unviable and, in Petry's narrative, a predatory contaminant of emergent black manhood.

While popular explanations held that "broken homes" produced homosexuals, these same perverts also threatened domestic stability. Pedophiles, observes Whiting in his reading of *Lolita*, "disrupted societal conceptions of reproduction, resemblance, and nature. Their infiltration of home and family posed a threat to notions of legitimate social and biological reproduction" ("Strange" 836). However, in Petry's and Demby's novels, such social upheavals are complicated as the familial structures are already nonnormative: Deceased fathers, estranged mothers, surrogate fathers, and extended kinships are themselves "perversions" of the nuclear family. While much of American literature from the 1950s critiques Cold War politics of containment and destabilized family structures, *The Narrows* and *Beetlecreek* suggest that mourning the nuclear family and clamoring for postwar hegemony are misguided desires. Thaddeus Russell notes that the increasing number of nonnormative African American families posed a challenge to the black media, which in the decade following the war often promoted the "norms of heterosexual citizenship" (121) as part of a growing civil rights agenda that initially promoted cultural assimilation.[22] Providing a valuable counternarrative equally committed to social freedom, these novels by Demby and Petry validate fractured families, tenuous racial communities, and familial identifications outside of the biological family and across racial divides.

Such nuanced critiques of the nuclear family have characterized trajectories within the African American literary tradition from its origins. As Hortense Spillers observes, the nonnuclear "African-American domestic unit," unrecognized by the "laws and practices of enslavement," had to be asserted in nineteenth-century African American literary projects intent on reimagining the meanings of family ("Permanent" 249). "In this moment outward from a nuclear centrality, the family has become an extension and inclusion—anyone who preserves life and its callings becomes a member of the family, whose patterns of kinship and resemblance fall into broader meaning," notes Spillers (249). Within explorations of U.S. society's collective alienation in the early Cold War—represented in these novels through cross-race identification and psychological longings, at times sexually ambiguous—queer characters threaten as well as illuminate social possibilities outside of traditional kinship. Although the homosexual has been perceived historically as a threat to familial life rather than an extension of it (the pedophile Mr. Valkill is our most immediate example), one might optimistically see a queer figure such as Bill Trapp, given his identification with African Americans' marginalization and his interracial sympathies, as part of a larger black literary tradition characterized by an expansive vision of kinship and desire—a welcomed queer member of this reimagined familial space.

Queer Initiations

In *Beetlecreek* as well as *The Narrows*, we find a black teenage boy who desires fatherly guidance and equally male affection as he navigates black masculinity in a segregated nation, but he is threatened by the erotic ambiguities and, for Link, outright sexual violations in these encounters across the color line. Eve Kosofsky Sedgwick's inclusion of "innocence/initiation" in her catalog of "definitional binarisms" that emerge from "the now chronic modern crisis of homo/heterosexual definition" (*Epistemology* 11) reminds us that the threat of the worldly homosexual lies partially in his potential to initiate unsuspecting but also curious youths into the perverse practices of homosexuality. In encountering the white pervert, African American teenagers such as Link Williams and Johnny Johnson risk losing sexual innocence, an assumed heterosexual normalcy, and a related sense of racial authenticity and communal belonging. Their attempts to understand their racial identities are inextricable from sexual discoveries, navigations of the body—desiring and being desired.

In his well-known discussion of Huck and Jim in "Twentieth-Century Fiction and the Black Mask of Humanity" (1953), Ralph Ellison characterizes adolescence as "the time of 'great confusion,' during which both individuals and nations flounder between accepting and rejecting the responsibilities of adulthood" (89). Johnny's "vague fear and shame" (229) are in part ambivalence about adulthood's strictures on gender identity, sexual expression, and racial respectability. Prohibitions and cautions about dangerous perversion are foundational to an adolescent's sexual education and initiation into adulthood. When Demby was twelve, he played clarinet in a Works Progress Administration orchestra located on the north side of Pittsburgh: "I had to leave home at sunset, get on a streetcar, and go to the other part of the city and rehearse. But my mother would always tell me, 'If a man sits around you, get up and move'" (interview). The novelist's father refused to let him sing in the Episcopalian choir because the organist was rumored to be "funny" (interview).[23] These recollections echo Weak Knees's warning to Link in *The Narrows*: "Don't you spend no time listenin' to any man who starts sweet talkin' to you. . . . [Y]ou always move off" (394). Such advice forms the cautionary education and its limits that young boys received in navigating the world and its perverts. These warnings are tinted with an anxiety about homosexuality, but they also reveal the ways that young African American men must learn to navigate being the objects of racial desire.

The vulnerability of youth became a pressing social concern after World War II. "Juvenile delinquency," D'Emilio notes, "emerged as a perplexing social problem," and these changes were often used to justify the harassment and arrest of homosexuals who might corrupt youth ("Homosexual Menace" 233).[24] Legislation in some states required attendants in movie theaters to "protect youth" from sexual predators (D'Emilio, "Homosexual Menace" 231). Magazines such as *Ebony* and *Our World* regularly documented changes in adolescent culture—a boom in sexually explicit reading material, increased drug use, and growing sexual experimentation, including interracial sex. An article in the April 1952 issue of *Ebony*, "Society Fails Youth Who Begin Earlier Sex Life," reported that by the age of fifteen, one-tenth of boys had experienced "homosexual approaches from older persons" and two-thirds had seen pornography (86). The same issue of *Ebony* uncovered "clubs" in Chicago and Milwaukee where teenage boys and girls were engaging in "a series of sex orgies, including acts of sodomy and other perversions" with older men, both white and black. Explaining the teens' behavior, the article posits, "Seeking outlets for their teen-age energy, they try different social activities—always seeking new thrills" ("Some Sex Clubs" 84–85). Another article targets the "contemptible charlatans" who lurk near schools and "sell to our youngsters everything from immoral literature to marihuana and dope" ("Peddlers" 30). These reports were often coupled with recommendations to parents to shield children from corrupting influences, supervise social visits between teens, and offer young people wholesome outlets for their inquisitive energy. When Bill Trapp sees Pokey, the young girl who later falsely accuses him of molestation, snooping in an anatomy book and ripping out a page, he remains silent, believing that her actions represent the natural curiosity of youth. But when Pokey's accusations spark the town's campaign against him, the page of the anatomy book, not unlike the supposed corrupting influence of comic books, becomes evidence of the pervert's potential to corrupt young minds.

This growing cultural interest in a transforming youth culture is also reflected in Demby's characterization of the Nightriders. Johnny is attracted to their risk-taking and cool personas as well as intimidated and repulsed by the teenagers' sexual sophistication. When they take him to their shanty and introduce him to pornographic cartoons, he is both disgusted and curious. As he witnesses the other boys subtly masturbating, he is surprised by this introduction to a larger sexual world, having previously viewed his own self-pleasuring as a "secret sin" (*Beetlecreek* 45). The interracial taboo of one of the cartoon images, "Little Orphan Annie in the Embrace of Punjab," with its pedophilic implications, offers transgressive appeal—an image Johnny finds impossible to forget (43). Not only does Demby's inclusion of the image underscore the association of interracial sex with pedophilia as forms of sexual deviance, but comic books were viewed as a corrupting influence on adolescents. Psychologist Fredric Wertham, a key commentator on the psychological damage of segregation in the *Brown v. Board of Education* case, attributed the rise in teenage violence in part to comic books that not uncommonly depicted "sadism, masochism, masturbatory situations, and homoerotic art" (Gilbert 92).[25] Confirming these connections among comics, delinquency, and homosocial practices, the shanty scene reveals the often-unacknowledged sexual and at times perverse dimensions that animate many inductions into adult racial identity. In such moments, the slippages and interdependencies between homo/heterosexual and innocence/initiation are made visible. Accepted by the Nightriders, Johnny is welcomed into a racial community defined by a "safe" homosociality that avoids the threatening homosexual initiation that the white pervert represents. Such accounts in literature and journalism demonstrate a cultural negotiation of changing sexual behavior, constructing teens exposed to these corruptive forces as perverts in the making.

Many otherwise insightful critical discussions of the sexual psychopath as pedophile, including those by Freedman, D'Emilio, and Edelman, have failed to consider adequately the subjectivity of the child, including attendant racial significance, in these social transgressions. Whiting notes that in 1950s legal constructions of the sex offender, "pedophiles and their victims were conceived as fixed categories of erotic identity," with children treated, in his terms, as "nonidentity" ("Strange" 857). For Whiting, such omissions indicate society's "resistance to examining the erotic subjectivity of children" (842). M. Carl Holman's observation, in a review of *Beetlecreek*, that Bill Trapp "learns too late that not all of the young are innocent" (289) offers an implicit challenge to the theorization of the Child found in Lee Edelman's *No Future: Queer Theory and the Death Drive*. Edelman provocatively argues for the radical potential in a queer politics that hedonistically embraces *sinthomo*sexuality, "the site where the fantasy of futurism confronts the insistence of a jouissance that rends it" through an embrace of the death drive (38). As its embodiment, the figure of the *sinthom*osexual, with all his negations, self-destructions, and rejections, argues Edelman, threatens the symbolic Child habitually invoked in the "sentimental futurism" of contemporary politics (48). But such a vision of futurity fails to account for the potential culpability of children and leaves unexplored the racial resonances found in such political rhetoric. Demby portrays children who are not void of sexual agency or blame; Petry, in contrast, reminds us that children can indeed be innocent victims, subject to the sexual and economic exploitation that too often converge in domestic work performed by African Americans in white homes. As these novels point out, invocations of the child, threatened by sexual psychopaths or other queer figures, can never be divorced from racial signifiers. This rhetoric about delinquency and "disadvantaged" youth, at risk for corruption and deviance, still circulates widely in media commentaries about African American teens. Through Petry's and Demby's depictions of adolescent sexuality and white queerness, the rhetoric of the destabilized family and its threatened/threatening child is referenced, reshaped, and refuted.

In Demby's novel, any romanticized future of familial cohesion and racial insularity is threatened as much by the community's juvenile delinquents as by the queer nonproductivity symbolized in Bill Trapp. In the coupling of white perversity with the deviance of black adolescents—trespassing, pornography, arson and existential shame—*Beetlecreek* offers substantive rejections of the sentimental futurism that Edelman critiques, yet both Petry and Demby seem concerned foremost with how perversion, as a more complicated denouncement of social protocols and identities, operates in the actual as much as the symbolic as a practice of racial as much as sexual deviance. Given the characterizations of juvenile delinquency and adolescents' perversions in these novels and their critiques of the black family's sustainability, we might understand the child, emerging into adolescence, not only as the desired object but also as the melancholic symbol of the postwar age. He—and often in the works of Gwendolyn Brooks, she—possesses a sadness that is not dissimilar to the alienation felt by the queer child. These sad, dislocated, nonwhite children upend the standard political rhetoric about postwar America's promising future.

Queer Dislocations

If, as Mia Bay argues, "black ideas about white people are inextricably entwined in [the] history of African-American intellectual resistance to racism" (8), then how do these portraits of white perversion function within larger commentaries on social changes and continued racial oppression in postwar America? When Abbie's dear friend, F. K. Jackson, herself a symbol of unconventional gender, states bluntly, "Mr. Valkill is a pervert, a sexual pervert" (*Narrows* 395), dissolving Abbie's innocence, and when the members of the Women's Missionary Guild of Beetlecreek shudder at newspaper reports of a "torso killer" and rumors of an unearthed child molester "destroying the innocence of the little ones" (*Beetlecreek* 144), history and the imagination collide. Journalistic accounts of the sexual psychopath become an all-too-real presence, a no longer abstract white intrusion into African American communities. Part of literature's power lies in its ability to canvass the intimate desires that animate history, to construct an embodied, aestheticized sexuality absent from most journalism and historical accounts—Mr. Valkill "delicately balancing the cup on his fingertips" (*Narrows* 393) or Bill Trapp's "familiar itchy nervousness" (*Beetlecreek* 9). This poetically rendered white archetype in the black literary imagination speaks to historical changes, including an anxiety about integration, and troubles racial stereotypes and sexual difference in politically useful ways.

Link's flight from Mr. Valkill's sexual advances and refusal to return, like Johnny's rejection of Bill Trapp to join the gang of boys who burn down the old man's house, can be understood as an act of sexual agency, a rejection of (white) perversity, as much as a statement of racial allegiance. Interracial intimacy, Petry's novel suggests, most often will result in exploitation or betrayal. In joining the Nightriders and their attack on Bill Trapp's home, Johnny accepts the segregationist ways of Beetlecreek for the racial and sexual normative security it affords. As Knadler observes, "Johnny had no unencumbered self that could choose his own identity apart from the aims and obligations imposed by his race" (*Fugitive* 166). In his 1950 review of the novel for the *Nation*, Ernest Jones reads Johnny's betrayal of Trapp as "double treachery, to friend and self" (139), underscoring the inadequacy of conservative racial communities for postwar youth and again invoking the Cold War discourse of loyalty and treason. Johnny's loyalty to race ultimately constitutes a betrayal of his interracial sensibilities as well as an implicit rejection of the era's integrationist politics. In a novel whose central concern is an existential investigation of the bounds of freedom, we might find more optimism, as an act of self-determination, in David's choice to leave family and community and join Edith, the woman from his youth who in the immediate symbolizes escape and more broadly his regret about life choices left unpursued. Whether or not we read this escape as a cowardly act, his decision, in contrast to Johnny's, represents a move, however belated, toward a more active self-fashioning that rejects both the obligations and comforts of racial kinship.

Of the novel's seemingly hopeless ending, Demby explained, "I think the only movement in my novels (and the novels I will be working on) will be more and more a trying to understand the relationships between small movements. That is, people think they move in a meaningful way, that they have come to a decision: They get on a bus. That is only movement.... I don't know why people expected that in the novel there should be something resolved.... [H]ope means that you still have options of movement" (O'Brien 4). Demby's interest in small movements as expressions, however mundane, of freedom aligns usefully with my conception of desegregation as not solely the movement of bodies into prohibitive spaces but also the shifts of mind into alien subjectivities and even the movement of a body, with hope, toward another tabooed body. Read as literature of desegregation, the novels and poems examined in this study often render these minor articulations of hope as an integral part of a larger civil rights discourse.

In his discussion of diaspora (a concept of community far more substantive than the fragile allegiances found in the literature explored here), Paul Gilroy posits that "the idea of movement can provide an alternative to the sedentary poetics of either soil or blood. Both communicative technology and older patterns of itinerancy ignored by the human sciences can be used to articulate placeless imaginings of identity" (111). In their attention to places of interracial contact, these novels certainly are interested in depicting postwar identities unmoored from segregated practices and traditional racial communities and family structures. But in depicting the psychological anguish that results from such dislocations, these narratives also question the political and social benefits of "placeless imaginings of identity." In her invocation of a postwar generation of changelings, discussed in the next chapter, novelist Jo Sinclair sees more possibilities for such identities and social movements unhinged from biological and topographical origins; in their shared focus on segregated African American communities beginning to be transformed by major social changes, however, Petry and Demby recognize the comfort and curse such place-bound identities could provide.

The Narrows and *Beetlecreek* confront what Gilroy calls "the disabling assumptions of automatic solidarity" (133), exploring the attraction and risks of attempting to define oneself outside of one's inherited racial community. In exploring cross-race identification and cross-race desire in an era of promised integration, these novels not only highlight the increasing porousness of formerly rigidly segregated places but also treat monoracial kinship and interracial sociality with equal suspicion. Link's restlessness and openness to an interracial affair (violently punished) compound a sense of dislocation that we find mirrored in David's search, now replicated in Johnny, for meaning in the mundane routines of segregated life. Although Link ends his relationship with Camilo because he is uncomfortable with the economic inequities and the gendered inversions it creates, the forces that police this interracial relationship have already been set in motion. In both novels, social critique is rooted not wholly in an indictment of white racism (though it is there) but also in the experience of African American men who seek escape from the oppressiveness—its limited choices, its conservative policing of sexuality—of the black community they have inherited. Both of these novels use encounters, traumatic and pleasurable, with whiteness as defining moments in which African American protagonists assess their loyalty to their racial communities. Figures literally on the edges of these communities, the white pervert and black men's disruptive exchanges with him emphasize the pervasive sense of dislocation felt by many Americans in the early Cold War.

In his essay on Norman Mailer's "White Negro," Whiting concludes that postwar domestic narratives, whether grounded in integrationist or containment ideologies, are "predicated on the systematic exclusion of homosexual relations" ("Stronger" 209) and argues that Mailer's particular depiction of the hipster, with his "vexed interest in homoerotic relations and masculine passivity" (208), complicates both of these narrative models.[26] The relevance of this compelling observation to my reading of the white pervert—an archetype who could be understood as the antithesis of hip—might not be immediately apparent; however, not only do these works by Petry and Demby highlight homoerotic relationships, but their representations of destabilized racial identities, particularly for black male characters, depend on these traumatic encounters with queer whiteness. The white pervert, like the hipster, might broaden conventional understandings of integrationist narratives, but his presence also complicates Whiting's conclusion that such narratives insist on his exclusion. The possibilities of queer kinship—homosexual, interracial, and perversely filial—that the white pervert represents are part of a spectrum of unconventional familial structures so prominently represented in *The Narrows* and *Beetlecreek*. The white pervert, then, might be read as a sort of White Negro (unlike Mailer's version), the sign of queer desire and social alienation that in African American novels of the 1950s is inextricably linked to integrationist impulses, both sexual and racial, and concerns about the meanings of family, race, and freedom. To embrace interracial sociality, to form a self beyond traditional racial communities, is to embrace the perversions associated with desegregationist practices.

The narrative attention to white perversion also highlights the slippage between racial and sexual pathology, showing that popular discourses on sexual deviance contain an often unspoken racial component. The white pervert provided an opportunity for these writers to invert and rupture the tired racial binaries that historically have rendered deviant all forms of black sexuality. They approach sexual pathology—understood at the time in part as homosexuality, pedophilia, and racial impropriety—with important differences. In emphasizing the often unremarked perversion in whiteness, they resituate black masculinity away from whites' stereotypes, aligning the white outsider with the social deviance and unchecked desire historically ascribed to black sexuality. Interracial sexuality in Petry's novel and the nonnormative gender identities in both her work and Demby's are to a degree normalized, while sexual perversion in the form of homosexual expression and pedophilic desire is distanced, embodied in white male characters. In writing the white pervert, these African American novelists dis/re-place the black body as the sign of sexual deviance; one might argue that they perversely move whiteness from center to margin.

Like the gay male writers in Corber's study, Petry and Demby "treated homosexuality as a subversive form of identity that had the potential to disrupt the systems of representation underpinning Cold War consensus," muddling our definitions of both queer writing and the African American postwar novel (*Homosexuality* 3). Though largely pessimistic in their vision of integration's potential, these novelists utilize the white pervert and homosexuality—whether explicit or allusive—as part of their critiques of racial and sexual politics, particularly a conservative nostalgia for traditional families and hegemonic gender identities. While Petry certainly is not exalting Mr. Valkill as a Cold War rebel worthy of emulation, his appearance not only reflects the pervasive "sex panic" but also illustrates the intersection between the era's discourse on threatened youth, the sociological fascination with deviance, and cultural anxieties about race mixing.

Embodying homosexuality and/or queer desires in white characters could be read as a way to distance homosexuality from African American experience; however, Jonathan Dollimore, alerting us to the "paradoxical perverse," has argued that perversion "is very often perceived as at once utterly alien to what it threatens, and yet, mysteriously inherent within it" (121). Though homosexuality is often positioned in opposition to blackness, a "white thing," the white pervert of these novels also serves as a reminder that queerness is also always present within blackness. Put another way, perversion, though utilized to contrast a normative black masculinity, also highlights the incongruities and hegemonic impossibilities of gendered black identities, always contested. Black gay men, argues Robert Reid-Pharr, "represent in modern American literature the reality that there is no normal blackness, no normal masculinity to which the black subject, American or otherwise, might refer" ("Tearing" 103). Similarly, the sexual and racial differences of the white pervert, as seen in these novels by Petry, Demby, and Ellison, highlight the queer instability of all sexual identities both in the middle of the previous century and today.

Along with the other six writers at the center of *Desegregating Desire*, Petry and Demby employ sexuality as an underutilized lens for understanding a range of social changes. In Petry's portrait, Mr. Valkill is unequivocally a pedophile and thus hardly a sympathetic model of homosexuality and sexual difference, but he is a useful figure in a novel that explores the communal restraints on desire and the sexual objectification of black men. Not only do Petry and Demby construct the Other and sexual deviance outside of an African American cultural context, but their turn to perversion allows for an exploration of the precarious position of the African American adolescent, including his coming to understand racial objectification and the limits of his social, including sexual, freedoms. These depictions of white deviance—an act of artistic desegregation—are part of a larger commentary on the increasing diffusion of African American communities previously bound for better or worse by Jim Crow. Segregation in Demby's and Petry's novels operates as a form of self-protection in these intimate yet stratified communities, but this strategy is increasingly vulnerable.

Rather than solely as the man with sticky palms and unnerving leers, ensconced in the shadowy alley, my reparative reading of the white pervert emphasizes his ambiguities—deviant, sympathetically alienated, rebelliously unconventional in matters of race and sex—and his centrality to new forms of social relations. Bill Trapp's existential sadness and his longing for acceptance allows for what José Muñoz has termed "revisionary identification," a nuanced process that includes "the recycling and rethinking of encoded meaning (26, 31)." In his essay on the homosexual as sad young man, Dyer notes that "a stereotype can be complex, varied, intense and contradictory, an image of otherness in which it is still possible to find oneself" ("Coming" 117). As an act of disidentification, the white pervert, then, can be both rejected and embraced. His sexual awkwardness and potential pedophilia make us nervous, but he also remaps racial boundaries, sexual identities, and definitions of family, community, and nation. From a contemporary perspective, I locate sympathy, political utility, lyricism, and a familiar depravity in this figure of deviance. The interracialist or race traitor whose unconventional acts, urges, and racial self-conception are always understood as perverse, instructs us, in our revisiting of this cultural moment, on other, potentially more liberated, ways of being.

In these literary depictions, racial subversion and sexual alienation are emphasized by the white pervert's countercultural urges: the Valkills' bohemian tastes (kimonos and leisurely sunbaths); Emerson Jr.'s love of Club Calamus's "continental flavor," with its interracial, queer decadence; or Bill Trapp's perch on the edges of blackness. Hidden in the office, in the jazz club, in the house on the hill, or on the edges of town in a rundown shack, the white pervert of the 1950s represented the newest anxiety about whites in "black spaces" that were once "safe"—home, family and their symbolic heterosexuality. As Estelle Freedman notes, "From the origins of the concept, the psychopath had been perceived as a drifter, an unemployed man who lived beyond the boundaries of familial and social controls" (204). The white pervert in these novels is deviant not only for his sexual impropriety but also because he violates the spatial boundaries of racial communities. Geographic dislocation is tethered to the queer. According to Demby, "We have always found white people who want to live on the edges of the black community because they feel comfortable there, whether or not the comfort that they feel is spiritual or intellectual. That is, they feel there is something superior about black people because of there being a fallen aristocracy inside African American life and they recognize that or they just want to be comfortable where they don't have to prove anything. They assume that black people are not class conscious" (interview). Echoing incidents of desegregation discussed elsewhere in this book, Mr. Valkill, Camilo Sheffield, and Bill Trapp exemplify racialized bodies in the "wrong" places—other figures in which to consider the meanings and dangers of whites in black locales. Like Bishop's Key West poems and Hurston's Floridian melodrama, the public and domestic places in Petry's and Demby's novels racialize whiteness and remove it from its commonly unremarked location. These novels acknowledge the historical reality that sexual desire has often fueled cross-race encounters and has facilitated as well as prevented the personal and social movements to end segregation.

My purpose in reading African American literary responses to sexual deviance—homosexual identities within the black community and perverse forms of racialized desire expressed by both whites and blacks—is twofold. First, the figure of the white pervert embodies the anxieties of African American communities faced with rapid social changes, particularly racial integration and an increasing candidness about sexual matters, including homosexuality and interracial sex. Second, a focus on white perversion allows postwar readers to critique the sexual conservatism in many African American communities and to question their resistance to these cultural shifts. Centering on the ways that African Americans deal with transgression—whether violence, silence, or shame—Petry and Demby also illuminate the marginal status of the black intellectual, another figure of deviance who by artistic necessity locates herself on the outskirts of the community. The critique of traditional family structures in both of these novels can be read in part as a desire for the black artist to produce her work outside of the often confining expectations of one's racial community, beyond the responsibilities that accompany racial belonging.

Although Petry's and Demby's depictions of the white pervert diverge, both novels document and challenge the era's prevailing homophobia. But they also engage the historical reality that black sexuality and queer sexuality have rarely been treated as distinct entities and cannot be easily bifurcated. These depictions of white perversion and inquiries into white forms of racialized desire have important implications for our understanding of the broader terrain of sexuality in postwar American literature. The interdependency of white perversion, racial treason, and queer kinship is important to a literature that explores desegregation and locates civil rights politics in the spatial, familial, and the sexual of everyday life.

Throughout *Desegregating Desire*, I complicate theories of racialized desire by looking at some of the specific ways whiteness, as an identity and as perverse expression, is represented and articulated in mid-twentieth-century American literature. Whiteness is made visible, as Mason Stokes has argued, through refraction, distorted by integrationist narratives, and compromised during moments of intimate conflict. In *The Narrows* and *Beetlecreek*, whiteness stands in for a range of social deviance. This chapter explores some of the ways that the white pervert, as a complex figure of social deviance, critiques white mythologies about black sexuality, reveals cultural anxieties about the sexual dimensions of integration, and illuminates the fractures within African American communities over sexual difference and interracial sexuality. In similar ways, the articulations of whiteness in Edwin Denby's poetry emerge through their often awkward alignment with blackness, particularly in contrast to Gwendolyn Brooks's experiments with gendered interiorities and desegregated public space.

Chapter 4 continues this inquiry, considering the meanings of whiteness and articulations of racial desire in an interracial as well as intracommunity context. Jo Sinclair's focus in *The Changelings* on the intergenerational conflicts within a Jewish American community and her placement of Jewish identity within a multiethnic neighborhood composed of immigrants from Poland, Italy, and Ireland further affirms the complexities and contradictions of whiteness analyzed in the preceding two chapters. My analysis of Carl Offord's *The Naked Fear* builds on this chapter's exploration of racial and sexual anxieties by looking closely at the phobias and traumatic memories attached to military desegregation and the aftermath of World War II. In this pulp novel, like the texts by Petry and Demby, social dysfunction is aligned with whiteness. This conceptual shift, a wresting away of sexual pathology from its historical associations with blackness, is another ideological strategy that unites much of the literature examined in *Desegregating Desire*.

Damaged Desires

Jo Sinclair, Carl Offord, and the Traumas of Integration

In a 1946 radio interview, Jewish novelist Jo Sinclair, assessing America's social ills in the wake of World War II, explained, "I call them ghettos. There's one named anti-Semitism and one called racial hatred. Any kind of segregation is a ghetto, whether it's mental, spiritual or physical segregation, and of any group, religion or race. The largest ghetto is one of the mind" (Sidney R. Williams).[1] Three years earlier, African American writer Carl Offord also cited the spatial segregation of the ghetto as a symptom of the nation's larger psychological dysfunction, warning, "The ghetto in our midst is like a stagnant pool, periodically a bubbling volcano" ("America's" 12). In evoking the ghetto as a site of desolation, disillusionment, and sublimated anger, Sinclair and Offord link the still-raw history of Jewish imprisonment during World War II to the plight of the urban poor, many of them African Americans, living in segregated, underserved neighborhoods. But within this metaphor, Sinclair also critiques the racist ideologies—the confinement of the mind— that justify such spaces. Offord, too, imagines an affinity between black Americans and European Jews through a shared experience of containment in policed, bounded physical spaces. In a 1943 essay on American fascism, Offord argues, "The pogrom and the ghetto go together and are trade marks of fascism. Here, they're imprinted on Detroit, and in the very existence of ghetto Harlem," both of which had experienced race riots that year ("America's" 11).[2] Sinclair and Offord formulate an integrationist politics as well as an aesthetic rooted in the analogous history of segregation for Jews and African Americans; the desegregationist gestures in their literature are also informed by a mission to psychologically liberate postwar citizens from segregated consciousness. Both writers see the ghetto as a space of segregation and psychological detachment, a sublimation of convoluted emotions—hatred and attraction—that inevitably will erupt.

Building on the transgressions of social spaces discussed in the previous three chapters, this chapter argues that desegregation was as much about the integration of the psyche as the creation of interracial spaces in neighborhoods and homes. Offord's nearly forgotten pulp novel, *The Naked Fear* (1954), and Sinclair's *The Changelings* (1955) depict social change less as reconfiguration of communal places—though their characters certainly traverse color lines—but as moments of psychological transformation, encounters with racial difference in which people develop new forms of social consciousness. Explicating Sinclair's contention that "the spirit can be the most intolerable ghetto of all" (*Seasons* 44), this chapter considers the way ordinary citizens defy racial customs and familial conservatism in literary texts reflective of a new spirit of pluralism and interracial cooperation.

Invoking the ghetto as both a spatial and psychological metaphor in their fiction as well as their journalism, Offord and Sinclair address the tensions and the interconnectedness of black and Jewish histories in postwar America, but they also dramatize the trauma—racial and sexual damage, communal as much as personal—of desegregation in the decade after World War II. In her study of black-Jewish relations, historian Cheryl Lynn Greenberg states that this "interconnectedness of minority concerns was not only an effective political strategy, it was an ethical imperative" (115). In many ways, the ethical imperative—indeed, the psychological interdependencies—that linked Jews and African Americans was inseparable from an artistic imperative for leftist writers, many of whom, like Sinclair and Offord, had roots in the Works Progress Administration (WPA).[3] In his important study of writers influenced by the Left's antifascist activism, including Sinclair and Offord, Wald argues that the era's politically committed art aimed "to restore historical consciousness to the reader by reproducing the forces shaping character, society, and belief" (14). The damages of racism, white supremacy, and fascism documented in the everyday lives of Sinclair's and Offord's characters required both political and psychological remedies. The era's literature about black-Jewish relations often located broader civil rights issues and antifascist sentiments within stories about ruptured families and emotional dislocation. As the literature by Gwendolyn Brooks, Ann Petry, and William Demby discussed earlier suggests, midcentury American literature often imagined desegregation as a traumatic affair.

Examining desegregation as a traumatic phenomenon, both communal and psychosexual, this chapter focuses on Sinclair's *The Changelings* and Offord's *The Naked Fear*, largely forgotten narratives that record a private history of desegregation in the ruptured psyches and shame-tinted experiences of returning soldiers and dispossessed youth. Although *The Changelings* peripherally includes the experience of a veteran, the novel is most concerned with exposing a form of Jewish communal trauma not directly associated with the Holocaust—that is, the struggle of Jewish families to uphold religious traditions within a changing social landscape, including African Americans' attempts to rent housing in a multiethnic Ohio neighborhood. Sinclair's heroine, Judy Vincent, a thirteen-year-old tomboy known simply as Vincent to her gang of friends, learns to navigate her ever-shifting beliefs about race, gender, and religion. In Offord's melodramatic street fiction, depictions of trauma are largely confined to the psychological war wounds of a white veteran, George Sutton, and the violent spats between him and his wife, Amy, after he brings home an abandoned child. Yet larger social forces, including the racial tensions of World War II, inform George's psychological transformation, on which the novel centers.

Segregation's ghettos, whether geographic or psychological, offer a useful lens for understanding an intersecting history of Jewish Americans and African Americans. U.S. race relations of the late 1940s and 1950s, shaped by the discourse of social psychology to which Sinclair alludes, were marked by both clashes and coalitions between African Americans and American Jews. Alternatively viewed as political allies or national threats, the fates of black and Jewish Americans were believed to be deeply intertwined. In 1942, L. D. Reddick conjectured on the origins of anti-Semitism in black communities in the second issue of the short-lived *Negro Quarterly*, edited by Ralph Ellison and Angelo Herndon, a well-known communist organizer who was tried for insurrection in the mid-1930s. The essay called for an alliance between African Americans and Jewish Americans that included "programs of education in terms of each others history and culture" (121). By the 1950s, such proposed political coalitions were condemned as threats to democratic unity. For example, George Kennan, draftsman of the containment doctrine that defined the Cold War, viewed both African Americans and Jews as "potentially subversive, 'maladjusted' groups" whose political loyalties, unlike white Americans, couldn't be taken for granted (Borstelmann 50). This conflation of the communist with the Jew, the homosexual and the Negro, defined this culturally paranoid moment in which various forms of social difference always held the potential for political disloyalty.

World War II proved to be a powerful catalyst for bringing together Jewish and African American organizations in the defense of civil rights. In the years leading up to the war, prominent African American leaders, among them Congressman Adam Clayton Powell Jr., W. E. B. Du Bois, and Walter White, the executive secretary of the National Association for the Advancement of Colored People (NAACP), decried Nazism and increasing anti-Semitism. Yet civil rights leaders remained critical of the lack of a similar indignation from Jewish leaders over the oppressive social conditions experienced daily by African Americans. Initiatives to combat anti-Semitism, such as those directed by the Anti-Defamation League, however, did find alliances with civil rights organizations focused on discrimination against African American soldiers and racial violence at home, including the *Pittsburgh Courier*'s NAACP-backed Double V campaign. Throughout the late 1940s and early 1950s, local chapters of the American Jewish Congress and the NAACP joined broader coalitions to address racial and religious discrimination and advocate on behalf of civil rights legislation on the local and state levels.

Describing the early years of the civil rights movement, Greenberg observes that "among the white organizations it was the Jewish ones that generally proved quickest to recognize the imperative of black civil rights and the necessity for strong coalitions, in part because they more quickly appreciated the danger of racism that Nazism raised" (94). As Greenberg notes, women often stood at the forefront of civil rights activism in both Jewish and African American organizations. The National Council of Jewish Women, for example, had been involved in antilynching measures since the early 1930s (a social issue that Sinclair addressed in her short fiction). Prominent Jewish organizations, including the Anti-Defamation League, also joined with the National Urban League, the NAACP, Catholic organizations, and labor unions to support the continuation of the Fair Employment Practices Commission beyond its wartime framework (Greenberg 96). In 1951, the Leadership Conference on Civil Rights, another coalition of civil rights organizations and labor unions, lobbied without success for a permanent commission and other antidiscrimination legislation.

This shared commitment to social equality that united Jewish Americans and African Americans extended to international politics. In 1948, the NAACP passed a resolution in support of the new state of Israel, and in the same year, the United States abstained from a provision to the Universal Declaration of Human Rights in part because its disputed definition of genocide encompassed the systemic oppression of African Americans. In a 1951 petition, the Civil Rights Congress argued that "segregation and continued racial violence in the United States qualified as acts of genocide" as defined by the Declaration; however, the American government, asserting itself as a defender of democracy against Nazi oppression, refused to address the ongoing racial violence within its own borders as an equally shameful genocide (Sundquist 217).

Despite political coalitions and historical commonalities, the meaning of desegregation and the barriers to integration differed profoundly for African Americans and American Jews. Eric Sundquist argues that the postwar assimilation of Jewish Americans was "comparatively seamless" relative to African Americans' integration, which was "halting and tormented, achieved only after constitutional upheaval, recurrent social disorder, and bloodshed and imprisonment for a number of courageous individuals" (23). Despite these important differences, alliances between African American and Jewish activists were central to civil rights achievements in the two decades after World War II. According to Sundquist, "some 30 percent of northern whites on the Freedom Rides were Jewish, as were up to 90 percent of the civil rights attorneys working in Mississippi during the 1960s." He also acknowledges, however, that many Jewish southerners were indifferent to the harsh Jim Crow restrictions and racial violence faced by African Americans living there (191). As part of their shared struggle for economic and educational equity, African American and Jewish American civil rights workers confronted both a complicated history of Jewish discrimination against black Americans and anti-Semitism within African American communities.

The social upheavals of the civil rights movement were not solely legislative but also communal and psychological. Sinclair and Offord narrate this history of political collaboration and intercommunity conflict not through the lens of public activism but within domestic conflicts from which characters gradually gain a greater social consciousness. "As an interpretation of the past," Kirby Farrell argues, "trauma is a kind of history," and both novelists were interested in the traumatic, psychological impact of interracial social relations (14). Their literary translations of the "damage thesis"—the claim, fundamental to the era's civil rights legislation, that segregation had debilitating psychological effects—demonstrate the ways that citizens' individual traumas facilitated social change and transformed communal consciousness. Traumatic events—prompted in both novels by sexual anxieties—become the spark for a pluralistic vision that Sinclair embodies and champions in the figure of the changeling.

Traumatic Subjects: Writing Black-Jewish Integration

For many writers of the 1950s—black and white alike—an integrationist politics, though later abandoned by many, offered an aesthetic opportunity to escape their respective ethnic and racial pigeonholes. For both Offord and Sinclair, desegregation was not only a literary theme but also an aesthetic risk, a branching out artistically to explore racial experiences outside of their lived experiences. Both blacks and Jews, observes Sundquist, have had "a tense but creative relationship with the mainstream, telling a story of absorption and resistance, of the aspiration to universalism and the retreat into particularism" (12). Not unlike Hurston's narrative displacement of African Americans in *Seraph on the Suwanee*, Sinclair's second novel, *Sing at My Wake* (1951) centers almost exclusively on non-Jewish characters and was perhaps her attempt to circumvent publishing strictures that categorized her solely as a writer of Jewish life. Offord's second novel, which tells the story of a white couple's racial phobias and marital troubles as a pulp fiction, reflects a similar desire to attract a broader readership. Although both Offord and Sinclair composed variations of the "white-life" novel, focused on white protagonists and outside of the conventions of racial protest, their writing still highlights interracial, usually contentious, encounters but focuses on the psychological impact of these confrontations. Both novelists faced a precarious balancing act, insisting on broad human experiences of communal and familial acceptance while still accounting for the fact that characters' struggles were shaped by the intricacies of race, gender, and sexuality.

In 1917, three-year-old Ruth Seid moved with her family from Brooklyn to Cleveland, a city that would become integral to her artistic identity. In the 1930s, after high school, Seid, who adopted the pen name Jo Sinclair, worked for the WPA at the Foreign Language Newspaper Digest, an experience she marked as critical to her political and artistic development. Editing the English translations of newspapers from Cleveland's various ethnic groups, Sinclair learned about Italians, Hungarians, and Spaniards, immigrants who, unlike her Russian parents, longed for their homelands and "seemed to touch two countries at once" (*Seasons* 4). As a publicist for the Red Cross during World War II, she continued to battle her "own wonderful inner war" (8), crafting her debut novel, *Wasteland*. The 1946 Harper Prize–winner startled critics with its candid portrait of a self-loathing Jew and his lesbian sister who turn to psychoanalysis in the hopes of achieving psychic and familial reconciliation. Many of Sinclair's short stories are set in the multiethnic and religiously pluralistic neighborhoods of her beloved Cleveland. The unpublished "I Want to Talk about Privilege," for example, centers on one of her treasured metaphors, the multicultural street, where the synagogue sits in patriotic coexistence with the Catholic and Baptist churches. Other stories, such as "Red Necktie" (1944), explore African Americans' encounters with Jewish immigrants, stressing the social parallels between these marginalized communities.

As a foundation for her broader critique of American politics, Sinclair documented this shared history of discrimination as well as Jewish Americans' mistreatment of black Americans. In 1939, at the start of her career, she published "Cleveland's Negro Problem" in the magazine *Ken*. In the piece, she described the work of the Future Outlook League, an organization that sought to end the discriminatory hiring practices of white businesses with a substantial number of black customers. This economic activism in Cleveland had parallels in Harlem, where members of black political organizations charged that Jewish business owners also engaged in unfair hiring practices and economic exploitation and that Jewish landlords overcharged African American tenants for substandard housing. The "Bronx Slave Market," where middle-class homeowners, often Jewish, went to hire day workers, often black women, encapsulated the interdependencies and tensions between blacks and Jews. As early as 1935, in an article for *The Crisis*, the civil rights activist Ella Baker and Marvel Cooke questioned the exploitation at the "market." In 1941, at the urging of the Anti-Defamation League, the American Jewish Committee, the NAACP, and the Harlem YMCA, two job centers were opened to deter such "street-corner hiring" and to "ensure fair wages" (Greenberg 108–9). Calling it a "stench in the nostrils of the New York and the Nation" (116), Reddick identified the Bronx Slave Market as one of the tense "areas of competition and conflict" between African Americans and Jews (114). Offord, too, included the notorious Bronx strip in his debut novel, *The White Face*: His disillusioned protagonist, Nella Woods, goes looking for employment as a domestic worker there.

Sinclair's personal and artistic interest in African American culture is evident in much of her early fiction and unpublished work. Though often overlooked, she should be read alongside Bucklin Moon and Carson McCullers, white writers identified by Lawrence Jackson as part of a noticeable trend in the 1940s of "imaginative depictions of blacks by white Americans" (153). Elizabeth Bishop's Key West poems might also be read within this trend, but overall they lack the psychological complexity that Jackson asserts that 1940s white writers were increasingly capable of rendering in their African American characters. Bishop often crafted imagistic portraits that depicted Cuban Americans, Brazilians, or African Americans as one-dimensional local color, racial writing that writers such as McCullers and Sinclair sought to avoid in their empathetic characterizations of expansive interior lives. Although her early writing focused on Jewish American experiences, Sinclair was equally interested in African American experiences. Many of her works, including the unpublished play "Sun on Negro Bodies" and "The Color of Rent or Love," a TV play, feature a diverse, interracial cast and embrace an integrationist ethos. Her play *Jesus Is a Dream*, written and revised between 1940 and 1945, for example, is set partially in the True Faith Baptist Church in a black neighborhood of Cleveland. Commissioned by a black arts center, Karamu House, the subject of Sinclair's essay "I, Too, Sing America," the play was never produced. Sinclair, however, remained an ardent supporter of the organization's mission to produce black-themed theater and dance.[4]

In other works, such as "Home in Duh Clouds" and "Songs My Mother Taught Me," Sinclair utilizes, with difficulty, black dialect. When Sinclair submitted "Songs" to *The Crisis* in 1942, she was reminded that a Jewish writer depicting African American lives could present artistic and editorial challenges. Roy Wilkins, the editor of the NAACP journal, accepted Sinclair's piece but expressed concern about the "language, the grammar, and the colloquial expression"; specifically, he questioned the plausibility of the story's narrator, a preacher "who uses English . . . unevenly" but despite this suggestion of a limited formal education is an expert on "Schubert or Handel or German lieder" (letter to Sinclair). Sinclair nevertheless retained the stilted dialect and questionable characterization. These acts of racial ventriloquism return us to Bishop's failures in crafting a convincing racial perspective radically different from her own. Sinclair's work at Karamu House and the WPA allowed for more substantial personal and work relationships with African Americans than Bishop achieved in her interracial relationships, which rarely involved black Americans who were her social equals. Such intimacies, of course, did not ensure artistic accuracy or psychological complexity in Sinclair's cross-race writing. *The Changelings* focuses only minimally on the experience of the African Americans attempting to rent housing in a hostile neighborhood.

Responding to the nation's growing political conservatism, both Offord and Sinclair composed short stories that commented on the compromised U.S. democracy and exposed the country's racist practices as a form of fascism that repeatedly obstructed citizens' promised freedoms. In complementary but certainly more overtly political ways than the writing of Elizabeth Bishop and William Demby, Sinclair's depictions of cross-race encounters and tentative spaces of interracial connection reference the nation's history of segregation and racial oppression. Though she mainly explores the influence of race on intimate relationships, her fiction also stresses the violent expression of racism in Jim Crow America. "Segregation is spiritual lynching," Lillian Smith wrote to the Southern Regional Council in 1944 (qtd. in McKay Jenkins 122), and Sinclair's focus on the vigilante injustice of lynching condemns a spiritually corrupted nation that refuses to confront the fascist elements on the domestic front as well as in wartime conflicts abroad. Sinclair, in fact, wrote several stories about lynching. In her first published story, "Noon Lynching," which appeared in *New Masses* in 1936, school officials coerce a black teenager into a false confession by cruelly pretending to proceed with his lynching. Another short story, "The Girl and the Traffic Light" (1937), in which a young Jewish woman is lynched by a fascist mob with pointed hats reminiscent of the Ku Klux Klan, recalls the real-life 1915 lynching of Leo Frank, a Jewish factory supervisor in Atlanta who despite his likely innocence was convicted and sentenced to death for the murder of a thirteen-year-old employee, Mary Phagen.[5] In "Courtesy of National Dairy Products," which Sinclair formatted as radio broadcast, a community eagerly gathers for the lynching of a black teenager, Jesse Hastings, described as a "boy-killer." The report is interrupted for a milk advertisement that ironically implores listeners to "Keep American youth safe and healthy" (3–4). The reality that the lives of some American youth are expendable while others need special protection underscores the schizophrenic nature of American democracy. In repeatedly evoking the horrific public spectacle of lynching, Sinclair crafts a transcultural narrative of social injustice and racial violence that links black Americans and Jewish Americans as maligned, displaced citizens despite glossing over the essential differences in their histories.[6]

Carl Offord shared Jo Sinclair's proletarian sympathies and interest in America's changing racial landscape, but his experience as an immigrant from the Caribbean and a U.S. Army veteran made his work distinctive from the other postwar writings examined in this project. Born in Trinidad, Offord migrated to the United States in 1929, when he was nineteen. He studied drama and writing at the New School in New York City and began reporting on black culture in the *Crusader News* in the 1930s and remained a journalist and fiction writer through the 1950s. In 1952, he founded African-American Industries, an import company whose mission was "to widen the growing orbit of independent all-Negro business" ("Negro Corp." 31.). Furthering his commitment to African Americans' cultural autonomy, he started his own newspaper, *Black America*, in 1961.[7]

Published in 1943, at the height of the war, Offord's first novel, *The White Face*, gave timely attention to fascist sympathies in Harlem. And, unlike Sinclair's fictional accounts of American anti-Semitism, which remain largely unknown, this debut novel generated critical interest. In her *New York Times* review, Rose Feld notes Offord's attention to "racial psychology" (BR 12), a subject he would explore with even greater melodrama in his second novel, *The Naked Fear* (1954), which focused on the damaged psyches of an embattled white couple.[8] Entering the army the same year that *The White Face* was published, Offord recognized that African Americans' loyalty to the war effort was a source of continual speculation in the popular press and would make a compelling subplot for his novel. As historian Thomas Borstelmann notes, the fear "that African Americans might serve more as a fifth column behind U.S. lines rather than as a loyal force" persisted into the Cold War (82). Both Jewish and black organizations monitored Harlem for fascist activity and anti-Semitic propaganda, fearing that "black communities could be Nazi breeding grounds" (Greenberg 84). Despite its pulpy sensationalism and implausible, often panicked plot, *The White Face* captured these cultural worries.

The novel begins with the flight of the Woods family to the North, a standard plot turn in many African American protest novels, but their struggles to survive in New York City are uniquely shaped by wartime politics and an increasingly anti-Semitic climate. Reeves, the novel's fascist agitator, rallies crowds by tapping into the era's anxiety over interracial sex, declaring that Jews "come to Harlem and they grab your daughters on every goddam corner" (*White Face* 119). He also paints Jews as sexually deviant, calling the practice of circumcision a way to "sleep kosher" (106). Part of Chris Woods's anxiety about his wife working for the Wallmans, the Jewish family that employs Nella from the Bronx Slave Market, is her close proximity to their son, Merve, a lawyer. In fact, when Chris is arrested for attacking Merve, Reeves sparks riots in the Harlem streets by falsely stating that Chris was defending Nella against rape. Such scenarios highlight not only the increasing visibility of Jewish Americans on the shifting racial landscape but also the melodramatic critiques of anti-Semitism sometimes found in stories of integration.

Alongside this novel about northern migration and communal unrest, Offord also commented on African Americans' disillusionment with the war effort in a 1943 editorial in *New Masses*, "America's Ghettos." Witnessing a new insistence among black Americans to extend the antifascist efforts of the war to the home front, Offord writes, "In the roots of Alabama, and Detroit, and Harlem run this new democratic determination of the Negro people. It is there when he strikes back at his attacker. It is there when he smashes Harlem businesses and puts a match to the rat-infested tenements" (12). Explicitly aligning African Americans with the violent oppression faced by Jews in Europe, Offord warns, "Hitler's guerrillas are conscious of this new determination of the Negro and are resolved to down it in fascist violence" (12). The editorial concludes by championing "economic integration" as a solution that both strengthens democracy on the domestic front and deters fascist factions within the United States.

Offord's interest in economic desegregation as an effective response to domestic fascism was part of a larger literary project that understood the internal U.S. racial divisions and economic exploitation in relation to the country's military presence in the Caribbean and West Indies. In between his two novels, Offord published short stories, variously set in America and his native Trinidad. "Low Sky," included in the 1945 collection *Cross Section*, examines the mundane but tender bonds between residents on a Harlem street.[9]

Appearing in *Story* magazine the same year, "So Peaceful in the Country" focuses on Viola, an African American domestic, who leaves her lover, Jim, in the city to work in a white couple's country home. In this tale of traumatic desegregation, the country is rendered as an alien, dislocating space, and Viola misses the familiar comforts of Harlem. Her hungover employer, Mr. Christian, gives her the afternoon off and offers her a swimming lesson. Viola is fascinated by his physical differences as well as frightened by his ambiguous attention and the absence of his wife to curtail it.

Offord's acknowledgement of both the allure of and panic over interracial sexuality recalls Mr. Valkill's disconcerting sexual advances on Link in Ann Petry's *The Narrows*, another scene where sexual transgression (albeit more disturbingly pedophilic) further complicates the racial politics of domestic work. Haunted by Jim's face and unsettled by her employer's aggressive attention, Viola flees, like Link, from the dangerous possibilities imagined in interracial sex. The domestic worker, as we witnessed in the work of Elizabeth Bishop as well as in all of Petry's novels, was a compelling figure for exploring changes in race relations. The presence of the paid employee in the private home demonstrated convincingly the tenuous nature of the lines between public and private citizenry, and Offord's attention to the curiosity across race as well as the exploitation that defined these dynamics demonstrated that social protest art could be extended to publicly invisible sexual politics as well as to the power asymmetries that typified American military presence in his native Trinidad.

Offord was interested in Americans' contentious, intimate encounters across racial, religious, or geographic difference and particularly in the role that World War II played in these encounters. Offord's wartime work with the Negro Port Company offered him a firsthand perspective on the decolonization movements that emerged following the war. The growing anti-imperialist movement sought to strengthen itself through global coalitions, uniting independence movements in Africa with those in Asia. Attending the historic 1955 Afro-Asian conference in Bandung, Indonesia (from which Israel was excluded), Richard Wright argued that black Americans shared with colonial subjects in Africa and Asia a "psychological distance, a feeling that one must regain something lost"—self-respect and autonomy (*White* 7). Wright envisioned a progressive anti-imperialist movement in the United States dedicated to mental health as well as economic and social equality. He characterized a similar 1957 conference in Paris, sponsored by *Présence Africaine*, as "a regrouping of psychological forces for constructive action" (39). Echoing the critiques of colonialism raised by other Caribbean intellectuals, including Frantz Fanon and fellow Trinidadian C. L. R. James, Offord's anticolonial politics aligned with Wright's, linking the oppression of black Americans to military occupations in the Caribbean, fascist movements at home and abroad, and the racial tensions among integrated troops stationed in Europe.

Offord's experiences in the military as well as his childhood in the West Indies informed his short stories "Gentle Native" (1948) and "The Green, Green Grass and a Gun" (1949), which pointedly critiqued the era's colonial and military paternalism. In "Gentle Native," a Trinidadian man swims to an anchored American steamer, rejecting the arrogance of the soldiers he finds there. In this tale, the Americans are the uncultured, unassimilated alien presence, dismissed by the local man for knowing nothing about "knife and fork" dining (11). In "The Green, Green Grass and a Gun," a "native" man (in Offord's parlance) who has lost his required pass is refused access to a beach near an American military barracks. An initially sympathetic "pudgy-faced" soldier grows increasingly hostile and threatens the man with a gun if he does not leave. The escalating tension between Trinidadians and American soldiers is described as a "thing that never sounded itself in words but only in bristling silence and a swift chilling of the air" (40). The local man attempts to challenge this colonial paternalism with its claimed property and contested borders. "This is my land," he protests, "I don't belong anywhere else. I belong here. But what are you-all doing here? Don't you know the war is over?" (43). Despite his vocal critique of military occupation, the Trinidadian man backs down, fearing violence. In referencing his experience as a colonial subject and a soldier, Offord reminds us that segregated places and challenges to them were not civil rights issues confined to the United States. These short stories define desegregation within broader anticolonial movements that the other writers addressed in this volume, with the exception of Zora Neale Hurston, fail to explore. The proletarian sympathies we find in Offord's early works became muted in *The Naked Fear*, a silencing that critics have read in other Cold War texts as a response to the era's censorship and political policing. However, *The Naked Fear*'s focus on an American soldier's difficult reintegration into society affirms Offord's continued interest in racial confrontations and the impact of war on midcentury America.

Decolonization and postwar integration—of returning soldiers, immigrants, and segregated black Americans—were in many ways complementary but also competing social movements. The foundational studies on racial melancholia by David Eng (both alone and with Shinhee Han) and Anne Anlin Cheng as well as Ron Eyerman's work on slavery and cultural trauma have argued convincingly that theories of trauma must account for the historical and racial particularities that produce it. In revealing desegregation as a form of racial and sexual trauma, Sinclair's and Offord's depictions of psychological damage reflect the cultural particularities of the early 1950s, including an emergent anticolonial movement, concerns about shell shock among returning soldiers, and the "damage thesis" that was central to the era's desegregationist legislature. Fanon's theories of alienated consciousness under colonialism spoke to American writers interested in psychoanalysis, among them Offord, Wright, Lillian Smith, and Sinclair, who explored the corollary yet distinct psychological traumas of an American society struggling to move beyond its segregationist history.[10]

Offord's short fiction and Wright's transnational lectures address the psychological impact of the American military on colonized people, but American writers were also interested in the war's impact on wounded returning veterans attempting to assimilate back into American life. The figure of the damaged soldier, for example, appears in Sinclair's unpublished "It Used to Be Called Shell Shock," written in October 1943, and again in Nate, Vincent's brother in *The Changelings*, who returns from the war "so changed, so terribly and mysteriously changed" (144). He disappoints the family by working as a bookie and socializing with gentiles. Like many returning soldiers, Nate represents a new generation of youth who rejected cultural traditions and embraced a newfound interracial world. As critic Laura Dubek notes in her reading of Petry's second novel, *Country Place* (1947), "Countless magazines as well as professional journal articles, books, novels, short stories, movies, government pamphlets, and newspapers focused on the social problems of demobilization" (59). In Truman Capote's 1944 short story "The Shape of Things," a corporal heading home to Virginia with his nerves "all torn up" disturbs diners on the train with his convulsions (18). In Petry's novel, white veteran Johnnie Roane's reacclimation into civilian life is complicated by the sexual and social freedoms claimed by his wife in his absence. The image of the shell-shocked soldier in these literary works reminded readers of war's traumatic legacy, but he also symbolized the broader struggle, experienced equally by American civilians, to acclimate to profound social change. In this moment of desegregation, the soldier's social and psychological barriers made him the overdetermined stand-in for all those unable to integrate into the U.S. mainstream, including African Americans, working-class women, immigrants, and gays and lesbians.

In Arthur Laurents's play, *Home of the Brave* (1946), one of the many "problem pictures" produced after the war, a disabled Jewish veteran struggles to gain his physical independence after returning home. The fact that the character was switched to a black veteran in the 1949 movie version underscores both the public's interest in situating America's racial tensions within the traumas of war and the overlapping and competing status of African Americans and Jews as marginalized populations fighting for social acceptance. In *The Naked Fear*, Offord reversed the formula, transposing shell shock with racial guilt and embodying it in a white veteran.

Offord's decision to focus on the difficult reintegration of a white soldier is curious given the fact that African American soldiers experienced the traumas of battle, harassment, and violence not only overseas but also after returning; in addition, African American servicemen found themselves excluded from many veterans' benefits. Discussing a 1956 comparative study of "psychoneurotic breakdown" in white and black soldiers during World War II, sociologist Arnold M. Rose reported that black soldiers had a higher incidence of precombat psychoneurotic symptoms—"fainting spells, trembling hands, nightmares, or pain in the head"—than did white soldiers (62).[11] The study acknowledged that race, including segregated units led by white officers, affected African American soldiers' mental health; in fact, these findings might lead to the conclusion that the psychological unease reported by black soldiers resulted not solely from persistent experiences with racism in the military but also from hostile social conditions in their civilian lives prior to the stresses of battle. Although the GI Bill's assistance in housing, employment, and education was intended to ease soldiers' reintegration, no single policy could effectively address veterans' psychological troubles. For African American soldiers, many of whom experienced physical violence and social discrimination after returning to the United States, these hardships were compounded. Because of redlining in real estate and with fewer educational institutions available to them, black veterans were excluded from many of the material and social benefits that facilitated the ascent of many working-class men into the middle class.[12]

The psychological traumas of war were paralleled in the social traumas of African Americans, former soldiers and civilians, fighting for educational access and economic equity. The importance of social psychology to these civil rights battles, particularly the 1954 *Brown v. Board of Education* decision, is now well documented. Revising the so-called damage thesis, which argued that contemporary African Americans were not only economically and socially disenfranchised by slavery and its Jim Crow legacy but psychologically injured as well, psychologists such as Kenneth Clark, Mamie Clark, and Fredric Wertham documented the ways that segregationist practices affected both black and white children.[13] Such studies were translated—some say misrepresented—by the plaintiffs of the *Brown* case into arguments of black Americans' learned inferiority under segregated conditions, thus necessitating desegregationist legislation and programs of social integration to remedy these psychological damages and social disparities.[14]

Discussing the importance of social psychology to legal challenges of segregation, Shelly Eversley notes that Ellison's and Wright's literary projects offered a complementary critique of America's "schizophrenic" politics that "celebrates democracy yet denies human equality" (454). According to Eversley, "Like the legal activists fighting segregation," Wright's and Ellison's "emphasis on interiority sought to explode the encrusted assumptions compromising black subjectivity" (457). While less existential than Demby's *Beetlecreek* or Wright's later novels, Sinclair's *The Changelings* and Offord's *The Naked Fear* also redirect the damage thesis to highlight, in concert with Kenneth Clark's research, racism's destructive psychological impact on white as well as black Americans. Located within ideological debates over the accuracy and utility of theorizing blacks as psychologically damaged, these novels acknowledge the ravages of racism while refusing to create a postwar subjectivity (of any race) wholly defined by racial damage. This reconception of racial damage operates as a reverse discourse that does not reify the ideology it seeks to upset; rather, as Judith Halberstam argues, "Its desire for reversal is a desire for transformation" (53). The reversal of the damage thesis, then, provides ways to imagine new identities shaped by trauma as well as to reconceptualize trauma's utility without sentimentalizing the victims of racial discrimination and sexual violence.[15]

The Changelings and *The Naked Fear* offer complementary visions of trauma—though in wildly different forms—that redirect the damage thesis and open up new ways of reading cross-race encounters. These novels can be read within a desegregationist aesthetic in that they universalize trauma while not ignoring its particular and varied racialized forms. Redirecting the pathologizing discourses used historically to subjugate African Americans, these literary texts show the destructive psychological impact of white racism on both white and black Americans. Furthermore, Offord and Sinclair offer versions of trauma focused on the social shifts occurring in the wake of World War II—a Jewish teenager's desire to live a life more expansive than that of her family and neighbors, African Americans' persistence in securing better housing despite humiliating refusals, and a white veteran's attempt to overcome his racial and sexual anxieties.

Trauma in both *The Changelings* and *The Naked Fear* is understood as necessary for social change. One might, in fact, argue that lunch counter sit-ins, mass marches, and Freedom Rides—the signature strategies of the civil rights movement—were acts of resistance intended to produce trauma.

"Nonviolent direct action," as Martin Luther King Jr. explained, "seeks to create such a crisis and foster such a tension that a community which has constantly refused to negotiate is forced to confront the issue" (291). This use of creative tension, forcing whites into traumatic situations, jarred the status quo of racial practices and prompted a public debate about remedies for segregation. Moreover, the fire hoses turned on marching students, the attacking police dogs, and the violent roundups of protesters that have become the iconic images of the civil rights movement suggest the centrality of trauma in the history of American integration not only for activists but also for the resisters. These novels explore the ways trauma productively unsettles the social practices of public, often contested places, including pubs and children's playgrounds as well as the intimate spaces of homes and psyches.

Desegregationist trauma—the violence and anxieties of interracial encounters and tentatively integrated places—was inseparably racial and sexual. The communal and individual traumas within these novels demonstrate the damage that occurs when people defy familial and communal practices of racial, ethnic, or sexual exclusion. In *The Naked Fear*, the animosities between black and white soldiers are rooted in an anxiety regarding interracial sex, and the revenge that a group of black soldiers takes on George Sutton is an act of sexual effacement. Suffering from these war traumas, he gradually distances himself from his wife's racism and hysteria and questions his racial prejudices after his first intimate and meaningful contact with African Americans. In *The Changelings*, Judy Vincent refuses to conform to gender norms, wearing boys' clothes and leading a gang. But when she is sexually attacked for this social nonconformity, an African American teen befriends her, and she enters a larger racially and religiously diverse world. Furthermore, the exile of Judy's sister from her Jewish American community because of her marriage to a Catholic reveals the personal cost of breaking social convention and the necessity of creating new domestic spaces that accommodate these more heterogeneous families. Here, the taboo against interfaith marriages stands in for a larger anxiety about interracial sex that many residents feared an integrated neighborhood would inevitably encourage.

Homeless in the Homeland: "Isn't This Street Like a Palestine to the Black Ones?"

Of all the literary works in this study, *The Changelings*, as its working title, *Now Comes the Black*, makes clear, is most explicitly about social integration: the arrival of the first black residents into an ethnic, working-class neighborhood. Started in the 1930s and published after the horrors of World War II,

Sinclair's novel does not substantially address the Holocaust but instead focuses on the psychological struggles of Jewish immigrants and their children in a diverse multicultural neighborhood. The novel illuminates the intricate fractures within the Jewish community and the complex hierarchies of power that exist between immigrants from different homelands. In imagining Jews as racial oppressors rather than solely as victims, Sinclair departs from conventional post-Holocaust narratives, transposing a Jewish conception of spiritual homelessness onto African Americans' search for a better neighborhood. The idea of a discovered modern Promised Land, a relief from the traumas of transience, resonated for both blacks and Jews. Mr. Levine, one of the residents of East 120th Street, reminds Judy's father, Abe Vincent, "Every man has his dream of a Homeland" (*Changelings* 268), suggesting that the street is a metaphorical Palestine for the African Americans hoping to live there. In many ways, integration is a narrative of tenuous homecoming, a reformulation of domestic and even more intimately psychological spaces. Not only did desegregation alter African Americans' sense of home as they moved from communities of same-race insularity to often hostile or indifferent spaces, but this social reconfiguration also threatened the economic privileges claimed by white Americans under a segregated system.[16]

As the earlier discussion of metaphorical ghettos illustrates, Sinclair employed a variety of spatial metaphors—most notably, the multicultural street—to represent the social changes and sexual traumas occurring within Jewish American communities. In *The Changelings*, East 120th offers a snapshot of mid-twentieth-century America: Jewish business owners, immigrants strategizing their way to the suburbs, and multigenerational Italian families contending with rebellious youth. In Sundquist's words, "A historical way station between the walled enclosures of anti-Semitic Europe and the self-selected, quasi-segregated American suburb, Sinclair's street is the American Jewish ghetto in disintegration, transformed into a 'Palestine to the Black Ones'" (45). Both Offord and Sinclair wrote during a transitional moment when Old World beliefs were being eclipsed by new attitudes about race and sexuality. For example, in Sinclair's novel, idealist Jules Golden criticizes the way the street operates like a proprietary "European village" and challenges his mother to sympathize with African Americans' desire for better living conditions (114). While both Offord and Sinclair contemplate the ways that traditional, racially homogenous homes and communities are altered by desegregation's subtle or pronounced intrusions of racialized bodies, they also assert the social value of symbolic communities not bound by physical borders and racially defined identities.

At the center of *The Changelings* is the interracial friendship that forms between Vincent and Clara, a Catholic African American teenager, whose family hopes to move into the neighborhood.[17] Both girls are discouraged from socializing outside of their race and faith, but after Vincent is sexually attacked by local boys, she and Clara begin a fragile friendship. Vincent's social nonconformity, Sinclair implies, makes her more responsive to others' maligned differences. A kind of gender "changeling," Vincent "had never actually called herself a boy, but neither had she ever thought of herself as one of the girls she despised for their soft, plaintive weakness" (*Changelings* 17). Although the rough, multiethnic gang accepts Judy as "Vincent," a cigarette-smoking tomboy who wears her brother's pants, the onset of puberty threatens her position as leader.

Early in the novel, the neighborhood gang taunts Vincent because of her unconventional gender identity; one teen suggests they search for bodily proof of her sex. The sexual violence and Vincent's resistance are described in disturbing detail: "One pair of hands with the strength of a hundred had her pinned to the ground. Gigantic hands—strangely powerful but still smelling of the Levine kids—were tearing off her blouse, peeling Nate's pants off her, down her thighs, down her legs and past her socks and shoes.... [S]he kicked and buckled against the grabbing weight, cursed like old Vincent, until they had her underpants off. The sensation of unshielded softness was so new and terrifying that she could not move suddenly" (*Changelings* 20). This traumatic act is intended not only to "prove" her gender but also to terrorize her into "returning" to conventional femininity and submissive behaviors. Explicating the social threat that the tomboy poses, critic Karin Quimby explains, "Because the tomboy is unhinged from and in turn unhinges the fiction that gender identity is natural, she in many ways only reveals in the extreme what is true for *all* children: that the possibilities of identification *and* desire are vast, perverse, and ultimately unmanageable" (2). Vincent's gender nonconformity, therefore, can be read within a larger context of social deviance that includes cross-racial identification. Desegregation transgresses racial boundaries but might also dismantle gender binaries. The attack in the Gully reveals the boys' desire to inhabit a managed world where everyone knows their place with regard to race and gender. The assault also marks Vincent's transition to a womanhood in which her adherence to social norms will be more overtly policed.

During the attack, Vincent says a prayer to a "gracious Lord" (*Changelings* 19). Asking for protection not for herself but for those she loves, she says the words faster and faster, as if "reaching for a miracle" (19). In her memoir, Sinclair wrote of finding the prayer in the library as a child. Although it was not from the Jewish tradition, she said it nightly "in case God was listening" (*Sea-*

sons 116). Offering a gendered explanation of the Christian prayer's appeal, Sinclair recounted, "The Jewish God and prayers (Orthodox) belonged to my father, to men and sons, and neither Pa nor the Hebrew made strength for me—or warmth" (116). Sinclair's fusion of religious symbols is another act of cross-cultural identification reflected in a desegregationist aesthetic. In this formulation, Christianity, particularly the Catholicism of *The Changelings*, becomes feminine and comforting—protective against sexual violence and associated for Vincent with her exiled sister's son, Manny, as well as Clara ("How could a *Schwartze* be a Catholic?" [*Changelings* 132]), who gives a St. Anthony medal to Vincent as further protection.

While both the medal and the knife offered after the attack are forms of symbolic masculinity, the two teenage girls connect, despite their racial and religious differences, because of a shared gender experience as maligned teenage girls. Characterized by critic Alan Wald as "proto-lesbian" (239), Clara and Vincent are unconventional tomboys, and the risk of sexual violence as a consequence of their nonconformity prompts a mutual identification as gendered Others. Vincent realizes how alike she and Clara are—not just their tomboy dress but also their "whole inner reflection of pride and arrogance" (*Changelings* 24). In lending the knife to Vincent, Clara takes pleasure in imagining herself as a perpetrator of sexual violence, responding to the historical legacy of black women's sexual subjugation. She explodes, "Why didn't you take your knife and cut off that damn thing they're always talking about?" (22). This intimate, cross-racial act of gender empowerment seeks to counter the shameful feelings connected to sexual abuse and racial oppression.[18]

This transgression occurs in the Gully, the wide-open field that separates East 120th, Vincent's street, from a black-occupied section of town. We are told that "the vastness of the Gully was like an ocean" but that this liminal geography is also "a children's space," apart from adult customs and prejudices (*Changelings* 2). Described as "East 120th's back door," the Gully, too, is an unsanctioned place that, like Dumble Street of Petry's literary geography, is wedged between racial and economic worlds and outside of mainstream visibility (2). Its existence as a space of social suspension, what Wald describes as a "fantasyland" (254) is confirmed when Santina is overhead in the Gully having sex in the clubhouse. Calling her dark-featured boyfriend "Blacky" (*Changelings* 13), she is wrongly thought to be sexually involved with a young African American man, an idea that scandalizes Vincent's neighbors. Through these rumors, this field is confirmed as an extrasocial space where transgressive acts are permitted.

Sinclair uses the tensions within the gang as a microcosm of the transforming neighborhood, where changes "loomed over her tight little, safe world like the black people standing in front of the empties" (*Changelings* 7). Here, sexual violence masks a larger racial anxiety, and the trauma Vincent experiences becomes a troubling catalyst for questioning her community's racial prejudice. Vincent comes to understand the attack as a psychological stripping that "left her mind naked, ready for a different kind of awareness" (103). Through acts of physical and mental desegregation, Vincent becomes increasingly freed from her neighborhood's racially stratified structures. As her father contemplates strategic homelessness, plotting to set fire to his home to finance a move to the suburbs, Vincent considers the possibilities of a life far more expansive than the physical and social boundaries of her home. Her emotional transformation is evident in the erosion of her carefully compartmentalized life: her parents' house, visiting her banished sister, and hanging out with the Gully gang. Succinctly describing the affective impact of desegregation that all eight writers in this study explore, the adolescent notices that "rather suddenly, lately, her worlds had begun jumping out of their boundaries" (12). Indeed, as Elisabeth Sandberg notes, both Sinclair's personal history and her fiction are "marked by displacement" (375). This sense of spiritual homelessness pervades *The Changelings*: Shirley's banishment after her intermarriage; Vincent's inability to fit in with her family's religious and racial conservatism; and the repeated attempts by African American families such as Clara's to find housing despite humiliating rejection.

Ironically, African Americans' literal exclusion from the multiethnic neighborhood of Sinclair's fictional midwestern town mirrors their narrative displacement to the margins of her plot. In the novel's afterword, Johnnetta Cole and Elizabeth Oakes question Sinclair's failure to create African American characters with the same complex interiorities as her other characters. Black characters such as Emma Savannah and her son, Chester, who are significant in earlier drafts disappear from the final version, as does, Sandberg contends (382), a more pronounced lesbian subtext. Sinclair acknowledged the skeletal depiction of African American life and the ways that blackness largely operates symbolically: "The novel, from beginning to end, is crammed with racial fear, yet only one Negro is brought to actual realized form—a teen-age girl whose dreams, groping, and actions throw the entire lie of race."[19] Even the novel's working title, *Now Comes the Black*, suggests that Sinclair's portrait of African American integration is more symbolic than evidential. Her editor, Ed Aswell, wrote to Sinclair that he found an early version of the novel too much of a "sociological treatise" but praised the final version for conveying the sense that racial integration was "a real issue of tremendous importance" in the lives of her characters. Sinclair's comment, however, about the novel being "crammed with racial fear" indicates the ways she wanted to depart from social realism and protest art and move toward a communal portrait focused, like Offord, on the psychological intricacies of racial prejudice. Despite Sinclair's decision to render Clara's family without the nuanced personalities found in the novel's other characters, the author still avoids the stock characterization and clichéd racial imagery found in Bishop's cross-race writing. The portrayal of Clara is compassionate and convincing because Sinclair imagines her with enough details about her religious faith, interests, and family life to make her fully human, unlike the fragmented subjectivity of Bishop's blues singer.

For many Americans in the 1950s, desegregation resituated the racial Other uncomfortably close. Vincent is afraid to walk in black neighborhoods; she "shivered as she pictured herself walking into an all-black street, past a thousand houses with black faces peering from porches, from behind windows" (*Changelings* 138). This expression of racial paranoia imagines an undifferentiated, dangerous blackness conspiring to cause harm. When Vincent goes to visit Clara (one of the few moments in the novel where Sinclair detours into a black cultural space), the white girl's anxiety turns out to be unwarranted. With her "poker face shivering like a loose mask" (240) and her heart beating "thunderous blows into her chest" (241), Vincent identifies with Clara, realizing that this fear is identical to the one she must feel when going to an all-white place.

Clara, too, is conscripted by the town's imaginary racial borders. For her own protection, her family warns of the dangers she will face if she challenges segregated practices. She repeats her parents' warnings to Vincent: "You colored, you stay with colored. Those white folks're waiting to get you. Take anything you got. Hurt you, kill you" (*Changelings* 137). Within this parental advice is an unspoken fear of the sexual violence that often accompanies acts of racial aggression. Integration, many observers feared, might compound rather than remedy this history of intersecting violence. Sinclair stresses not only the physical danger of crossing racial boundaries but the recurrent emotional trauma of pushing against accepted social protocols. For postwar youth who felt trapped by communal prohibitions and desired desegregated places, these dangers had to be faced.

The most racially rebellious teenager in neighborhood is Vincent's friend, Jules Golden, a sickly young man who writes poetic manifestos of an integrated future from his bed. Read as a figure of leftist activism by Wald (254–55), Jules uses poetry to expose "the relationship between racism and self-hatred" (255). His attempts to unsettle the polite racism of his house, however, are not confined to the literary. He enrages his mother by showing their empty flat to a black woman and taunts Mrs. Golden by saying the woman has touched everything—the chairs, the toilet, her daughter's hand. The idea of African Americans intruding into the most private of spaces, the home, paralyzes the woman with anxiety. Unable to fathom her son's identification with African Americans, Mrs. Golden bluntly admits, "I'm afraid of a black face" (*Changelings* 156). Jules angrily responds, "You've got to open up your heart. I have to breathe, that's all I know" (156). But he admits to a larger fear—a fear of dying—and believes somehow that his fevered allegiance to "the Black Ones" (31) will save him. An admirer of Jules's poetic sensibility, Vincent comes to understand the difference between art and life through her interactions with Clara, who describes the racial discrimination her family has faced. Through Vincent's assessment that "this girl had just made the poems real. She had put people's faces in them, and crying and cursing" (130), Sinclair offers a critique of social protest or other literary forms that espouse high-minded political ideals divorced from the real violence and tangible emotions of people disenfranchised by those injustices.

Violence, symbolic and literal, sparked by these racial fears, becomes in Sinclair's and Offord's novels the catalyst that transforms self and family. Vincent, for example, finds the courage to end a racial attack. When an African American man dressed in his Sunday best asks about a vacant flat, Ross, the streetwise son of an Italian family on the block, brutally beats him. Vincent, initially paralyzed like the rest of neighbors by the bloody fight, is compelled to step in after imagining the black man as Clara's father or even her own. While little attention has been paid to the traumas of integration in the everyday lives of many African Americans, the psychological impact of legal segregation, with its daily indignities and routine incidents of physical violence and verbal insult, were lasting and certainly catastrophic. The rhetoric of integration asked African Americans to reconcile this history of racial violence with a newfound intimacy with whites that promised, at least ostensibly, to be less charged. Still, black people who attempted to move into previously all-white neighborhoods were likely to experience a range of racial trauma from feigned indifference to polite refusal to physical violence.[20] Mrs. Golden, Jules's mother mentions the violence in other American cities where African Americans had begun to integrate neighborhoods, including rocks thrown through windows and firebombings. She uses her fear of similar attacks to justify her refusal to rent to African American tenants.

"The burden of exile, their 'certain homelessness in the world' passed on generation to generation," Sundquist asserts, "was accentuated for Jews and blacks alike by their common heritage of racist violence" (26–27). In illuminating intergenerational trauma and inherited dislocation, both Sinclair and Offord insist that the racial traumas of America's postwar desegregation often are inextricably sexual traumas as well. In *The Changelings*, Ruth Miller, another resident of East 120th Street, witnesses Ross's brutal attack on the African American man; the violence triggers a memory of watching anti-Semitic peasants with "rocks and heavy chunks of wood in their hands that sunny afternoon" as they attacked her brother in the Hungarian village of their youth. Once again that "tiny frightened girl," Ruth conflates the two racially charged incidents (235). In this moment of traumatic recollection, Ruth also returns to a memory of being called *kurveh*, a whore, throughout her teenage years as she "struggled to get away from the clinging hands, the heavy body" of her molesting father (166). This overlapping sexual and racial violence is treated as a kind of shameful cultural inheritance. Emotional and sexual abuse are passed on from generation to generation, connecting the women in this novel—both Jewish and black—to a legacy of gendered violence and shame resulting from war, immigration, and women's social and sexual disempowerment. Vincent, we are told, "sensed the long moment between the generation, the hurt of it, the way it could go on endlessly, like a clock stopped by a senseless, groping hand" (181). Her family's experience with anti-Semitism as well as resistance to it are part of this hidden history of hurt, and the sexual attack Vincent experiences in the Gully links her viscerally to Ruth and to persistent gendered violence. The molestation evoked in this temporal image of the stopped clock appropriately yokes a legacy of racial damage to the traumatic sexual histories that defined postwar life for some Jewish American women.

Sinclair's exploration of desegregation is the most literal of the writers treated in this study: the arrival of the first African American families in a multiethnic neighborhood. However, in also exploring cultural assimilation, most pointedly represented in the marriage of Shirley, Vincent's sister, to an Irish Catholic, a central conflict in the novel, Sinclair critiques rifts fostered by interfaith marriage and younger residents' willingness to leave family businesses and cultural traditions that were often preserved through chosen physical isolation from middle America. Her writing extends desegregation outside of the white/black binary as a religious and cultural issue for Jewish Americans navigating assimilation into white institutions and intercultural families. Vincent, for example, understands but cannot speak Yiddish. Identifying racial integration as the first level of the narrative, Sinclair's artist statement for *The Changelings* explains the connection between the preservation of Jewish identity and desegregation: "On the second level, the book digs into relationships between parents and children, and lights up blindly repeated patterns clamped by one generation upon another. The threat of the

Negro is the psychological sword that shears open personalities and hearts."[21] Sinclair's reference to "repeated patterns" confirms her interest in the inherited traumas that the novel exposes as well as the cultural traditions that the younger generation increasingly rejects.

Interfaith marriage, as with interracial sex, was viewed as an inevitable and for some Jewish Americans dreaded outcome of assimilation. The Jewish community's resistance to racial integration in Sinclair's novel reveals an anxiety about changing social customs as well as a fear that mixed marriages would threaten religious traditions and community cohesion. Shirley is expelled from the family after she marries an Irish Catholic, and her devout grandmother refuses to acknowledge her great-grandson, Emmanuel O'Brien, whose hybrid name symbolizes the cultural contamination that the elderly woman fears. Vincent recognizes that for her grandmother "Manny was an enemy, like a *Schwartze*" (*Changelings* 101), seeing the connection between religious and racial prejudice that Sinclair is intent on exposing.[22] As sites of trauma, both desegregation and religious intermarriage were defined by "forbidden tastes" (38) and exemplified a changing American social landscape that this community of immigrants was reluctant to embrace. Indeed, the placelessness that Vincent, Shirley, and Clara feel is not unconnected to the larger postwar cultural dispersals that this younger generation must navigate to shape previously unimagined identities within their respective diasporas.

The Changelings in many ways records an affective American history, extending Richard Wright's idea of a psychology of loss to address the gender oppression in America's multiethnic communities that is missing in his formulation.[23] When Vincent's mother shows her the family Bible, with generations of names written in it, including those of her mother's brothers and sisters as well as their children, "all murdered by Hitler" (*Changelings* 186), her daughter notices that her and her siblings' names are absent. "In America the habits are different," her mother explains (186). Although this family tradition and its implied historical record of religious oppression ended with American assimilation, the trauma still continues. Vincent, then, begins to question why the private histories of race and sexuality are left unrecorded. Through much of the novel, Vincent struggles with these generational rifts, maintaining a relationship with her sister and eventually introducing Manny to his grandfather. When she defiantly adds Manny's name to the family Bible, along with his mother's and her own, Vincent not only writes them into a Jewish legacy that extends back to the Old World but also asserts a contemporary family history that is particularly American, a community that extends across religion, ethnicity, and in her mind race. In fact, she associates her first black friend, Clara, also Catholic, with her nephew, imagining an integrated family where "Manny and Clara stood close as a brother and sister" (133). Vincent attributes the intimacy she feels for Clara to Manny and tellingly describes it as a "queer closeness" (133). This hint of homoeroticism underscores the fact that new postwar identities, created from a merging of cultural influences, also ushered in forms of sexual expression previously hidden from public life.

The Changelings is ultimately a Jewish novel where African Americans' reactions to the hostilities of desegregation hover at the margins. Still, by focusing on Vincent's rejection of her family's prejudices against African Americans and interreligious marriages, the novel powerfully illustrates segregation's damaging effects, including the emotional and social alienation experienced by postwar adolescents, white and black. As a victim of a sexual assault, a witness to the violent attack of a black man, and a member of a changing religious community, Vincent has personal experiences that exemplify larger shifts in Americans' attitudes about gender, race, and religion. Sinclair labeled the postwar generation navigating these social traumas "changelings," figures of a desegregated future who, like the folk shape-shifter for which they were named, found themselves in alien homes and recognized in themselves alien desires.

Desegregation's Secrets and Scars

The sense of placelessness and spiritual dislocation experienced by Sinclair's protagonist in *The Changelings* was evoked in much of the African American literature of the 1940s and 1950s, including Offord's work. In his short stories, native Trinidadians are disrupted and displaced by military occupation, and the main characters of his novels, both white and black, are outlaws who are repeatedly expelled, fleeing from violence or the threat of the law and in search of safe havens. Home in the wake of war had become a strained place defined by the overlapping feelings of racial estrangement and spiritual dislocation. Offord's last novel, *The Naked Fear*, like William Demby's *Beetlecreek*, is a tale of reverse integration, with all its ironies and complex cross-race identifications. A white man discovers a sense of home and psychological resolution through his symbolic integration into an African American family.

A case study of racial trauma, *The Naked Fear* diverts the dominant narrative of black pathology onto George Sutton, a white veteran who mysteriously suffers from amnesia and collapses at the sight of blood and black people. After George finds a child abandoned in a city lot, he hides out in Harlem with his wife, Amy, fearing that they will be linked to a high-profile kidnapping case. Because of a housing shortage in New York City and despite George's racial phobia, they are forced to rent a room from the Joneses, a sympathetic African American family whose members gradually become intolerant of the couple's constant, violent fights. After their plan to garner ransom money fails, Amy maniacally shifts between tender caretaker and enraged vixen and tries to poison the baby in jealousy. Identifying with the social vulnerability that the orphaned baby symbolizes, George laments, "there just wasn't enough love for all the poor, little, wonderful, marvelous children" (*Naked Fear* 29). Already rescued from a near-fatal illness, the child, whom they have called Sue, is saved again by Ma Quilly, the religiously armored matriarch of the Jones family. This mammy figure, who rescues with folk remedies, stoic resilience, and prayers, is one of the many stock characters—among them the femme fatale, misogynistic brute, and the selfless wife—on which Offord and the pulp genre depend.

Rather than return to the conventions of social protest used in his first novel, Offord employs pulp fiction to explore racial trauma in troubled whites. The Suttons are transient, unethical, and psychologically troubled and live in sharp contrast to the generous, protective, and stable African American family. In Ma Quilly's worldview, white racists "fear a black skin like the devil fears the name of the Lord" (*Naked Fear* 85), an analogy that not only equates whites with the devil but elevates blacks to a Christlike piety. Ultimately, it is George's interactions with the members of the Jones family—their repeated concern for his child despite racist comments from Amy—that, as Ma Quilly might put it, save him, helping him to overcome his racial trauma and question his racism.

This symbolic integration into the domestic space of an African American family helps George renounce Amy's racism and leave her, pledging to care for his daughter and regain his wounded masculinity. The couple's retreat into the back room of a Harlem basement apartment recalls the hibernation of Ellison's Invisible Man as well as several of Wright's protagonists who recede into the underground. When he first enters their rented room, George calls it a "hole" and observes, "Feels like we're cut off from the outside world" (*Naked Fear* 67). For Amy and George, this retreat into blackness is also a psychological unsettling of whiteness. As with *Beetlecreek*'s Bill Trapp, white people living in proximity to blacks is read as a sign of social deviance. Fearing the police, Amy recognizes that their trespassing of racial boundaries will draw attention, noting, "the fact that she shared the basement dump with Negroes would be enough to cause suspicion in the average person" (82). The couple's transience and ambivalent presence on the edges of an African

American community offers another example of ruptured domesticity traced throughout *Desegregating Desire*.

Amy's paranoia couples with George's racial phobia to provide the psychological suspense readers expect in a pulp thriller. Less restricted than the Hollywood film industry of the 1950s, pulp fiction, notes Woody Haut, represented "paranoia as both a social and a psychological phenomenon" (17) and thereby offered a sly commentary on Cold War censorship. This cultural paranoia, including concern that social ills would erode family stability, often encompassed "a sexual anxiety based on fears concerning women and homosexuality" (17); Offord's portrayals of women betray this anxiety. His largely misogynistic and one-dimensional characterizations warrant a larger feminist inquiry than can be offered here, but in an era anxious about women's empowerment, the male protagonists in both of his novels exhibit an explosive anger at their wives, often trying unsuccessfully to suppress their violent urges. Amy is depicted as a volatile femme fatale—nagging, often hysterical, obsessive, and ultimately emasculating. In the fury of one of their many arguments, Amy taunts, "Choke Me!... Think you're well, don't you? Think you're a man now don't you?" (25). George repeatedly attempts to prove his suspect manhood by trying to strangle Amy into silence. In one scene, his hands, as if beyond his control, are described as "itching to fly at her bare throat" (25). When he discovers that Amy has tried to kill the baby, George nearly beats her to death, but after he sees her slumped over and bloody, he regrets his actions and begins to care for her. The couple perversely repeats this cycle of escalating aggression followed by tender nurturance; their sadomasochistic relationship recalls Hurston's equally troublesome portrait of marital dysfunction in *Seraph on the Suwanee*.

Much of the tension in *The Naked Fear* resides in Amy's ambivalence about George's inability to be a "complete" man; at times she is attracted to his frailty—the back cover announces, "Amy Liked Her Men Weak"—but she then insults George for not defending her from Slim, the leering janitor who calls Amy's man a "queer duck" (62). George cannot satisfy Amy sexually; when he cuddles with her but is unable to go further, Amy declares, "I need more. I'm dried up for something more. More real man. This is half-stuff" (41). Amy's aggressive sexual advances begin to fill George with dread, and he begrudgingly follows her to bed, "feeling trapped" (39). His fainting and bouts of hysteria also affirm his suspect masculinity. When some brash, young women at the movie theater where George works corner him and forcefully strip him, they discover his sexual disfigurement. Seeing that "George's waist to his thighs his milk-white body was a snarled mass of shining chop-chop scars" (132), the girls conclude that he is physically incomplete and therefore not a real man.[24]

These portraits of conniving, predatory white women stand in sharp contrast to the compassionate, respectable African American women in Offord's novel, and together they offer a spectrum of gender identities, problematically racialized, that can be positioned as an instructive counterpoint to the disparate representations of black masculinity in Petry's *The Narrows*. In these novels as well as *The Changelings*, we find writers articulating Cold War anxieties regarding the loss of traditional gender roles through depictions of nonnuclear family structures that deviate from social norms but ultimately provide emotional refuge. The era's changing ideas and practices regarding gender and sexuality challenged heteronormative concepts of family. George's decision to raise his adopted daughter on his own and his acceptance within a multigenerational African American household hint at new models of kinship and domestic space also envisioned by Sinclair in *The Changelings*. The potential radicalism of Offord's narrative, however, is compromised by its gender and racial stereotypes, such as those found in the characters of Amy and Ma Quilly.

The Naked Fear's atmosphere of cultural paranoia extends beyond domestic anxieties about gender and sexuality to include the racial fears of Americans confronting social upheavals and integrationist legislation after the war. With George Sutton's racial phobia—he at times urinates at the sight of black people—the most heavy-handed example, both *The Naked Fear* and *The Changelings* are invested in capturing the psychology of racial fear to dismiss the irrational anxieties about blackness that often lay at the heart of white people's resistance to integration. Amy tries to protect George, even cutting out images of African Americans from magazines to avoid triggering another breakdown, but she holds her own stereotypes about black people. Alleviating her fears about moving to Harlem, she reminds herself that "colored people" "possess a certain simple quality of kindness" in addition to being "terrific dancers" who "could sing like mad" (*Naked Fear* 52). She later finds herself flirting with Sam, her landlord's war-damaged brother, and her revulsion at his blackness quickly turns to sexual passion. Sam offers her a necklace (which he claims to have received from a white woman as payment for her sexual curiosity) in exchange for the permission to kiss her feet. Fetishizing white femininity, he professes, "Only a white woman could look so good," "like a queen in the movies" (109). The scene emphasizes the sublimation of erotic attraction within racial fear. These nuances of racial identification and the complexities of desire, moments where revulsion and longing converge, are central to the affective terrain of both Offord's and Sinclair's novels.

The pulp packaging and, to be blunt, mediocre writing of *The Naked Fear* masks the novel's radicalism but ensured its critical neglect.[25] Nevertheless, more than any other writer examined in *Desegregating Desire*, Offord directly confronts two critical issues of the era: the difficult assimilation of returning veterans into American society and many white Americans' pronounced though politely avoided fear of black Americans' gradual integration into workplaces and schools. Offord also subtly explores cross-race attraction, the specter that most conservatives and many liberals felt lurked under integrationist reforms. Amy accuses George of lusting after Justine, Ben Jones's wife, which George flatly denies; later, however when his racial prejudice has begun to lessen, he admires Justine's "trim figure snugly waisted in a house print" and admits to himself that "in their own way colored women were good looking" (*Naked Fear* 143). Through the flirtations between Amy and Sam, Offord offers a more sensationalized portrait of interracial desire. Represented as cognitively damaged, Sam commits a sexual transgression that is explained by his disability, but Amy is reluctantly aroused by his erotic attention and later manipulates his desire to get his help in her scheme to trick George. Providing this undercurrent of interracial desire, Offord indulges in the taboo sexual thrills expected of pulp, but he also treats these exchanges with a straightforward nonchalance that argues for the normalcy of these "perversions," questioning the necessity of complex psychological explanations of interracial attraction of the sort offered by Petry in *The Narrows*.

Offord saves his most forceful social critique for the novel's end, when the cause of George's racial phobia (the only compelling suspense in the plot) is revealed. We learn that George's racial anxieties and sexual disfigurement are the results of a wartime incident with African American soldiers directly related to the era's anxiety about integration. When black GIs stationed in England begin to "josh and smooch with the rosy-cheeked barmaids" in the Bristol pubs, the white soldiers, unaccustomed to overt expressions of interracial desire, begin to randomly attack black soldiers (*Naked Fear* 151). Later, a white soldier, Red, with George in the jeep, purposely runs over an injured black GI lying in the road. A group of black soldiers witnesses the heartless act and viciously retaliates by attacking George and Red. The repressed memory of black soldiers with "knives flashing in their hands" (156) resurfaces in George as a phobia of black people, a wartime memory defined by sexual trauma and racial shame.

For the white soldiers in Offord's story, black masculinity is threatening, unbounded and encroaching on a white femininity in a way that was previously prohibited. After being attacked, George fears both sexually forward women, such as Amy and the delinquent girls at the movie theater, and the

African Americans he encounters, particularly black men, who represent for him an aggressive sexuality, a corporeal completeness, now unavailable to him. George's guilt about his complicity in the black GI's death as well as his shame at his disfigured body translate into a racial phobia that, as Lillian Smith argues, is inseparable from sexual anxieties. George's "naked fear" is in actuality a form of projected shame, a phobia that occludes the guilt of the wartime attack and is channeled into a fear of and desire for black masculinity. The revulsion felt in these interracial encounters is a perverse form of identification, like that in *The Narrows* and Elizabeth Bishop's poetry, and is a critical component of desegregationist literature's goal of dissecting the racist psychologies that undergirded segregation.

Offord's portrait of racial trauma has striking parallels to a wartime incident of interracial violence in Bamber Bridge, Lancashire. On 24 June 1943, white military policemen came to a pub in the town to arrest black soldiers, ostensibly for disorderly conduct but likely because they were socializing with white women, a scenario that often rankled white MPs. When white residents came to the defense of the black GIs, white and black soldiers fought violently for several hours (Borstelmann 35). Such tensions in large part constituted a patriarchal showdown over white women as sexual possessions. Historian Thomas Borstelmann explains that "many white American males were determined to export their definition of racially appropriate socializing, seeing themselves as protectors of white womanhood in England just as at home, where most states in the South and West banned interracial marriages" (33). Witnessing British women's unfamiliar acceptance of and even sexual desire for African American men, many white U.S. soldiers sought to discipline black soldiers into returning to the (at least publicly) segregated sexual practices of the United States.

More expansive than Sinclair's depictions, sexual trauma in *The Naked Fear* is always located within interracial confrontation. The heavy-handed symbolism of George's "naked fear" suggests an unmasked, primal anxiety about blacks as well as a panic over bodily exposure, his actual genital scars revealed. Through this concrete evidence of psychological wounds and interracial hostility, Offord alerts us to the sexual dimensions of war trauma and the slippage between racial and sexual phobia. Again, as with Demby and Petry, the discourses of racial damage and pathology are redirected onto white characters, a desegregationist strategy that unsettles calcified racial and racist associations. Fully aware of America's tradition of vigilante justice, in which black men were regularly lynched for purported sexual violations of white women, Offord foregrounds the castration that often accompanied such lynchings and its homoerotic implications. He writes a revenge scenario, reminiscent of Clara's fantasy of using her knife against the gang of boys, in which inversely the white phallus is pursued and destroyed. The violent altercation in essence feminizes George, but it also offers a subversive vision of black retaliatory agency. Indeed, the larger narrative could be read as a form of wish fulfillment: a castrated white man at the mercy of black people in the urban ghetto. These revisions of clichéd racial scenarios signal another way that desegregationist literature employed sexuality to comment on social issues—in this case, the resisted integration of the military in World War II and, though sensationally rendered as a phobia, white Americans' fears of African Americans and race liberals' pressing need to confront these fears.

Offord's turn to melodramatic pulp to contemplate the war's legacy is a curious one, an aesthetic choice markedly different from the multifamily "social problem" narrative of *The Changelings*. Wald attributes both Offord's and Sinclair's move away from urban protest in these later novels to the silencing effect of the Cold War. This political climate of censorship intersected with an aesthetic climate and particularly a popular interest in social psychology and psychoanalysis that propelled postwar writers to experiment with new depictions of racial identities and social issues, including mixed marriages and interracial sexuality. In crafting a domestic drama and pulp thriller, respectively, Sinclair and Offord argued that individual citizens' psychological upheavals were as important in advancing social change as were public demonstrations. Furthermore, with conclusions emphasizing psychological healing and interracial dependency, these novels offer cultural narratives of mid-twentieth-century American identity that do not depend solely on metaphors of domestic containment and social division.

In the 1960s, critic Robert Bone argued that postwar novelists who sought to write outside of the protest tradition largely embraced one of three aesthetic options—pulp fiction, the assimilationist novel (which avoids racial material), or a novel that pursued "an intensive exploration of racial material" (distinct from racial conflict) but also attempted to break new aesthetic ground (*Negro Novel* 171).[26] Critical of the "escapist" impulses in pulp, a genre that traditionally "poses no problem concerning race" (166), Bone overlooks writers such as Offord who revise the popular form to address racial issues while still employing the genre's heightened suspense and sexual thrills. *The Naked Fear* in many ways elides Bone's taxonomy of the postwar African American novel. Pulp fiction, with its attention to the seedy underworld of crime, sexualized violence, and psychological suspense, offered Offord an ideal genre for exploring white America's racial and sexual pathologies. In applying the consciousness-raising imperative of the social protest novel to pulp fiction, he replaces a heavy-handed critique of racial politics in the U.S.

military with a portrait of a white veteran's psychological terror. Offord's interest in extending the idea of racial damage to explore the impact of racism on whites themselves and the confrontation of race-based fears precisely captures the political currents and aesthetic experimentation of this desegregationist moment. Though regarded as a failed novel, completely ignored by critics, *The Naked Fear* is a hybrid work of pulp protest that complicates the lineage of "white-life" novels by African American authors such as Zora Neale Hurston, Richard Wright, Ann Petry, and Frank Yerby as well as troubles more broadly the borders of the American protest tradition.

The assimilationist novel, Bone contended, varied little from the protest novel in that both served a propagandistic function; he argued, however, that the "propaganda needs" changed in the postwar years, making it "more important today to demonstrate that the Negro is prepared for integration than getting a raw deal" (*Negro Novel* 170). The "milder assimilationist novel" (170) is an apt description of Sinclair's approach to racial politics in *The Changelings*, which locates the struggle for desegregation not on the courtroom steps or even the factory floor but in the quotidian friendship of two teenage girls. However, Bone's assessment in the 1960s that assimilationalist literature aims to persuade a skeptical public of African Americans' ability to integrate not only assumes a conservative white readership and critical establishment but also neglects other desegregationist strategies used in these novels, particularly their engagement with new forms of sexuality and gender and their importance to changing race relations. Furthermore, the radicalism of Offord's and Sinclair's novels partially rests in their challenge to the idea of race as biological fact or even as a basis for social identity. Turning now to explore this desegregationist critique of racial definitions more fully, we return again to questions regarding Jewish Americans' liminal identity within America's unsettled racial landscape.

"Nothing to Do with Blood": Rethinking Racial Identity

Many literary projects focused on postwar race relations chose to address the definition of race itself. The belief in a biological basis for racial difference, already rejected by the scientific community, was by the 1950s steadily losing its hold in the general population. "Strictly biological understandings of race," notes historian Matthew Frye Jacobson, "gave way to cultural and environmental explanations" (*Whiteness* 99). Seeking to challenge the idea of race as a biological, external reality, many postwar writers confronted the growing ambiguity over racial definitions, a practice that generated its own kind of trauma. *The Changelings* and *The Naked Fear* question racial identity in at least two important ways. Sinclair refuses to depict whiteness as an invisible, monolithic identity, and Offord debunks medical classifications of race. These novels collectively forward a vision of common humanity, an increasingly popular political sentiment that often undergirded the era's integrationist legislation and civil rights activism.

The Changelings challenges the idea of one-dimensional whiteness by situating Jewish identity alongside other ethnicities, including Polish and Italian immigrants. These groups, David Roediger notes, were initially kept out of American whiteness through designations as "foreigners" or "racials," effectively labeling them "not-yet-white" and therefore excluded from routes to middle-class mobility (*Working* 23, 75, 13). The residents of Sinclair's multiethnic neighborhood recognize themselves as distinctly different than Anglo-Saxon America even as some of them attempt to emulate an assimilated, nonethnic American identity. Ethnicity was mobilized to support, perhaps paradoxically, the era's embrace of universalism; as Jacobson explains, "The ascendance of ethnicity as an analytic category was one element in a powerful tendency in American social thought at mid-century to revise away from the concept of biological 'difference' and move toward universalism" (*Roots* 32). American Jews such as Vincent's father perceived their tenuous economic gains as at risk and their provisional whiteness as under assault by the social integration of African Americans who could not as easily escape the rubric of race. The novel, however, critiques Jewish assimilation and middle-class aspirations of moving to the suburbs to avoid living alongside blacks. In addition to illuminating the class conflicts within Jewish communities, *The Changelings* critiques how the adoption of racist beliefs about African Americans and the rejection of political coalitions with other racial and ethnic minorities are essential but lamentable steps in the process of enculturation. Describing the acquisition of racism as a recognizable step in assimilation, L. D. Reddick wrote in 1942, "Some Jews were willing to change their names, their religion, residences and to make other adjustments including the assumption of certain prejudices toward the Negro, which identified them with *white* America" (120).

Crucial to these discussions of assimilation to whiteness were meditations on blood. As shown in Esta Diamond's short story "Something for the War," World War II blood drives became a recurrent symbol of patriotism, a tangible contribution that civilians could make to the war effort. As a symbol, however, blood has a longer troubled history in the United States as a pseudoscientific marker of racial identity as evidenced in a pervasive anxiety about miscegenation, including the "one-drop" rule for designating second-class Negro citizenship and the mythology of the physically degenerate mulatto. As a publicist for the Red Cross, Sinclair wrote about the role blood played in expressions of both American patriotism and the nation's racial anxieties during World War II. As with Hurston, Offord, and Demby, her wartime service informed her literary production. In Sinclair's "Brother-Sister Act," an unpublished story from 1943, Virginia, an African American social worker (notably with the same name as an African American friend of the novelist), and her brother Paul, a postal clerk, argue over the value of donating blood. Virginia sees her donation as an act of subversion, gleefully requesting that they take her blood and "merge it with all the other blood." Paul, however, objects to his sister's patriotism, disgusted that in America's hypocritical democracy, the blood of black donors is kept separate to pacify white Americans' anxieties.[27] Here, integration and the resistance to it are located in the body; the desegregation of physical spaces is extended not only to the psychic inhabiting of racial differences as imagined by Jules in his poetry but also to the mixture of fluids, a progressive counterpoint to the panic over miscegenation in the early twentieth century.

In her short story "Second Blood: A Rosh Hashonoh Story," published in the *Jewish Spectator* in 1944, a young man, attending a blood drive during the celebration of the Jewish New Year, thinks about the images he has seen of Jews in Nazi-occupied ghettos. With a growing sense of ethnic pride as he drives through the city's Jewish district after his blood donation, he declares that "he had given not only as an American but as a Jew" (140). Evoking the image of a Jewish ancestral bloodline, Sinclair asserts that Jews who are proudly American need not abandon their ethnic and religious identifications. Her work often expresses a politics that simultaneously espouses patriotism and quashes racial and ethnic prejudices. This literary interest in blood symbolism exposed America's wartime contradictions: Blood represented a common humanity—all one blood—united for democracy, but it was also foundational to a racial classification system, biologically unfounded, used to construct racial hierarchies and justify social discrimination.

The notion of "Jewish blood," painfully associated with the rhetoric of Nazi propaganda, both affirmed and troubled such racist practices. Jewish identity has often been theorized as a liminal racial identity, representing an assimilated whiteness or a provisionally white ethnic identity; others have perceived Jewish identity as a murky "black" identity. As Sundquist notes, Jewishness often "constitutes an ambiguous zone between color and its absence" (81). Inhabiting this fluid identity between white and black—"belonging neither to one category or the other" according to Sundquist (81)—Jews were often envisioned in American literature as the mediators of racial issues. Vincent certainly is the intermediary in family conflicts over her sister's intermarriage, and she begins to challenge her neighbors' resistance to integration, stepping in during racist incidents. Sinclair tinkers with these significations in *The Changelings*. Vincent is nicknamed *schwartze kuter* (the black cat) because of her tough "black alley cat" ways as well as presumably for her dark physical features (131). Jules later imagines her as a "shadow in the street," inhabiting a spectral blackness that steadily pervades the entire neighborhood "like an insistent wind full of questions and accusations" (199). In contrast to the Nazi propaganda that imagined degenerate Jews possessing "black blood," Sinclair evokes the blackness of Jewish physicality and the dualities within Jews' social identity as Americans to highlight a shared history of oppression and to advocate for a collective integrationist politics. A liberal sympathetic to the struggles of working-class Americans, Sinclair highlights the battle for civil rights shared by African Americans and Jewish Americans. Her fiction repeatedly questions the conservative strands of the Jewish community that shunned women's rights, interreligious marriage, and interracial political coalitions.

Despite its populist packaging, Offord's novel also addresses the pressing issue of racial indeterminacy, ultimately asserting the popular liberal belief in a universal humanity rather than discernible racial categories. In a scene near the end of *The Naked Fear*, George panics when Amy insinuates that the child he rescued, now "his" daughter, is black. Offord uses this dilemma to mock many popular racial myths, including the belief that blacks "have an instinct for telling their own" (*Naked Fear* 14) and the lore that imperceptible blackness can be detected by looking at a child's gums. George's scrutiny of his daughter's nose and eyes further illustrates the era's reluctance to move beyond a racial discourse centered on physiological differences. Though he suspects that Amy is again merely attempting to get rid of the infant, George visits a doctor in hopes of definitively determining the girl's race. He is confident that science is "able to do almost anything" (146). After the doctor explains, with humored indignation, that such a blood test is impossible because "pigmentation is under the skin" and "has nothing to do with blood" (147), George is forced to rethink popular understandings of racial difference. Still he worries that if Sue were black, she "was not doomed by any visible difference but by a force mountainous and indefinable; he was conscious of this force but could not grapple with it" (143). In this short dramatic phrase, Offord underscores the privilege of white Americans to distance race as a monumental burden that is impossible for them to understand. Race, then, was less about physical difference than about perception and about the discriminatory practices habitually enacted in a racist society because of those perceived differences, a social reality that George cannot quite grasp.

Articulating this cultural moment when the significance or meaninglessness of race was being debated, George confronts the physician's question about race: "What does it mean, really?" (*Naked Fear* 148). He initially feels that his desire to care for his child, "to give of himself to the cause of goodness" (142), will dissolve if Sue turns out to be black. But George quickly comes to accept the reality that his child's race cannot be medically determined and decides to raise her alone, away from Amy's violence and racism. Voicing a new ethics for a pluralistic age, the doctor insists that George should care more about a "sense of righteousness" than about race (148). This call for a color-blind society would be seen as a naive impossibility a decade later by a generation becoming increasingly disillusioned by the slowness of social change. In the mid-1950s, however, it was a comforting ideology that asked Americans to turn away from a divisive sense of identity based on physical differences and toward a belief in a common humanity individualized by our diverse psychological interiorities.

Vincent's and George's shared desire to move beyond racial and gender particularities and cultural borders resembles the sentiments of universalism found in the poetry of Gwendolyn Brooks and Edwin Denby as well as the aesthetic balancing acts between racial and sexual particularities and common humanity faced by all the writers in this project. *The Changelings* and *The Naked Fear* redefine racial damage and question the social value of trauma, but these interracial narratives also argue for postwar identities and communities not centered on racial distinctions. Both Sinclair and Offord employ blood imagery and raise questions about the potency of cultural origins to support their larger exploration of imagined kinship. The idea of a chosen family offered a powerful metaphor for the political alliances and symbolic communities across racial and spatial differences that both writers advocated. Less literal than the racially reconfigured physical places found in the literary works discussed in previous chapters, these imagined kinships are nonetheless essential symbolic spaces within a desegregated geography.

Changeling Nation

Of the new models of family and community traced throughout this book, Sinclair's idea of an emergent generation of "changelings" is perhaps the most poetic. These postwar youth hoped to form an integrated society and to fashion identities that, though not yet visible, reflected the modern complexities of race, gender, and sexuality—including multiracial, homosexual, transgender, and multinational subjectivities. Many Americans in the 1950s were interested in transforming youth cultures—in particular, increasing expressions of juvenile delinquency. In *The Naked Fear*, it is a group of sexually forward girls, smoking marijuana in the movie theater bathroom, who discover George's sexual secret. The adolescents in *The Changelings*, however, though members of a neighborhood gang, are imagined not as a delinquent contingent but as America's progressive future, a postwar generation that embraces new attitudes about race, religion, and gender.

Explaining the term to her new confidant, Vincent tells Clara that a changeling is "somebody who's left in a place secretly, instead of the person who's supposed to be there," but she goes on to explain that in its modern form, as imagined by the poet Jules, the swap is internal, on "the *insides*" (*Changeling* 135).[28] This postwar spiritual orphan who "thinks entirely different" is of a new generation of Americans who seek "different things out of life" (135). The changeling is the odd kid in the family: She might be a tomboy or the effeminate lad who has friends of another race or of another faith or who might, by extension, love differently. Christening this generation "changelings," Jules implores them in his poetic manifesto to reject their "strange parents," who sustained them on "bread made of their fears and ignorance" (304). These changelings—a name suggestive of liminal identities that blur racial, gender, and sexual binaries—were raised within conservative ideologies, but they reject the anxieties of their parents, who fear the disintegration of traditions and social boundaries.

In declaring to her first black friend that "maybe you're a changeling, too" (*Changelings* 137), Vincent naively seeks to bring Clara into a world that transcends difference. Through Clara and Vincent, Sinclair envisions a model of interracial kinship and queer belonging (one more socially appropriate than the bond in Demby's version between adult Bill and child Johnny). She expressed the hope that her novels might "un-torment a lot of kids to come" (*Seasons* 114). Indeed, this integrationist novel is marked by moments of racial and gender rebellion, acts admired as a kind of courage instructive for postwar youth intent on change. In writing of her own mentor and maternal figure, Helen Buchman, Sinclair admits, "I've always had some older women (strong, warm) for friends—to respect, admire, do things for. . . . And I find myself writing about them a lot. Some day, I'll write the definitive book about the waif, motherless in her emotions, who's always looking for a substitute mother" (112).[29] *The Changelings* in many ways is that book about children who are emotionally motherless, with Vincent as the waif who has a strained relationship with her religiously devout grandmother and seeks a spiritual sisterhood with fellow tomboy Clara.

After hearing about the changeling folktale, Clara toys with this idea of the maternal surrogate, mischievously imagining a white woman discovering

Clara in her child's bed: "My little old black face peeping up at her. 'Mama, Mama!' I'd holler" (*Changelings* 137). In her trickster revision of the changeling folktale, Clara subversively turns the sentimentalized mammy narrative on its head. In claiming the identity of changeling, both young women begin to imagine the possibilities of creating family outside of biological bonds and in symbolic spaces outside the physical home. Vincent's rewriting of family history to include her banished sister's Irish-Jewish son is part of Sinclair's larger attempt to redefine kinship, envisioning a queer family that is bound by ideology rather than blood and crosses racial, religious, and sexual difference. As an activist writer, she sees herself as one of these socially transitional figures, believing in integration's potential to trouble racial, gender, and sexual binaries, to desegregate psyches as well as social spaces.

In becoming a changeling, Vincent begins to understand the complexity of emotions that animate cross-race identification. She observes her grandmother's reactions to her "half-and-half" great-grandson, the fact that she "must have wanted to put her arms around Manny and hated him and loved him and wanted to cry—all at the same time" (*Changeling* 227). In this emotionally ambiguous response, Vincent recognizes her conflicted reactions to Clara, an indiscriminate mix of attraction and revulsion, fear and longing. Illustrating what Toni Morrison has described as the "parasitical nature of white freedom" (*Playing* 56), Vincent and George in *The Naked Fear* reevaluate religious and/or racial beliefs through their first meaningful interactions with African Americans. In acknowledging the complex feelings beneath their phobias and attractions—the reality that desire can be both possessive and destructive—they begin to align themselves with African Americans, identifying with and wishing they could possess a racial difference they believe will, if not free them, transform them or cure them from social ills.

In trusting white people despite historical reasons for not doing so, Clara Jackson and, for a time, Johnny Johnson in Demby's *Beetlecreek* also confront their revulsion and fear, recognizing that their desire for a more expansive future is bound, despite all its perversions, to this suspect whiteness. Informed by their individual traumas and despite their differences, black and white characters in these novels embrace a developing ethics of integration. In redirecting the damage thesis put forward by the era's social psychologists, Offord's and Sinclair's novels question traditional narratives of racial oppression, pursuing postwar subjectivities informed but not wholly defined by incidents of trauma.

Stephen Knadler's reading of nineteenth-century passing narratives in which "traumatic gaps call attention to those moments in which the self is unable to pass into, or be constituted according to, any kind of normative or counterhegemonic racial performance" ("Traumatized" 65–66) is instructive for understanding trauma's function in these postwar integrationist novels. Vincent is unable or unwilling to embrace the conventional gender practices in which 1950s popular culture was reinvesting, and George's whiteness and the robust masculine superiority assumed in its privileges are assaulted by military integration. Rather than being a barrier to identity formation, trauma—inextricably racial as well as sexual—is foundational to these characters' changing sense of self. These postwar subjectivities and the performances of racial ventriloquism found in the writing of Hurston, Bishop, and Demby emerge from traumatic events. However, unlike the passing narratives of the previous century, in which trauma is "not fully scripted" (Knadler, "Traumatized" 66), racial and sexual violations in these novels are highly visible and central to narrative development. These postwar texts are compelling responses to Anne Anlin Cheng's call for new formulations of the "connection between subjectivity and social damage" (7). As Sinclair and Offord remind us, to adequately render an emergent postwar consciousness, an integrationist literature must directly engage citizens' traumatic personal histories.

In both *The Changelings* and *A Naked Fear*, interracial contact and attempts at social integration prompt fear and, in the extreme, sexual violence, but amiable relationships across race also offer the potential for psychological healing and new social identities in which redefinitions of race reflect an emergent postwar racial consciousness. In depicting the traumatic impact of desegregation and cultural assimilation, these novels reveal how societal change in America is often prompted not only by the catastrophic events of history but also by the seemingly minor psychological conflicts, subtle indignities, and silences in daily life. Early in Sinclair's novel, the arrival of African Americans into the neighborhood is described as catastrophic, aligned with floods, the Great Depression, and Hitler (*Changelings* 42). Despite their importance as catalysts for cultural transformation, private incidents and the literary projects (often aesthetic anomalies) that depict them remain largely invisible in the official history of the American civil rights movement.

The Changelings and *The Naked Fear* were written during a historical moment in which documenting the psychological effects of racism on both whites and blacks was a crucial approach for advancing integrationist politics. Witnessing the heightened tensions in his neighborhood, Herb Miller explains to his sister, "A thing like *Schwartze* coming into a neighborhood— you know, it can smack you like a psychiatrist's talk—medicine. It has an effect on stuff that's been there all along—hidden" (*Changelings* 206). Desegregation, Sinclair suggests, forces introspection, demanding citizens to confront traumatic racial histories and their often hidden emotions, including guilt, shame, anger, and sexual desire. In detailing the racial and sexual traumas of everyday life and in questioning archaic notions of racial distinctiveness, these novels stress psychological interiorities over public identities. Aesthetically, these works also anticipate the more complex portraits of racial subjectivities, particularly interiorities of shame, found in the work of Toni Morrison, Gayl Jones, Dorothy Allison, and others.

For Offord and Sinclair, this shame is often revelatory; trauma repeatedly prompts personal epiphany. In Sinclair's novel, Herb draws an apt analogy between his personal revelations, triggered by racial changes, and war trauma. Comparing the street's immigrant residents to traumatized soldiers who "break down because they've been ready to break down anyway" (*Changelings* 206), he suggests that the community—already grappling with the loss of religious traditions, increasing intermarriage, and changing attitudes about gender and race—was already poised for a crisis. Martin Luther King Jr., in fact, argued that the intent of nonviolent direct action was to foster "crisis-packed" situations (292). The arrival of African Americans in the neighborhood, like "guns and bombs just start the ball rolling" (*Changelings* 206), as Sinclair phrases it, forces the residents of East 120th Street to confront long-standing issues—whether religious prejudice, hidden sexual traumas, or intergenerational rifts. Vincent speculates about whether she would have been transformed by her friendship with Clara if her sexual assault had not prompted their connection: "Would they ever have known each other if it hadn't been for that day? Would she ever have gone to a *Schwartze* street, into a church? Would she ever have discovered that Manny was not really an outcast" (252). Her questions point not only to an unexpected gratitude for the trauma but also to its necessity in changing social habits.

For *The Naked Fear's* George to overcome his phobia, he must literally reside in a black family's home, replacing his violent urges and fears with a newfound tenderness. The narrative reflects on the mundane forces in his transformation: "Something had happened in him. But what? He had been forced to meet them closely. That was all. To be face to face with them, to share words, and, too, to share the common anxiety over the child" (123). Through his interactions with the Jones family, particularly as a witness to Ma Quilly's religious fervor and fierce protection of his child, he begins to see African Americans differently and wonders how one could draw any conclusions about black people when "you didn't know anything at all about them except what you read, and that couldn't be too accurate" (99). Offord offers a version of racial reconciliation that does not require legislation or an elaborate reckoning with the past; instead, simple conversation, physical proximity, and examples of compassion erode his phobia. This resolution is hardly without its problems, particularly since George never publicly acknowledges the phobia's origins in the death of a black soldier and a racially charged, retaliatory attack. When the troubled veteran is no longer willing to respond to Amy's violent rages or parrot her racist comments, she accuses him of being "niggerfied" (158), suggesting that his fear has turned to emulation or even attraction. For the postwar integrationist, phobia is potentially replaced with identification; for its critics, fear will dissolve dangerously into desire to mimic identities across color lines. Chip, another character in *The Changelings*, succinctly articulates the minute shifts of consciousness that accompanied these social alterations in American culture. He speaks of being "charged with a peculiar strength and tenderness," feeling "as if the mysterious Negro figure stalking the mind of the street so long has turned familiar enough to see, to know as intimately as he knew his own desires" (163). Reflecting the emotional complexities of racial identification seen throughout this study, the African American citizen, literally desegregating the community, here is being integrated into the minds of the neighborhood's Jewish residents as a paradoxically familiar alterity.

In insisting on trauma's utility, Sinclair and Offord distance themselves from the disempowering aspects of the damage thesis, stressing instead the inevitable interpersonal struggles, the ambivalent expressions of agency, and the nearly invisible psychological transformations that desegregation demanded. These novels also offer other understandings of assimilation, arguing that the process need not be a soulless one of cultural erasure. In a moment when pressures to desegregate American society were mounting, African Americans became not only white people's moral mirror but also psychoanalytically a mimetic identity. When Vincent first sees Clara, she notes the physical similarities—height, hairstyle, chosen dress—that temporarily occlude their different skin shades: "It was like staring into a mirror" (*Changelings* 22). And in his earnest social poetry, Jules writes, "Now comes The Black / From out of the secret dark cell of my heart," insisting later in the poem, "His face is mine!" (33).[30] Residing in a place so intimate—for some, the mind; for others, the heart—this spectral figure of blackness, problematically undifferentiated, not only knows the integrationist's desires but often mirrors them. Despite its narcissism, the poem's psychoracial geography also narrates a migration from psyche to public consciousness. This image—the racial other residing within—illuminates a form of cross-racial identification that reoccurs in this desegregationist literature. The physical spaces of desegregation—the diner in Gwendolyn Brooks's poetry, Edwin Denby's city park, or the bedroom in Ann Petry's literary imagination—becomes the interior spaces of mind and altered heart in these later novels.

Placing Offord's and Sinclair's novels in conversation across aesthetic and cultural differences, across their individual structural flaws—including their failures to convincingly represent the subjectivities of other races, their implausible plot turns, and their underdeveloped characters—exemplifies some of the challenges of cross-race writing. These messy aesthetic moments are themselves a kind of racial trauma—writers' individual attempts to break free of psychological and artistic constraints to imagine a world informed by but not restricted to their respective racial identities. The novels explored in this chapter reflect the era's renewed interest in trauma by psychologists, sociologists, and the general public. *The Naked Fear* translates the racial and sexual traumas of war into a pulp thriller. *The Changelings* imagines trauma as communal and quotidian, stressing the importance of gender and queer sexuality to social change. Both works, with their motifs of homelessness and bloodlines, are shadowed by the Holocaust, yet they depart from this catastrophe, still incomprehensible, to consider forms of racial and sexual violence imprinted on the everyday lives of Americans in the 1950s. When Jules, *The Changelings*'s resident poet, urges "Come Changeling, let us look into our hearts for identity" (305), he privileges a postwar subjectivity that is self-discovered rather than one that mimics the discriminatory customs of family, community, and nation. Imagining an integrated society where Vincent, a Jewish changeling; her Jewish-Irish nephew, Manny; and Clara, her Catholic tomboy friend, can live, worship, and write history together, he invites readers to engage in a similar introspection, composing self-selected, integrated queer families outside of the confining ghettos of tradition.

Conclusion: Intimate Failures

Returning to America in 1957 to report on the expanding civil rights movement, James Baldwin confessed, "I have always been struck, in America, by an emotional poverty so bottomless, and a terror of human life, of human touch, so deep that virtually no American appears able to achieve any viable, organic connection between his public stance and his private life" ("Take" 385). The dissonance between private desire and public expression that Baldwin bemoans is central to the understanding of desegregation pursued throughout this project. We might read the literature discussed in *Desegregating Desire* as a diverse body of writing that not only recognizes this emotional poverty but also attempts to circumvent it via emotionally rich depictions of interracial relationships and cross-race identifications that embody the public complexities of private feelings. Baldwin later notes that this "failure of the private life has always had the most devastating effect on American public conduct, and on black-white relations" (386). Like the writers discussed in the introduction—Margaret Halsey, Ralph Ellison, and Wallace Thurman—who insisted on the importance of sexuality to racial divisions and interracial reconciliation, Baldwin highlights the intimate failures and tentative bonds of desegregation that are central to the poems, essays, and novels discussed in these pages.

Evaluating desegregated cultural spaces in mostly neglected literary texts by writers not associated with an overt integrationist politics, this study constructs a history of intimate desegregation that is distinct from the well-documented events of the civil rights movement, including the desegregation of Little Rock's Central High School, the Freedom Rides, and the monumental March on Washington. This desegregation occurs outside of the public record, in small towns, neighborhoods, homes, and the minds of American citizens. In interpreting the racial and sexual discourses of literary works from the late 1940s and 1950s as an earlier chapter of the civil rights movement, I have acknowledged World War II's importance in ushering in substantial changes in the ways race, sexuality, and gender were lived and perceived in American society. Military service and an expanded wartime economy increased the visibility of homosexual men and women, provided African Americans with new economic and cultural opportunities, and disrupted conventional gender roles. These major changes, in turn, facilitated integration and shaped the politics and aesthetics of American writers interested in exploring the interdependencies of race and sexuality in this transitional cultural moment.

In the ten years following World War II, many Americans expressed a belief that desegregation must and could occur, though some conceded that government intervention might be required to get the process started. Despite their ambivalence about integration's viability, the novelists and poets on whom I have focused challenge the prescriptions of American protest writing and segregated literary traditions: They wanted their work to be much more than artistic propaganda; they wanted it to capture the changes in Americans' feelings about race and sexuality, about home and public space. These eight writers characterize desegregation as a tentative impulse, more than a route to publicly recognizable, achieved integration; instead, their novels and poems record transformations of racial consciousness still in progress. Not without its critiques and moments of cynicism, this literature also pays attention to the awkward exchanges, the ambivalent identifications, and the intimate failures that occur when discontented citizens venture across social boundaries

The writers of *Desegregating Desire* ultimately circumvent artistic prescriptions, including long-standing racial and sexual prohibitions, embracing their own flexibility as artists to render a range of racial and sexual affiliations. In addition to sentiments of universalism and occasional color-blind depictions of postwar life, these eight writers use cross-race writing to highlight the emotional interdependencies of black and white Americans. Crossing the literary color line, Elizabeth Bishop and Jo Sinclair attempted to inhabit discursively black subjectivities and the postwar experiences of African Americans, highlighting the often-contradictory emotions that interracial encounters elicit. This muddled terrain of longing and revulsion is also found in the cross-race writing of Ann Petry, William Demby, Zora Neale Hurston, and Carl Offord, black writers who sought to craft psychologically complex white characters.

Desegregation, their literature reminds us, was a remapping of internal as well as social spheres. These writers, like many of their contemporaries, turned to psychoanalysis, a discipline whose language had seeped into popular culture, and reformulated theories about sexual difference, racial damage, neurosis, and cross-race identification to complicate their representations of fragmented families, sexual deviance, and interracial desire. In privileging interiorities, shifts of consciousness, and the psychologies of racial desire as sources for identifying social change, these poets and novelists explore the neuroses, traumatic scars, identifications, and desires for belonging that in part define the affective landscape of integration. Bishop's "Songs for a Colored Singer" publicly performs her murky cross-racial identification through a blues singer's surrealist song. In Hurston's *Seraph on the Suwanee*, Arvay Henson journeys from neurotic isolation to a welcomed sense of communal, interracial belonging. Annie Allen and Maud Martha, black female protagonists in Brooks's writing from the early Cold War era, articulate emotionally textured responses to the racial indignities and gender injustices of daily life, sentiments largely invisible to their families and larger communities in which they live.

Denby's urban poetry explicitly upsets the private/public dualism, infusing city streets, luncheonettes, and apartment houses with previously private feelings of erotic attraction, buried rage, and sexual abjection. In *The Narrows*, Petry exposes the familial rifts that result from emotional withdrawal and recognizes the dangers of expressing interracial desire within the confines of a small town's racially fragmented community. Characters in Demby's *Beetlecreek* attempt to escape this cultural isolation by exploring a tentative companionship across racial boundaries despite a societal distrust that discourages such bonds. Sinclair's *The Changelings* imagines a midwestern neighborhood as a microcosm of America's larger struggles to adapt to changing racial and sexual protocols, and the youth influenced by these cultural tensions become the agents of change, altering their families from the inside out. And in *The Naked Fear*, Offord, echoing Baldwin, critiques the emotional poverty of racism: George Sutton, recovering from racial phobia and shell shock, literally emerges into a fledgling interracial community and resolves to embrace a politics of racial interdependence.

In focusing on racialized desire and cross-race identifications, these eight postwar writers foreground the importance of sexuality to desegregation, its imprint visible in transforming public and private spheres. Denby's and Brooks's contributions to a poetics of sexual containment; the varied expressions of same-sex and interracial desires found in the writing of Bishop, Petry, Sinclair, Demby, and Offord; and the progressive portraits of black female sexuality in the work of Brooks and Petry collectively emphasize the irrefutable importance of sexuality and gender—reimagined and articulated in countless ways—to postwar American race relations. Vincent's allegiance to Clara in *The Changelings*, for example, is defined by both homoerotic attraction and a fear of blackness that was learned within the intimacies of family. The acts of submission and dominance, often tinged with sexual ambiguities, that are explored in the domestic relationships between white and black women in Bishop's and Hurston's writing are additional overlooked sites of interracial intimacy. Oscillations between attraction and revulsion can also be found in the unconventional queer pairing of a black teenaged boy and a white old man in *Beetlecreek*, a novel that questions traditional practices of racial belonging. Cross-race identifications, as these varied forms suggest, played a crucial role in desegregating postwar communities and individuals' behavior, but they also thwarted social change. Anxieties about homosexuality, interracial sex, and racial loyalty as well as long-held gender and racial prejudices are also explored in this literature as potent cultural forces that prevented some Americans from moving beyond segregated communities and belief systems.

The inversions of sexual deviance, situating the rhetoric of sexual pathology onto white subjects rather than black, in *Beetlecreek* and *The Naked Fear* also reflect this growing interest in the psychologies of race. Such gestures might be understood as attempts by African American writers to disassociate blackness from queerness. Indeed, there is something queer about whiteness in many of these texts; in *Seraph on the Suwanee*, *The Narrows*, and *The Naked Fear* as well as in the works of white authors such as Bishop and Denby, whiteness is not only deviant but possesses a strangeness, a nonconformity to sanctioned sexual and racial practices. This scrutiny of whiteness, including its abnormality and complex dependencies on a mythologized blackness, is another characteristic of the desegregationist writing examined in this study.

While *Desegregating Desire* identifies some of the ways Cold War activists and writers were reimagining the relationship between race and sexuality in America, including a more expansive definition of civil rights, the crossfertilization between the burgeoning gay and lesbian movement and the civil rights movement during the 1950s and 1960s warrants further research. The ideological tensions that John D'Emilio identifies within the early gay liberation movement have clear parallels to debates among activists in the civil rights movement. Mirroring the debates among African Americans and Jewish Americans over the merits of maintaining cultural distinctiveness or assimilating into a dominant, white-defined culture, gay men and lesbians in the 1950s also struggled to determine whether they "should accommodate themselves to the mores of society or assert their difference" (*Sexual Politics* 90). Without ignoring the very real historical differences between these various liberation movements, we can see from the literary projects discussed in this volume that the dilemmas of integration—the liabilities of assimilation, the tenuousness of communal belonging—were remarkably similar, underscoring the need for further scholarship that explores the sexual dimensions of the civil rights movement as well as continued research focused on the racial politics and gendered practices within various U.S. lesbian and gay liberation movements.

The fluctuations and interdependencies between a minoritizing view of identity and a universalizing one, famously theorized by Eve Kosofsky Sedgwick in *Epistemology of the Closet*, surface as strategic disagreements within both the gay and lesbian liberation movement and the civil rights movement. Such tensions were evident in many literary texts from the early Cold War, which struggled to convey racial and sexual particularities within a politics of universalism. The queer aesthetic in Denby's poetry, for example, although at times homoerotic, refuses an overt allegiance to homosexual politics. In Petry's *The Narrows*, Link Williams's decision to act on his desire for Camilo, despite still-pervasive prohibitions against interracial sex, is an act of individualism that defies conservative mores regarding racial allegiance. Bill Trapp's attempt to connect with Beetlecreek's African American community is condemned and eventually punished, suggesting that individual acts of desire cannot always transcend the strictures found within "minority" communities that organize around and often police social difference.

By the end of the 1950s, the optimism over integration, a faith in Americans' willingness to confront and correct their nation's history of racial injustice, had largely dissolved. According to historian Howard Zinn, "By 1965, ten years after the 'all deliberate speed' guideline of the Court, more than 75 percent of the school districts in the South were still segregated" (124–25). Unsurprisingly, a growing cynicism regarding race relations began to shape American literature of the 1960s. Eric Sundquist, for example, notes a pronounced pessimism about the viability of black-Jewish alliances in the era's literature (362). This move away from sentiments of universal humanity and an integrationist politics, which began to be perceived by some artists as a disempowering strategy of assimilation, suggested a changing cultural climate. Many writers in the Black Arts movement returned to earlier works of social protest fiction and crafted literature dominated by racial themes or retreated to a separatist and at times deeply homophobic rhetoric of black nationalism. As more statements of black authenticity emerged in American literature, many white writers, fearing harsh critiques, avoided depictions of African American identities and culture.

James Baldwin's 1962 novel, *Another Country*, seems to rest between these two impulses, crafting a fully mature desegregationist aesthetic through his complex treatment of homosexual, interracial desires but also voicing the growing disillusionment with the integrationist imperative embraced by liberal artists and intellectuals. In his composite picture of 1950s New York City, Baldwin critiques social alienation as well as compassionately examines the interconnectedness of men and women, white and black, heterosexual and homosexual, in self-selected communities. These imagined kinships nurture and wound lovers and friends. His character, Vivaldo Moore, to take one example, embodies the desegregationist desire to flee from the racism and sexual repression of his childhood neighborhood, but the social freedoms toward which he is running remain unrealized. Writing of Vivaldo's repeated trips to Harlem for parties and sex with prostitutes, Baldwin critiques a postwar version of slumming: "He had merely been taking refuge in the outward adventure in order to avoid the clash and tension of the adventure proceeding inexorably within" (*Another* 133). The distracting allure of the "outward adventure," the public and often reckless interactions between white and black Americans across racial, geographic, and sexual barriers, rarely prompts confrontations with the unseemly anger, fear, and predatory desires fostered in our deeply fractured nation. Interracial intimacies, Baldwin concludes, mean little unless they are accompanied by a courageous introspection, unless private feelings are placed into public light.

Written before this growing disillusionment with American race relations, the novels and poems examined in *Desegregating Desire* document racially unsettled places, conflicted interior lives, and forms of integrated intimacies not yet fully realized. The attention to transformed identities, imagined queer families, and reconstituted homes and public places were equally assertions of a new public identity for the postwar American writer. Desegregation—psychological and topographical—invited writers to rethink the equally rigid divisions between public life and private feelings. Finding many literary forms, including the protest novel and the metered sonnet, insufficient structures for conveying postwar social complexities, these novelists and poets experimented with cross-race writing, fragmented narratives, or the poetic cadences in everyday speech as a means of examining interracial spaces, cross-race identification, and the psychologies of racial desire. Rather than dealing with racial and sexual difference in sanitized forms or from an impersonal sociological approach, these writers contended that the creative intellectual in postwar America must grapple publicly with private intimacies. But literature about a haltingly desegregating America also seeks to capture the queer feelings of postwar life, including the ambivalence, shame, envy, lust, and even love that Baldwin confronts pointedly in *Another Country*. Moreover, in stressing the existential dilemmas of postwar existence— an alienation from calcified notions of race and sexuality; the possibility of belonging to a community that is racially or sexually different from one's community of origin; and the inevitable fragmentations of self in modern life—the writers examined in *Desegregating Desire* composed work that desegregated desire. That is, they integrated sexuality into their renderings of race, muddled the line between public protest and personal confession, and simultaneously questioned the sharply drawn lines between black/white and heterosexual/homosexual in mid-twentieth-century American culture.

Sensing a useful distance from the events of World War II and the civil rights movement, artists and critics have begun to reflect on the legacies and failures of integration. In our revisiting of the 1950s, always vulnerable to nostalgic misinterpretations, and in our warranted pessimism over the persistent inability to form integrated communities in schools, neighborhoods, or workplace in the U.S., we must pay attention to desegregation's complex meanings, including the intricacies and cultural significances of a midcentury literature that explores America's vexed interracial histories. In particular, we need to revisit the decade after World War II and the failings of integration, mindful of the crucial roles that sexuality, cross-race identification, and artistic innovation played in these histories.

Sharing Ralph Ellison's commitment to understanding the "inter-relatedness of blackness and whiteness" ("Change" 109) in American life, I have focused on integrationist themes and interracial intimacies in American literature from the early Cold War as a way of better understanding one chapter in this complex history of cultural interdependence. Although their fiction is not a primary focus here, Ellison and Baldwin loom over this project. Their investigations into the inextricability of whiteness and blackness and the entangled significance of race and sexuality in American society—cultural criticism that I admire for its always visible personal investment—inform my critical practices at every turn. It seems fitting, then, to conclude with Ellison, whose ruptures of the private and public return us to Baldwin and his attention to our private failures. Our guide Ellison leads the descent: "Down at the deep dark bottom of the melting pot, where the private is public and the public private, where black is white and white black, where the immoral becomes moral and the moral is anything that makes one feel good (or that one has the power to sustain), the white man's relish is apt to be the black man's gall" ("Change" 104). I locate an integrated imaginary within this desegregated space of inversions—indeed, cultural perversions—and muddled identifications. Risking gall, I traverse the "deep dark bottom" of this pot, relishing the public private desires that I find and feel within its gradually illuminated recesses.

NOTES

Introduction

1. Beyond its significance as a tool for social and economic equity, the FEPC illuminates the broader American politics of the 1940s. The commission was created by Franklin Roosevelt by executive order in 1941 in response to Randolph's planned Washington, D.C., march. An interracial effort involving Jewish organizations, including the National Council of Jewish Women, and African American civil rights groups organized to have the legislation extended beyond the war. Boris notes that protection against gender discrimination was excluded from the original order, and Giddings discusses the reality that the FEPC did little to improve African American women's economic situation. See also Dudziak, "Desegregation"; Greenberg.

2. Discussing the relationships between race and ethnicity during World War II, historian Matthew Frye Jacobson notes that "ethnicity itself provided a paradigm for assimilation which erased race as a category of historical experience for European and some near Eastern immigrants" (*Whiteness* 110). For a thoughtful analysis of the shifting definitions of *whiteness* in the United States and European immigrants' claims to it after World War II, see Jacobson, *Whiteness*.

3. Jackson notes that according to 1950 Census data, 2.2 percent of the 15 million black Americans were college graduates, many from segregated institutions (338).

4. Historians have questioned the standard narrative of postwar American abundance, particularly for African American men and women of all races. Despite many Americans' anticipation of increased economic opportunities in the immediate postwar years, Zinn notes that the era "saw no basic change in the traditional distribution of American income in which the top fifth of the population made ten times the income of the bottom fifth" (96). Sacks has also documented that the means by which many white veterans acquired middle-class economic and social status—that is, the GI Bill and federal housing incentives—were unavailable to many black veterans as a consequence of systemic discriminatory practices.

5. For other historical overviews of African Americans in the post–World War II era, see Kelley; Sugrue; Deborah Gray White; Kryder; Dudziak, *Cold War Civil Rights*.

6. For more details about Brooks's receipt of the Pulitzer Prize and the family's housing hardships, see Kent, *Life*, 92–95.

7. "Pills for Prejudice," 39; "Negro, White Youngsters," 36; "When Negroes Go to School with Whites"; "Mixed Couples," 52. For other commentary on changes in U.S. race relations as documented in the press and popular culture, see Judith Smith; Sklaroff. Information cited on Hollywood's codes regarding interracial intimacy taken from Patterson, 24. For a discussion of interracial marriage in the Cold War era, see Lubin, *Romance*; Randall Kennedy; Moran.

8. For a full account of the federal government's discriminatory campaigns against gay men and lesbians, which began in the 1940s and continued well into the 1960s, see David K. Johnson.

9. For a more comprehensive discussion of homosexuality in mid-twentieth-century America, see Kunzel; Chauncey, *Gay New York*; D'Emilio, *Sexual Politics*; David K. Johnson; Elizabeth Lapovsky Kennedy and Davis.

10. Sagarin, who published the pioneering book under the pseudonym Donald Webster Corey, famously recanted his homosexuality at twenty-five and married. His continued, lifelong partnership with an African American man is one of the many nearly forgotten stories in America's interracial history. See Kaiser 126.

11. Both Carl Offord and Ann Petry had short stories published in Seaver's anthology, which was applauded for its integrationist editorial policy.

12. In July 1945, critic Philip Butcher challenged African American writers to not turn away from the nation's racial issues, which required "artistically mature spokesmen," in favor of "raceless" subject matter (115). Kenneth W. Warren characterizes Walker's and Butcher's claims that African American literature was reaching a new complexity as a "prospective posture" adopted by critics who constructed a "progressive narrative of a literature moving toward maturity" (*What Was* 67, 68). African American literature is often described as reaching a new aesthetic sophistication during this period, but white artists' maturation in addressing racial matters with greater complexity also defined the decade after World War II.

13. Evaluating the precarious benefits of a 1950s civil rights politics organized around claims of universalism, Singh notes that "struggles to claim universality for black people have challenged not only particularism masquerading as a universalism, but a universalism distorted by its long monopolization against blacks" (44).

14. Matthew Frye Jacobson (*Whiteness*), Karen Brodkin Sacks, and Thomas Schaub are among the scholars who discuss a shift in both cultural representations of and scientific theories about race after World War II: from physical to psychological, from biological to cultural, and from economic to behavioral.

15. Robert Corber, Ruth Feldstein, Alex Lubin, Judith E. Smith, and Frederick Whiting are among the recent scholars who have argued persuasively for the importance of race in the shaping of American Cold War literary culture.

16. For an insightful discussion of the retrospective condemnation of the 1950s optimism about race relations by a later generation of activists and writers, see Warren, *What Was* 55–80. Singh (134–73) traces a mid-twentieth-century history of black radicalism as a more politically palatable counternarrative to the assimilationist politics and universalizing aesthetic embraced by elite liberals in the 1950s.

17. In her excellent discussion of Petry's use of domestic labor as a lens for broader social critiques of capitalism, sexual exploitation, and racial hierarchies, Peterson argues that "Petry's domestics make interventions into our understanding of class struggle via their unique access to the private sphere" (76).

18. Recent scholarship by Christina Klein, Alex Lubin, and Frederick Whiting has offered important new directions for evaluating Cold War culture outside of the framework of containment. See Klein, *Cold War Orientalism*; Lubin, *Romance*; Whiting, "Stronger."

19. In his comprehensive study of whiteness in relation to U.S. immigration, *Whiteness of a Different Color*, Jacobson notes, "The contest over whiteness—its definitions, its internal hierarchies, its proper boundaries, and its rightful claimants—has been critical to American culture throughout the nation's history, and it had been a fairly untidy affair" (5). See also Roediger, *Working*; Roediger, *Wages*; Lipsitz, "Possessive Investment."

Chapter 1

1. According to historians Mintz and Kellogg, "By the end of World War II, there were 2.5 million fewer single women than in 1940, and by the end of the 1950s, 70 percent of all women were married by the age of twenty-four, compared to just 42 percent in 1940 and 50 percent today" (179). Given these cultural trends, Bishop's and Hurston's decisions to be single women without children in many ways anticipates the social shifts of the 1960s. Their life choices, which might be read as progressive anomalies, depart from the dominant narratives about gender in the 1950s.

2. Hurston was married to Herbert Sheen, a medical student, from 1927 to 1931 (though they separated in 1928). In June 1939, when she was forty-eight, she married Albert Price III, a twenty-three-year-old whom she met in the education department of the Works Progress Administration; she filed for divorce in February 1940, though it was not finalized until 1943. She married James Pitt, a Cleveland businessman eight years her junior, in January 1944, and they were divorced ten months later. Her final two marriages were largely kept a secret from her extensive network of friends (Valerie Boyd 149–50, 160–61, 325–26, 337–38, 373).

3. Bishop, *One Art*, 109. Hereafter cited in the text as *OA*.

4. Hurston's world travels included Jamaica, the Bahamas, Honduras, and Haiti. In addition to spending fifteen years in Brazil, Bishop traveled to England, France, Morocco, Ecuador (including the Galapagos Islands), and Peru, among other countries.

5. In a 29 March 1944 letter, Hurston invited Harold Jackman and his friend (and rumored lover) Countee Cullen to stay on the *Wanago*. The novelist admitted, "I could use two men to pull on ropes when coming into a dock" (Kaplan 498). She also told writer Katherine Tracy L'Engle to consider the *Wanago* her "second home" (485).

6. During this nautical domesticity, Hurston was writing about Cudjo Lewis, who was considered to be the last African-born slave living in the United States and whom she had interviewed in the late 1920s. Published in *American Mercury* in March 1944, her article, "The Last Slave Ship," begins with the image of the ship's hull peeking from an Alabama marsh. This receding history of American slavery, including enslaved people's relationship to the water, was the subject of Hurston's writing as she made her home on these houseboats and her friend Fred Irvine's boats and as she navigated the segregated worlds of Miami and New York. Hurston's invocation of the slave ship—its receding form and the bodies carried within it—reminds us of the necessary modulation between physical structure and metaphysical experience that characterizes places, particularly those marked by race.

7. This research expedition reveals that the writing process for *Seraph* began much earlier than the 1947 Honduran trip during which she produced a full draft of the novel in about six months.

8. The accuser was a ten-year-old boy, "Billy," from whose mother Hurston had rented a room on 124th Street in Harlem in November 1946. The case was dismissed after it was determined that Hurston was in Honduras at the time of the purported abuse and that the child was likely covering up his own sexual experimentation with two other neighborhood boys. For a full account of the trial, see Valerie Boyd 387–400.

9. Critics have not fully explored Bishop's interest in Cuban American culture in Key West, evident in her essays "Gregorio Valdes" and "Mercedes Hospital" and the poems "Jerónimo's House" and "Faustina, or Rock Roses."

10. Bishop, *Collected Poems*, 34. Hereafter cited in the text as *CP*.

11. Alice Quinn, the editor of Bishop's posthumous *Edgar Allan Poe and the Juke-Box* (2006), locates the poem in a notebook from the mid-1940s (289).

12. Bishop's ever-fascinating letters are dotted with references to hotels that she or her friends resided in or worked from, but a letter from 27 June 1950 (around the time when Bishop began her post as poetry consultant in Washington, D.C.) to Robert Lowell is particularly alluring in relation to the poem "In a cheap hotel." She wrote, "Did I tell you I am now living at a hotel—sort of—called 'Slaughter's?'—run entirely by colored people for Eurasians, strange gray people, poets, etc. I like it much better than the boardinghouse" (*OA* 204). Not only do I like the thought of Bishop as both a poet and a strange gray person, it is tempting to imagine that the perverse encounter with the night clerk of her poetic imagination was inspired by her stay at Slaughter's.

13. The poem's sadomasochistic fantasy recalls the primitivist imaginary of Ten-

nessee Williams's "Desire and the Black Masseur," where whiteness is also cannibalized and obliterated by interracial sexuality. Artist Wardell Milan, whose image, *Champions #1*, serves as the cover for this book, created a series of images, *Desire and the Black Masseur*, based on Williams's short story.

14. Bishop calls it "Penn's Garden of Roses" in a June 1941 letter (*OA* 100).

15. Diary, 1938–42, 36, File 77.3, Elizabeth Bishop Papers, Special Collections, Vassar College Libraries, Poughkeepsie, N.Y.

16. The poem was published posthumously in the collection *Edgar Allen Poe and the Juke-Box* (2006). It also appeared in the 6 March 2006 issue of the *New Yorker* without any editorial commentary to contextualize a poem with a reference to "nigger-town" appearing in a twenty-first-century publication.

17. Diary, 1938–42, 36, Bishop Papers.

18. Hurston's skepticism toward whites is understandable. Her patron from 1927 to 1932, Charlotte Osgood Mason, was notoriously controlling over both Hurston's folklore material and her finances (her expense reports were detailed enough to include Kotex). The anthropologist's research was legally Mason's, and Hurston, a budding novelist, had to be quite strategic and subversive in using her research in her fiction and theatrical productions. Also, the rejection of a novel set in black middle-class society and editorial censures of her autobiography, *Dust Tracks on a Road*, informed Hurston's understanding of white business practices. Richard Rochester, a white acquaintance, tried to sue Hurston for money owed and sullied her name with stories of marijuana smoking and indecent exposure (Valerie Boyd 389). Furthermore, Hurston's mentor, noted anthropologist Franz Boas, oscillated between enthusiastic support and professional betrayals.

19. A section in Hurston's 1926 "Eatonville Anthology" called "Turpentine Love" reveals the seeds for *Seraph*. This brief folktale of Jim Merchant nearly mirrors the early scene in *Seraph* where Jim Meserve exposes Arvay's false hysteria by dropping turpentine in her eye.

20. For a discussion of the critical reception of "white-life" novels, including Langston Hughes's admiration of postwar African American writers such as Frank Yerby, Ann Petry, and Willard Motley, who extended beyond African American subject matter, see Dubek.

21. For a discussion of the U.S. involvement in anticolonial movements of the early Cold War and particularly their intersections with the U.S. civil rights movement, see Von Eschen; Borstelmann.

22. Jackson, for example, states that the "impolite" term "Pet Negro" could be suitably applied to James Baldwin in the 1950s, given his role as the sole black spokesman in the journal *Commentary* (281).

23. The phrase *assimilationist novel* comes from Bone (*Negro Novel* 169). For commentary on African American writers moving away from race and social protest to-

ward "universal" themes, see Bernard; Bone, *Negro Novel*; Arthur P. Davis; Dubek; Ro; Walker.

24. For a thorough discussion of American modernist writers, visual artists, and collectors who engaged in forms of racial ventriloquism, see Gubar 139–68. DuPlessis also investigates the racial poetics of modernist poets, including Wallace Stevens and T. S. Eliot.

25. This essay was published literally alongside Gwendolyn Brooks's war sonnet, "piano after war." (*Blacks* 68). The poem's reference to lost soldiers and placement next to Hurston's critique of aesthetic conservatism reveal the ways that American writers in this era were gauging both the war's impact and the role literature would play in documenting and forwarding the social changes that began with World War II.

26. Valerie Boyd makes a similar point: "Hurston had endured a good deal of criticism and misunderstanding for her portrayals of black people; one way to take a break from this kind of scrutiny was to write about whites" (393).

27. duCille reads the ending as a "spoof" (139) and Arvay's submission as "enlightened or calculated" (141), a strategy that strokes the male ego and ultimately obscures the strategic power negotiation beneath the tactic. Tate views the apparent patriarchal romance as Bakhtinian masquerade, arguing that Arvay's acceptance of Jim's authority is a "subversive commentary on female masochism" ("Hitting" 388).

28. For a discussion of Bishop in relation to Cold War politics, see Roman; Axelrod, "Elizabeth Bishop."

29. Louise Crane was an obsessive Billie Holiday fan and initiated Bishop into jazz cafés and the singer's songbook. For Holiday's memorable account of her relationship with Crane, see *Lady Sings the Blues* (1956). According to Holiday, "Brenda"—her pseudonym for Crane—"was crazy about my singing and used to wait for me to finish up. I wasn't blind. I hadn't been on Welfare Island for nothing. It wasn't long before I knew I had become a thing for this girl" (87). I find Holiday's theory on interracial sex fascinating. Reflecting on this white woman's attraction, Holiday says, "These poor bitches grow up hating their mothers and having the hots for their fathers. And since being in love with our father is taboo, they grow up unable to get any kicks out of anything unless it's taboo too. And since Negroes in America walk around with big 'Do Not Touch' signs on them, that's where we come in. And I'm telling you it can be a drag. Sometimes simple little mess-ups like this take years to unravel; and that's how these doctors with the couches make their loot" (88). Lloyd Schwartz notes that Bishop hoped the poem would be set to music "so that Billie Holiday could record it" and recalls Bishop telling him a story of coming home to find a friend, probably Crane, in bed with Holiday, most likely when they were living in New York City in 1936 (Fountain and Brazeau 328). Bishop's affection for the blues, her association of Holiday

with Crane, and her ambiguous identification with black women haunt "Songs for a Colored Singer."

30. Griffin's study of Holiday counters dominant narratives of Holiday as a victim, getting "under the layers of myths that have formed like a callus around" the legendary singer (*If You* 33). See also Margolick.

31. Roman's notable reading of the poem engages its racial implications and the "quasi-(in)visible lesbian subtext" (76) that emerges from the connections among Bishop, Crane, and Holiday, but her analysis could go further to explore how the poem desegregates race and sexuality—specifically, the way that lesbian desire for Bishop is often expressed within a poetics of racial longing.

32. In *Playing in the Dark*, Morrison writes, "It as if the realms of fiction and reality were divided by a line that, when maintained, offers the possibility of winning, but, when crossed, signals the inevitability of losing" (18).

33. Desegregation, its necessity and impossibilities, remained a topic of discussion in Hurston's correspondence. In a March 1956 letter, she criticized the NAACP's approach to integrating the University of Alabama: "As a Negro, you know I can't be in favor of segregation, but I do deplore the way they go about ending it" (Kaplan 747). While many people mistakenly interpreted such comments to mean that Hurston supported segregated institutions, her essays of the late 1940s and early 1950s frequently contradict this charge and reflect a complex, shifting racial politics.

34. Steven Gould Axelrod ("Is Elizabeth Bishop"), Renée Curry, Lorrie Goldensohn, and Camille Roman are among the scholars who have interpreted Bishop's complicated, often conservative, racial politics, particularly her intimate and problematic relationships with servants. See also Ellis's fascinating discussion of Bishop's characteristically ambivalent early politics in "'Curious Cat'" as well as Millier's discussion of Bishop's anticommunist sentiments (97–98).

35. Rodman's *New Anthology of Modern Poetry* included African American folk songs; he also wrote the first monograph on African American folk painter Horace Pippin (Martin B8).

36. Bishop, *Complete Prose*, 65. Hereafter cited in the text as *CPR*.

37. Kaplan notes the irony in the fact that Hurston was working as a maid when the short story came out, a situation noted in the *Miami Herald*. While Kaplan is largely critical of the troublesome racial politics of the story, calling it "stereotypical, sentimental, and bathetic" and arguing that Hurston did not intend the tale, including its ending as ironic, she does acknowledge the ways that the courtroom scenarios allowed Hurston to address "racism, sexism, and the difficulty of attaining public recognition" (595). Read within a postwar context in which the concept of universal human rights and the role of the newly formed United Nations in protecting them were being widely debated, Hurston's seemingly retrograde story about a servant's loyalty uses

ironic humor to raise questions about the limits of privacy as well as the rhetorical and racial blind spots in human rights discourse.

38. Singh rightly cautions against romanticized interpretations of African Americans' embrace of American nationalism during and after World War II: "It is certainly the case that in World War II, as in the past, black thinkers took up liberal and republican ideas about American exceptionalism and exemplarity, adapting them to their own ends. In doing so, they reinvested it with the symbolic power of their own struggles" (126). While Hurston, often chastised for her conservative politics, is not likely to be an intellectual placed in Singh's genealogy of black radicalism, I think her writing exemplifies this reinvestment strategy, infusing universal aspirations for human rights with the historical particulars of racial oppression as well as interracial intimacy.

Chapter 2

1. According to historian Paula Giddings, "The percentage of Black workingwomen earning wages in the industrial sector in 1940 tripled by 1944" (238). For other historical overviews of African Americans in the post–World War II era, see Kelley; Sugrue; Deborah Gray White; Kryder; Dudziak, *Cold War Civil Rights*.

2. Histories of gay and lesbian Americans in the post–World War II era and their impact on urban centers include Bérubé; D'Emilio, *Sexual Politics*; David K. Johnson; Kaiser; Elizabeth Lapovsky Kennedy and Davis.

3. Denby, "Summer," *Complete Poems*, 9. Hereafter cited in the text as *DCP*.

4. Brooks, "One Wants a Teller in a Time Like This," *Blacks*, 132. Hereafter cited in the text as *BL*.

5. Walker and Smethurst locate Brooks within a modernist context; for feminist readings of Brooks, see Spillers, "Gwendolyn"; Tate, "Anger"; Mary Helen Washington.

6. Even in recent reassessments of the New York School, Denby is still neglected. Stephen Paul Miller and Terence Diggory's *The Scene of My Selves*, for example, makes no mention of Denby, and Lehman's revisionist study, *Last Avant-Garde*, contains only the briefest discussion of Denby, again treating him as a "minor" figure in the circle. In Davidson's recent and important reassessment of Cold War poetics, *Guys Like Us*, Denby remains invisible.

7. Arna Bontemps and Conroy, a leftist activist and proletarian writer, coauthored *They Seek a City* (1945), an account of African Americans' northern migration. He also edited *The Anvil*, the literary magazine that first published Richard Wright in 1934. A friend of Conroy's from their time at the South Side Art Center in the 1940s, Brooks presented Conroy with the Literary Times Prize in 1967. See Wixson.

8. Warren also describes Locke's advocacy, ten years later, of an art that fuses racial particularity with a universal relevance. Characterizing the aesthetic reorientation

of African American writers after World War II, Warren notes, "The matter to be determined was not whether African American writers should write about African Americans, but rather under what conditions and in which way ought they do so" (*What Was* 59–60). Locke's embrace of a precarious balance between racial subject matter and universality was one of many directives given to this postwar generation of writers. The challenge that postwar critics posed to the era's black writers, as Warren encapsulates it, was to "see the particular plight of black Americans in relation to what was deemed the broader human condition" (68).

9. See Najar's discussion of African American poet Margaret Danner and Loeser Katinka, a white associate editor of *Poetry*, as another "point of contact between a burgeoning African American art movement and the tradition of literary modernism" in which in the South Side Community Art Center played a crucial role (320).

10. Gwendolyn Brooks, "Has It Been Hard Miss Brooks?," 2–3, Carton 3:33, Gwendolyn Brooks Collection, Bancroft Library, University of California, Berkeley. The essay was likely written in the early 1950s as her list of prizes ends with a mention of a novel (*Maud Martha*) being published in the fall, which would have been 1953.

11. Borstelmann notes that there were "at least sixty known violent deaths of black Southerners at the hands of whites between the end of the summer of 1945 and the end of 1946" (55).

12. For a discussion of the important role movies played in "wedging open spaces for critical thought" for African American viewers, see Green, *Battling the Plantation Mentality*, 148.

13. Both Mullen and Giddings discuss the expansion of black consumer culture after World War II as a strategy for claiming class mobility and social respectability. See also May's discussion of domestic consumerism as a form of national security in an anxious age (153–73). May notes the relationship between this domestic consumerism and sexual containment as conservative ideologies that "required conformity to strict gender assumptions that were fraught with potential tensions and frustrations" (172). As Mary Helen Washington's famous reading of *Maud Martha* attests, Brooks compellingly depicts the sublimated anger produced in public and domestic environments informed by these ideologies.

14. Despite the treasured narrative of the 1950s as an era of postwar abundance, the median income for black women in the late 1940s was 57 percent that for white women (Giddings 256).

15. I recognize that my use of the terms *gay* and *queer* throughout this study is problematic; though I use them at times as a kind of shorthand for a range of homosexual, homosocial, and homoerotic activity and sentiment, I remain aware that none of these men would have identified themselves or their cultural practices as "gay" or in many cases even "homosexual." For a discussion of the increasing use of the term *gay* by homosexual men as an identity marker in the 1930s and 1940s, see Beemyn 197–98.

16. O'Hara was an even more enthusiastic fan of Mitchell, gushing about his performance as Puck in the 1962 premiere of *A Midsummer Night's Dream*. See Gooch, *City Poet*, 386.

17. Denby's critical tastes could be quite varied. He reviewed the Museum of Modern Art's Coffee Concerts, a series organized in 1942 by writer and art patron Louise Crane, Elizabeth Bishop's close friend. The program included flamenco, tap, and Yemeni dance.

18. A figure who connects Brooks and Denby, Dunham was also active at the South Side Community Art Center.

19. Leslie had dated painter Grace Hartigan, a dear friend of O'Hara, the previous year. Leslie's paintings included a series on O'Hara's death, and in the 1990s, he painted a series of African American nudes, including *Jaleel Mohammed* and *Betty Moore*, a bodybuilder. The artist is also known for his 1959 film, *Pull My Daisy*, an adaptation of a Jack Kerouac story (Hoban AR33; Gooch 211).

20. In a review from a 1962 production, Van Vechten delighted in the young Ailey and Carmen de Lavallade as they "plunged into *House of Flowers* like two young animals . . . a happy explosion"; Van Vechten also gushed over Ailey's "perfect body" and early promise as a dancer (44).

21. Another figure who exemplifies this integrationist moment of convoluted connections between African American and white artists in the 1950s is John LaTouche. Both Denby and LaTouche appeared in Rudy Burkhardt's first film. In 1940, Strayhorn commissioned LaTouche, a librettist, to write the lyrics for "Day Dream." He also wrote the lyrics to accompany Vernon Duke's music for the 1941 Broadway musical *Cabin in the Sky*, starring Ethel Waters and Lena Horne. As a white artist with a "track record with black-themed material," LaTouche collaborated with Strayhorn and Duke Ellington on *Beggar's Holiday*, a 1946 musical that shocked audiences with its interracial romances (Hajdu 101). Before his death in 1956, LaTouche was the partner of writer Kenward Elmslie, another figure of the New York School scene. LaTouche also produced a film version of James Schuyler's *Presenting Jane* in 1952, the same summer Schuyler was dating Denby. See Hajdu. LaTouche's "Ballad for Americans," written with Earl Robinson, was sung by Paul Robeson at many of his concerts (see Smethurst 225–26).

22. Thomson evidently thought Denby would also enjoy the company of Alice Toklas, Stein's lover; in a June 1948 letter to Denby, Thomson wrote, "If you are in Paris I wish you would you to see Alice Toklas. You would love each other" (226).

23. Hajdu's *Lush Life* documents the importance of salons and social clubs in providing both social support and professional connections for black artists. The Neal Salon, for example, started by dancer/painter Frank Neal and his wife, Dorcas, brought together an interracial (though largely black) group of artists, many of them gay. Artists who participated in the Neal Salon included the choreographer Talley

Beatty, musician John Cage, Harry Belafonte, artist Charles Sebree, Billy Strayhorn, and occasionally James Baldwin. Strayhorn was also a founding member of the social club the Copasetics, which consisted of African American dancers, musicians, and comedians, mainly gay men, who together produced small events and wildly popular musical revues. These types of salons and social clubs, essential networks for mid-twentieth-century African American artists, have been largely omitted from gay cultural studies and racial histories of America but offer promising research possibilities for contemporary scholars (Hajdu 114–20).

24. Elizabeth Lee discusses the prevalence of visual representations of the emotional and sexual connections between soldiers during World War II as well as various artistic depictions of queer desire within a military context throughout the twentieth century.

25. In her biographical sketch of the poet, Melhem is cryptic about Brooks's marital problems: "There was a hiatus in the marriage from 1969 to 1973, when the Blakelys lived apart" (8). In her autobiography, *Report from Part One*, Brooks is more forthcoming, offering a model for marriage and its progressions that departs from the heteronormative: "The relationship between a man and a woman properly develops from one stage to another, and it sometimes *properly* occurs that the last stage, to somebody's or nobody's surprise, is a dignified separation. In such a case, both man and woman may then proceed to arrivals, to adventures, to a peace, to personal shapings not possible before" (58).

26. Roi Ottley's December 1950 contribution to the same magazine, "What's Wrong with Negro Women," does not claim racial distinctiveness, concluding that "what's wrong with Negro women is, in fact, what is wrong with women generally" (72).

27. The tributes in *Ballet Review* after Denby's death in 1983 are almost completely silent about his homosexuality. While many observers would argue that his sexual identity has no direct relevance to his dance criticism, many of the reminiscences were personal and journeyed into other intimate biographical details yet neglected the largely gay worlds in which he lived.

28. The warehouse or artist loft, a particular New York School version of the bachelor pad, served both public and private functions for artists. It was a place to create, dine, have sex, and present art. It is a queer space that should be added to those theorized as essential in gay cultural life.

29. The large number of portraits of Denby, often by friends, are a fascinating layer of this ghostly persona; paintings by Alex Katz and Neil Welliver and a drawing by Willem de Kooning depict his skeletal physique, his gaunt face, his tufts of snowy hair. Reva Wolf offers a compelling reading of the "visual gossip" in Andy Warhol's double portrait of Edwin Denby and Gerard Malanga for a 1963 cover of *C: A Journal of Poetry*. She characterizes Denby as "a model of gentility and urbanity" (21). On

the magazine's back cover, Denby, wrapped in Malanga's arms, looks corpse-like, the kiss easily confused for an act of resuscitation. The image echoes the ghostly persona evoked in many of the tributes to Denby as well as in his poetry.

30. Baker was an icon of transnationalism and integration as a performer and activist, and her 1947 marriage to Jo Boullion, a white Frenchman, was one of the era's most famous interracial marriages and was widely reported in the black press. For an announcement of Baker's marriage, see the October 1947 issue of *Ebony*.

31. Notley, "Intersections," notes that Denby "read Stein constantly and told others to do so too." Melhem also links Brooks's linguistic compression to Stein (85).

32. Corber discusses the influence of Gunnar Myrdal's *An American Dilemma* (1944) on Corey's political beliefs about homosexuals as a minority group best served by an assimilationist strategy (*Homosexuality* 91–92).

33. For succinct overview of the predominance of the minoritarian model within gay and lesbian civil rights discourse and the now well-known critiques by queer theorists of this political strategy, see Corber, "Queer," which also discusses some of the theoretical and political liabilities of the analogy between race and homosexuality as shared oppressions requiring state protections.

34. In his discussion of the integrationist ethos among African American critics in the early 1950s, Warren writes, "Broadly speaking, the fact that the civil rights gains of the 1950s and 1960s did not end racial disparity, particularly at the bottom end of the economic scale, made it possible to paint the writers and critics who in the 1950s through the mid-1960s expressed optimism about the imminent collapse of racial inequality as naïve dupes of a power structure that had recognized it could seize as putative color blindness of liberal humanism to contain demands for racial egalitarianism" (*What Was* 67).

Chapter 3

1. For a fuller discussion of the conflation of the homosexual with the sexual psychopath, see Neil Miller, an account of a child murder in Sioux City, Iowa, in the 1950s and the sexual hysteria that surrounded it. See also Chauncey, "Post-War."

2. Ann Petry, "Ann Petry," 253. Hereafter cited in the text as "AP."

3. In addition to a children's book, *The Legends of Saints* (1970), Petry wrote a picture book, *The Drugstore Cat* (1949), as well as two historical nonfiction books for young adults, *Harriet Tubman: Conductor on the Underground Railroad* (1955) and *Tituba of Salem Village* (1964), which renders the famous witch trials from the perspective of an accused black woman.

4. Both Lubin ("Introduction" 7–11) and Peterson (72–81) provide excellent overviews of Petry's political commitments and status as an "ambivalent radical" (Lubin, "Introduction" 8).

5. Both Wald (113–37) and Jackson (144–45) critique Petry's reluctance to claim

her connections to communist-affiliated or leftist organizations and her general distancing from activist politics with the rise of the Cold War. Petry's daughter, Elisabeth Petry, describes her mother as a member of the Harlem Left but also explains her lifelong membership in the Republican Party as commonplace in local New England politics (8, 114–15). Petry's political commitments and their evolution defy easy encapsulation.

6. The 11 September 1958 issue of *Jet* reported the deal, calling Petry the "first Negro script writer in Hollywood" ("Ann Petry," 61).

7. I am leery of the term *masculinist*. The distinction between feminist and masculinist approaches and the latter's potential to overlap with patriarchal practices raise a potentially troubling divide that suggests that literary projects such as Petry's focused on masculinity or critical studies of gender focused predominantly on masculinity sit somewhere outside feminism. In fact, the more thoughtful strands of feminist criticism have always critiqued gender in all its forms, including masculinity. Maurice Wallace's fear that black masculinity studies "has lost its black feminist moorings" is warranted (34). In exploring masculinity and in unearthing the ideologies of whiteness, we must be careful not to reify existing power structures; instead, critics need to consistently acknowledge earlier feminist scholarship and literature, including Petry's, that have made possible our more recent investigations of masculinity and race.

8. Critic Michael Barry similarly only gestures in a footnote to Petry's exploration of same-sex parenting in his essay, "'Same Train.'"

9. McDowell notes that in *The Narrows*, Petry includes "memorable eccentrics" who "are peripheral to the plot but add mystery" (134), offering Cesar the Writing Man, Weak Knees, and Cat Jimmie as examples. She fails to mention the Valkills, also eccentric figures whose bohemian lifestyle and sexual transgressions become central to Link's racial consciousness and sexual education.

10. Similarly, Alfred Kinsey's reports also chipped away at many of the stereotypes surrounding black sexuality, including myths about penis size, promiscuity, and virility. For some of Kinsey's findings, see *Ebony*, December 1948.

11. "Let's Be Honest" warns of homosexuality's irreversibility, noting that a homosexual "cannot be unmade." One expert recommends that adult homosexuals marry and have children as a "solution" (49).

12. Petry's depiction of the white pervert is clearly intended to alarm as it avoids the absurd comic layers of Richard Wright's "Man of All Work" (1957), in which an African American man, unable to find work, disguises himself as a woman to work as a domestic and must ward off the sexual approaches of both husband and wife. In Wright's "radio play," the sexual danger is never taken seriously.

13. For a fuller discussion of Petry's representations of domestic labor and their uses in forwarding racial and economic critiques of Cold War society, see Peterson. Peterson convincingly links the Valkill incident to other moments in the novel where

white people's wealth and racial paternalism facilitate and obfuscate "the sexual exploitation of domestics" (160).

14. Box 4, Folder 9, Ann Petry Collection, Gotlieb Archival Research Center, Boston University.

15. Ibid.

16. In her writing notebook, Petry is clear about the function of this flashback to Mr. Valkill's sexual advances: "It is necessary in order to do what—to explain how [Link] comes to love at Last Chance—how Abbie tried to build his character by forcing him to keep at a job that was intolerable—because of the type of people—because only an exploiter would hire a twelve-year-old-boy and expect him to do the work of a trained female servant." This illuminating comment suggests that the Mr. Valkill is abhorrent not only for his sexual advances but also for his inappropriate use of a child for domestic labor as well as his nonconformity to gender norms for domestic work. The exploitative figure of homosexual pedophilia is positioned as the antithesis of familial love. Valkill reveals that Abbie's belief in white respectability is a dangerous myth. The traumatic encounter is, in fact, crucial to Petry's narrative progression as it propels Link toward an alternative family unit that is racially affirming and in which, to use Petry's phrase, "he comes to love." See Box 19, Folder 2, Petry Collection.

17. Demby's marriage to Drudi was announced in a 1953 issue of *Jet*. See "Negro Author," 21. For further details on Demby's career, including his novel in progress, see Biggers 12–13.

18. For a detailed account of the federal government's twenty-year efforts to purge gay and lesbians from its ranks, deeming them "security risks," communist sympathizers, and easy targets for blackmail by Cold War enemies, see David K. Johnson.

19. Cultural examples of an idealized pederasty offered by Demby include Denton Welch, *In Youth is Pleasure* (1944), William Maxwell, *The Folded Leaf* (1945), and works by Italian filmmaker and writer Pier Paolo Pasolini. See also Campbell's discussion in *Paris Interzone* of Maurice Girodias, the controversial publisher of Nabokov's *Lolita* (1955) and William Burroughs's *Naked Lunch* (1959). Girodias's father, Jack Kahane, published James Hanley's banned novel, *Boy* (1931).

20. David K. Johnson notes the pervasiveness of Waldeck's article, initially published in 1952, and its paranoid thesis; it was read into the *Congressional Record* and often cited by those who contended that gays and lesbians posed a serious security risk within the federal government in positions at home and abroad (34).

21. For a discussion of Africana existentialism see Gordon, *Existence in Black*, particularly the introduction, for an overview of existential investigations in specifically African American contexts.

22. According to Russell, "After World War II the numbers of African Americans living outside heterosexual family norms only increased, and at a far faster rate than for whites. The illegitimacy rate among African Americans rose from 16.8 percent in

1940 to 23.6 percent in 1963, while the rate among whites remained relatively tiny, moving from just 2 percent to 3.07 percent during the same period. . . . The divorce rate for both groups was 2.2 percent in 1940, but for African Americans it grew to 5.1 percent by 1963, while the white rate increased to only 3.6 percent" (120).

23. Demby also elaborated on the nuanced indirections used to discuss sexuality in middle-class African American communities in the 1930s.

24. According to Gilbert, the rise of a new youth culture after World War II and sociologists' and psychologists' fervor to explain the deviant elements within it can be attributed to a combination of factors: an increase in marriages and childbearing; demographic shifts as a consequence of migration, urbanization, and suburbanization; and radical changes in mass communication and advertising (130).

25. Gilbert offers a full discussion of Wertham's controversial crusade against comic books, *The Seduction of the Innocent* (1954). Gilbert notes that Wertham saw a connection between comics and segregation, arguing that their racist imagery and story lines promoted "destructive ideas" and contributed to racial tension (101). For a discussion of representations of racialized sexuality in 1950s comic books, see Lubin, *Romance* 39–65. Lubin observes that the era's comics "represented interracial intimacy in fantastic ways to foreclose the possibility of interracial sexuality" (58) and concludes that the medium often employed nonwhite sexuality to critique normative ideas about class and gender and Americans' increasing anxiety about the stability of these norms.

26. Of the many critics who have critiqued Mailer's troublesome fetishism regarding black sexuality and cultural freedom, few have discussed the origins of the essay. Schaub notes that "White Negro" was conceived as a "metaphor for integration" in response to a bet Mailer made with Lyle Stuart, who challenged him to "write something about integration that would be too controversial for a major newspaper to publish" (139). Demby and Petry should be read as producers of their own metaphors of integration, but they do so in modes that consciously challenge the sort of sexual stereotypes and racial essentialism found in Mailer's essay.

Chapter 4

1. This interview took place in 1946, which Sandberg labels "a peak year of anti-Semitism" in America (378).

2. In response to the hiring of black workers, twenty-six thousand white workers at Detroit's Packard Motor Company went on strike. According to McKay Jenkins, "thirty-four people died, including seventeen blacks who were killed by police" (24). In Harlem, nearly four hundred African Americans were injured and five killed when racial violence erupted after a confrontation between a black soldier and a white police officer after the policeman's mistreatment of a black woman (24).

3. Wald notes that Sinclair worked with African American novelist Chester Himes,

another important documentarian of the sexual politics of postwar America, as part of a WPA project at the Cleveland Public Library in the 1930s (242). Himes also orchestrated Richard Wright's review of Sinclair's *Wasteland* (242).

4. Cultural institutions as well as midcentury artists faced this balancing act between capturing a common human condition and documenting cultural and individual distinctiveness. For example, Karamu House's mission statement announced the cultural center's "two goals of professional integration and forging a self-determined mode of African American cultural expression as complementary goals" (Morgan 6). Dan Levine, a Jewish writer and editor of the journal *Crossroad*, was also involved in Karamu House's interracial theatrical productions (Wald 236–47).

5. For a fuller account of Frank's controversial trial, including its racial and sexual politics, see Sundquist 194–97; Jacobson, *Whiteness* 62–67. The fervent anti-Semitism and vigilante justice of Frank's case prompted the creation of the Anti-Defamation League.

6. For other examples of other literary works by Jewish writers that center on lynching and other forms of racial violence against African Americans, see Sundquist 27.

7. As a prominent publisher in African American media, Offord stayed active in politics. In 1979, he was one of one hundred black Americans invited to Libya by the United African Nationalist Movement Harlem Council for Economic Development to promote cross-cultural dialogue and future financial investment in Harlem ("Negro Corp." 31).

8. For a survey of critical responses to Offord's first novel by left-leaning American critics, see Wald 138–40.

9. Marjorie Farber's review of Seaver's anthology praises Offord's story for having "more than a didactic value," in contrast to other stories in the collection about race, which she finds lacking in literary merit. Farber offensively concludes, "The Negro writers—well represented here—were trained in the protest school of writing, and it is hardly surprising if they have had neither the time nor the inclination to develop a purely literary tradition" (BR4). African American writers in the decade after World War II were always writing against this assumption, many of them challenging the opposition set up by Farber that social critique sullied the purity of literature.

10. According to McKay Jenkins, Lillian Smith's long-standing interest in psychoanalysis "led her to her most dramatic claims about racism's legacy of broad spiritual damage" (119).

11. Rose reports that the differences between white and black soldiers leveled off after combat and that black soldiers experienced an overall stronger sense of morale than white soldiers.

12. Sacks discusses how the GI Bill excluded most African Americans and women of all races through discriminatory admissions policies at universities, redlining in

urban districts, and restrictive covenants that prevented African Americans from buying in the burgeoning suburbs (86–98).

13. Ralph Ellison was a supporter of Wertham's Lafargue Clinic in Harlem, which sought to address the "personality damage" that resulted from America's racist social system ("Harlem").

14. Scott includes a thoughtful distillation of the role social scientists played in legitimizing the damage thesis, including the reversal of the conclusion, arrived at in many studies, that proximity to rather than segregation from discriminatory white people and institutions more negatively affected African Americans' self-image (96–136).

15. The impact of slavery, segregation, and daily social discrimination on African Americans' identity and mental health would remain a contentious topic. Controversial studies, including Stanley Elkins's 1959 *Slavery*, which in its discussion of learned inferiority complexes drew parallels between Holocaust survivors and slaves on southern plantations, and the infamous 1965 Moynihan Report, which constructed a pathology out of single black motherhood, prompted many black intellectuals and artists increasingly to challenge psychological discourses focused on "damage," "inferiority," and "pathology." Warren notes that Ellison's embrace of a "culture-as-resistance" model of African American life directly challenged the damage thesis asserted by Elkins and others. Warren notes, however, that Elkin argued that "it had never been sufficiently proved that the culture produced by African Americans under slavery had been more nurturing than damaging" (*So Black* 69). For a discussion of black nationalist responses to the damage thesis, see Warren, *So Black* 73–75. Sundquist argues that black nationalists' critiques of and revisions to the damage thesis were substantially influenced by the Holocaust, including survivor testimony and its iconography (436–39). Finally, for an expansive history of conservatives' as well as liberals' use of damage imagery in U.S. race relations, see Scott.

16. Both Sacks and Lipsitz have documented the ways that whiteness was solidified and middle-class status obtained by working-class and ethnic whites through unofficial affirmative action after World War II. Sacks describes the various social forces and federal programs, including the GI Bill and the Federal Housing Authority, which, though they excluded most African Americans, made middle-class professions and suburban housing available to Jewish Americans previously barred from these sources of upward social mobility. In "The Possessive Investment in Whiteness: Racialized Social Democracy and the 'White' Problem in American Studies," Lipsitz discusses how urban renewal programs and suburbanization increased segregation while permitting immigrants to shed ethnic identities and claim the social and material benefits of whiteness.

17. Black, Catholic, and a tomboy, Virginia Houston, Sinclair's lifelong friend, was clearly the model for Clara. Houston, a poet and social worker whose multiracial fam-

ily history Sinclair mentions in her memoir, *The Seasons* (1993), was Sinclair's sounding board while she wrote the novel, verifying the authenticity of her black characters. She supported Sinclair's decision to write a novel about blacks attempting to integrate a neighborhood, urging, "You write the book. One thing this world doesn't need, baby, is another nigger book by a nigger" (*Seasons* 109). Although Houston found the integrationist tale of resistance compelling, she warned Sinclair not to be too optimistic about the novel's potential to challenge racism: "Even if your book's the great American novel, baby, it won't change that black-white garbage" (*Seasons* 114). Sinclair was deeply interested in people's racial, sexual, and emotional "garbage." Explaining the title of her novel *Wasteland*, Sinclair said, "I wanted it to mean uselessness, wasted lives because the heart and the energies are unused" (Sidney R. Williams 1). Psychological wastelands became one of her favored metaphors and rescuing people from them her literary mission.

18. Sinclair's progressive explorations of racial phobia and sexual trauma might be placed as a mid-twentieth-century contribution to the queer "archive of feelings" that Cvetkovich convincingly configures. There are, however, ironies in placing Sinclair along this historical trajectory given that the novelist's occluded (closeted?) homosexuality appears to stand in opposition to Cvetkovich's inquiry into the more visible "sites of lesbian public culture" (3). Typical of her generation, Sinclair, like Elizabeth Bishop, wrapped her lesbianism in ambiguity and innuendo. Her purposefully gender-ambiguous penname—Jo—as well as her tomboy manner (the inspiration for Judy Vincent) fueled the open secret of Sinclair's homosexuality. Despite the pathbreaking portrait of lesbianism in *Wasteland*, which placed her as a pioneer of queer American literature, Sinclair's 1995 *New York Times* obituary mentions euphemistically her "companion," Joan Soffer ("Jo Sinclair" B10).

19. Jo Sinclair, statement, Box 35, Folder 9, Sinclair Collection.

20. In his history of racial damage, Scott documents the ongoing debates among social scientists on whether "proximity rather than distance was more damaging to blacks" (xii; see also chapters 4, 5).

21. Jo Sinclair, statement, Box 35, Folder 9, Sinclair Collection.

22. The largely unflattering portrait of Vincent's conservative grandmother whose life is wholly defined by her faith (she decides to move to Israel at the end of the novel) is a pronounced departure from Toni Morrison's optimistic reading of ancestral figures as "timeless people whose relationships to the characters are benevolent, instructive, and protective, and they provide a certain kind of wisdom" ("Rootedness" 343). The social instruction provided by the Vincent family's matriarch is largely one of intolerance, gender conformity, and cultural isolation, lessons that Vincent defiantly rejects. Sinclair's unsentimental portrait of community elders is typical of the all of the postwar texts discussed in this project. Ancestral figures fail to be the bearers of tradition, and adults are mostly depicted as morally corrupt, emotionally unavailable,

or socially constricted. Ancestry, it seems, is an impediment to younger characters' self-realization rather than a resource.

23. Sinclair's passion for psychoanalysis is evident not only in *Wasteland* but also in stories such as "From the Letter File of a Psychiatrist," about a patient's obsessive necrophilia, and "Fascism: Headquarters in Ohio," which documents the pathologies of a white supremacist organization.

24. This subplot is an odd echo of the speculation over Leo Frank's alleged sexual deformity. Sundquist notes that testimony during Frank's trial for the murder of Mary Phagan suggested that he had some type of "genital deformity," a reference possibly to circumcision or a physical difference that was never confirmed (195). In both cases, these bodily scars—evidence of trauma—were used to explain and condemn social deviance.

25. One of the few critics to examine Offord's writing, Wald locates Offord within a leftist, proletarian tradition but offers no analysis of *The Naked Fear*, suggesting that the paperback thriller represented Offord's distancing from communist publications and circles. Offord's discussion in *The Naked Fear* of desegregation in the military and the tensions it fostered as well as his depictions of interracial sexuality and white people's racism demonstrate that the novel is far more political than Wald acknowledges.

26. For Bone's survey of postwar African American novels that depart from the protest tradition, see *Negro Novel* 160–72.

27. In 1942, the American Red Cross approved the segregation of blood supplies according to the race of donors (Borstelmann 32). In "Many Thousands Gone" (1951), James Baldwin also cites the appalling racism of the act, lamenting that for black Americans "in our most recent war, his blood was segregated as was, for the most part, his person" (20).

28. For an overview of the changeling tale and its cultural variations, see JoAnn Conrad 179–80. At the center of most changeling narratives is the abduction of a baby by a supernatural spirit who then masquerades as the child. Beyond the direct reference to the folktale in Clara's comments, Sinclair uses the changeling as a figure of social change, a shape-shifter who can infiltrate families and communities across race and religious differences as well as adapt into kinship structures of her/his own creation.

29. The married Buchman supported Sinclair through psychological upheavals and struggles to survive as a writer. Scattered between stories of gardening at Buchman's home in Cleveland, where Sinclair lived and worked, Sinclair's odd memoir, which she calls her "obituary" for Buchman, also records painful memories of mental breakdowns and hard drinking (*Seasons* 98). Buchman, who was well versed in psychoanalysis but had "no official qualifications" (85), treated her "patient-friend" as she struggled to confront her "hurt and self-disgust and bitter, shamed confusion" (87)—a

textbook definition of queer self-loathing. The intimacy of Sinclair's relationship with Buchman and the intensity of emotion described in *The Seasons* becomes, like *The Changelings*, another coded, though less veiled, lesbian text. In this potentially messy dynamic, Buchman becomes the therapist-mother, nurturing the writer and chipping away at Sinclair's emotional numbness, freeing her from her psychological ghettos.

30. Jules also recognizes the role that African Americans played for integrationist writers as a surrogate moral consciousness, a relationship he imagines stereotypically as cannibalistic. He reflects on his transformation: "I started to know why the *Schwartze* were in me like that. Eating out my guts" (*Changelings* 279).

WORKS CITED

"100 Blacks Off to Libya in August." *New York Amsterdam News*, 4 August 1979, 7.

"Ann Petry to Write Script for Kim Novak Movie." *Jet*, 11 September 1958, 61.

Aswell, Ed. Letter to Jo Sinclair. 7 February 1955. Box 44. Jo Sinclair Collection. Gotlieb Archival Research Center, Boston University, Boston.

Axelrod, Steven Gould. "Elizabeth Bishop and Containment Policy." *American Literature* 75.4 (December 2003): 843–67.

———. "Is Elizabeth Bishop a Racist?" *"In Worcester, Massachusetts": Essays on Elizabeth Bishop*. New York: Lang, 1999. 345–56.

Baker, Ella, and Marvel Cooke. "The Bronx Slave Market." *The Crisis* 42.11 (November 1935): 330–40.

Baldwin, James. *Another Country*. 1962. New York: Vintage, 1993.

———. "Many Thousands Gone." 1951. *Collected Essays*. New York: Library of America, 1998. 19–34.

———. "Notes of a Native Son." *Collected Essays*. New York: Library of America, 1998. 63–84.

———. "Preservation of Innocence." *Collected Essays*. New York: Library of America, 1998. 594–600.

———. "Take Me to the Water." From *No Name Is the Street* (1972). *Collected Essays*. New York: Library of America, 1998. 353–403.

Baraka, Amiri (LeRoi Jones). *Blues People: Negro Music in White America*. 1963. New York: HarperCollins, 2002.

Barry, Michael. "'Train Be Back Tomorrer': Ann Petry's *The Narrows* and the Repetition of History." *MELUS* 24.1 (Spring 1999): 141–59.

Bay, Mia. *The White Image in the Black Mind: African-American Ideas about White People, 1830–1925*. New York: Oxford University Press, 2000.

Beaver, Harold. "Homosexual Signs (In Memory of Roland Barthes)." *Critical Inquiry* 8.1 (Autumn 1981): 99–119.

Beemyn, Brett. "A Queer Capital: Race, Class, Gender, and the Changing Social Landscape of Washington's Gay Communities, 1940–1955." *Creating a Place for Ourselves: Lesbian, Gay, and Bisexual Community Histories*. Ed. Brett Beemyn. New York: Routledge, 1997. 183–210.

Bernard, Emily. "'Raceless' Writing and Difference: Ann Petry's *Country Place* and the African-American Literary Canon." *Studies in American Fiction* 33.1 (Spring 2005): 87–117.

Bérubé, Allan. *Coming Out under Fire: The History of Gay Men and Women in World War II*. New York: Free Press, 1990.

Betsky, Aaron. *Queer Space: Architecture and Same-Sex Desire*. New York: Morrow, 1997.

Biggers, Jeff. "William Demby Has Not Left the Building: Postcard from Tuscany." *Bloomsbury Review* 24.1 (January–February 2004): 12–13.

Bishop, Elizabeth. *The Collected Prose*. New York: Farrar, Straus, and Giroux, 1984.

———. *The Complete Poems, 1927–1979*. New York: Farrar, Straus, and Giroux, 1983.

———. *Edgar Allen Poe and the Juke-Box: Uncollected Poems, Drafts, and Fragments*. Ed. Alice Quinn. New York: Farrar, Straus, and Giroux, 2006.

———. *One Art*. Ed. Robert Giroux. New York: Farrar, Straus, and Giroux, 1994.

Bland, Aldon. "Let's Go Fishing." *Negro Story*, May–June 1944, 20–22.

Bone, Robert. *The Negro Novel in America*. Rev. ed. New Haven: Yale University Press, 1965.

———. "Richard Wright and the Chicago Renaissance." *Callaloo* 9.3 (Summer 1986): 446–68.

Bontemps, Arna, and Jack Conroy. *They Seek a City: A Study of Negro Migration*. New York: Doubleday, 1945.

Boris, Eileen. "'You Wouldn't Want One of 'Em Dancing with Your Wife': Racialized Bodies on the Job in World War II." *American Quarterly* 50.1 (March 1998): 77–108.

Borstelmann, Thomas. *The Cold War and the Color Line: American Race Relations in the Global Arena*. Cambridge: Harvard University Press, 2003.

Bousfield, Maudelle B. "Sex in High School." *Ebony*, December 1950, 24–32.

Boyd, Nan. *Wide-Open Town: A History of Queer San Francisco to 1965*. Berkeley: University of California Press, 2003.

Boyd, Valerie. *Wrapped in Rainbows: The Life of Zora Neale Hurston*. New York: Scribner, 2003.

Brodovitch, Alexy. *Ballet*. New York: Augustine, 1945.

Brooks, Gwendolyn. "Chicago Portraits." *Negro Story*, May–June 1944, 49–50.

———. *Blacks*. Chicago: Third World, 1987.

———. *Maud Martha*. 1953. *Blacks*. Chicago: Third World, 1987.

———. *Report from Part One*. Detroit: Broadside, 1972.

———. *Report from Part Two*. Chicago: Third World, 1996.

———. "Why Negro Women Leave Home." *Negro Digest* 9 (March 1951): 26–28.

Brown, Ashley. "An Interview with Elizabeth Bishop." *Shenandoah* 17.2 (Winter

1996). *Elizabeth Bishop and Her Art.* Ed. Lloyd Schwartz and Sybil P. Estess. Ann Arbor: University of Michigan Press, 1983. 289–302.

Browning, Alice C., and Fern Gayden. "Just to Mention That." *Negro Story*, December–January 1945–46, 2, 59–64.

———. "A Letter to Our Readers." *Negro Story*, May–June 1944, 1.

Burkhardt, Jacob. "Martens Bar." *Jacket*, 21 February 2003. http://jacketmagazine.com/21/denb-jacob.html.

Burkhardt, Rudy. "Edwin Denby Remembered." *Ballet Review* 12.1 (Spring 1984): 12–14.

Burroughs, William. *Naked Lunch.* 1959. New York: Grove, 2009.

Butcher, Philip. "Our Raceless Writers." *Opportunity* 26 (Summer 1948): 113–14.

Byrd, James W. "Ineffective Sequel to Brilliance." *Phylon* 19.4 (4th Quarter 1958): 433–35.

Campbell, James. *Paris Interzone.* London: Vintage, 1994.

Capote, Truman. "The Shape of Things." 1944. *The Complete Short Stories of Truman Capote.* New York: Vintage, 2005. 15–19.

Carby, Hazel V. Foreword. *Seraph on the Suwanee* by Zora Neale Hurston. 1948. New York: Harper Perennial, 1991.

Chafe, William. *The Unfinished Journey: America since World War II.* New York: Oxford University Press, 1986.

Chauncey, George. *Gay New York.* New York: Basic Books, 1994.

———. "The Post-War Sex Crime Panic." *True Stories from the American Past.* Ed. William Graebner. New York: McGraw-Hill, 1993. 160–78.

Cheng, Anne Anlin. *The Melancholy of Race.* New York: Oxford University Press, 2001.

Cherokee, Charles. "National Grapevine." *Chicago Defender*, 27 November 1948, 6.

Clark, Keith. "'From a Thousand Different Points of View': The Multiple Masculinities of Ann Petry's 'Miss Muriel.'" *Ann Petry's Short Fiction: Critical Essays.* Ed. Hazel Arnett Ervin and Hilary Holladay. Westport, Conn.: Praeger, 2004. 79–96.

Cole, Johnnetta B., and Elizabeth Oakes. "On Racism and Ethnocentrism." *The Changelings.* New York: Feminist Press, 1985. 339–47.

Conrad, Earl. "I Heard a Black Man Sing." *Negro Story*, October–November 1944, 63–64.

Conrad, JoAnn. "Changeling." *The Greenwood Encyclopedia of Folktales and Fairytales.* Westport, Conn.: Greenwood Press, 2007. 179–80.

"A Conversation with Author Toni Morrison." *Charlie Rose.* 10 November 2008. www.charlierose.com/view/interview/9464.

Coontz, Stephanie. *The Way We Never Were: American Families and the Nostalgia Trap.* New York: Basic Books, 1992.

Corber, Robert J. *Homosexuality in Cold War America*. Durham, N.C.: Duke University Press, 1997.

———. "Queer Regionalism." *American Literary History* 11.2 (Summer 1999): 391–402.

Corey, Donald Webster. *The Homosexual in America*. New York: Greenberg, 1951.

Couch, William. "To a Soldier." *Negro Story*, May–June 1944, 60.

Coughlan, Robert. "Changing Roles in Modern Marriage." *Life*, 24 December 1956, 108–18.

Cuordileone, K. A. *Manhood and American Political Culture*. New York: Routledge, 2005.

———. "'Politics in an Age of Anxiety': Cold War Political Culture and the Crisis of American Masculinity, 1949–1960." *Journal of American History* 87.2 (September 2000): 515–45.

Curry, Renée. *White Women Writing White: H.D., Elizabeth Bishop, Sylvia Plath, and Whiteness*. Westport, Conn.: Greenwood, 2000.

Cvetkovich, Ann. *An Archive of Feelings*. Durham, N.C.: Duke University Press, 2003.

Davidson, Michael. *Guys Like Us: Citing Masculinity in Cold War Poetics*. Chicago: University of Chicago Press, 2004.

Davis, Angela. *Blues Legacies and Black Feminism*. New York: Random House, 1999.

Davis, Arthur P. "Integration and Race Literature." *Phylon* 17.2 (2nd Quarter 1956): 141–46.

Davis, Frank Marshall. *Livin' the Blues: Memoirs of a Black Journalist and Poet*. Madison: University of Wisconsin Press, 1992.

———. "Peace Quiz for America." *Black Moods: Collected Poems*. Ed. John Edgar Tidwell. Champaign: University of Illinois Press, 2002. 131–37.

de Kooning, Elaine. "Edwin Denby Remembered." *Ballet Review* 12.1 (Spring 1984): 29–30.

"A Delicate Problem." *Newsweek*, 14 June 1954, 99–100.

Demby, William. *Beetlecreek*. 1950. Jackson: University Press of Mississippi, 1998.

———. *The Catacombs*. New York: Pantheon, 1965.

———. Interview by author. 1 December 2005, 10 September 2012.

———. *Love Story Black*. New York: Reed, Cannon, and Johnson, 1978.

D'Emilio, John. "The Homosexual Menace: The Politics of Sexuality in Cold War America." *Passion and Power: Sexuality in History*. Ed. Kathy Peiss and Christina Simmons. Philadelphia: Temple University Press, 1989. 226–40.

———. *Sexual Politics, Sexual Communities*. 2nd ed. Chicago: University of Chicago Press, 1998.

Denby, Edwin. "A Completely Civilized Art." 1943. *Looking at the Dance*. 1949. New York: Horizon, 1968. 362–66.

———. "Against Meaning in Ballet." 1949. *Dance Writing and Poetry*. New Haven: Yale University Press, 1998. 188–93.

———. *The Complete Poems*. New York: Random House, 1986.

———. "Concert Dancers in Night-Clubs." 1943. *Looking at the Dance*. 1949. New York: Horizon, 1968. 377–79.

———. "Dancers, Buildings, and People in the Street." *Dancers, Buildings, and People in the Street*. New York: Horizon, 1965. 191–202.

———. "Miss Dunham in Review." 1943. *Looking at the Dance*. 1949. New York: Horizon, 1968. 366–69.

———. "Not Tied to Any Apron Strings." 1944. *Looking at the Dance*. 1949. New York: Horizon, 1968. 340–41.

———. "Three Sides of *Agon*." *Dancers, Buildings and People in the Street*. New York: Horizon, 1965. 119–27.

———. "The Variety in African Dancing." 1943. *Looking at the Dance*. 1949. New York: Horizon, 1968. 361–62.

De Vore, Jesse. "Article on Homosexuals Drew Fire." *New York Amsterdam News*, 12 October 1957, 28.

———. "Singer Says Many Men in Harlem Choirs Are 'Queer.'" *New York Amsterdam News*, 5 October 1957, 1, 23.

Diamond, Esta. "Something for the War." *Negro Story*, December–January 1944–45, 23–25.

Dickie, Margaret. *Stein, Bishop, and Rich: Lyrics of Love, War, and Place*. Chapel Hill: University of North Carolina Press, 1997.

Diggory, Terence. *Encyclopedia of the New York School Poets*. New York: Infobase, 2009.

Dodson, Owen. "Open Letter." *Negro Story*, March–April 1945, 48.

Dollimore, Jonathan. *Sexual Dissidence: Augustine to Wilde, Freud to Foucault*. New York: Oxford University Press, 1991.

Douglas, Ann. *Terrible Honesty: Mongrel Manhattan in the 1920s*. New York: Farrar, Straus, and Giroux, 1996.

Drexel, Allen. "Before Paris Burned: Race, Class, and Male Homosexuality on the Chicago South Side, 1935–1960." *Creating a Place for Ourselves*. Ed. Brett Beemyn. New York: Routledge, 1997. 119–44.

Dubek, Laura. "White Family Values in Ann Petry's *Country Place*." *MELUS* 29.2 (Summer 2004): 55–76.

duCille, Ann. *The Coupling Convention: Sex, Text, and Tradition in Black Women's Fiction*. New York: Oxford University Press, 1993.

Duckett, Alfred. "The Third Sex." *Chicago Defender*, 2 March 1957, 7.

Dudziak, Mary L. *Cold War Civil Rights: Race and the Image of American Democracy*. Princeton: Princeton University Press, 2001.

———. "Desegregation as a Cold War Imperative." *Stanford Law Review* 41.1 (November 1988): 61–120.

Duncan, Robert. "The Homosexual in Society." 1944. *Young Robert Duncan: Portrait of the Poet as Homosexual in Society*. Ed. Ekbert Fass. Santa Barbara, Calif.: Black Sparrow, 1983. 319–22.

Dunning, Jennifer. *Alvin Ailey: A Life in Dance*. Boston: Addison-Wesley, 1996.

DuPlessis, Rachel Blau. *Genders, Races, and Religious Cultures in Modern American Poetry, 1908–1934*. New York: Cambridge University Press, 2001.

Dyer, Richard. "Coming Out as Going In: The Image of the Homosexual as a Sad Young Man." *The Culture of Queers*. New York: Routledge, 2002. 116–36.

———. "The Matter of Whiteness." *White*. New York: Routledge, 1997. 1–40.

Edelman, Lee. *No Future: Queer Theory and the Death Drive*. Durham, N.C.: Duke University Press, 2004.

Elkins, Stanley. *Slavery: A Problem in American Institutional and Intellectual Life*. Chicago: University of Chicago Press, 1959.

Ellis, Jonathan. "'A Curious Cat': Elizabeth Bishop and the Spanish Civil War." *Journal of Modern Literature* 27.1–2 (Autumn 2003): 137–48.

Ellison, Ralph. "The Art of Fiction: An Interview." 1955. *The Collected Essays of Ralph Ellison*. Ed. John F. Callahan. New York: Modern Library, 2003. 210–24.

———. "Change the Joke and Slip the Yoke." 1958. *The Collected Essays of Ralph Ellison*. Ed. John F. Callahan. New York: Modern Library, 2003. 100–112.

———. "Harlem Is Nowhere." 1948. *The Collected Essays of Ralph Ellison*. Ed. John F. Callahan. New York: Modern Library, 2003. 320–27.

——— "Indivisible Man." 1970. *The Collected Essays of Ralph Ellison*. Ed. John F. Callahan. New York: Modern Library, 2003. 359–99.

———. *Invisible Man*. 1952. New York: Vintage, 1995.

———. "The Little Man at Chehaw Station." 1977. *The Collected Essays of Ralph Ellison*. Ed. John F. Callahan. New York: Modern Library, 2003. 493–523.

———. "Twentieth-Century Fiction and the Black Mask of Humanity." 1953. *The Collected Essays of Ralph Ellison*. Ed. John F. Callahan. New York: Modern Library, 2003. 81–99.

———. "The World and the Jug." 1964. *The Collected Essays of Ralph Ellison*. Ed. John F. Callahan. New York: Modern Library, 2003. 155–88.

Eng, David. "Melancholia in the Late Twentieth Century." *Signs* 25.4 (Summer 2000): 1275–81.

Eng, David, and Shinhee Han. "A Dialogue on Racial Melancholia." *Loss: The Politics of Mourning*. Ed. David Eng and David Kazanjian. Berkeley: University of California Press, 2002. 343–71.

Erkkila, Betsy, "Elizabeth Bishop, Modernism, and the Left." *American Literary History* 8.2 (Summer 1996): 284–310.

Eversley, Shelly. "The Lunatic's Fancy and the Work of Art." *American Literary History* 13.3 (Autumn 2001): 445–68.

Eyerman, Ron. *Cultural Trauma: Slavery and the Formation of African American Identity*. New York: Cambridge University Press, 2001.

Faderman, Lillian. *Odd Girls and Twilight Lovers: A History of Lesbian Life in Twentieth-Century America*. New York: Penguin, 1992.

Farber, Marjorie. "The Younger Writers." *New York Times*, 18 May 1944, BR4.

Farrell, Kirby. *Post-Traumatic Culture: Injury and Interpretation in the Nineties*. Baltimore: Johns Hopkins University Press, 1998.

"Federal Vigilance on Perverts Asked." *New York Times*, 16 December 1950, 3.

Feld, Rose. "Flight to Harlem." *New York Times*, 23 May 1943, BR12.

Feldstein, Ruth. *Motherhood in Black and White: Race and Sex in American Liberalism, 1930–1965*. Ithaca: Cornell University Press, 2000.

Ferguson, Roderick A. "The Parvenu Baldwin and the Other Side of Redemption." *James Baldwin Now*. New York: New York University Press, 1999. 233–61.

Fiedler, Leslie. "'Come Back to the Raft Ag'in, Huck Honey.'" *Huck Finn among the Critics*. Ed. M. Thomas Inge. Frederick, Md.: University Publications of America, 1985. 93–101.

Ford, Nick Aaron. "A Blueprint for Negro Authors." *Phylon* 11.4 (4th Quarter 1950): 374–77.

Fountain, Gary, and Peter Brazeau. *Elizabeth Bishop: An Oral Autobiography*. Amherst: University of Massachusetts Press, 1994.

Freedman, Estelle. "'Uncontrolled Desires': The Response to the Sexual Psychopath, 1920–1960." *Passion and Power: Sexuality in History*. Ed. Kathy Peiss and Christina Simmons. Philadelphia: Temple University Press, 1989. 199–225.

Fuller, Hoyt, Eugenia Collier, and George E. Kent. "Interview with Gwendolyn Brooks." *Conversations with Gwendolyn Brooks*. Ed. Gloria Wade Gayles. Jackson: University Press of Mississippi, 2003. 67–73.

Fuss, Diana. *Identification Papers: Readings on Psychoanalysis, Sexuality, and Culture*. New York: Routledge, 1995.

Gayles, Gloria Wade, ed. *Conversations with Gwendolyn Brooks*. Jackson: University Press of Mississippi, 2003.

Gebhard, Paul H., John H. Gagnon, Wardell B. Pomeroy, and Cornelia V. Christenson. *Sexual Offenders: An Analysis of Types*. New York: Harper and Row, 1965.

Giddings, Paula. *When and Where I Enter: The Impact of Black Women on Race and Sex in America*. New York: Morrow, 1993.

Gilbert, James. *A Cycle of Outrage: America's Reaction to the Juvenile Delinquent in the 1950s*. New York: Oxford University Press, 1988.

Gilroy, Paul. "Identity, Belonging, and the Critique of Pure Sameness." *Against Race*. Cambridge: Harvard University Press, 2002. 97–133.

Glicksburg, Charles I. "Racial Attitudes in *From Here to Eternity*." *Phylon* 14.4 (4th Quarter 1953): 384–89.
Gloster, Hugh. "Race and the Negro Writer." *Phylon* 11.4 (4th Quarter 1950): 369–71.
Goldensohn, Lorrie. *Elizabeth Bishop: The Biography of a Poet*. New York: Columbia University Press, 1992.
Gooch, Brad. *City Poet: The Life and Times of Frank O'Hara*. New York: Knopf, 1993.
Gordon, Lewis R. "Black Existential Philosophy." *Existence in Black: An Anthology of Black Existential Philosophy*. Ed. Lewis R. Gordon. New York: Routledge, 1997. 1–9.
———, ed. *Existence in Black: An Anthology of Black Existential Philosophy*. New York: Routledge, 1997.
———. "Existential Dynamics of Theorizing Black Invisibility." *Existence in Black: An Anthology of Black Existential Philosophy*. Ed. Lewis R. Gordon. New York: Routledge, 1997. 69–79.
Gorham, Thelma Thurston. "Authors Discuss Sex Behavior in Males." *Pittsburgh Courier*, 27 March 1948, 15.
Goulden, Joseph C. *The Best Years, 1945–1950*. New York: Atheneum, 1976.
Green, Laurie Boush. *Battling the Plantation Mentality: Memphis and the Black Freedom Struggle*. Chapel Hill: University of North Carolina Press, 2007.
Greenberg, Cheryl Lynn. *Troubling the Waters: Black-Jewish Relations in the American Century*. Princeton: Princeton University Press, 2006.
Griffin, Farah Jasmine. "Hunting Communists and Negroes in Ann Petry's *The Narrows*." *Revising the Blueprint: Ann Petry and the Literary Left*. Ed. Alex Lubin. Jackson: University Press of Mississippi, 2007. 137–49.
———. *If You Can't Be Free, Be a Mystery: In Search of Billie Holiday*. New York: Free Press, 2001.
Gross, Mimi. "Edwin Denby Remembered—Part III." *Ballet Review* 12.3 (Fall 1984): 87–91.
Grubb, Davis. "Rest Stop." *Negro Story*, October–November 1944, 27–32.
Gruen, John. *The Party's Over Now: Reminiscences of the Fifties*. New York: Viking, 1972.
Gubar, Susan. *Racechanges: White Skin, Black Face in American Culture*. New York: Columbia University Press, 2000.
Hajdu, David. *Lush Life: A Biography of Billy Strayhorn*. New York: North Point, 1996.
Halberstam, Judith. *In a Queer Time and Place: Transgender Bodies, Subcultural Lives*. New York: New York University Press, 2005.
Halsey, Margaret. *Color Blind: A White Woman Looks at the Negro*. New York: Simon and Schuster, 1946.

Hammonds, Evelyn. "Black (W)holes and the Geometry of Black Female Sexuality." *Differences* 6.2–3 (June 1994): 126–45.
Handlin, Oscar. "Where Equality Leads." *Atlantic Monthly*, November 1956, 50–54.
Hanley, James. *Boy*. 1931. Paris: Obelisk, 1946.
Harris, Sydney J. "Why Many Women Won't Marry." *Science Digest*, May 1945, 79–82.
Harrison, Victoria. *Elizabeth Bishop's Poetics of Intimacy*. New York: Cambridge University Press, 1993.
Harvey, Frank. "The Bedroom Door." *Negro Story*, August–September 1945, 28–30.
Haut, Woody. *Pulp Culture: Hardboiled Fiction and the Cold War*. London: Serpent's Tail, 1995.
Hayden, Robert. *The Lion and the Archer*. Nashville, Tenn.: Hemphill, 1948.
Hemenway, Robert E. *Zora Neale Hurston*. Champaign: University of Illinois Press, 1977.
Herbert, Helen. "The Masterpiece: A Story about a Colored Girl and a White Man." *Negro Story*, May–June 1944, 32–43.
"Here's Kinsey's Report on Women." *Chicago Defender*, 29 August 1953, 2.
Higgins, Ross. "Bath, Bushes, and Belonging: Public Sex and Gay Community in Pre-Stonewall Montreal." *Public Sex/Gay Sex*. Ed. William L. Leap. New York: Columbia University Press, 1999. 187–202.
Hoban, Phoebe. "The Alfred Leslie School of Everything." *New York Times*, 21 November 2004, AR33.
Holiday, Billie, and William Duffy. *Lady Sings the Blues*. 1953. New York: Penguin, 1984.
Holladay, Hilary. *Ann Petry*. New York: Twayne, 1996.
Holman, M. Carl. "History of a Nightmare." *Phylon* 11.3 (3rd Quarter 1950): 289.
hooks, bell. "Representations of Whiteness." *Black Looks: Race and Representation*. Boston: South End, 1992. 165–78.
Howard, John. "The Library, the Park, and the Pervert: Public Space and Homosexual Encounter in Post–World War II Atlanta." *Radical History Review* 62 (Spring 1995): 166–87.
Hughes, Langston. "Here to Yonder." *Chicago Defender*, 6 October 1945, 1.
Hull, Gloria T., and Posey Gallagher. "Update on Part One: An Interview with Gwendolyn Brooks." *Conversations with Gwendolyn Brooks*. Ed. Gloria Wade Gayles. Jackson: University Press of Mississippi, 2003. 85–103.
Hurston, Zora Neale. "Art and Such." 1938. *Zora Neale Hurston: Folklore, Memoirs, and Other Writing*. Ed. Cheryl Wall. New York: Library of America, 1995. 905–11.
———. "The Conscience of the Court." *Saturday Evening Post*, 18 March 1950, 22–23, 112–22.

———. "Crazy for This Democracy." *Negro Digest* 4 (December 1945). *Zora Neale Hurston: Folklore, Memoirs, and Other Writing.* Ed. Cheryl Wall. New York: Library of America, 1995. 945–49.

———. *Dust Tracks on the Road: An Autobiography.* 1942. Philadelphia: Lippincott, 1971.

———. "Eatonville Anthology." *The Messenger,* September 1926. *Zora Neale Hurston: Folklore, Memoirs, and Other Writing.* Ed. Cheryl Wall. New York: Library of America, 1995. 813–25.

———. *Go Gator and Muddy the Water.* Ed. Pamela Bordelon. New York: Norton, 1999.

———. "The Last Slave Ship." *American Mercury,* March 1944, 351–58.

———. "My Most Humiliating Jim Crow Experience." *Negro Digest* 2 (June 1944). *Zora Neale Hurston: Folklore, Memoirs, and Other Writing.* Ed. Cheryl Wall. New York: Library of America, 1995. 935–36.

———. "Negroes without Self-Pity." *American Mercury,* November 1943, 601–3.

———. "The 'Pet Negro' System." *American Mercury,* May 1943, 593–600.

———. *Seraph on the Suwanee.* 1948. New York: Harper Perennial, 1991.

———. "What White Publishers Won't Publish." *Negro Digest* 8 (April 1950): 85–89.

Jackson, Lawrence. *The Indignant Generation: A Narrative History of African American Writers and Critics, 1934–1960.* Princeton: Princeton University Press, 2011.

Jacobson, Matthew Frye. *Roots Too: White Ethnic Revival in Post–Civil Rights America.* Cambridge: Harvard University Press, 2008.

——— *Whiteness of a Different Color: European Immigrants and the Alchemy of Race.* Cambridge: Harvard University Press, 1998.

JanMohamed, Abdul R. "Sexuality on/of the Racial Border: Foucault, Wright, and the Articulation of 'Racialized Sexuality.'" *Discourses of Sexuality from Aristotle to AIDS.* Ed. Domna C. Stanton. Ann Arbor: University of Michigan Press, 1992. 94–116.

Jenkins, Candice M. *Private Lives, Proper Relations: Regulating Black Intimacy.* Minneapolis: University of Minnesota Press, 2007.

Jenkins, McKay. *The South in Black and White: Race, Sex, and Literature in the 1940s.* Chapel Hill: University of North Carolina Press, 1999.

"Jo Sinclair, Novelist and Memoirist, 81." *New York Times,* 13 April 1995, B10.

Johnson, David K. *The Lavender Scare: Cold War Persecution of Gays and Lesbians in the Federal Government.* Chicago: University of Chicago Press, 2004.

Johnson, E. Patrick. *Appropriating Blackness: Performance and the Politics of Authenticity.* Durham, N.C.: Duke University Press, 2003.

Jones, Ernest. "Beetlecreek" (review). *The Nation,* 11 February 1950, 138–39.

Jowitt, Deborah. "Edwin Denby Remembered—Part II." *Ballet Review* 12.2 (Summer 1984): 28–30.

Kaiser, Charles. *The Gay Metropolis: The Landmark History of Gay Life in America*. New York: Harcourt Brace, 1997.

Kaplan, Carla, ed. *Zora Neale Hurston: A Life in Letters*. New York: Doubleday, 2002.

Karpman, Benjamin. "The Sexual Psychopath." *Journal of Criminal Law, Criminology, and Political Science* 42.2 (July–August 1951): 184–98.

Katz, Alex. "Edwin Denby Remembered—Part II." *Ballet Review* 12.2 (Summer 1984): 21–25.

Kelley, Robin D. G. "Looking Backward: African Americans in the Postindustrial Age." *Columbia Guide to African American History since 1939*. Ed. Robert L. Harris Jr. and Rosalyn Terborg-Penn. New York: Columbia University Press, 2008. 101–19.

Kennedy, Elizabeth Lapovsky, and Madeline D. Davis. *Boots of Leather and Slippers of Gold: The History of a Lesbian Community*. New York: Routledge, 1993.

Kennedy, Randall. *Interracial Intimacies: Sex, Marriage, Identity, and Adoption*: New York: Pantheon, 2003.

Kent, George E. "Aesthetic Values in the Poetry of Gwendolyn Brooks." *A Life Distilled: Gwendolyn Brooks, Her Poetry and Fiction*. Ed. Maria K. Mootry and Gary Smith. Champaign: University of Illinois Press, 1989. 30–46.

———. *A Life of Gwendolyn Brooks*. Lexington: University Press of Kentucky, 1990.

King, Charles E. "Family Life Trends." *Phylon* 11.3 (3rd Quarter 1950): 258–63.

King, Martin Luther, Jr. "Letter from Birmingham City Jail." 1963. *A Testament of Hope: The Essential Writing and Speeches of Martin Luther King Jr.* Ed. James M. Washington. New York: HarperCollins, 1986. 289–302.

Kirstein, Lincoln. "Comment." *Dance Index* 5.2 (February 1946): 27.

———. *Paul Cadmus*. New York: Chameleon, 1996.

Klein, Christina. *Cold War Orientalism: Asia in the Middlebrow Imagination*. Berkeley: University of California Press, 2003.

———. "The Sentimental Culture of Global Integration." *Minnesota Review* 55–57 (2002): 153–66.

Knadler, Stephen. *The Fugitive Race: Minority Writers Resisting Whiteness*. Jackson: University Press of Mississippi, 2007.

———. "Traumatized Racial Performativity: Passing in Nineteenth-Century African-American Testimonies." *Cultural Critique* 55 (Fall 2003): 63–100.

Koestenbaum, Wayne. *Hotel Theory*. Berkeley, Calif.: Soft Skull, 2007.

Kryder, Daniel. *Divided Arsenal: Race and the American State during World War II*. New York: Cambridge University Press, 2001.

Kunzel, Regina. *Criminal Intimacy: Prison and the Uneven History of Modern American Sexuality*. Chicago: University of Chicago Press, 2008.

Laurents, Arthur. *Home of the Brave*. New York: Random House, 1946.

"Leading Sociologists Discuss Sex Fears and Integration." *U.S. News and World Report*, 19 September 1958, 77–90.

Lee, Don L. [Haki Madhubuti]. "Gwendolyn Brooks: Beyond the Wordmaker—The Making of an African Poet." *Report from Part One*. Detroit: Broadside, 1972. 13–30.

Lee, Elizabeth. "When Soldiers Kiss: Picturing Homosexuality in Post–World War II America." *Journal of American Culture* 32.4 (December 2009): 318–31.

Leeming, David. *Amazing Grace: A Life of Beauford Delaney*. New York: Oxford University Press, 1998.

Lehman, David. *The Last Avant-Garde: The Making of the New York School of Poets*. New York: Doubleday, 1998.

LeSueur, Joe. *Digressions on Some Poems by Frank O'Hara*. New York: Farrar, Straus, and Giroux, 2003.

"Let's Be Honest about Homosexuals." *Our World*, August 1954, 48–49.

Lewis, Ida. "My People Are Black People." *Essence*, April 1971. *Conversations with Gwendolyn Brooks*. Ed. Gloria Wade Gayles. Jackson: University Press of Mississippi, 2003. 54–66.

Lipsitz, George. "The Possessive Investment in Whiteness: Racialized Social Democracy and the 'White' Problem in American Studies." *American Quarterly* 47.3 (September 1995): 369–87.

———. *Rainbow at Midnight: Labor and Culture in the 1940s*. Champaign: University of Illinois Press, 1994.

Locke, Alain. "Chicago's New Southside Art Center." *Magazine of Art* 34.6 (December–January 1941): 370–74.

———. "More Than Blasting Brick and Mortar." *Survey Graphic*, January 1947, 88–89.

Lombardi, Marilyn May. *The Body and the Song: Elizabeth Bishop's Poetics*. Carbondale: Southern Illinois University Press, 1995.

Longenbach, James. "Elizabeth Bishop's Social Conscience." *Journal of Modern Literature* 62.2 (Summer 1995): 467–86.

Lott, Eric. *Love and Theft: Blackface Minstrelsy and the American Working Class*. New York: Oxford University Press, 1993.

Lubin, Alex. "Introduction." *Revising the Blueprint: Ann Petry and the Literary Left*. Ed. Alex Lubin. Jackson: University Press of Mississippi, 2007. 3–14.

———. *Romance and Rights: The Politics of Interracial Intimacy, 1945–1954*. Jackson: University Press of Mississippi, 2009.

Lynn, Susan. "Gender and Progressive Politics: A Bridge to Social Activism of the 1960s." *Not June Cleaver: Women and Gender in Postwar America, 1945–1960*. Ed. Joanne Meyerowitz. Philadelphia: Temple University Press, 1994. 103–27.

Mackenzie, Catherine. "Harlem Mothers Fight Delinquency." *New York Times*, 2 September 1946, 14.

Madhubuti, Haki. "Black Books Bulletin Interviews: Gwen Brooks." *Conversations with Gwendolyn Brooks*. Ed. Gloria Wade Gayles. Jackson: University Press of Mississippi, 2003. 74–84.

"Manpower: Sex in the Factory." *Time*, 14 September 1942, 21.

Margolick, David. *Strange Fruit: Billie Holiday, Café Society, and an Early Cry for Civil Rights*. New York: Running Press, 2000.

Margolies, Edward. *Native Sons: A Critical Study of Twentieth-Century Negro American Authors*. New York: Lippincott, 1968.

Martin, Douglas. "Selden Rodman, Writer and Folk Art Advocate, Dies at 93." *New York Times*, 11 November 2002, B8.

Mauro, Nicole. "Ode (to Edwin Denby)." *Jacket*, 21 February 2003. http://jacketmagazine.com/21/denb-mauro.html.

Maxwell, William. *The Folded Leaf*. London: Harper, 1945.

May, Elaine Tyler. *Homeward Bound: American Families in the Cold War Era*. New York: Basic Books, 1999.

Mayfield, Julian. "Into the Mainstream and Oblivion." *The American Negro Writer and His Roots*. New York: American Society of African Culture, 1960. 29–34.

McCabe, Susan. *Elizabeth Bishop: Her Poetics of Loss*. University Park: Pennsylvania State University Press, 1994.

McDowell, Margaret B. "A Fuller View of Ann Petry." *The Critical Response to Ann Petry*. Ed. Hazel Arnett Ervin. Westport, Conn.: Praeger, 2005. 131–42.

McKay, Nellie Y. "Ann Petry's *The Street* and *The Narrows*: A Study of the Influence of Class, Race, and Gender on Afro-American Women's Lives." *Women and War*. Ed. Maria Diedrich and Dorothea Fischer-Hornung. New York: Berg, 1990. 127–40.

Melhem, D. H. *Gwendolyn Brooks: Poetry and the Heroic Voice*. Lexington: University Press of Kentucky, 1987.

Miller, Neil. *Sex-Crime Panic: A Journey to the Paranoid Heart of the 1950s*. Los Angeles: Alyson, 2009.

Miller, Stephen Paul, and Terence Diggory, eds. *The Scene of My Selves: New Work on New York School Poets*. Chicago: National Poetry Foundation, 2001.

Millier, Brett C. *Elizabeth Bishop: Life and the Memory of It*. Berkeley: University of California Press, 1993.

Mintz, Steven, and Susan Kellogg. *Domestic Revolutions: A Social History of American Family Life*. New York: Free Press, 1988.

"Mixed Couples in 3 Big Cities Form Clubs to Fight against Social Bans." *Ebony*, November 1950, 52–53.

Mlinko, Ange. "Scoured Light." *The Nation*, 7 June 2010, 38–41.

Moon, Bucklin. *Primer for White Folks*. New York: Doubleday, 1945.

Moore, Brenda L. "African Americans in the Military." *The Columbia Guide to African American History since 1939*. Ed. Robert L. Harris Jr. and Rosalyn Terborg-Penn. New York: Columbia University Press, 2006. 120–35.

Mootry, Maria K. "'The Step of Iron Feet': Creative Practice in the War Sonnets of Melvin B. Tolson and Gwendolyn Brooks." *Reading Race in American Poetry*. Ed. Aldon Lynn Nielsen. Champaign: University of Illinois Press, 2000. 133–47.

Moran, Rachel. *Interracial Intimacy: The Regulation of Race and Romance*. Chicago: University of Chicago Press, 2003.

Morgan, Stacey I. *Rethinking Social Realism: African American Art and Literature, 1930–1953*. Athens: University of Georgia Press, 2004.

Morrison, Toni. *Playing in the Dark: Whiteness and the Literary Imagination*. Cambridge: Harvard University Press, 1992.

———. "Rootedness: The Ancestor as Foundation." *Black Women Writers (1950–1980)*. Ed. Mari Evans. New York: Doubleday, 1984. 339–46.

Moynihan, Daniel P. *The Negro Family: The Case for National Action*. Washington, D.C.: Office of Policy, Planning, and Research, U.S. Department of Labor, 1965.

Mullen, Bill V. *Popular Fronts: Chicago and the African-American Cultural Politics, 1935–46*. Champaign: University of Illinois Press, 1999.

Mumford, Kevin J. *Interzones: Black/White Districts in Chicago and New York in the Early Twentieth Century*. New York: Columbia University Press, 1997.

Muñoz, José. *Disidentifications: Queers of Color and the Performance of Politics*. Minneapolis: University of Minnesota Press, 1999.

Nabokov, Vladimir. *Lolita*. 1955. New York: Vintage, 1989.

Nadel, Alan. *Containment Culture: American Narrative, Postmodernism, and the Atomic Age*. Durham, N.C.: Duke University Press, 1995.

Najar, Lubna. "The Chicago Poetry Group: African American Art and High Modernism at Midcentury." *Women's Studies Quarterly* 33.3–4 (2005): 314–23.

"Negro Author Marries Italian Poet." *Jet*, 18 June 1953, 21.

"Negro Corp. Is Founded." *New York Amsterdam News*, 2 February 1952, 31.

"Negro, White Youngsters Lived Together and Liked It." *Ebony*, January 1946, 36.

Nelson, Deborah. *Pursuing Privacy in Cold War*. New York: Columbia University Press, 2002.

North, Michael. *The Dialect of Modernism: Race, Language, and Twentieth-Century Literature*. New York: Oxford University Press, 1998.

Notley, Alice. "Edwin Denby: *Collected Poems*." *Poetry Project Newsletter* 37 (July 1976): 2–6.

———. Email to the author. 19 November 2006.

———. "Intersections with Edwin's Lines." *Jacket*, 21 February 2003. http://jacket-magazine.com/21/denb-notl.html.

O'Brien, John. "An Interview with William Demby." *Studies in Black Literature* 3.3 (Autumn 1972): 1–6.

O'Connor, William Van. *The Grotesque: An American Genre and Other Essays*. Carbondale: Southern Illinois University Press, 1962.

Offord, Carl. "America's Ghettos." *New Masses*, 21 September 1943, 11–12.

———. "Gentle Native." *Masses and Mainstream*, September 1948, 8–16.

———. "The Green, Green Grass and a Gun." *Masses and Mainstream*, February 1949, 39–43.

——— "Low Sky." *Cross Section 1944: A Collection of New American Writing*. Ed. Edward Seaver. New York: Fischer, 1944.

———. *The Naked Fear*. New York: Ace, 1954.

———. "So Peaceful in the Country." *Story*, May–June 1945, 81–86.

———. *The White Face*. 1943. New York: AMS, 1975.

O'Hara, Frank. *The Collected Poems of Frank O'Hara*. Ed. Donald Allen. Berkeley: University of California Press, 1995.

———. "The Poetry of Edwin Denby." Edwin Denby, *The Complete Poems*. New York: Random House, 1986. 179–81.

Ottley, Roi. "What's Wrong with Negro Women?" *Negro Digest* 9 (December 1950): 71–75.

Padgett, Ron. "Introduction." *The Complete Poems of Edwin Denby*. New York: Random House, 1986. xi–xxvi.

Pasolini, Pier Paolo (director). *The Decameron (Il Decameron)*. 1975.

——— (director). *Salo*. 1971.

Patterson, James T. *Grand Expectations: The United States, 1945–1974*. New York: Oxford University Press, 1996.

"Peddlers Prey on Youngsters." *Ebony*, December 1950, 30–32.

Peterson, Rachel. "Invisible Hands at Work: Domestic Service and Meritocracy in Ann Petry's Novels." *Revising the Blueprint: Ann Petry and the Literary Left*. Ed. Alex Lubin. Jackson: University Press of Mississippi, 2007. 72–96.

Petry, Ann. "Ann Petry." *Contemporary Authors Autobiography Series*. Ed. Adele Sarkissiah. Detroit: Gale Research, 1988. 6:253–69.

———. *Country Place*. 1947. New York: Houghton Mifflin, 1953.

———. *The Drugstore Cat*. New York: Crowell, 1949.

———. "The Great Secret." *The Writer* 61.7 (July 1948): 215–17.

———. *Harriet Tubman: Conductor on the Underground Railroad*. New York: Crowell, 1955.

———. *The Legends of Saints*. New York: Crowell, 1970.

———. *Miss Muriel and Other Stories*. New York: Houghton Mifflin, 1971.

———. "My Most Humiliating Jim Crow Experience." *Negro Digest*, June 1946, 63–64.

———. *The Narrows*. 1953. New York: Houghton Mifflin, 1988.

———. "The Novel as Social Criticism." 1950. *African American Literary Criticism, 1773 to 2000*. Ed. Hazel Arnett Ervin. New York: Twayne, 1999. 94–98.

———. "On Saturday the Siren Sounds at Noon." *The Crisis*, December 1943, 368–69.

———. *The Street*. New York: Houghton Mifflin, 1946.

———. *Tituba of Salem Village*. New York: Crowell, 1964.

———. "What's Wrong with Negro Men?" *Negro Digest*, March 1947, 5–7.

Petry, Elisabeth. *At Home Inside: A Daughter's Tribute to Ann Petry*. Jackson: University Press of Mississippi, 2009.

"Pills for Prejudice." *Ebony*, March 1946, 39.

Quimby, Karin. "The Story of Jo: Literary Tomboys, *Little Women*, and the Sexual-Textual Politics of Narrative Desire." *GLQ: A Journal of Lesbian and Gay Studies* 10.1 (2003): 1–22.

Rawlings, Marjorie Kinnan. *The Selected Letters of Marjorie Kinnan Rawlings*. Ed. Gordon E. Bigelow and Laura Monti. Gainesville: University Presses of Florida, 1983.

Reddick, L. D. "Anti-Semitism among Negroes." *Negro Quarterly* 1.2 (Summer 1942): 112–22.

Redding, J. Saunders. "Cellini-Like Lyrics." *On Gwendolyn Brooks: Reliant Contemplation*. Ed. Stephen Caldwell Wright. Ann Arbor: University of Michigan Press, 1996. 6–7.

Reid-Pharr, Robert. *Once You Go Black: Choice, Desire, and the Black American Intellectual*. New York: New York University Press, 2007.

———. "Tearing the Goat's Flesh." *Black Gay Man: Essays*. New York: New York University Press, 2001. 99–134.

Rich, Adrienne. "The Eye of the Outsider: Elizabeth Bishop's *Complete Poems, 1927–1929*." In *Blood, Bread, and Poetry: Selected Prose, 1979–1985*. New York: Norton, 1994. 124–35.

Ro, Sigmund. "Coming of Age: The Modernity of Postwar Black American Writing." *The Black Columbiad: Defining Moments in African American Literature and Culture*. Ed. Werner Sollors and Maria Diedrich. Cambridge: Harvard University Press, 1994. 226–33.

Rodman, Selden. "Carefully Revealed." Rev. of *North and South*, by Elizabeth Bishop. *New York Times*, 21 October 1946, 161.

———, ed. *A New Anthology of Modern Poetry*. New York: Modern Library, 1946.

Roediger, David R. *The Wages of Whiteness: Race and the Making of the American Working Class*. New York: Verso, 1991.

———. *Working toward Whiteness: How America's Immigrants Became White: The Strange Journey from Ellis Island to the Suburbs*. New York: Basic Books, 2006.

Roman, Camille. *Elizabeth Bishop's World War II–Cold War View*. New York: Palgrave, 2001.

Rose, Arnold M. "Psychoneurotic Breakdown among Negro Soldiers in Combat." *Phylon* 17.1 (1st Quarter 1956): 61–69.

Rowe, Ann E. *The Idea of Florida in the American Literary Imagination*. Baton Rouge: Louisiana State University Press, 1986.

Rowell, Charles, and Fred Moten. "'Words Don't Go There': An Interview with Fred Moten." *Callaloo* 27.4 (Autumn 2004): 953–66.

Russell, Thaddeus. "The Color of Discipline: Civil Rights and Black Sexuality." *American Quarterly* 60.1 (March 2008): 101–28.

Sacks, Karen Brodkin. "How Did the Jews Become White?" *Race*. Ed. Steven Gregory and Roger Sanjek. New Brunswick, N.J.: Rutgers University Press, 1994. 78–102.

Sancton, Thomas. "Editorial." *Survey Graphic*, January 1947, 9–11.

Sandberg, Elisabeth. "Jo Sinclair." *Contemporary Jewish-American Novelists*. Ed. Joel Shatzky and Michael Taub. Westport, Conn.: Greenwood, 1997. 375–84.

Sass, Herbert Ravenel. "Mixed Schools and Mixed Bloods." *Atlantic Monthly*, November 1956, 45–49.

Schaub, Thomas Hill. *American Fiction in the Cold War*. Madison: University of Wisconsin Press, 1991.

Schweik, Susan. *A Gulf So Deeply Cut: American Women Poets and the Second World War*. Madison: University of Wisconsin Press, 1991.

Scott, Daryl Michael. *Contempt and Pity: Social Policy and the Image of the Damaged Black Psyche, 1880–1996*. Chapel Hill: University of North Carolina Press, 1997.

Seaver, Edward, ed. *Cross Section 1945: A Collection of New American Writing*. New York: Fischer, 1945.

Sedgwick, Eve Kosofsky. *Epistemology of the Closet*. Berkeley: University of California Press, 1990.

———. "Queer and Now." *Tendencies*. Durham, N.C.: Duke University Press, 1993. 1–20.

———. "A Response to C. Jacob Hale." *Social Text* 52–53 (Autumn-Winter 1997): 237–39.

Silver, Kenneth E. "Modes of Disclosure: The Construction of Gay Identity and the Rise of Pop Art." *Hand-Painted Pop: American Art in Transition, 1955–62*. Ed. Russell Ferguson. Los Angeles: Museum of Contemporary Art, 1992. 197–203.

Sinclair, Jo. "Brother-Sister Act" (unpublished short story). September 1943. Jo Sinclair Collection. Box 26. Gotlieb Archival Research Center, Boston University, Boston.

———. *The Changelings*. 1955. New York: Feminist Press, 1998.

———. "Cleveland's Negro Problem." *Ken*, 15 December 1938, 76, 79.

———. "The Color of Rent or Love" (undated television play). Box 24. Gotlieb Archival Research Center, Boston University, Boston.

———. "Courtesy of National Dairy Products" (unpublished radio broadcast). Undated. Jo Sinclair Collection. Box 26. Gotlieb Archival Research Center, Boston University, Boston.

———. "Fascism: Headquarters in Ohio" (unpublished short story). Undated. Jo Sinclair Collection. Box 26. Gotlieb Archival Research Center, Boston University, Boston.

———. "From the Letter File of a Psychiatrist" (unpublished short story). Undated. Jo Sinclair Collection. Box 26. Gotlieb Archival Research Center, Boston University, Boston.

———. "The Girl and the Traffic Light" (unpublished short story). 1937. Jo Sinclair Collection. Box 27. Gotlieb Archival Research Center, Boston University, Boston.

———. "Home in Duh Clouds." Undated. Box 27. Gotlieb Archival Research Center, Boston University, Boston.

———. "I, Too, Sing America." *Common Ground*, Autumn 1942, 99–106.

———. "I Want to Talk about Privilege" (unpublished short story). Undated. Jo Sinclair Collection. Box 27. Gotlieb Archival Research Center, Boston University, Boston.

———. "It Used to Be Called Shell Shock" (unpublished short story). October 1943. Jo Sinclair Collection. Box 27. Gotlieb Archival Research Center, Boston University, Boston.

———. *Jesus Is a Dream*. Undated. Box 23. Gotlieb Archival Research Center, Boston University, Boston.

———. "Noon Lynching." *New Masses*, September 1936, 16–18.

———. "Red Necktie." *America in Literature*. Ed. Tremaine McDowell. New York: Crofts, 1944. 315–19.

———. *The Seasons: Death and Transfiguration*. New York: Feminist Press, 1993.

———. "Second Blood: A Rosh Hashonoh Story." 1944. *America and I: Short Stories by Jewish Women Writers*. Ed. Joyce Antler. Boston: Beacon, 1990. 134–41.

———. "Songs My Mother Taught Me (A Sermon)." *The Crisis*, May 1942, 158–74.

———. "Sun on Negro Bodies" (unpublished play). Undated. Box 24. Gotlieb Archival Research Center, Boston University, Boston.

———. *Wasteland*. New York: Harper, 1946.

Singh, Nikhil. *Black Is a Country: Race and the Unfinished Struggle for Democracy*. Cambridge: Harvard University Press, 2004.

Sitkoff, Harvard. "Racial Militancy and Interracial Violence in the Second World War." *Journal of American History* 58.3 (December 1971): 661–81.

Sklaroff, Lauren Rebecca. *Black Culture and the New Deal: The Quest for Civil Rights in the Roosevelt Era*. Chapel Hill: University of North Carolina Press, 2009.

Slaughter, Frank G. "Freud in Turpentine." Rev. of *Seraph on the Suwanee*, by Zora Neale Hurston. *New York Times*, 31 October 1948, BR24.

Smethurst, James Edward. *The New Red Negro: The Literary Left and African American Poetry, 1930–1946*. New York: Oxford University Press, 1999.

Smith, Alfred E. "Adventures in Race Relations." *Chicago Defender*, 22 December 1945, 13.

Smith, Gary. "Gwendolyn Brooks's 'Children of the Poor,' Metaphysical Poetry and the Inconditions of Love." *A Life Distilled: Gwendolyn Brooks, Her Poetry and Fiction*. Ed. Maria K. Mootry and Gary Smith. Champaign: University of Illinois Press, 1989. 165–76.

Smith, Judith E. *Visions of Belonging: Family Stories, Popular Culture, and Postwar Democracy, 1940–1960*. New York: Columbia University Press, 2004.

Smith, Lillian. "Addressed to White Liberals." *New Republic*, 18 September 1944, 331–33.

———. *Killers of the Dream*. 1949. New York: Norton, 1994.

Smith, Simon, and Ron Padgett. "A Conversation about Edwin Denby." *Jacket*, 21 February 2003. http://jacketmagazine.com/21/denb-smith-padg.html.

"Society Fails Youth Who Begin Earlier Sex Life." *Ebony*, April 1952, 86–88.

Somerville, Siobhan. *Queering the Color Line: Race and the Invention of Homosexuality in American Culture*. Durham, N.C.: Duke University Press, 1999.

"Some Sex Clubs Practice Perversion, Are Interracial." *Ebony*, April 1952, 84–85.

Spillers, Hortense J. "Gwendolyn the Terrible: Propositions on Eleven Poems." *Black, White, and in Color: Essays on American Literature and Culture*. Chicago: University of Chicago Press, 2003. 119–30.

———. "'The Permanent Obliquity of an In(pha)llibly Straight': In the Time of the Daughters and the Fathers." *Black, White, and in Color: Essays on American Literature and Culture*. Chicago: University of Chicago Press, 2003. 230–50.

Starbuck, George. "'The Work!': A Conversation with Elizabeth Bishop." *Ploughshares* 3.3–4 (1977). *Elizabeth Bishop and Her Art*. Ed. Lloyd Schwartz and Sybil P. Estess. Ann Arbor: University of Michigan Press, 1983. 312–30.

Stein, Gertrude. "Miss Furr and Miss Skeene." *A Stein Reader*. Ed Ulla E. Dydo. Evanston, Ill.: Northwestern University Press, 1993. 255–59.

Stockton, Katherine Bond. *Beautiful Bottom, Beautiful Shame: Where "Black" Meets "Queer."* Durham, N.C.: Duke University Press, 2006.

Stokes, Mason. *The Color of Sex: Whiteness, Heterosexuality, and the Fictions of White Supremacy*. Durham, N.C.: Duke University Press, 2001.

Sugrue, Thomas. *Sweet Land of Liberty: The Forgotten Struggle for Civil Rights in the North*. New York: Random House, 2009.

Sundquist, Eric J. *Strangers in the Land: Blacks, Jews, Post-Holocaust America*. Cambridge: Harvard University Press, 2005.

Tate, Claudia. "Anger So Flat: Gwendolyn Brooks's *Annie Allen*." *A Life Distilled: Gwendolyn Brooks, Her Poetry and Fiction*. Ed. Maria K. Mootry and Gary Smith. Champaign: University of Illinois Press, 1989. 140–52.

———. "Hitting 'A Straight Lick with a Crooked Stick': *Seraph on the Suwanee*, Zora Neale Hurston's Whiteface Novel." *The Psychoanalysis of Race*. Ed. Christopher Lane. New York: Columbia University Press, 1998. 380–94.

———. "An Interview with Gwendolyn Brooks." *Conversations with Gwendolyn Brooks*. Ed. Gloria Wade Gayles. Jackson: University Press of Mississippi, 2003. 104–10.

Terkel, Studs. "A Conversation with Gwendolyn Brooks." *Conversations with Gwendolyn Brooks*. Ed. Gloria Wade Gayles. Jackson: University Press of Mississippi, 2003. 3–12.

Terry, Walter, and Edwin Denby. "Dance Critic at War: Cairo Letter." *New York Herald Tribune*, 9 March 1944, 8.

Thompson, Edgar. "Sex Fears 'Vague but Real.'" *U.S. News and World Report*, 19 September 1958, 86–90.

Thomson, Virgil. *Selected Letters of Virgil Thomson*. Ed. Tim Page and Vanessa Weeks Page. New York: Summit, 1988.

Thurman, Wallace. "The Perpetual Bugaboo." *The Collected Writings of Wallace Thurman*. Ed. Amritjit Singh and Daniel M. Scott III. New Brunswick, N.J.: Rutgers University Press, 2003. 281–82.

Valien, Preston. "Sex Argument Is Emotional." *U.S. News and World Report*, 19 September 1958, 84–86.

Van Vechten, Carl. *The Dance Writings of Carl Van Vechten*. Ed. Paul Padgette. New York: Dance Horizons, 1974.

Vendler, Helen. "Domestication, Domesticity, and the Otherworldly." *World Literature Today* 1 (Winter 1977). *Elizabeth Bishop and Her Art*. Ed. Lloyd Schwartz and Sybil P. Estess. Ann Arbor: University of Michigan Press, 1983. 32–48.

Von Eschen, Penny. *Race against Empire: Black Americans and Anticolonialism, 1937–1957*. Ithaca: Cornell University Press, 1997.

Wald, Alan. *Trinity of Passion: The Literary Left and the Antifascist Crusade*. Chapel Hill: University of North Carolina Press, 2007.

Waldeck, R. G. "Homosexual International." *Human Events* 17:39 (29 September 1960): 453–56.

Walker, Margaret. "New Poets." *Phylon* 11.4 (4th Quarter 1950): 345–54.

Wallace, Maurice. "What Nellie Knew." *African American Review* 40.1 (Spring 2006): 33–35.

"War Baby." *Newsweek*, 5 January 1942, 27.

Warren, Kenneth W. *So Black and Blue: Ralph Ellison and the Occasion of Criticism*. Chicago: University of Chicago Press, 2003.

———. *What Was African American Literature?* Cambridge: Harvard University Press, 2011.

Washington, Mary Helen. "'Taming All That Anger Down': Rage and Silence in Gwendolyn Brooks's *Maud Martha*." *Massachusetts Review* 24.2 (Summer 1983): 453–66.

Washington, Robert E. *The Ideologies of African American Literature: From the Harlem Renaissance to the Black Nationalist Revolt*. Lanham, Md.: Rowman and Littlefield, 2001.

Watson, Steven. *Prepare for Saints: Gertrude Stein, Virgil Thomson, and the Mainstreaming of American Modernism*. Berkeley: University of California Press, 2000.

Welch, Denton. *In Youth Is Pleasure*. London: Routledge, 1944.

Wertham, Fredric. *The Seduction of the Innocent*. New York: Rinehart, 1954.

West, M. Genevieve. *Zora Neale Hurston and American Literary Culture*. Gainesville: University Press of Florida, 2005.

"What South Really Fears about Mixed Schools." *U.S. News and World Report*, 19 September 1958, 76–90.

"When Negroes Go to School with Whites." *U.S. News and World Report*, 24 September 1954, 24–29.

White, Deborah Gray. *Too Heavy a Load: Black Women in Defense of Themselves, 1894–1994*. New York: Norton, 1993.

White, William. "Inquiry by Senate on Perverts Asked." *New York Times*, 20 May 1950, 8.

Whiting, Frederick. "'The Strange Particularity of the Lover's Preference': Pedophilia, Pornography, and the Anatomy of Monstrosity in *Lolita*." *American Literature* 70.4 (December 1988): 833–62.

———. "Stronger, Smarter, and Less Queer: 'The White Negro' and Mailer's Third Man." *WSQ* 33.3-4 (Fall–Winter 2005): 189–214.

Wilkins, Roy. Letter to Jo Sinclair. 16 March 1942. Jo Sinclair Collection. Box 33. Gotlieb Archival Research Center, Boston University, Boston.

Williams, Oscar. "North but South." *New Republic*, 21 October 1946, 525. *Elizabeth Bishop and Her Art*. Ed. Lloyd Schwartz and Sybil P. Estess. Ann Arbor: University of Michigan Press, 1983. 184–85.

Williams, Sidney R. Interview with Jo Sinclair (from WJW radio show, *Minority Opinion*, Cleveland, Ohio, 25 March 1946). Jo Sinclair Collection. Box 23. Gotlieb Archival Research Center, Boston University, Boston.

Williams, Tennessee. "Desire and the Black Masseur." *Tennessee Williams: Collected Stories*. New York: New Directions, 1985. 205–12.

Williams, William Carlos. *In the American Grain*. 1925. New York: New Directions, 1956.

Wixson, Douglas. *Worker-Writer in America: Jack Conroy and the Tradition of Midwestern Literary Radicalism, 1898–1990*. Champaign: University of Illinois Press, 1994.

Wolf, Reva. *Andy Warhol, Poetry, and Gossip in the 1960s*. Chicago: University of Chicago Press, 1997.

Wonham, Henry. "Introduction." *Criticism and the Color Line: Desegregating American Literary Studies*. Ed. Henry B. Wonham. New Brunswick, N.J.: Rutgers University Press, 1996. 1–15.

Wright, Richard. "Man of All Work." 1957. *Eight Men*. New York: Harper Collins, 2008. 109–54.

———. *White Man, Listen!* New York: Harper Perennial, 1995.

Zinn, Howard. *Postwar America, 1945–1971*. Indianapolis: Bobbs-Merrill, 1973.

INDEX

Adams, Diane, 107
adolescence: delinquency and, 65, 170, 214–15; femininity and, 196–97; masculinity and, 166; sexuality and, 167–69; vulnerability and, 21, 139, 147–49, 186–87, 201, 203
Agee, James, 103
Ailey, Alvin, 106–7, 109, 110, 128, 238n20
alienation: familial, 60, 152, 163, 170; as postwar condition, 34, 88, 110, 115–16, 133–34; social, 16–17, 85, 88, 158, 167, 203, 226
Allison, Dorothy, 218
Almyda, Hannah, 55
American Jewish Committee, 182
American Jewish Congress, 185
anticolonialism, 61, 164, 189–91, 233n21
Anti-Defamation League, 182, 185, 244n5
Ashbery, John, 90, 106, 108
Aswell, Ed, 198
Axelrod, Steven Gould, 69, 72–73

Bailey, Pearl, 109
Baker, Ella, 185
Baker, Josephine, 107, 131, 240n30
Baldwin, James, 25, 27, 103, 140, 151, 221, 223, 227, 233n22, 239n23, 247n27; *Another Country*, 225–26
Barnett, Claude, 77
Bay, Mia, 171

Beaver, Harold, 90
Beemyn, Brett, 12, 237n15
Bell, Bernard, 33
Belo, Jane, 41, 45
Bernard, Emily, 25, 33
Berrigan, Ted, 90
Bérubé, Allan, 12, 102
Bethune, Mary MacLeod, 145
Bishop, Elizabeth, 5, 16, 20, 23, 24, 25, 26, 28, 30–32, 38, 39, 40–43, 45–48, 49–50, 52, 54, 55–58, 62–82, 84–85, 94, 128, 137, 165, 176, 185, 186, 199, 208, 223, 224, 235n34; "Cootchie," 48, 55–56, 57, 58, 62, 63, 69, 72, 73, 82; "Faustina, or Rock Roses," 32, 54, 55, 56–58, 62, 68, 69, 72, 73, 74, 75, 82, 85, 232n9; "In a cheap hotel," 47, 232n12; "In the Waiting Room," 50; "Jerónimo's House," 43, 46, 48, 232n9; "Mercedes Hospital," 39, 81–82, 84, 232n9; "Roosters," 78; "Something I've Meant to Write about for 30 Years," 50–52; "Songs for a Colored Singer," 57, 58, 64, 69–73, 74, 79, 82, 85, 223, 235n29
blackness: ambiguity and, 25, 213; gender and, 58, 148, 149; identification with, 31, 165; representations of, 33, 70–73, 177, 198–99, 206, 213, 219; sexuality and, 156, 175, 224
Blakely, Henry, 92

271

Bland, Aldon, 95, 116
blood, 21, 95–96, 172, 203, 211–13, 247n27
Blough, Frani, 55
Bone, Robert, 15, 19, 92, 158, 160, 164, 209, 210, 233n23
Boris, Eileen, 53
Borstelmann, Thomas, 7, 14, 29, 96, 181, 187, 208, 237n11
Bowles, Paul, 101
Boyd, Nan, 102
Boyd, Valerie, 41, 234n26
Brainard, Joe, 126
Brodovitch, Alexy, 130
Brook, Peter, 109
Brooks, Gwendolyn, 5, 9, 15, 23–24, 25, 85, 88–94, 96–101, 107, 110–11, 112, 114–23, 129–35, 170, 180, 214, 223, 234n25, 236n7, 239n25; "Anniad," 117–18, 120; *Annie Allen*, 91, 96, 97, 114, 116–18, 120, 125, 132; "Appendix to the Anniad," 120–23; "Beverly Hills, Chicago," 97, 98–99; "The Children of the Poor," 114, 123; "flags," 105; "Gay Chaps at the Bar," 94, 96, 113, 114, 120; "Has It Been Hard Miss Brooks?," 93; "I love those little booths at Benvenuti's," 97–98, 107, 110; *In the Mecca*, 91; *Maud Martha*, 92, 99–101, 119, 143, 159, 237n13; "Memorial to Ed Bland," 116–17; "One Wants a Teller in a Time Like This," 88; *Report from Part One*, 91; *Report from Part Two*, 98, 100, 120; *A Street in Bronzeville*, 91, 116; "Why Negro Women Leave Home," 119, 145; "The Womanhood," 97, 114
Browning, Alice C., 94, 95
Brown v. Board of Education, 4, 14, 77, 169, 192

Buchman, Helen, 215, 247n29
Burkhardt, Jacob, 103
Burkhardt, Rudy, 101–2, 103, 104, 112, 238n21
Burroughs, Margaret, 92, 93, 115
Burroughs, William, 103
Butcher, Philip, 63, 230n12
Byrd, James, 59

Cadmus, Paul, 106
Cannon, Poppy, 152
Capote, Truman, 109, 191
Carby, Hazel, 66
Carroll, Diahann, 109
Chauncey, George, 12, 102, 104, 106, 130, 140
Cheng, Anne Anlin, 165, 190, 217
civil rights movement, 4, 5, 14, 19, 29, 61, 182–83, 193–94, 217, 221, 224, 225
Clark, Keith, 146
Clark, Kenneth, 192, 193
Clark, Mamie, 192
Cole, Johnnetta B., 198
color prejudice, 99, 117, 119, 120, 131
Conrad, Earl, 92, 94–95
Conroy, Jack, 92, 236n7
containment: alternatives to, 29–30, 155, 209; cultural, 66; domestic, 39, 53, 114–15, 117–19, 166; gender/sexual, 25, 26, 44–45, 120, 122, 132, 136, 223; political, 10, 19, 115, 152, 181; racial, 19, 39, 99, 115, 137, 179
Cooke, Marvel, 185
Coontz, Stephanie, 40
Copland, Aaron, 101, 106, 127
Corber, Robert, 140, 150, 174, 240n32, 240n33
Corey, Donald Webster, 133–34, 230n10, 240n32
Couch, William, 92

Coughlan, Robert, 40
Crane, Hart, 109
Crane, Louise, 41, 45, 48, 55, 234n29, 235n31, 238n17
cross-race writing, 29–31, 32–35, 63–64, 109, 186, 199, 220, 222; "white-life" novels, 33–34, 59, 184, 210, 233n20
Cullen, Countee, 41, 232n5
Cuordileone, K. A., 9, 10, 26, 65, 74, 102
Curry, Renée, 69

damage, 40, 169, 217, 244n10; "damage thesis," 77, 183, 190–94, 219, 245n14, 245n15; racial, 71, 83, 208, 222, 245n13; sexual, 201, 216
Daniels, Jimmie, 109, 128
Danner, Margaret, 92, 237n9
Daughters of Bilitis, 13
Davis, Arthur P., 14, 33, 35, 37
Davis, Frank Marshall, 92, 96
de Kooning, Elaine, 104, 108, 110, 129
de Kooning, William, 104, 239n29
Demby, William, 5, 17, 23, 24, 25–26, 34, 137–38, 140–42, 157–77, 203, 217, 222, 242n17, 243n26; *Beetlecreek*, 17, 36, 137, 157–78, 215, 216, 223; *The Catacombs*, 158; *Love Song Black*, 158
D'Emilio, John, 133, 139, 140, 163, 168, 169, 224
Denby, Edwin, 5, 13, 16, 17, 24, 25, 36, 85–86, 88–90, 91, 94, 101–11, 112–13, 114–16, 117, 123–35, 136, 177, 214, 223, 224, 225, 236n6, 238n17, 238n21, 239n27, 239n29; "Aaron," 127; "Against Meaning in Ballet," 125; "Dancers, Buildings, and People in the Street," 90, 129; "Elegy—The Streets," 105; *In Public, in Private*, 88, 90, 103, 112, 116, 132; "Lunchroom," 104; "Meeting in the Postoffice," 128;

"Miss Dunham in Review," 107–8; "New York dark in August, seaward," 123–24; "On the Home Front—1942," 112–13; "People on Sunday," 105, 129; "A Sonnet Sequence: Dishonor," 123–25; "Standing on the Streetcorner," 105; "The Subway," 105; "Summer," 88, 105–6, 111; "Writing poems, an employee," 128–29
desegregated desire, 4, 26, 27–28, 31, 97, 110, 148, 152, 166, 177, 207, 226, 227
desegregation, 6, 17, 19, 75, 85, 111, 188; affect and, 44, 74, 88, 91, 99, 116, 127, 180, 198, 219; containment and, 115, 137–38; as critical practice, 23–26, 89; definitions of, 3–4, 6, 19, 20–21, 23, 27, 134, 182–83, 222; interfaith marriage and, 201–2; as private phenomenon, 5, 18, 22, 27, 44, 61, 85, 87, 96–97, 119, 172, 179, 210, 222; schools and, 3, 21, 77, 106–7, 136, 139, 221, 225; sexuality and, 87–88, 94, 104–5, 136–37, 156; trauma and, 23, 112, 143, 148, 173, 180, 190–94, 200–201, 202, 208, 217; of U.S. military, 5, 6–7, 76, 191, 209; versus integration, 18–19, 22
desegregationist literature: American identity and, 34; characteristics of, 14–15, 16, 21–22, 23, 29–30, 94, 153, 172, 197, 221; racial interdependency and, 4, 53, 63, 64, 108, 219; as social critique, 84, 95, 175, 208
Diamond, Esta, 95–96, 211
Dickie, Margaret, 57
dislocation, 17, 51, 79, 88, 101, 112, 116, 125, 172, 173, 176, 180, 200, 202, 203
Dodson, Howard, 94
Dollimore, Jonathan, 174
domestic labor, 8, 23, 28, 53–63, 80, 145, 149, 170, 185, 189, 231n17, 242n16

Donne, John, 93
"Double V" campaign, 7, 182
Douglas, Ann, 23
Drexel, Allen, 13, 14
Dubek, Laura, 191
Du Bois, W. E. B., 8, 14, 181
duCille, Ann, 66, 67, 68, 234n27
Dudziak, Mary L., 19, 29, 61
Dunbar, Paul Laurence, 93
Duncan, Robert, 13, 133–34
Dunham, Katherine, 107–8, 109, 131, 145, 238n18
DuPlessis, Rachel Blau, 23, 127
Dyer, Richard, 137, 151, 175

Edelman, Lee, 169, 170
Eliot, T. S., 93, 116
Ellington, Duke, 108, 238n21
Ellis, Havelock, 140
Ellis, Jonathan, 30
Ellison, Ralph, 4, 22, 28, 30, 31, 33–34, 55, 80, 85, 137, 141, 167, 175, 181, 193, 204, 221, 227, 245n13, 245n15; *Invisible Man*, 161, 162, 163, 176, 204
Emerson, Ralph Waldo, 93
Eng, David, 165, 190
Engle, Paul, 93
Erkkila, Betsy, 82
Eversley, Shelly, 85, 193
existentialism, 17, 37, 74, 118, 158, 164, 242n21
Eyerman, Ron, 190

Faderman, Lillian, 41
family: intergenerational trauma, 201; reinvented, 29, 35, 62, 102–3, 146–47, 156–57, 162–63, 165–67, 202–3; social stability and, 10, 39–40, 42–44, 54, 68, 141, 204–5, 242n22
Fanon, Frantz, 189, 191

Farrell, Kirby, 183
Federn, Paul 123
Feld, Rose, 187
Feldstein, Ruth, 29
feminism, 53, 68, 80, 114, 117–19, 120, 144–47, 205, 241n7
FEPC (Fair Employment Practices Commission), 5, 182, 229n1
Ferguson, Roderick A., 10, 11, 133
Fiedler, Leslie, 141, 162
Ford, Nick Aaron, 59
Frank, Leo, 187, 247n24
Freedman, Estelle, 138, 139, 169, 176
Frost, Robert, 93
Fuss, Diana, 30, 31, 57, 63

Gayden, Fern, 92, 94, 95
gay rights movement, 11, 13, 78, 87, 133–34, 224, 225, 240n33
Giddings, Paula, 8, 101, 236n1
Gilbert, Douglas, 77
Gilbert, James, 169, 243n24, 243n25
Gilroy, Paul, 42, 54, 172
Ginsberg, Allen, 103, 123, 131
Glicksburg, Charles, 140, 141
Gloster, Hugh, 84
Gooch, Brad, 103
Gordon, Lewis, 164
Goulden, Joseph, 6
Green, Paul, 41
Greenberg, Cheryl Lynn, 180, 182, 185, 188
Greenberg, Marilyn, 152
Griffin, Farah Jasmine, 146, 235n30
Grubb, Davis, 95
Gruen, John, 123, 127, 128
Gubar, Susan, 32

Halberstam, Judith, 91, 193
Halsey, Margaret, 4, 5, 221

Hammonds, Evelyn, 53
Han, Shinhee, 165, 190
Handlin, Oscar, 21
Hansberry, Lorraine, 37, 39
Hartigan, Grace, 108, 238n19
Harvey, Frank, 95
Haut, Woody, 205
Hayden, Robert, 89, 157
Hemenway, Robert E., 61
Herbert, Helen, 94, 95
Herndon, Angelo, 181
Higgins, Ross, 103
Holiday, Billie, 70, 71, 107, 110, 234n29, 235n30
Holladay, Hilary, 146, 151
Holman, M. Carl, 169
Hopper, Edward, 124
Horne, Lena, 145
Horton, Lester, 106
Howard, John, 130
Howe, Irving, 34, 150
Hughes, Langston, 41, 93, 156, 233n20
Hurst, Fannie, 41, 66
Hurston, Zora Neale, 5, 20, 23, 24, 25, 26, 33, 34, 38, 40–45, 53, 63–65, 73–77, 84–85, 94, 137, 150, 176, 212, 217, 222, 231n2, 231n4, 232n5, 232n6, 232n8, 233n18, 235n33; "The Conscience of the Court," 39, 75, 83, 235n37; "Crazy for This Democracy," 52, 61; "My Most Humiliating Jim Crow Experience," 49–50, 143; "The 'Pet Negro' System," 60–62, 83; *Seraph on the Suwanee*, 30, 33, 35, 43, 54, 55, 58–63, 65–68, 71, 74–75, 183, 205, 223, 232n7, 233n19; "What White Publishers Won't Publish," 64–65

identification, 3, 29–32; cross-racial, 53, 57–58, 63, 72–73, 158–59, 164–66, 196–97, 206, 216, 219, 224; familial, 17, 162; racial marginalization and, 100, 142; sexual, 41, 70, 158–59, 175–76, 208
interracial sexuality, 10–11, 17–18, 20–22, 95, 103, 119, 136–37, 152–56, 169, 188, 189, 194, 234n29
Irvine, Fred, 44

Jackman, Harold, 41, 232n5
Jackson, Lawrence, 54, 69, 185
Jackson, Mahalia, 109
Jacobson, Matthew Frye, 210, 211, 229n2, 231n19
James, C. L. R., 189
Jenkins, Candice, 28
Jenkins, McKay, 25, 186, 243n2
Jewish identity, 201, 211, 212–13
Johnson, David K., 138, 161, 242n18, 242n20
Johnson, E. Patrick, 150
Johnson, James Weldon, 93
Jones, Ernest, 171
Jones, Gayl, 218
Jowitt, Deborah, 128

Kaiser, Charles, 102, 112
Kaplan, Carla, 42, 235n37
Karamu House, 185, 186, 244n4
Karpman, Benjamin, 138
Katz, Alex, 109, 239n29
Kennan, George, 181
Kent, George E., 98, 114, 115, 117, 121, 132, 133
Khama, Prince Seretse, 152
King, Charles, 8
King, Martin Luther, Jr., 194, 218
Kinsey, Alfred, 12, 102, 241n10
Kirstein, Lincoln, 106, 109, 124
Klein, Christina, 29, 35

Knadler, Stephen, 62, 165, 171, 216–17
Koestenbaum, Wayne, 47
Kunzel, Regina, 11, 12

Larsen, Nella, 33
LaTouche, John, 238n21
Laughlin, James, 48, 49
Laurents, Arthur, 191
Lee, Elizabeth, 129
lesbians, 11–12, 13, 30, 41, 42, 46, 69, 70, 80, 87, 102, 104, 112, 133, 161, 184, 197, 198, 224, 246n18, 247n29
Leslie, Alfred, 108, 110, 238n19
LeSueur, Joe, 126
Lindsay, Vachel, 127
Lipsitz, George, 16, 87–88, 245n16
Locke, Alain, 93, 236n8
Lombardi, Marilyn May, 58
Longenbach, James, 72
Lorca, García, 108, 109
Lott, Eric, 57, 72, 73
Lowell, Robert, 79, 232n12
Lubin, Alex, 11, 14, 18, 28, 110

Machiz, Herbert, 108
Madhubuti, Haki, 116, 122
Mailer, Norman, 140, 150, 173, 243n26
Margolies, Edward, 160
Mason, Charlotte Osgood, 45, 66, 233n18
Mattachine Society, 13, 87
Mauro, Nicole, 126
May, Elaine Tyler, 26, 39, 40, 68, 74, 120, 237n13
Mayfield, Julian, 33, 34, 140–41
McCabe, Susan, 57
McCullers, Carson, 185
Mershon, Katharine, 45
Millier, Brett, 77
Mitchell, Arthur, 107, 109, 110, 238n16

Mitchell, Burroughs, 66
Moon, Bucklin, 14, 33, 185
Moore, Marianne, 42
Mootry, Maria K., 96
Morgan, Stacey, 15, 115
Morrison, Toni, 17, 23, 30, 31, 55, 70, 216, 218, 235n32, 246n22
Moten, Fred, 117, 122, 131
Motley, Willard, 33, 59, 63, 92, 233n20
Mullen, Bill V., 16, 92, 93, 94, 96, 97
Mumford, Kevin J., 17, 48
Muñoz, José, 175
Myers, John Bernard, 108

NAACP, 18, 181, 182, 185, 186, 235n33
Nadel, Alan, 115
National Urban League, 182
Neal Salon, 238–39n23
Negro Story, 94–96
Nelson, Deborah, 26–27, 53, 74, 84
neomodernism, 17, 89, 116, 132–33
Neruda, Pablo, 42
New York School, 89, 90, 103, 106, 108, 110, 126, 127, 129, 236n6, 238n21
North, Michael, 23
Notley, Alice, 90, 102, 124, 125, 126, 132, 240n31
Novak, Kim, 144
Nugent, Richard Bruce, 41

Oakes, Elizabeth, 198
Offord, Carl, 5, 9, 15, 18, 23, 25–26, 35–37, 152, 179, 183–84, 187–92, 191–93, 195, 220, 223, 230n11, 244n7; "America's Ghettos," 179, 188; "Gentle Native," 190; "The Green, Green Grass and a Gun," 190; "Low Sky," 188, 244n9; *The Naked Fear*, 17, 20, 35, 178, 180–81, 190, 192, 203–10, 213–14, 215, 217–19, 247n25; "So

Peaceful in the Country," 189; *The White Face*, 185, 187–88, 244n8
O'Hara, Frank, 78, 102–3, 106, 108, 109, 110, 113–14, 123, 124, 126–27, 132, 238n16, 238n19
Ottley, Roi, 145, 239n26

Padgett, Ron, 90, 102, 105, 107, 128
Pepper, Claude, 79
perversion, 11, 155, 168–70, 207; artistic, 141, 227; familial, 166; homosexuality as, 103, 105, 138–40, 148–51, 153, 163–64; racial, 160–61, 174–77, 224; as security risk, 161
Petry, Ann, 5, 15, 18, 23, 24, 33, 34, 59, 63, 137, 140–46, 160, 166, 170–73, 175, 177, 180, 189, 210, 222, 230n11, 231n17, 233n20, 240n3, 240n4, 240n5, 241n6, 243n26; *Country Place*, 59, 142, 191; *Miss Muriel and Other Stories*, 142, 146; "My Most Humiliating Jim Crow Experience," 143; *The Narrows*, 3, 9–10, 19, 28, 35, 137, 141, 146–57, 165, 171, 174, 189, 197, 206, 207, 223, 225, 241n9, 242n16; Negro Women Incorporated, 144; "The Novel as Social Criticism," 141, 142; "On Saturday the Siren Sounds at Noon," 142–43; *The Street*, 142, 152; "What's Wrong with Negro Men?," 145
Plath, Sylvia, 74
Pollack, Peter, 92
Pound, Ezra, 93, 116
Powell, Adam Clayton, Jr., 144, 181
Présence Africaine, 189
Primus, Pearl, 107–8, 131
psychoanalysis, 17, 29–30, 47, 65–66, 74, 101, 123, 165–66, 184, 191, 209, 222–23

queer kinship, 35, 80, 137, 159, 165–67, 173–74, 177, 206, 214–16, 226
Quimby, Karin, 196

race traitor, 141, 158, 160, 161, 162, 163–64, 176
racial belonging, 16, 17, 33, 123, 158, 162, 177, 223
racial ventriloquism, 31, 39, 58, 63–64, 66–67, 73–74, 97, 186, 217, 234n24
Randolph, A. Philip, 5
Rawlins, Marjorie, 45, 66
Reddick, L. D., 181, 185, 211
Redding, J. Saunders, 116
Reid-Pharr, Robert, 140, 175
Rey, Frederick, 107
Reynolds, Grant, 76
Rich, Adrienne, 73
Ro, Sigmund, 33, 133, 158
Robbins, Jerome, 106
Robeson, Paul, 5, 94, 238n21
Robeson, Paul, Jr., 152
Robinson, Dollie Lowther, 144
Rodman, Selden, 79, 235n35
Roediger, David R., 211
Roman, Camille, 69, 71, 235n31
Rose, Arnold M., 192
Ross, Herbert, 109
Russell, Thaddeus, 166, 242n22
Rustin, Bayard, 5

Sacks, Karen Brodkin, 244n12, 245n16
Sandberg, Elisabeth, 198, 243n1
Sartre, Jean Paul, 158
Sass, Herbert Ravenel, 21
Schuyler, James, 90, 108, 112, 238n21
Schweik, Susan, 89, 113, 114
Seaver, Edwin, 14, 230n11, 244n9
Sedgwick, Eve Kosofsky, 43, 89, 151, 167, 225

segregation, 4, 7, 11, 13, 17, 19, 21, 22–23, 26, 38, 41, 44, 49–52, 84, 103, 119, 143–44, 169, 175, 179, 182, 186, 192–93
Sexton, Ann, 74
Shook, Karel, 106–7
Silver, Kenneth E., 105
Sinclair, Jo, 5, 9, 15, 16, 18, 23, 25, 30–31, 35, 179, 182, 184–87, 191, 209, 222; *The Changelings*, 17, 19, 34–35, 36, 37, 180–81, 186, 191, 193, 195–203, 206, 210–11, 213, 214–20, 223, 245n17, 246n18, 247n29; "Cleveland's Negro Problem," 184–85; "Courtesy of National Dairy Products," 187; "The Girl and the Traffic Light," 186–87; "It Used to Be Called Shell Shock," 191; *Jesus Is a Dream*, 185; "Noon Lynching," 186; "Red Necktie," 184; *The Seasons*, 180; "Second Blood: A Rosh Hashonoh Story," 212; *Sing at My Wake*, 183–84; "Songs My Mother Taught Me," 186; *Wasteland*, 184, 244n3, 246n17, 247n23
Singh, Nikhil, 19, 29, 230n13, 236n38
Slaughter, Frank G., 66
slumming, 52, 98, 226
Smethurst, James, 14, 92, 119–20, 133
Smith, Alfred E., 98
Smith, Judith E., 17–18, 28, 29, 39
Smith, Lillian, 16, 20, 22–23, 38, 49, 52, 56, 62, 186, 191, 208, 244n10
Soares, Lota de Macedo, 42, 79, 80
social protest literature, 15, 17, 29, 65, 89, 94, 101, 112, 120, 122, 140, 189, 200, 204, 209–10, 225
social realism, 14, 16–17, 142, 198–99
Somerville, Siobhan, 19
South Side Community Art Center, 92–93, 236n7, 237n9, 238n18
space: desegregated, 27–28, 97–100, 114–15, 153, 227; domestic, 28, 44–45, 46–47, 53, 60, 68–69, 83, 154–55, 204; interracial/integrated, 11, 138, 204; liminal, 42–43, 47, 71, 155, 197; public, 3, 18, 27, 39, 50, 81, 85, 90–91, 96, 101, 104–5, 110–11, 114, 117, 122, 133, 138, 153–54; queer, 12–13, 87–88, 90–91, 97, 102–4, 105, 106, 129–30, 136, 139, 140, 150, 239n28; racialized, 96–97, 153, 159–60
Spillers, Hortense, 166–67
Stark, Inez Cunningham, 92–93
Stein, Gertrude, 109, 127, 132, 240n31
Stevens, Marjorie, 41, 42
Stevens, Wallace, 127
Stockton, Katherine Bond, 4, 30
Stokes, Mason, 129, 177
Strayhorn, Billy, 108–10, 128, 238n21, 238n23
Sugrue, Thomas, 19
Sundquist, Eric, 182–83, 195, 200, 212, 225

Tate, Claudia, 58, 66, 67, 68, 114, 117, 118, 234n27
Terkel, Studs, 92
Terry, Walter, 106, 107
Thompson, Edgar T., 20
Thomson, Virgil, 101, 106, 109, 238n22
Thurman, Wallace, 6, 221
Tolson, Melvin, 89
Toomer, Jean, 33, 80
Truman, Harry S., 6
Tuskegee Airmen, 7

universalism, 13, 15–16, 22, 33, 64, 71, 80, 83, 110, 114, 129, 131, 211, 222, 225, 231n16; versus cultural/racial particularities, 34, 59, 62, 88–89, 92–93,

119–20, 133–34, 183–84, 214, 230n13, 236n8

Valdes, Gregorio, 45, 46
Valien, Preston, 20
Van Vechten, Carl, 41, 44, 45, 238n20
Veterans Benevolent Association, 13
Von Eschen, Penny, 29, 61

Wald, Alan, 15, 23, 180, 197, 199, 209
Waldeck, R. G., 163
Walker, Margaret, 15, 35, 89, 115–16, 131, 230n12, 236n5
Warhol, Andy, 90, 239n29
Washington, Booker T., 93
Washington, Mary Helen, 237n13
Washington, Robert E., 164
Waters, Ethel, 41, 238n21
Wertham, Fredric, 169, 192, 243n25, 245n13
West, M. Genevieve, 77
White, Walter, 76, 152, 181
whiteness: definitions of, 16, 25, 211, 229n2, 231n19; deviance and, 151, 224; interrogation of, 16, 32, 98; production of, 151, 245n16; representations of, 34, 57, 65, 72, 127–29, 147–48, 173–74, 177
Whiting, Frederick, 140, 166, 169, 173
Wilkins, Roy, 186
Williams, Ruth, 152
Williams, Tennessee, 48, 103, 109, 131, 233n13
Works Progress Administration, 180, 184, 186, 243n3
World War II: homosexuality and, 10, 11–13, 41, 87, 112, 113–14, 239n24; race and, 6–8, 14, 61, 76–77, 95–96, 113, 181–82, 190, 207–9, 211–12; reconversion and, 8, 20, 97–98, 190–91; veterans and, 7, 11, 13, 14, 76, 78, 96, 98, 152, 190–92, 229n4, 245n16; women and, 8–9, 11–12, 41, 53, 95–96, 120–21, 184
Wright, Richard, 25, 33, 61, 63, 144, 189–90, 191, 193, 202, 204, 210, 236n7, 241n12, 244n3

Yerby, Frank, 59, 210, 233n20

Zinn, Howard, 225, 229n4

CPSIA information can be obtained at www.ICGtesting.com
Printed in the USA
BVOW07*0626050913

330221BV00003B/4/P